UNDERSTANDING
FORTRAN

*

UNDERSTANDING FORTRAN

Michel Boillot

Pensacola Junior College

WEST PUBLISHING CO.

St. Paul / New York
Los Angeles / San Francisco

COPYRIGHT © 1978 By WEST PUBLISHING CO.
50 West Kellogg Boulevard
P.O. Box 3526
St. Paul, Minnesota 55165

Library of Congress Cataloging in Publication Data

Boillot, Michel H.
   Understanding Fortran.
   Includes index.
    1. FORTRAN (Computer program language)
I. Title.
QA76.73.F25B64   001.6'424   77–19356
ISBN 0–8299–0205–8

1st Reprint—1978

PREFACE

This text represents a unique approach to teaching and learning FORTRAN. All chapters are divided into five or six sections, each with a specific purpose. In the first section, a completely defined problem is presented with a programmed solution and flowchart. The display of the complete program before any discussion of the material to be covered in the chapter is to stimulate the reader's curiosity by confronting him with a "conceptual whole." The reader may capture the essence of the program without much difficulty. This complete program illustration serves to introduce the new language features and syntax to be discussed in the chapter. The reader is warned not to spend too much time on this introductory programming example, since subsequent sections will clarify the program; details, at this point, are unimportant.

The second section contains explanations of the new features, syntax and programming techniques. Numerous short, illustrative examples are included to show both correct and incorrect coding, usage of programming techniques, and so on.

The third section, entitled "You might want to know," is in question-and-answer format. It attempts to anticipate commonly asked questions and provides informally phrased answers. This section represents a compilation of predictable pitfalls for novice programmers.

The fourth section displays two or three "worked-out problems" which apply the language features and programmed techniques covered in the preceding sections. These problems are taken from a variety of disciplines reflecting both scientific and business areas of applicability. The reader at this stage should be able to comprehend all program details and may wish to refer back to the program example of the first section for further study.

Many chapters feature an optional fifth section containing material deemed desirable for the sake of a complete presentation of the FORTRAN language, but not necessarily essential to all students. Each instructor may elect to cover or omit these optional sections.

All chapters conclude with a section containing exercises and programming problems. The first part of the sixth section, entitled "Self test," enables the reader to test his understanding of the material covered in the chapter. Answers to the self test are provided at the end of each chapter for immediate feedback. The second part of the sixth section contains an extensive collection of problems ranging over a wide variety of subject matter areas and levels of difficulty. Problems are generally presented in graduated order of difficulty. The instructor or reader should be able to find problems impacting his own area of interest. There are "fun" problems often dealing with the simulation of a process or an environment (a random number generator function is supplied in Chapter 9 for use in these problems), "total" problems requiring the student to design a complete system, and, of course, traditional-type problems. Some instructors may wish to select some of these problems to present as the first programming example of the chapter instead of using the one given in the first section. In any event, the abundance of problems in the sixth section will allow the instructor to give his students different problems semester after semester.

Other features, in addition to the overall organization of the text, are as follows. Initial discussions of input/output are placed in separate chapters. This enables the student to concentrate on each topic separately rather than having to master both simultaneously. This approach has been used successfully at Pensacola Junior College as well as at other institutions. Chapter 7 centralizes all information on alphabetic data, number and data representation, DOUBLE precision, logical and complex data. To many, the presentation of this material in Chapter 7 may seem too premature, or even totally unnecessary. For some classes, Chapter 7, excepting the section on alphabetic data, should be optional. Omitting Chapter 7 does not break the logical continuity between Chapters 6 and 8. The instructor may always cover this chapter at a time he deems propitious. Structured programming is included in an independent chapter. There is a great deal of interest at present in the concepts and techniques of structured programming, and, while not every class will cover this topic, the author feels that most readers will profit from a brief exposure to these ideas.

Many people have attempted to "debug" this book, but inevitably some errors will remain. The author would appreciate any correspondence with users regarding errors or suggestions dealing with the improvement of this book.

Acknowledgments

I have come to realize that no successful textbook can be produced without the assistance and better judgment of colleagues and reviewers. I am greatly indebted to Wayne Horn of Pensacola Junior College, without whose assistance this book would never have materialized. I am also indebted to Carol Shingles at Virginia Polytechnic Institute and State University for her superb reviews and many suggestions, including problems and explanations, the results of an obvious deep concern for students and how they learn. I would also like to thank Betty Whitten of the University of Georgia, Don Bishko of the State University of New York at Albany, Arnold McEntire of Appalachian State University, and Edward Suppiger, Professor Emeritus, Princeton University, for their helpful comments and constructive criticisms. To Greg Hubit, my sincere appreciation for the thorough and excellent work performed during the editing and typesetting stages. His patience, assistance and understanding have contributed greatly to the format of the book. My thanks also go to Charles D. Cox for his critical editing and proofreading of the book. Additionally I wish to thank Gary Woodruff, West's College Department Editor, for his advice and encouragement during the writing process. Finally I must thank my wife Mona and children Marc and Laura for their understanding and patience during the birth of this book.

M. Boillot

*

CONTENTS

1 Computers and Computing 1

Computer organization and concepts
A model computer
Computer hardware and software
The punched card
Computer access modes

2 Flowcharting 26

Algorithms and programs
Program flowcharting
System flowcharting?

3 Introduction to FORTRAN—Part 1 47

FORTRAN character set and coding form
Constants, variables, and expressions
Replacement statement, WRITE, FORMAT, STOP, END
Format codes I, F
Carriage control

Introduction to FORTRAN—Part 2   92

READ, GO TO, arithmetic and logical IF, computed GO TO,
   comment card
Format codes I, F, T, X and literal data

The Counting Process   141

INTEGER, REAL, DATA, IMPLICIT
End of file checking and the END-option
Counting
Format code slash /

6

The Accumulation Process   186

Accumulation
DO loops and the CONTINUE statement
Flowcharting the DO statement
Random numbers

7

Data Representation   220

Integers, real numbers
A format code
DOUBLE PRECISION, COMPLEX, LOGICAL

8

One-Dimensional Arrays   260

Subscripts and arrays
The DIMENSION statement
Implied DO
Frequency distribution and sorting

Two-and Three-Dimensional Arrays   317

Implied DO
Graphing

10   **Functions**   362

FORTRAN supplied functions
User written functions
FORTRAN statements FUNCTION, RETURN
Statement functions

11   **Subroutines**   400

FORTRAN statements CALL, SUBROUTINE, RETURN, COMMON,
   EQUIVALENCE
Flowchart symbols for subroutines
Variable DIMENSIONS
Named COMMON

12   **File Processing**   441

Sequential file concepts
Unformatted READ/WRITE
FORTRAN statements END FILE, REWIND, BACKSPACE,
   DEFINE FILE
Direct access files
Direct access READ and WRITE
File flowchart symbols

13   **Structured Programming**   465

Pseudo code
Top-down program design
DO WHILE, DO UNTIL, and SELECT

Index   485

†

1

COMPUTERS AND COMPUTING

1-1 The Electronic Brain

News Item: When the Apollo 13 flight was jeopardized by unforeseen events, new flight plans produced by computers were available in just 84 minutes. One person working on the problem could have performed the task in 1,040,256 years. With a desk calculator, the time could have been cut to 60,480 years.

News Item: Mathematical Application Group, Inc., has announced a commercially available animation technique called Synthavision using the computer to construct visuals, which, when photographed, resemble conventionally produced cartoons.

News Item: At Loch Ness, Scotland, a group of scientists are using a computer to continuously monitor sonar signals in an effort to find the famous and elusive Loch Ness monster. When a sonar image of a large object is detected by the computer, a camera system is activated which takes a photograph of the object.

News Item: At Bell Laboratories in Murray Hill, New Jersey, a computer has been programmed to produce synthetic human speech. No prerecorded voice is utilized; the computer "reads" sentences and commands a voice synthesizer to produce the proper sounds.

The computers mentioned in the above news items are the high-speed, internally programmed, electronic computers that have become the unseen "brain" behind most of the business transactions of everyday life. Computers have also had an incalculable influence on government, science and the arts in the years since the first fledgling computer was invented in the mid-1940s. Today, computers are being applied to every conceivable problem. One has only to pick up any popular magazine to read about newer, larger and more complex problems being solved by computers. The computer has become an indispensable tool in all scientific and commercial endeavors.

1-2 Computers —What Are They?

Computers are automatic electronic machines that can accept and store vast amounts of information and perform arithmetic at high speeds, to produce answers to complex problems. Without human intervention, computers can process long sequences of instructions (called a *program*) to solve a variety of problems ranging from payroll calculations to satellite trajectory computations.

1-2-1 Organization of a Computer

The computer may be thought of as a system composed of five components, as shown in Figure 1-1. These components and their functions are as follows:

1. The *input* unit feeds information from the outside world to the computer. This information includes both data and instructions (program).[1] Input units are capable of reading information recorded on such different mediums as punched cards, magnetic tape and terminal keyboards. The information read from these devices is placed into appropriate memory locations.

2. The *memory* unit stores information. It holds the program necessary to solve a problem and any data that will be processed by the program. The memory is divided into locations (cells) each of which has an address. Instructions and data are stored in these cells.

3. The *control* unit fetches the instructions and data from memory and executes instructions one at a time with the assistance of either the input, output or arithmetic/logical unit. All of the other components operate as directed by the control unit.

---

[1] Data are the information (raw facts) to be processed by a program. For example, if a program is designed to sort names into alphabetical order, then the names to be sorted would be the data for that program.

4. The *arithmetic/logical* unit consists of the electronic circuitry, which performs arithmetic operations such as addition, multiplication, subtraction and division, and logical operations, such as comparison of numbers.

5. The *output* unit can transfer (copy) the contents of certain memory locations onto some external medium such as punched cards, punched paper tape, magnetic tape, a printed page produced by a teletype or line printer or a cathode ray tube (CRT) screen for visual display.

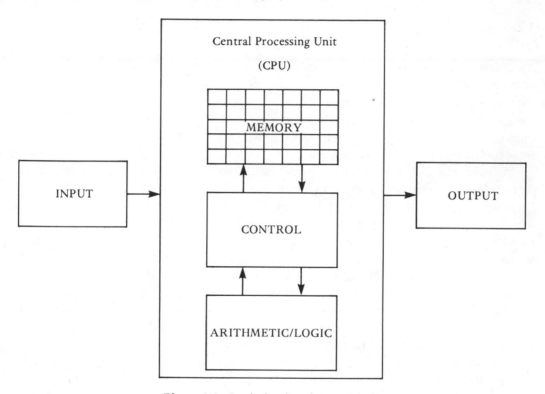

Figure 1-1   Logical units of a computer.

It is quite common to refer to the memory, control and arithmetic/logical units collectively as the *central processing unit (CPU)*. The CPU is the heart and brain of the entire computer system. The input and output functions may be performed by devices located at some distance (a few feet or many miles) from the CPU.

1-2-2 Why Use a Computer?

A computer is a problem-solving machine. However, it cannot be said that the computer is suitable for solving all problems. It is sometimes more economical to solve relatively simple problems, or problems that occur infrequently, by some other means—such as mechanical or manual. If, on the other hand, a problem requires the processing of a large volume of input or output, is repetitive in nature or requires great processing speeds and accuracy, it may be worthwhile or even necessary to use a computer. Some problems cannot be solved without computers. For example, data relayed to the ground by a spacecraft must be analyzed instantaneously to allow controllers to make on-the-spot decisions; only a computer can record and analyze the mass of data fast enough for such decisions to be practical.

1-2-3   Computer Programs

An electronic computer may be called an electronic "brain," but its function and problem-solving ability depend on the intelligence of a human being who directs and controls the machine. This person is called a *programmer* and is responsible for giving the computer a set of instructions consisting of the necessary steps required to derive a solution to a given problem. This set of instructions, which controls the computer, is called a *program*.

A program can be executed (processed) by the computer only when it is stored in the computer's memory and is in machine language code. Machine language is the only language the computer can understand. It is a language in which all operations are represented by machine-recognizable numeric codes and in which memory locations containing data and program instructions are represented by numeric addresses. Machine language programs are very detailed and hence difficult to write. Machine languages will vary from one computer manufacturer to another; such languages are machine dependent, reflecting the design of the particular computer. Other types of languages (called *high-level languages*) have been developed to allow the user to formulate his problem in a much more convenient and efficient manner. Such languages are problem oriented, rather than machine oriented. High-level languages are machine independent, which means that programs written in such languages can be processed on any type of computer. Programs written in a high-level language must ultimately be translated into machine language before they can be executed by the computer. Special programs called *language translators* or *compilers* have, therefore, been developed to provide this translation service. FORTRAN is an example of a high-level language. FORTRAN is an acronym for FORmula TRANslation.

The following will help you understand how and why a language like FORTRAN, instead of the machine language of the computer, is used by the programmer:

Each memory location has an "address." Suppose we wanted to add the data contained in memory locations 065 and 932 and store the result in location 752. The machine instruction for this might be "43065932752." The first two numbers are called the *operation code*. The operation code is used by the control unit to determine what action (add, multiply etc.) is to be performed on the data in the specified memory locations. Following the specification of an operation, the operands are given. Operands represent the addresses of the data to be used. The data we wish to add is located in memory locations 065 and 932. We are going to store our result in location 752. The machine language instruction is broken down as follows:[2]

	43	065 932	752
	↑	↑	↑
	Operation code	Memory address of first and second operands	Address for result

In FORTRAN programs, arithmetic operations are indicated by the symbols + (addition), − (subtraction), * (multiplication), / (division) and ** (exponentiation). Each memory location is assigned a symbolic name. Let us agree to call location 065 by the symbolic name P, location 932 by X, and location 752 by A. Then the FORTRAN instruction equivalent to the machine language instruction "43065932752" would be

$$A = P + X$$

In practice, the high-level language programmer never need worry about machine addresses or operation codes. The FORTRAN programming system takes care of all such details, allowing the programmer to focus his attention on the logic of the problem.

1-3 You Might Want to Know

1. Just how fast do computers operate?

   Answer: The latest model computers operate at speeds measured in *nanoseconds* (1 nanosecond = 1 billionth of a second). For example, the ILLIAC IV computer is capable of executing 100 to 200 million instructions per second, i.e., one instruction takes 5 to 10 nanoseconds to execute.

2. I can't conceive of how fast a nanosecond is. Can you help me?

   Answer: Perhaps. One nanosecond is to one second as one second is to 32 years. In other words, there are approximately one billion seconds in 32 years. One nanosecond is the approximate time required for light to travel one foot.

3. Is there any limit to the internal speeds of a computer?

   Answer: Electrical signals are propagated at speeds approaching the speed of light (1 nanosecond/foot). Integrated circuits packing many thousands of tran-

---

[2] In memory, the machine language instruction would be represented in binary (1's and 0's).

sistors per square inch have been designed to minimize the length of interconnections through which electrical signals are propagated, thereby reducing the time it takes a signal to travel from one transistor to another in that circuit. Figures 1-2 and 1-3 illustrate the size and density of an integrated circuit "chip."

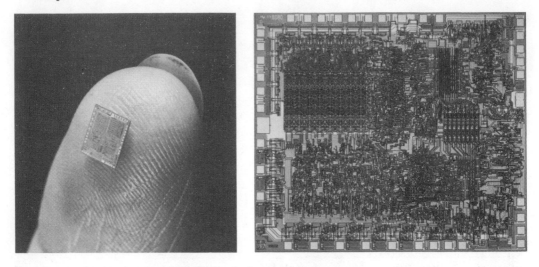

Figure 1-2   The Intel 8080 CPU of the Altair 8800 minicomputer.

Figure 1-3   A magnified view of the Intel 8080 microprocessor. The arithmetic/logic unit occupies most of the lower half of the silicon chip. The CPU registers, which serve as a "scratchpad" during calculations, are at left just above center. The control unit occupies most of the remaining area. Wires attached to the square pads around the rim of the chip connect it to the computer's memory, the input/output devices and a power supply.

4. Computers may be very fast and powerful devices, but aren't there problems that even the fastest and largest computer cannot handle?

   Answer: Yes. If a computer one billion times faster than the fastest available today were to analyze all possible outcomes of a chess game, it would require on the order of 10^{100} hours (many billions of years) to make the first move in the game.

5. Do computers make mistakes?

   Answer: Unless a computer component malfunctions (an extremely rare occurrence), computers do not make mistakes. Of course, the programmer may cause the computer to err because of incorrect instructions in a program. Most "computer errors" are attributable to human error rather than to actual machine malfunction.

6. What computer languages are there other than machine language and FORTRAN?

Answer: One survey reported over 600 computer languages in more or less widespread use. Many of these were special-purpose languages oriented to a single application. Some of the better-known languages include

BASIC	*Beginner's All-Purpose Symbolic Instruction Code*
COBOL	*COmmon Business-Oriented Language*
RPG	*Report Program Generator*
PL/I	*Programming Language I*
ALGOL	*ALGOrithmic Language*
SNOBOL	String Manipulation Language
GPSS	*General-Purpose Simulation System*
APL	*A Programming Language*
WATFOR	*WATerloo FORTRAN*—FORTRAN-like language developed at the University of Waterloo primarily for student usage
WATFIV	A version of WATFOR

7. How many versions of FORTRAN are there?

Answer: Every manufacturer implements FORTRAN in a slightly different way. In fact, a given computer installation might have several different versions of FORTRAN available all running on the same computer. All FORTRAN compilers are measured against a "standard" description of the language formulated by the American National Standards Institute (ANSI), which is a subdivision of the Bureau of Standards. Most FORTRAN compilers meet these standards and have other features which are classified as extensions of the language. A technical reference manual developed by the computer manufacturer for the FORTRAN used at the reader's computer installation is a worthwhile investment and may save hours of frustration and inconvenience. The serious student should consult a FORTRAN user's guide as he or she studies this text.

8. Is there any way I could possibly "hook" up my brain to a computer to assist me in my studies and intellectual pursuits?

Answer: Perhaps someday this will be possible. Dr. Adam V. Reed, a neurologist, computer engineer and now a mathematical psychologist at the Rockefeller University, predicts that within a few years it will be possible to implant a miniscule computer within one's own head. This operation will allow one to store an almost infinite amount of data with near-instant recall capability. This will sharpen man's mental processes with the speed and accuracy of a computer.

1-4   A Model Computer

Let us consider a very simple model computer which operates conceptually in much the same way as its larger real-life counterparts (see Figure 1-4). The input medium consists of pieces of paper onto which numbers have been written. The memory unit consists of a group of sequentially numbered "pigeonholes." Each "hole" or location in the memory can hold one instruction or one number. Locations can be referred to either by name or by address. The arithmetic/logical unit is represented by a desk calculator capable of performing arithmetic and logical operations. The role of the control unit is played by a human operator who can fetch instructions from memory one at a time and execute them; he can also fetch data from or store data into various memory locations. The types of instructions he is capable of executing include:

1. *Input.* Read a value from the input medium and store that value in a specified memory location. For example, the instruction

READ X

will cause one value on the input medium to be read and stored in a memory location called X.

2. *Output.* Copy a value from a memory location onto the output medium. For example, the instruction

WRITE X

will cause the contents of X to be written out on the output pad.

3. *Calculations.* Perform calculations in coordination with the arithmetic unit and place results in desired memory locations. For example, the instruction

$$Y = X * 2 + 1$$

will cause the control unit to fetch the value contained in memory location X and activate the arithmetic unit to multiply that value by 2, and then add 1 to the result. The final result is then stored in memory location Y.

4. *Unconditional branching.* Take the next instruction from a specified memory location. For example, the instruction

GO TO 3

causes the control unit to fetch the next instruction from location 3 rather than from the next sequentially numbered location. Unconditional branching, then, simply means transfer directly to a particular instruction in memory.

5. *Conditional branching.* Perform a comparison test between two values in coordination with the logical unit and branch to a specified memory location if the test condition is met. If the condition is not met, no transfer occurs and

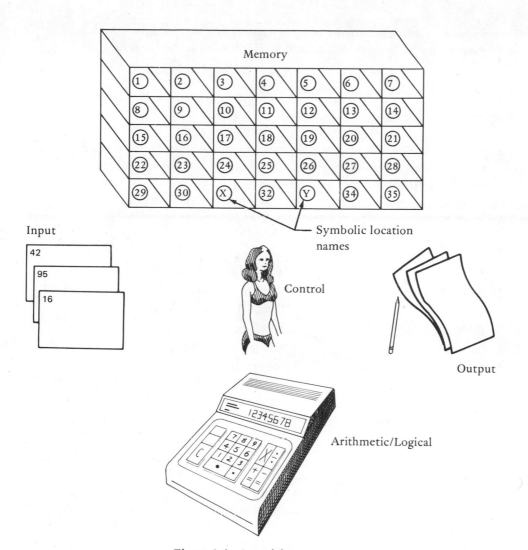

Figure 1-4   A model computer.

the following instruction is taken from the next memory location. For example, the instruction

IF X < 4 GO TO 60

causes the control unit to first fetch the value X from memory and then request the logical unit to compare that value with 4. If the logical unit reports that the value of X is less than 4, the control unit fetches the next instruction from location 60. If the value of X is greater than or equal to 4, the next instruction is taken from the next sequentially numbered location. Hence a conditional transfer allows a program to process a particular instruction(s) if a certain condition is met, or process another different instruction(s) if that condition is not met.

6. *Termination.* Cease execution of instructions for this program and wait for a new program to be loaded into memory. For example, the instruction

STOP

causes the program to terminate. No more instructions in this program are executed.

To illustrate the concepts just discussed, let us write a short program to calculate and write out an amount of pay owed to an employee who is paid $2 an hour with time and a half for all hours in excess of 40. The number of hours worked is punched on a time card. The complete set of instructions to solve this problem might be as follows:

1	READ HRS	Determine the number of hours worked from time card.
2	IF HRS > 40 GO TO 5	Check if number of hours is greater than 40.
3	PAY = 2*HRS	If not, compute regular pay
4	GO TO 6	and go to print pay.
5	PAY = 80 + 3*(HRS − 40)	If hours are greater than 40, compute regular pay, which is $80, plus overtime at rate of $3 per hour.
6	WRITE PAY, HRS	Print pay and number of hours.
7	STOP	Stop.

Suppose now this program has been loaded in memory as shown in Figure 1-5. After execution of the instruction at location 1, the value read from the input unit (38, in this example) is placed in location HRS (see Figure 1-6). The computing system will have automatically reserved a location for HRS. In the second instruction, the logic unit will determine that the contents of location HRS are not greater than 40; hence, the next instruction to be executed comes from location 3. After the instruction in 3 is executed, the contents of location PAY become 2*38 = 76. The instruction at location 4 causes the control unit to take its next instruction from location 6. The instruction at location 6 will cause the contents of locations HRS and PAY to be copied onto the output medium. The instruction at location 7 causes the control unit to stop and wait for the next program. The status of the model computer after execution of this program is shown in Figure 1-6.

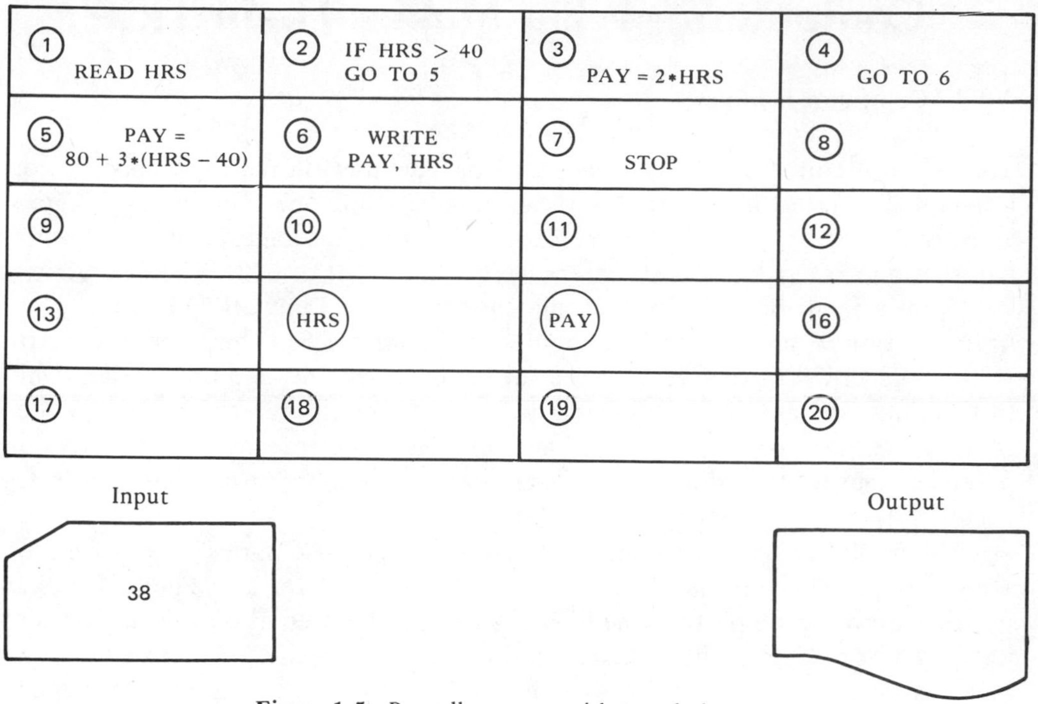

① READ HRS	② IF HRS > 40 GO TO 5	③ PAY = 2*HRS	④ GO TO 6
⑤ PAY = 80 + 3*(HRS − 40)	⑥ WRITE PAY, HRS	⑦ STOP	⑧
⑨	⑩	⑪	⑫
⑬	(HRS)	(PAY)	⑯
⑰	⑱	⑲	⑳

Input

38

Output

Figure 1-5 Payroll program with sample input.

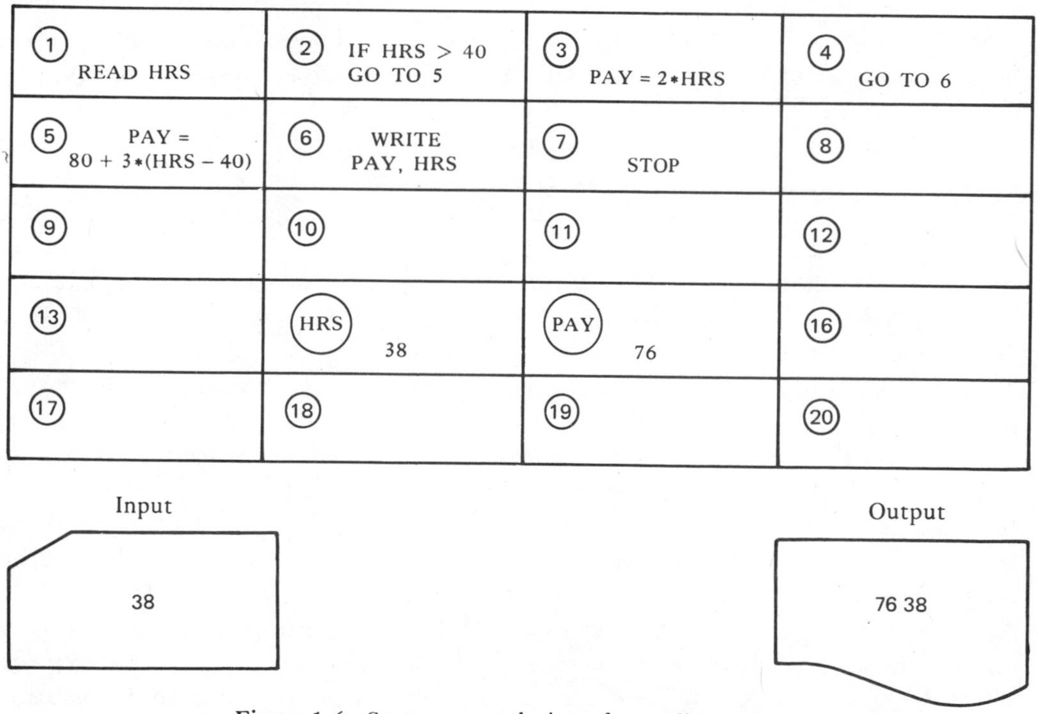

① READ HRS	② IF HRS > 40 GO TO 5	③ PAY = 2*HRS	④ GO TO 6
⑤ PAY = 80 + 3*(HRS − 40)	⑥ WRITE PAY, HRS	⑦ STOP	⑧
⑨	⑩	⑪	⑫
⑬	(HRS) 38	(PAY) 76	⑯
⑰	⑱	⑲	⑳

Input

38

Output

76 38

Figure 1-6 Status at conclusion of payroll program.

1-5 Computers—What Makes Them Tick?

1-5-1 Computer Hardware

The physical configuration (the *hardware* or machinery) used for the logical components illustrated in Figure 1-1 varies greatly from one computing system to another. Typically the memory, control and arithmetic/logical units are grouped together and referred to as the *central processing unit* or *CPU*. The CPU varies in size from a small box in a typical minicomputer (see Figure 1-7) to a fairly large unit in a typical medium-scale computer (see Figure 1-8). The internal construction of the CPU, the technology used for the memory unit and the speed at which instructions are executed vary greatly from one computer to another. Modern systems tend to make great use of microminiaturized integrated circuits making possible significant reduction in sizes and increase in processing speeds (see Figure 1-2).

The hardware used for input and output devices also varies greatly from one system to another. Some devices, such as the line printer (see Figure 1-9), card punch and the graph plotter (see Figure 1-10), can be used as output devices only. Other devices, such as the punched-card reader (see Figure 1-11), can be used as input devices only. Some devices can be used both for input and output purposes, although generally not simultaneously. Such devices include the Teletype (see Figure 1-12), the punched-paper tape reader/punch, the CRT (cathode ray tube) console (see Figure 1-13), the magnetic disk, the magnetic drum and magnetic tape. The latter three devices are sometimes referred to as *mass storage* devices because they are capable of storing large quantities of data and can be accessed by the CPU very rapidly.

The input/output devices for a particular system may be located physically close to the CPU or at some distance—in an adjacent room or miles away. In the latter case, data may be transmitted to the CPU via telephone lines. This technique is called *telecommunication*. The user may dial up the computer's number to initiate communication, identify himself, transmit a program and/or data and receive results at his terminal. When the user is finished, he can release the telephone line for other use.

A typical computing system will generally include a great variety of input/output devices. Most of these devices are electromechanical and thus operate at far slower speeds than CPU internal processing speeds where processing is wholly electronic. Therefore, if the CPU were required to wait for such devices to perform a complete operation (a data transmission from a Teletype, for example), the advantage of the tremendous internal speeds of the CPU would be greatly reduced. In most computer installations, the CPU is equipped with one or more channels. A *channel* is a special-purpose device which controls input/output operations; it relieves the CPU of the task of communicating directly with input/output devices. The CPU, for example, will instruct a channel to perform an output operation (e.g., write out results on a printer), and while the channel is busy servicing this

Figure 1-7   A Central Processing Unit (courtesy Hewlett-Packard Company).

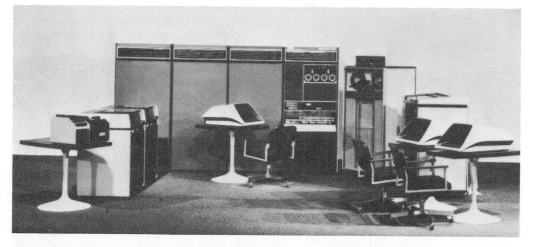

Figure 1-8   DEC System-10 Central Processing Unit (courtesy Digital Equipment Corporation).

Figure 1-9   A line printer (courtesy IBM).

Figure 1-10   A plotter (courtesy Hewlett-Packard Company).

Figure 1-11   A card reader (courtesy IBM).

Figure 1-12   Teletype terminal (courtesy Teletype Corporation).

Figure 1-13   A CRT console (courtesy Hewlett-Packard Company).

output request the CPU can continue processing instructions. In this way CPU computations are carried out concurrently with I/O operations, which greatly increases the efficiency of the computer system.

Computers can be used in many different types of operating environments, each reflecting different organizational needs, hardware configurations, and economic bases. Of special interest are multiprogramming and time-sharing environments. In a multiprogramming setting several programs are present in memory at one time. While a channel is servicing an I/O request for a particular program, the CPU can start processing a new program, or resume processing a program temporarily interrupted by a previous I/O request or each program may be interrupted sequentially to allow execution of other programs in memory. In a time-sharing environment, numerous terminals (Teletypes, CRT's etc.) are attached to the CPU by ground cables or telephone lines. These terminals allow users to communicate directly (*on-line*) with the computer. Users enter their programs directly into the system at the terminal rather than submitting the program in punched card form. To the user at the terminal, it appears that he has the computer all to himself and that only his program is being executed by the CPU. In reality, the CPU may be servicing several other users concurrently. This is accomplished by allowing each user a small slice of time and by processing each user's program in turn. Thus while one user is typing FORTRAN instructions on a Teletype the CPU may be processing another user's program. The most significant advantage of time sharing is that the user has immediate access to the computer; feedback is instantaneous. In addition, computer utilization costs can be significantly lowered by multiuser participation.

1-5-2 Software

The term *software* is generally used to describe the set of programs, written by the programmer, which causes the computer hardware to function. There are three basic software categories:

1. Translation programs.

2. Operating system programs.

3. User processing programs.

Translation programs (compilers) are programs used by the computer system to translate high-level languages or problem-oriented languages into machine language. These translation programs are generally supplied by the hardware manufacturer.

Operating system programs are usually supplied by the computer manufacturer to assist in the overall operation of the computer system. They are used to regulate and supervise the sequence of activities going on at any time in the system. These programs minimize operator intervention in the actual operation of the computer and ensure a smooth, fast and efficient transition among the varied tasks performed by the system. Other operating system programs aid the programmer in his own work; examples of such programs are utility and library programs. Following is a list of functions performed by some operating system programs:

1. Load programs into memory from mass storage.

2. Print messages for the operator and the programmer regarding the status of the program.

3. Perform job accounting by keeping track of who uses the computer and for how long.

4. Handle requests for input/output from executing programs.

5. Handle the collection of data from telecommunication lines (in a time-sharing system).

6. Schedule the slice of time to be allocated each user's program (in a time-sharing or multiprogramming system).

7. Perform some routine processing of data, such as sorting and copying the contents of one data set onto a specified device.

8. Maintain the store of programs on the mass storage device—adding programs to the store, deleting those no longer needed and so forth.

9. Attempt to recover from and/or correct errors that may occur in any segment of the computing system.

10. Interpret the job set up and job control instructions specified by the programmer.

At the heart of most operating systems is a program variously called the *supervisor*, the *executive* or the *monitor*. This program is usually resident in memory at all times and performs many essential tasks such as program loading and error checking. This resident portion of the operating system loads other less-often used routines as they are required.

User processing programs, sometimes called *applications programs*, are those programs written by individual users to solve particular problems. They may be written in a generalized fashion and modified as needed to fit the peculiar requirements of a particular system, or they may be constructed exactly to satisfy specific needs. For example, a company may construct its own payroll system or it may purchase (or rent) a general set of payroll programs and modify them if necessary. Companies guard their processing programs as a very important company asset. Extensive security measures are taken to avoid the loss or theft of programs. A considerable store of programs is usually available to a computer user; in fact, the usefulness of a computer may well depend more on the variety and efficiency of the available software than on any single aspect of the hardware.

It is of interest to note that over the last decade or so computer hardware has undergone dramatic cost reductions, which have not been accompanied by corresponding reductions in computer software costs. On the contrary, software development costs have soared to the point where now in a typical computer operation approximately 85 percent of the total computer system budget is earmarked for software costs, as opposed to only 5 percent in 1950.

1-5-3   The Punched Card

One of the most widely used media for communication with a computer is the punched card. Many computer systems require the user to punch his program and data on punched cards before these can be processed by the card reader (see Figure 1-11). The most widely used version of the punched card is shown in Figure 1-14. The card is divided into 80 vertical columns; each column can be used to record one character. A character is represented by one or more punched holes. Each column is divided into 12 horizontal punch positions or rows. Rows 0, 1, 2, . . .,9 are usually numbered on the card; rows 12 and 11 are at the top of the card and usually are not numbered. The top area of the card is usually left blank for interpretation (printed translation) of the data punched on the card.

The code used to represent data on a punched card is called the Hollerith code, in honor of Herman Hollerith who, around 1890, pioneered the use of punched-card equipment for data-processing machines. The Hollerith code is summarized in Figure 1-14. Each alphabetic character is represented by two punches—a zone punch (12, 11 or 0) and a numeric punch (1, 2, . . .,9). Numeric characters require only a single numeric punch (0, 1, 2, . . .,9). Other characters are assigned other combinations of punches. The codes used for these vary from one system to another. The card illustrated in Figure 1-12 was punched on an IBM 029 keypunch machine.

Cards are punched on a keypunch machine such as the one shown in Figure 1-15. The keypunch is equipped with a keyboard similar to the keyboard of a typewriter (see Figure 1-16). Depressing a key causes the appropriate character to be punched on a card. The ALPHA and NUMERIC keys are used to punch characters from the lower half of a key (ALPHA) or the upper half of a key (NUMERIC). The device is ordinarily in ALPHA mode, which means that depressing a key will cause the character on the lower half of the key to be punched. To punch a character on the upper half of a key, both the NUMERIC and the key for the desired character must be depressed at the same time, similar to depressing the shift key on the typewriter.

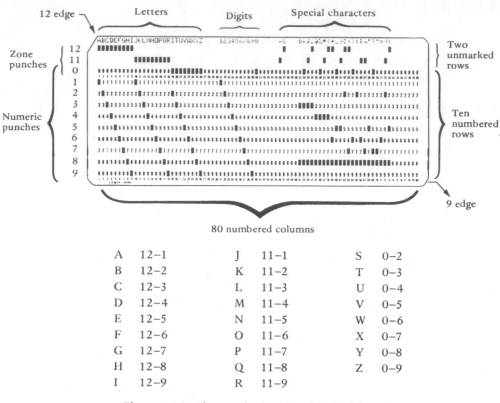

Figure 1-14   The punched card and Hollerith code.

A	12–1	J	11–1	S	0–2
B	12–2	K	11–2	T	0–3
C	12–3	L	11–3	U	0–4
D	12–4	M	11–4	V	0–5
E	12–5	N	11–5	W	0–6
F	12–6	O	11–6	X	0–7
G	12–7	P	11–7	Y	0–8
H	12–8	Q	11–8	Z	0–9
I	12–9	R	11–9		

Figure 1-15   Keyboard of IBM 029 keypunch
(courtesy IBM).

Figure 1-16   IBM 029 keypunch
(courtesy IBM).

1-5-4 Computer Access Modes

From a user standpoint, communications (submission of programs) with a computer can be established in two different methods or modes: *batch-processing* and *conversational* mode. Both of these access methods may or may not be available on the user's particular computer system. Some systems will support batch-processing mode only, while others will support conversational mode only. Some systems will support both.

Batch-processing can be characterized as an indirect method to communicate with a computer (see Figure 1-17). The user must first punch the instructions on cards, which must then be read by a card reader (Figure 1-13) to transmit the instructions to the computer system. Thus, the punched card acts as an intermediary agent between the user and the computer. In conversational mode, the user communicates directly (or enters into a dialogue) with the computer by keying in instructions line by line on a terminal (see Figures 1-9 and 1-10). The computer may then immediately react to each line by specifying whether any grammatical errors have been made. The user can then key in corrections. If no errors are present in the complete program, the computer will print results on the user's teletype or visual screen, thus providing the user with near instantaneous feedback. Such a quick-response system is highly desirable both in terms of time saving and learning benefits. In a batch-processing environment, on the other hand, hours or even days may elapse before the user obtains his output (results). Typically, the computer operator may wait until a sufficient number of punched-card programs have collected; the operator then creates a batch (queue) of programs, which is submitted to the card reader. The computer then processes these programs sequentially in the order encountered in the input stream. Results are then printed (first one in, first one out) on a printer on continuous output forms, which must then be separated by the operator and distributed to each owner (punch cards and result listing). This sequence of activities, over which the user has no control, is time consuming, which explains the time delay (turnaround time) between submission of a program and receipt of the output. If mistakes (keypunching or other) are made, many program submissions may be required before receiving an error-free output. Figure 1-17 illustrates the logistics of batch-processing.

In systems which support conversational computing, the communication link between the terminal and the computer takes many forms. Telephone links are quite commonly used. To initiate communications via the telephone, the user must dial the number of the computer and place the telephone receiver in a special device (called a *modem*) which is attached to the communications terminal. When other types of links are used, it is usually unnecessary for the user to take special action to establish communications.

In all but the smallest systems, the user must establish his identity to the computer before making use of the computing facility. This is done to enable the system to account for the time used, to bill users accordingly and to establish what resources are available to individual users. Before a person can make use of a

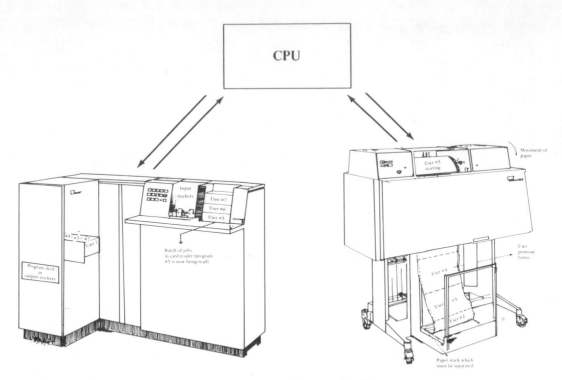

Figure 1-17   Batch-processing flow.

conversational system, it is generally necessary to have an assigned account number and perhaps also a special password. After establishing the communications link, if necessary, the user enters his account number and password. If these match a list kept by the computing system, the user is allowed to proceed; if not, the user may not have access to the computing facility. These steps, called a *sign-on procedure*, are quite specific to a particular computing system. An equally important operation is the *sign-off procedure*, which is followed when the user is finished. Almost all systems have a command such as GOODBYE or BYE which terminates the user's communications with the system and releases the terminal for another user. It is important that the sign-off procedure be followed after each session at a terminal. If a user does not sign off, the next person may continue without signing on, and the time used by both persons will be charged to the first user's account.

It will be necessary for the reader to familiarize himself with the system he plans to use. A user's manual is normally available for this purpose. Before attempting to write a FORTRAN program on a given system, the user should learn the sign-on/sign-off procedures and other idiosyncracies of his particular computing system. A coworker or fellow student who has just made a run on the system may also be helpful in this regard.

1-5-5   A Typical Job

The FORTRAN program shown in Figure 1-18 will perform the task outlined in Section 1-4. Comparison of this program with the program in Section 1-4 should reveal many similarities as well as some differences in the actual code. The requirements for writing FORTRAN code are the subject of the remainder of this text, so the reader need not be concerned with the technical details of the program at this time.

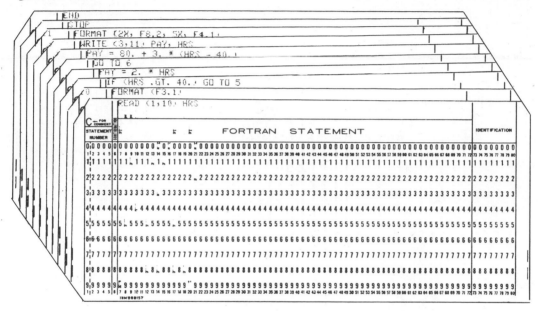

Figure 1-18   FORTRAN program.

Let us assume for the moment that the program has been written and is available in the form shown in Figure 1-18. The program and data it will process must still be prepared in some suitable form for submission to the computer. In a conversational computing environment, the program and data will be entered one line at a time at a terminal (see Section 1-5-3). In a batch-computing environment, the program and data will be punched onto cards and submitted to the computer as a complete "job." In both conversational and batch environments, certain instructions must be included to inform the operating system how the job is to be processed. In a conversational environment, these instructions are specified at the terminal; in a batch environment, these instructions are punched onto cards and submitted with the program and data. Figure 1-19 shows a complete job deck for the compilation and execution of the program shown in Figure 1-18. Note the inclusion of operating system instructions (job control cards) before, between and after the program and data. The operating system instructions will vary greatly from one computing system to another; hence the reader must determine local requirements for these instructions.

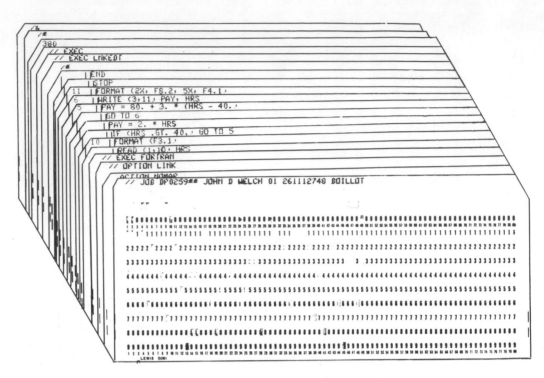

Figure 1-19 Complete job deck for sample FORTRAN program.

1-6 Exercises

1-6-1 Self Test

1. List five parts of a computer and explain the function of each.

2. Define the following:

   a. CPU
   b. CRT
   c. Program
   d. Data
   e. Nanosecond
   f. ANSI
   g. Machine language
   h. Unconditional branch
   i. Conditional branch
   j. Batch environment
   k. Conversational computing
   l. Hollerith code

3. What value will be written by the program in Figure 1-5 if the input value is 47.5 instead of 38?

4. If the punches 0–3, 12–8, 12–5, 12–5, 11–5 and 12–4 are found on a punched card, what is the meaning of the message?

5. The card used for keypunching is divided into ___ vertical columns and ___ punching positions (rows).

6. Which of the following is used for input as well as output?
   a. Card reader   b. Printer   c. Magnetic tape
   d. All of the above   e. None of the above

7. A compiler is
   a. A program which translates machine code into a high-level language.
   b. Another name for FORTRAN.
   c. A program which loads FORTRAN into memory.
   d. A program which translates a high-level language program into machine code.

8. The part of the machine-language instruction which tells the computer what to do is called
   a. An operand   b. A compiler   c. An operation code   d. A translator

9. Determine whether each of the following statements is true or false.
   a. Each memory location has a corresponding address.
   b. A machine language operand may indicate where the result of a particular operation is to be placed.
   c. Computer hardware consists of all the physical components which make up a computer system.
   d. High-level languages are machine-independent.
   e. The term *software* refers to such material as punched cards, magnetic tape, paper tape etc.
   f. In a batch-processing environment, the user receives an almost instantaneous response to his program.
   g. Time sharing is made possible by the use of time slices.
   h. Multiprogramming means that instructions from two or more programs can be processed at the same time by the CPU.
   i. A single card column may accommodate any number up to and including the number 99.

1-6-2 Other Problems

1. Modify the program in Section 1-4 to read both the number of hours worked and the rate of pay from one input card. The output line should contain the pay, the hours worked and the rate.

2. a. If you will be working in a conversational computing environment, determine sign-on, sign-off and other procedures necessary to compile and execute a FORTRAN program. Try out these procedures with the program shown in Figure 1-17.

b. If you will be working in a batch-processing environment, determine the operating system instructions and the exact makeup of the job deck necessary to compile and execute a FORTRAN program. Try out these procedures with the program shown in Figure 1-17.

3. Make a list of tasks to which computers have been applied. Pool the list you make with others in your class. The variety and number of applications will probably surprise you and will give you a feeling for the important role the computer plays in our society.

4. List some problems that would not be suitable for solution by means of a computer. Are there any conditions which would change your assessment of the feasibility of a computer solution?

1-6-3 Answers to Self Test

1. Input: Device which reads information from some medium.
    Output: Device which writes information onto some medium.
    Memory: Stores program instructions and data.
    Arithmetic/logical: Circuitry which performs arithmetic and decisions on the data.
    Control: Executes program instructions.

2. a. CPU: Central processing unit—Memory, arithmetic/logical and control units.
    b. CRT: Cathode ray tube—Input/output visual display device.
    c. Program: Instructions to solve a problem.
    d. Data: Information to be processed by a program (numbers, lists of names etc.).
    e. Nanosecond: One billionth of a second.
    f. ANSI: American National Standards Institute.
    g. Machine language: Numerical language inherent in the design of the particular computer.
    h. Unconditional branch: GOTO—branch or transfer to same location each time the instruction is executed.
    i. Conditional branch: IF—branch based on whether a condition is true or false.
    j. Batch environment: Computing system in which programs and data are processed some period of time after submission of programs.
    k. Conversational computing: Computing system in which user's instructions and data are analyzed and processed immediately.

1. Hollerith code: Punched-card code.

3. 102.5; 47.5   4. THEEND.   5. 80, 12.

6. c.   7. d.   8. c.

9. a. T.   b. T.   c. T.   d. T.   e. F.   f. F.   g. T.   h. F.   i. F.

FLOWCHARTING

2-1 Algorithms, Programs and Flowcharts

As a problem solver, the computer can function only if it is given instructions as to how to proceed. A set of instructions for solving a problem is called an *algorithm*. Algorithms of one type or another are used daily by people to solve such routine problems as baking a cake, operating an electrical appliance or solving a quadratic equation. Algorithms may be expressed in verbal or in symbolic form. A useful algorithm must be expressed in a way that can be understood and executed by the person (or machine) for which it is intended. A computer *program* is a specific example of an algorithm intended for a machine. It is expressed in a symbolic language which the computer can readily understand and execute.

Because of the logical organization and sequencing of program instructions and because of requirements of specific computer languages, it is usually difficult to write a computer program without first expressing the algorithm in some preliminary form. For a simple problem, a verbal outline of the steps required may suffice; for more complex problems, however, a widely used tool is the program *flowchart*. A flowchart is a pictorial representation of the logic (method) used to solve a particular problem. It is a diagram illustrating the sequence of steps (instructions) that a person or machine must execute to arrive at the solution to a problem. A flowchart is particularly useful for visualizing paths through the logic of an algorithm. For example, the algorithm of Figure 1-5 (computing pay given the number of hours worked) could be expressed in flowchart form as shown in Figure 2-1. Note that there are two paths through the algorithm; the path taken depends on the particular value of HRS supplied at execution time. Since there is generally more than one correct method to solve a problem, one should expect that there might be any number of flowcharts to describe various methods for solving a given problem.

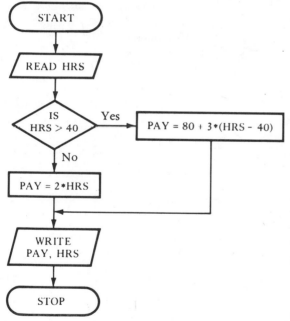

Find the number of hours (HRS) punched on a card (the data card is not shown).

Is the number of hours greater than 40? If so, compute total pay, which includes overtime ((HRS − 40) times time-and-a-half rate) and go and write PAY and HRS. Otherwise compute regular PAY, meaning HRS is less than 40. The asterisk (∗) means multiplication.

Write out the value of PAY and HRS and stop.

Figure 2-1   Flowchart for the algorithm of Figure 1-5.

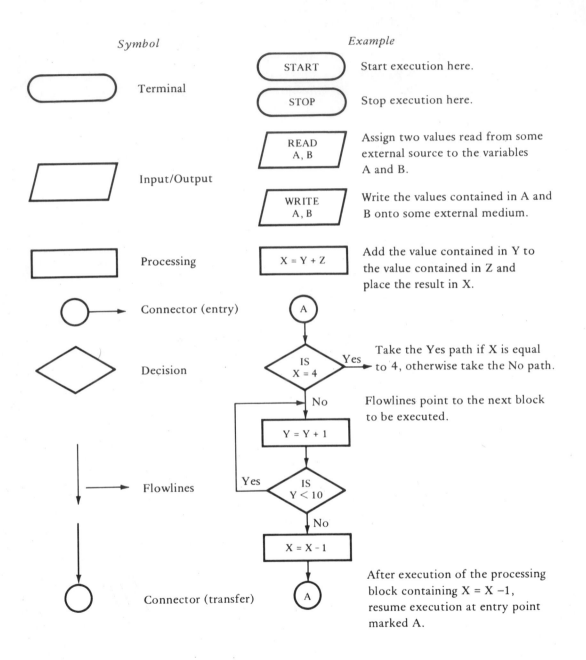

Figure 2-2 Program flowchart symbols.

2-2   Flowchart Symbols

In program flowcharts, the symbols shown in Figure 2-2 are generally used. Each symbol or *block* represents a different type of operation. Written within the blocks are instructions to indicate (in general terms) what operation is to be performed. It is not necessary to express the instructions used in a flowchart block in any particular computer language; it is sufficient that the instructions reflect the general functional operations used in the computing system. From the flowchart, it will be possible to write computer programs in a number of different languages. The emphasis in the flowchart is on the logic required for solving a problem rather than on the mechanics or specifics of a programming language.

2-2-1 The Terminal Block

An oval-shaped symbol (   ) is used to mark the point at which execution of instructions is to begin and end. The instruction START may be used to mark the beginning point; the instruction END or STOP may be used to mark the ending point.

2-2-2 The Input/Output Block

A symbol shaped like a parallelogram /   / is used for input and output instructions. For an input operation the instruction (command) READ followed by a list of names (called *variables*) separated by commas is used. These variables can be thought of as symbolic names given to memory locations into which the

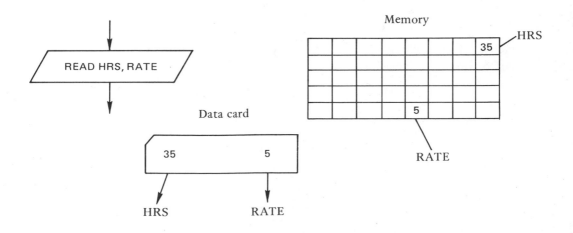

Figure 2-3   Meaning of the READ block.

data is to be stored. Rather than give each memory location a numerical address, which would be difficult to remember and which would not be very meaningful, symbolic names are used to represent the data. The computer, not the programmer, determines which exact memory cell is to be used to store the particular data. Variable names can be chosen to convey the nature of the data to be processed. For example, the flowchart segment in Figure 2-3 shows that two numbers are to be read from a record (card) and stored in two memory locations called HRS and RATE. Other names, such as X and Y, could have been used instead of HRS and RATE. Here again, judicious selection of HRS and RATE serves to better identify and document the nature of the transaction under consideration. For an output operation, the instruction WRITE, followed by a list of symbolic locations (variables), is used. The value of each of the locations is to be written onto some output device. For example, the block $\overline{\text{WRITE PAY, HRS}}$ indicates that values in locations PAY and HRS are to be displayed on some device.

2-2-3 The Processing Block

A rectangular-shaped symbol $\boxed{}$ is used for processing instructions. The most common form for expressing these instructions is the *replacement statement*. A replacement statement specifies the arithmetic operations to be performed on constants and/or variables and the location (variable) into which the value computed is to be placed. For example, the block $\boxed{X = Y + Z}$ specifies that addition is to be performed on the contents (value) of Y and Z and the results are to be placed into X. Any sequence of operations can be performed, but there must be a single variable specified as the destination for the value calculated (only one variable on the left-hand side of the equal sign).

2-2-4 The Decision Block

A diamond-shaped symbol $\diamondsuit$ is used to denote decisions. A common means of expressing a decision is in terms of a question which can be answered yes or no. The question must involve only mathematical relations, such as equality (=), less than (<), greater than (>), less than or equal to (≤), greater than or equal to (≥) or not equal to (≠). The decision block is the only block from which two different logical paths may be selected. Flowlines indicate the path to be taken, depending on the decision made. For example, consider the following decision block:

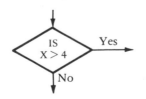

If the value of X is greater than 4, the path marked YES is taken; otherwise, the NO path is taken.

Another way of expressing decision is in terms of a comparison between two values. The two values being compared are separated by a colon (:) in the decision block; the two paths are marked with the relation symbols that are appropriate for the decision in question. For example, the decision above could also be written:

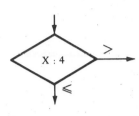

If X is greater than 4, the path marked ">" will be taken; otherwise, the path marked "≤" will be taken.

2-2-5 Flowlines

The sequence of instructions to be executed in a flowcharted algorithm is denoted by straight lines with an arrowhead such as ⟶ or ↓ . The direction of flow is always in the direction pointed out by the arrowhead.

2-2-6 Connector Blocks

When it is inconvenient to draw flowlines to connect one area of the flowchart to another, connectors are often used. Connectors serve two purposes:

1. To identify a block by a label for reference purposes, and

2. To indicate transfer to another labeled block.

The symbol used for a connector is a small circle ◯ .
A numeric or alphabetic label is placed in the connector block. When the flowline points away from the connector such as ◯⟶ , the connector is being used to denote an entry point, that is, a block to which transfer will be made from some point in the flowchart. When the flowline points toward the connector as in ⟶◯ , the connector is being used to indicate a transfer, that is, execution should resume at an entry point with the same symbol as used in the connector at the transfer point. For example, consider the following flowchart segment:

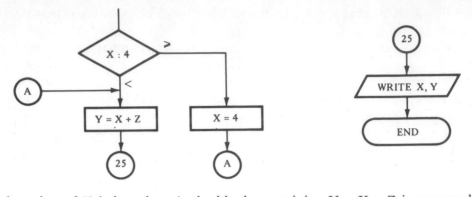

If the value of X is less than 4, the block containing Y = X + Z is executed and transfer is made to the entry point marked "25" which contains the WRITE instruction. If the value of X is not less than 4, the block containing X = 4 is executed and transfer is made to the entry point labeled "A." The flowchart above is equivalent to the following:

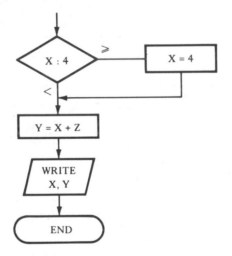

Note that in a flowchart it is possible to have many transfer connectors such as ——▸(A) . Only one entry connector such as (A)——▸ may be designated in a flowchart, however.

2-3 You Might Want To Know

1. Are program flowcharts of any use once a program has been written?

   Answer: Yes, program flowcharts serve as documentation of the logic used in the program. Any changes that need to be made to a program may be visualized more easily by referencing the flowchart rather than the actual program.

2. How does one learn to draw flowcharts?

Answer: Flowcharting involves not only understanding the way in which computing systems work but also (as in any problem-solving environment) the ability to think logically. A systematic approach is necessary: One must analyze what is known and what is wanted and generate a sequence of instructions required to proceed from what is known to obtain the desired output. With experience, one will find the language of flowcharts a very useful aid in making a problem analysis complete and logically correct.

3. What kinds of flowcharts other than program flowcharts are there?

Answer: In relation to computers, other kinds of flowcharts are system flowcharts which show the relationship among various programs in a system (see Section 12-5-5). In other technological fields, flowcharts may be used as an aid in visualizing relationships among entities of various systems or processes.

4. Are the program flowchart symbols standard?

Answer: There is a fair degree of standardization in the use of flowchart symbols. Older books may use a set of symbols that are somewhat different. For example, the input/output block may be represented by the symbol ⬡ . In some texts, the symbol ⬠ is used for input, and the symbol ⬓ is used for output.

5. Often computer output consists of alphabetic as well as numeric characters. How can this be indicated on a flowchart?

Answer: A common means of indicating alphabetic or *literal* data to be written onto an output device is to use quotations around the desired characters in an output block. For example, the block ⬦WRITE "PAY=",P⬦ would indicate that the characters 'PAY=' are to be printed followed by the value in location P.

2-4 Examples

2-4-1 A Compound Interest Problem

Compute the interest on $100 at 5 percent compounded yearly for four years and write out the principal and interest for each year. The flowchart for this problem is shown in Figure 2-4. This flowchart involves a sequence of instructions which are executed repeatedly (a *loop*).

The variable P (principal) is initially set at 100. At the end of the first year, when the interest I has been computed, the new principal P is equal to the old principal P plus the interest I. This is accomplished by the statement P = P + I (the first time through the loop, the new P = old P + I = 100 + 5 = 105). The next time through the loop, the interest is computed on this new principal. The values that are assumed by the variables may be tabulated as shown in Figure 2-4. Each time a new value is computed for a variable, the new value replaces whatever value was previously assigned to the variable.

Note how the variable K is used to count the years. K is initially set to 0. Each time the interest and principal have been computed for one year K is incremented by one. In this way we are keeping track of the number of times the principal and interest are computed. When K reaches the value N (4 in this example), processing is terminated since the principal and interest will have been computed N times.

Note that in the flowchart of Figure 2-4 the block $\boxed{N = 4}$ could be omitted; the decision would then be $\langle K : 4 \rangle$.

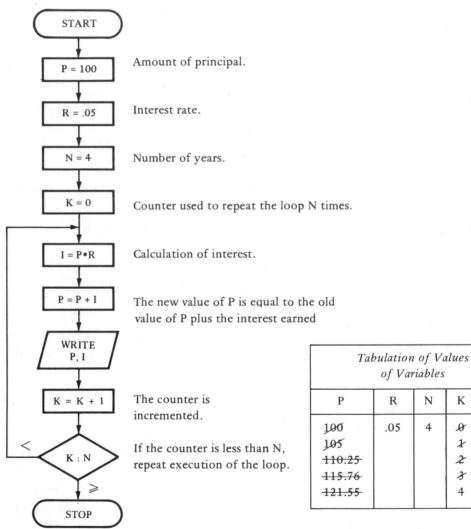

Figure 2-4   Flowchart and table of values for the compound interest problem.

2-4-2 Computation of an Average

Six grades are recorded on six data cards. We wish to compute the average grade and write it out. The flowchart for this problem is shown in Figure 2-5. Note that the sum SUM is initially set to 0, as it should be when no grades have yet been read. Each time a grade GRADE is read it is added to SUM, thereby reflecting the sum of the grades read so far. Note also the use of the counter I to keep track of how many values are read. When I has a value of 6, six grades have been read, and the average is computed and printed.

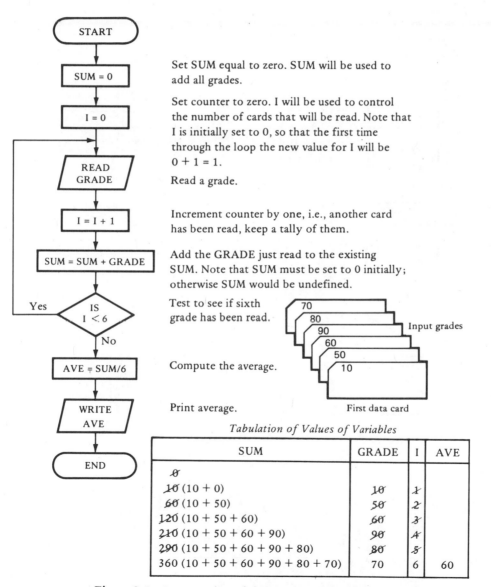

Figure 2-5   Computation of the average of six grades.

2-4-3 Calculation of N! (N! = N-factorial)

Let us construct an algorithm for the calculation of N! = 1 · 2 · 3 · 4 · · · · N for a value of N accepted from input. In general, the factorial function N!, where N is an integer, represents the product of the first N integers starting with one. For example, 15! = 1 · 2 · 3 · · · · · 15. The flowchart for this problem is shown in Figure 2-6. Note the use of the counter K and an accumulator PROD. The prod-

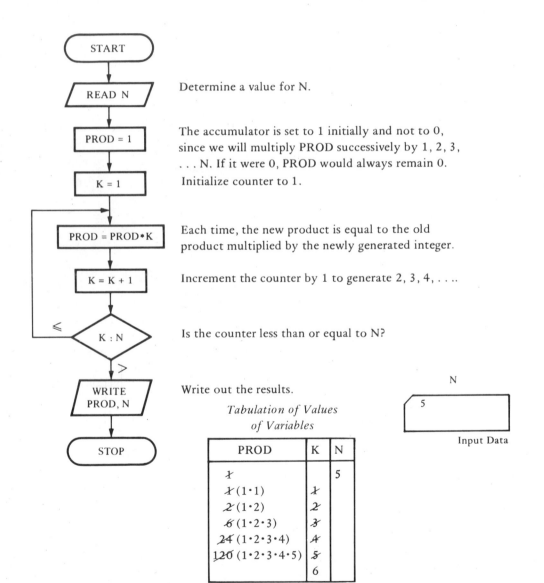

Determine a value for N.

The accumulator is set to 1 initially and not to 0, since we will multiply PROD successively by 1, 2, 3, . . . N. If it were 0, PROD would always remain 0.

Initialize counter to 1.

Each time, the new product is equal to the old product multiplied by the newly generated integer.

Increment the counter by 1 to generate 2, 3, 4, ...

Is the counter less than or equal to N?

Write out the results.

Tabulation of Values of Variables

PROD	K	N
1̶		5
1̶ (1·1)	1̶	
2̶ (1·2)	2̶	
6̶ (1·2·3)	3̶	
2̶4̶ (1·2·3·4)	4̶	
1̶2̶0̶ (1·2·3·4·5)	5̶	
	6	

Input Data

Figure 2-6 Computation of N!.

uct of all the values of K is accumulated in location PROD. When K has been incremented to a value larger than N, the value of N! has been calculated and so the desired output is produced. It should be noted that factorials grow very quickly in magnitudes and that 16! on most computers is even too large to represent as an integer value.

2-5 Exercises

2-5-1 Self Test

1. Is a recipe found in a cookbook an example of a flowchart? An algorithm? A program?

2. Determine the output produced by the following flowcharts, given the following data cards:

a.   b.

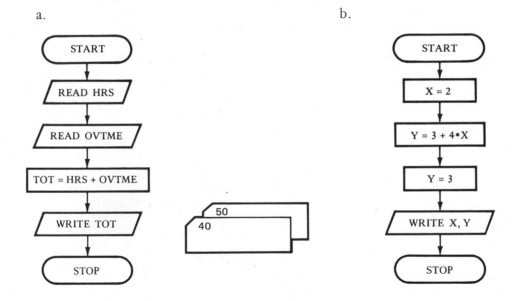

3. Determine the number of cards read by each of the following flowcharts:

a.   b.

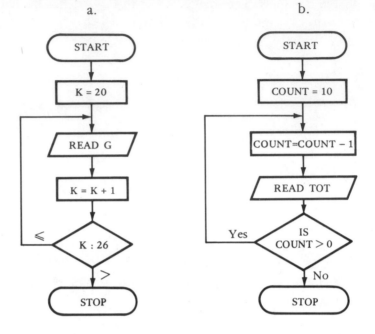

c.

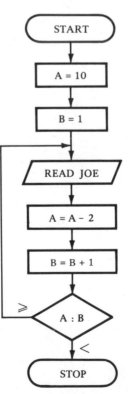

4. Write down any six numbers on six simulated data cards and determine what process the following flowcharts represent (assume that each pass through a READ block specifies the reading of exactly one card).

a.   b.   c.

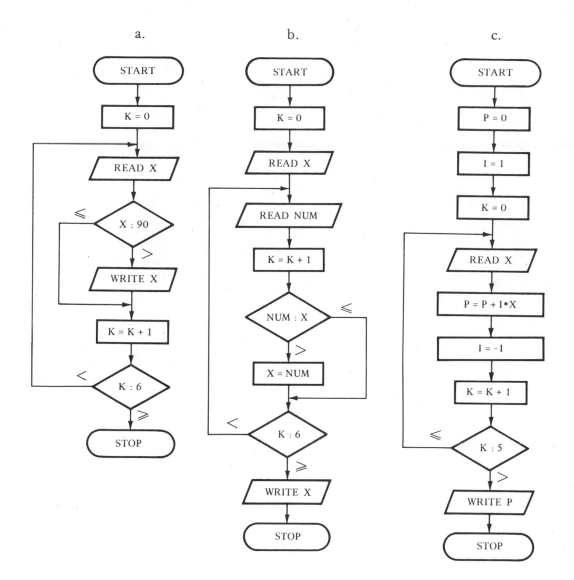

5. Tabulate the values of K, X and Y given the following flowchart and data cards. Indicate what values will be printed for K, X and Y. Is this a valid flowchart?

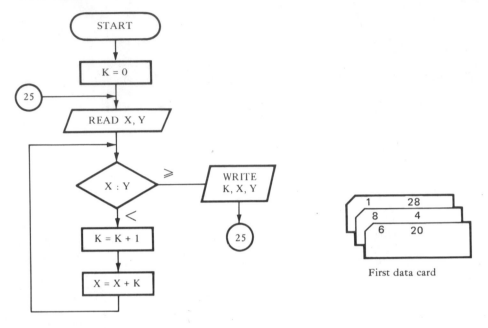

First data card

6. A deck of 16 cards contains one temperature reading per card which can be either positive, negative or zero. Draw a flowchart to print the count of positive, negative and zero temperatures to obtain a printout similar to the following (assume each WRITE block causes just one line of output to be printed).

a.   b.

```
TEMPERATURE
     -3
      2
      0
     -3
      0
      1

COUNT    POSITIVE IS   1
COUNT    NEGATIVE IS   3
COUNT    ZERO IS       2
```

```
TEMPERATURE    -3
                2
                0
               -3
                0
                1

COUNT + = I    COUNT - = 3    COUNT 0 = 2
```

7. How could the flowchart of Figure 2-5 be modified to compute interest compounded twice a year? Monthly? Daily?

8. Modify the flowchart of Figure 2-5 to accept the principal, rate and number of quarters as input.

9. How would one modify the flowchart of Figure 2-6 to compute the average of 20 grades?

10. In Figure 2-4 could the years N have been used as a counter (instead of K) and decremented each time through the loop by 1 until it reached the value 1 or 0? Draw a flowchart to reflect this approach.

11. Modify the flowchart of Figure 2-7 to compute the product of the odd integers up to 57, that is, $P = 1 \cdot 3 \cdot 5 \cdots \cdot 57$ (assuming the computer can process a number of that magnitude). Write out the results and do *not* use a READ statement.

12. What would happen to the flowchart in Figure 2-7 if the value read for N were either 0 or 1? Can you change the flowchart in Figure 2-7 to account for values of N equal to 0 or 1? (Recall that $0! = 1! = 1$.)

2-5-2 Flowcharting Problems

1. Draw a flowchart to read a temperature in Fahrenheit and print the equivalent Celsius temperature by using the formula $C = \frac{9}{5}(F - 32)$ where F is the Fahrenheit temperature read.

2. Suppose you are given the lengths and widths of certain rectangles. Draw a flowchart to find the area of these rectangles.

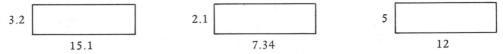

3. Draw a flowchart to read three student test scores from one data card and determine whether the student is passing or failing. If the average exceeds 73 a "PASS" grade is awarded; otherwise, a "FAIL" grade is given.

4. Draw a flowchart to read a deck of 20 cards, each card containing an employee number and number of hours worked. Find how many worked exactly 40 hours, more than 40 and less than 40.

5. Draw a flowchart to read a value X from a card and compute and print the absolute value. Recall that $|X| = X$ if $X \geqslant 0$ and $|X| = -X$ if $X < 0$.

6. A deck of cards contains 25 cards with each card containing one exam score. Find the average of the scores greater than or equal to 60 and how many people failed (less than 60).

7. Draw a flowchart to compute $S = 2 + 4 + 6 + 8 + \cdots + 200$ by generating internally (not reading from data cards) the numbers 2, 4, 6, 8, and so on and accumulating the sum.

8. Draw a flowchart to input two numbers and print the larger. Do the same for three numbers accepted from input.

9. Draw a flowchart to calculate and write out the area of a rectangle for values of length and width accepted from input.

10. A salesman is assigned a commission on the following basis:

Sales	Commission
$00–$500	2% of sales
Over $500	5% of sales

Draw a flowchart to input an amount of sale and compute and print out the salesman's commission.

11. You work in a diner. Every time a meal is sold, a card is punched with the cost of the order and then a 1, 2 or 3; a 1 means breakfast meal, a 2 means lunch and a 3 means dinner. At the end of the day, 116 cards are collected. Draw a flowchart to

    a. Compute the total sales.
    b. Determine the average cost of a breakfast meal.
    c. Find out what the minimum cost of a dinner was.

12. Draw a flowchart to read a value for X and compute and print:

$$y = \frac{x^2 - 2x + 3}{x + 2}$$

13. Draw a flowchart to produce as output an amortization schedule for a loan when the principal, interest rate and amount of each payment is accepted from input.

14. Draw a flowchart to solve quadratic equations of the form $ax^2 + bx + c = 0$ for values of a, b, and c accepted from input. Recall that

$$x = \frac{-b \pm \sqrt{b^2 - 4ac}}{2a}$$

(Don't forget that the discriminant $b^2 - 4ac$ may be negative! If the discriminant is negative, print the message "Complex solution.")

2-5-3 Answers to Self Test

1. A recipe, if very carefully written, may be an example of an algorithm.

2. a. 90.   b. 2, 3.

3. a. 7.   b. 10.   c. 4.

4. a. Read six cards and print those numbers above 90.

   b. Print largest value contained on the six data cards.

   c. Compute $X_1 - X_2 + X_3 - X_4 + X_5 - X_6$ where $X_1, X_2, \cdots, X_6$ are the six values read.

5.

K	X	Y
0	6	20
1	7	
2	9	
3	12	
4	16	
5	21	
	8	4
	1	28
6	7	
7	14	
8	22	
9	31	

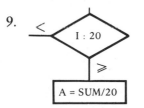

K	X	Y
5	21	20
5	8	4
9	31	28

6. Flowcharts are shown on pages 44–45.

7. Twice a year $Y = 4 * 2$ $I = P * (R/2)$
    Monthly $Y = 4 * 12$ $I = P * (R/12)$
    Daily $Y = 4 * 365$ $I = P * (R/365)$

8. ⟋ READ P, R, Y ⟋

9.

    $<$ ⟨ I : 20 ⟩

    ⟩

    [A = SUM/20]

10. Flowchart shown on page 46.

11. Flowchart shown on page 46.

12. If the value of N is 0 or 1, the value written for F will be 1. The flowchart does not require modification.

6. a.

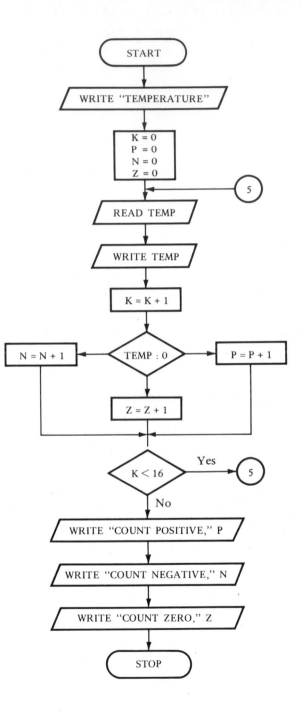

b.

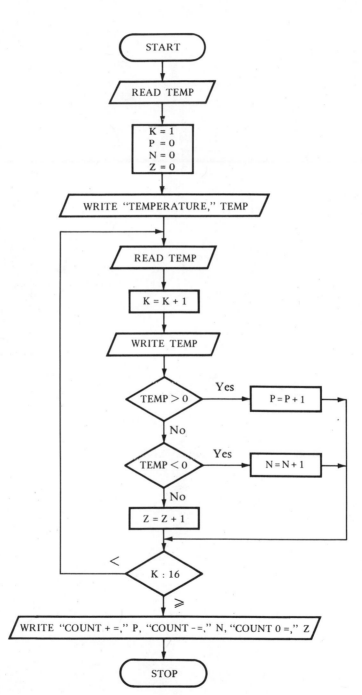

10.

11.

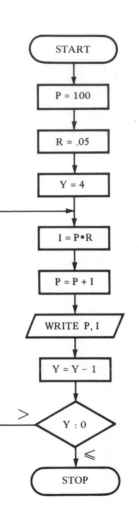

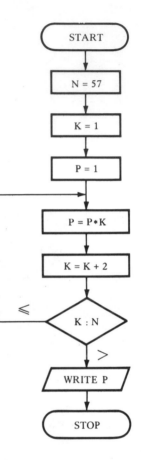

INTRODUCTION TO FORTRAN — PART 1

3-1 Problem Example

Mr. X. has two rectangular lots of land. The width (W1) of lot 1 is 75.6 and its length (E1) is 121.5. The width of lot 2 is 98.5 and its length (E2) is 110.6. Calculate and print the area of each lot and the combined area of both lots. An example of a FORTRAN program to solve this problem is shown in Figure 3-1. Analyze carefully Figures 3-2 and 3-3 to see how the FORTRAN program is punched on the cards. Also look at the computer printout sheet and notice the listing of the original program and the results printed by the FORTRAN program. Note the five types of FORTRAN statements in the program of Figure 3-1:

1. The replacement (assignment) statement used for calculations; for example A1 = W1*E1

2. The WRITE statement used to identify which variables are to be printed.

3. The FORMAT statement used to position the numeric values (results) and the alphabetic messages on the output line.

4. The STOP statement to terminate execution of the program.

5. The END statement which *must* be the last statement in any FORTRAN program.

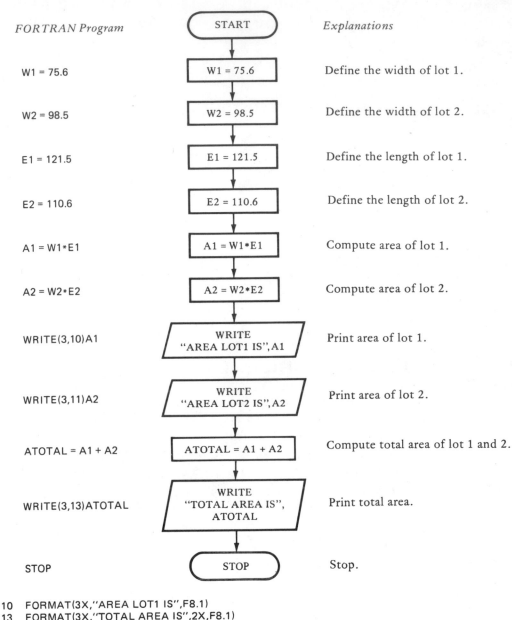

FORTRAN Program

W1 = 75.6

W2 = 98.5

E1 = 121.5

E2 = 110.6

A1 = W1*E1

A2 = W2*E2

WRITE(3,10)A1

WRITE(3,11)A2

ATOTAL = A1 + A2

WRITE(3,13)ATOTAL

STOP

Explanations

Define the width of lot 1.

Define the width of lot 2.

Define the length of lot 1.

Define the length of lot 2.

Compute area of lot 1.

Compute area of lot 2.

Print area of lot 1.

Print area of lot 2.

Compute total area of lot 1 and 2.

Print total area.

Stop.

```
10   FORMAT(3X,"AREA LOT1 IS",F8.1)
13   FORMAT(3X,"TOTAL AREA IS",2X,F8.1)
11   FORMAT(3X,"AREA LOT2 IS",F8.1)
     END
```

Figure 3-1 Calculation of the area of two lots.

```
      W1 = 75.6
      W2 = 98.5
      E1 = 121.5
      E2 = 110.6
      A1 = W1*E1
      A2 = W2*E2
      WRITE(6,10)A1
      WRITE(6,11)A2
      ATOTAL = A1+A2
      WRITE(6,13)ATOTAL
      STOP
10    FORMAT(3X,'AREA LOT1 IS',F8.1)
13    FORMAT(3X,'TOTAL AREA IS',2X,F8.1)
11    FORMAT(3X,'AREA LOT2 IS',F8.1)
END
```

```
      AREA LOT1 IS   9185.4
      AREA LOT2 IS  10894.1
      TOTAL AREA IS 20079.5
```

Figure 3-2   Computer-produced FORTRAN listing and results.

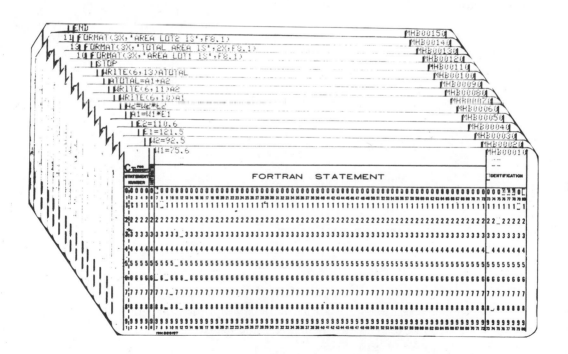

Figure 3-3   FORTRAN program on punched cards.

3-2 Getting Started

3-2-1 Character Set

The characters used in FORTRAN are grouped into three classes:

Alphabetic. The alphabetic characters are

A B C D E F G H I J K L M N O P Q R S T U V W X Y Z

Numeric. The numeric characters are

0 1 2 3 4 5 6 7 8 9

Special. The special characters are

. , ( ) ' + − * / =

3-2-2 Constants

A constant is a quantity whose numerical value is fixed and explicitly stated; in other words, it is a number. A constant may be expressed in *integer* mode or *real* mode. An integer constant is always written without a decimal point; a real constant is always written with a decimal point. Either type may be preceded by a sign (+ or −) if desired.

Examples

300	−2	63247	+4	0	are integer constants.
6.32	−3.21	.0005	+63.04		are real constants.

An imbedded blank (blanks between the first and last digit) in a constant has no effect on the value of the constant.

Example The following constants have the same value:

$$6\quad32\qquad632\qquad6\ 3\ 2$$

No characters other than the above described may be used in writing constants.

Example The following constants are invalid:

632,000	No commas allowed.
23.34.	Only one decimal point is permitted.
$30.50	Special character $ is invalid.
111-333-444	Special character − is invalid.

The allowable size (magnitude) of integer and real constants and their internal representation on a computer is discussed in detail in Chapter 7. Integers and real numbers have different internal representations.

3-2-3 Variables

Unlike a constant, a variable may assume different values. Variable names may be from 1 to 6 characters in length. One can think of a variable as the name given to a memory location into which data is to be stored. Judicious choice of variable names can help understand the purpose of a particular FORTRAN statement as in PAY = HRS*RATE where PAY, HRS, RATE are variable names. The first character of a variable name must be alphabetic; succeeding characters may be alphabetic or numeric. No "special" characters may be used in a variable name.

Examples The following are valid variable names:

$$X \qquad Q1 \qquad COUNT$$
$$ABC \qquad SUM \qquad X12345$$

The following are invalid variable names:

INVOICE	Too long.
A – B	Special character (–).
1PAY	Numeric first character.
LIGHT.	Period is invalid.

Any blanks used between characters in a variable name are ignored.

Example The following are names for the same variable:

$$ABC \qquad A\ BC \qquad A\ B\ C$$

A variable may contain integer data or real data. Data which is in integer mode may *not* contain any fractional part; real type data may or may not contain a fractional part (3.12 or 9). The mode of a variable (whether integer or real) is implicitly defined by its name. If the first letter of the variable name is either

$$I, \ J, \ K, \ L, \ M \text{ or } N$$

the variable is integer; otherwise the variable is real.

An integer variable name represents a memory cell in which the number stored will have no decimal point while a real variable represents a cell in which there is a decimal point. Consider the following real and integer variables with corresponding arbitrary memory contents.

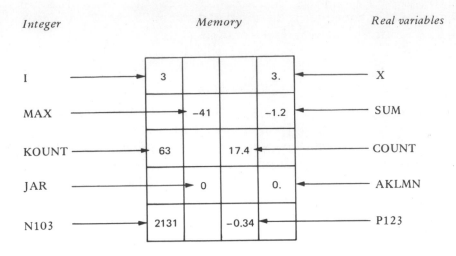

Variable names are automatically assigned to memory locations by the computer system.

3-2-4 Integer and Real Arithmetic

The primary distinction between integer and real data is that real data can contain a fractional part, while integer data cannot. When arithmetic is performed using two integer constants and/or variables, no decimal part is retained (everything to the right of the implied decimal point is truncated); with two real constants, the fractional part is retained.

Examples

Expression	Value	
3/4	0	3 and 4 are integers. No fractional part retained.
8/3	2	Same for 8 and 3.
3./4.	.75	3. and 4. are real; fractional result is computed.
8./3.	2.66667	Note: round off for 8./3.
1/2 + 1/2	0	Both operands evaluate to 0.
1./2. + 1./2.	1.	Result is real.

3-2-5 Expressions

An expression may be a constant or a variable or any combination of constants and/or variables linked by arithmetic operators. Parentheses may be included to denote the order of computations. The arithmetic operators are:

+	Addition
−	Subtraction
*	Multiplication
/	Division
**	Exponentiation

Examples The following are valid expressions:

FORTRAN expression	Algebraic expression
A	a
14	14
(A/B)*C	$\dfrac{a}{b} \cdot c$
A*B − 30.	$a \cdot b - 30$
− C	$-c$
(A*B)**2	$(ab)^2$
(− C + B)*D	$(-c + b)d$
A**B	a^b
− 3.7	-3.7
A**.5	$\sqrt{a}$
((A − B)**3)**.25	$\sqrt[4]{(a - b)^3}$

Following are some examples of invalid expressions:

3(A + JB)	Operator missing after the 3.
A − (B + C*(K)	Unpaired parentheses. Should be A − (B + C*(K)).
X* − 3	Two operators side by side.

When parentheses are present in an expression, the operation within the parentheses is performed first.

Example

Expression	Evaluation
3*(4 + 5)	3*(4 + 5) = 3*9 = 27

If parentheses are nested in an expression, then the innermost set of parentheses is performed first.

Example

Expression	Evaluation
3*(4 + (8/2))	3*(4 + 4) = 3*(8) = 24

When no parentheses are present in an expression, operations are performed according to the following rules of precedence:

Operation	Precedence
**	high
* or /	intermediate
+ or −	low

Operations with higher precedence are performed before operations with lower precedence. The operations addition/subtraction, multiplication/division are performed in order from left to right according to the rules of precedence. Exponentiations are performed in order from right to left.

Examples

1. A − B + C

   3. − 2. + 5.

   B is subtracted from A and the result is added to C

   (3. − 2.) + 5. = 1. + 5. = 6.

2. A + B*C

   Since multiplication has priority B*C is computed, the result is then added to A giving A + (B*C).

   3. + 2.*3.

   3. + (2.*3.) = 3. + 6. = 9.

3. A/B*C

   Since multiplication and division have same priority, B is first divided into A (A/B), and the result of the division is multiplied by C. This is different from A/(B*C).

   9./4.*2.

   (9./4.)*2. = 2.25*2. = 4.50

4. A/B/C

   First A/B is performed, and the result is then divided by C. You will get the same answer if you calculated A/(B*C).

   8./4./2.

   $\dfrac{8.}{4.} \div 2. = 2. \div 2. = 1.$

5. (A + B)/C*D

   The parentheses indicate that the sum of A + B is to be performed first. The sum is then divided by C and the result is multiplied by D, giving

   $$\dfrac{A + B}{C} * D \quad \text{not} \quad \dfrac{A + B}{C*D}$$

   (3. + 6.)/3.*6.

   $\dfrac{9.}{3.} *6. = 3.*6. = 18.$

6. A + B*C**2

   Since exponentiation has highest priority, C^2 is computed. This result is then multiplied by B, since multiplication has the next highest priority. Finally, this result is added to A giving A + (B + (C**2))

   3. + 3.*2.**2.

   $3. + (3.*2.^2) = 3. + (3.*4.) = 3. + 12. = 15.$

7. A**B**C   Exponentiations are evaluated from right to left; therefore, B is raised to the power C. This result is used as the power of A giving

$$A**(B**C) \quad not \quad (A**B)**C$$

3.**2.**3.   3.**(2.**3.) = 3.**8. = 6561. not

(3.**2.)**3. = 9.**3. = 729.

3-2-6 The Replacement Statement

A replacement statement specifies arithmetic operations to be performed and the location (variable) into which the value computed is to be placed. The general form of the replacement statement is

variable = expression

The value of the expression is first computed, and the result is placed (stored) in the variable in the left-hand part of the statement. The equal sign used in a replacement statement must be understood as a replacement sign rather than a mathematical equality.[1] Accordingly, the statement X = X + 1 is quite legal, since it means add 1 to whatever value is currently in memory cell X and store the result in X. The following are valid examples of replacement statements:

X = 3.123   Define X to be 3.123 (place 3.123 in location X). Whatever value was in X before is now destroyed (replaced).

C1 = (A + B)/C   Compute A + B, divide by C and call result C1.

Z = 3.**2.   Let Z be equal to 3. squared.

SK = (Z + 4.)**.5   SK is computed as the square root of Z + 4.

The following are examples of invalid replacement statements:

3.16 = X   A variable and not a constant must occur on the left-hand side of the equal sign; besides which, how can one store the value of X into 3.16?

X + Y = 1   An expression cannot occur on the left-hand side of the equal sign; besides which, how could one store a 1 in the sum of two memory locations?

HRS*RATE + BONUS   There is no variable specified into which the result is to be stored.

---

[1] Many texts use the symbol ← to denote the replacement to avoid the ambiguity of the two meanings of the = sign.

3-2-7 Mixed-Mode Expressions

A mixed-mode expression is an expression in which constants and/or variables of different modes (integer, real) are present. The general evaluation rule is as follows: If an integer and a real constant are involved in an arithmetic operation, the integer value is converted to real before the operation is performed and the result becomes a real quantity. If two integers or reals are involved in an arithmetic operation, the resulting mode for that operation will be the same as the mode of the operands.

Examples

Expression	*Value of Expression*	
3/2.	1.5	The integer 3 is converted to real 3.
3./2	1.5	The integer 2 is converted to real 2.
4. + 3/2	5.	The operation 3/2 involving integers is performed, resulting in 1. Then 4. + 1 is a mixed-mode expression evaluating to 5.
4. *3/2	6.	The operation 4.*3 is performed first, yielding 12., which is then divided by 2 to give 6.
4.*(3/2)	4.	(3/2) is performed first, giving 1, which is then multiplied by 4. yielding 4.
4 + 3/2.	5.5	3/2. is mixed mode, which evaluates to 1.5, which is added to 4 giving 5.5.
I + 7.2	6.2	If I = −1, the expression evaluates to 6.2. In memory, however, the value stored in I is still the integer −1.

3-2-8 Mixed-Mode Replacement Statements

A mixed-mode replacement statement is a replacement statement in which the mode of the variable on the left is different from the mode of the evaluated expression on the right. In this case the mode of the value of the expression is converted to the mode of the variable on the left-hand side of the equal sign before the resulting value is stored in the variable. In essence, the mode of the variable on the left-hand side of the equal sign determines the mode of the final value of the expression; that is, the expression on the right is evaluated first, using the rules of hierarchy, and the final answer is stored in the mode of the variable on the left.

Examples

IX = 3.2	The value stored in IX will be the integer 3 When a real value is converted to integer, any fractional part is truncated.
X = 3 + 2	The value of X will be 5., not 5
J = 3./2	The value of the expression is 1.5, but the value stored in J will be 1, since J is an integer variable.
KX = 4/3 + 6.8	4/3 is 1, since both numbers are integers. 1 + 6.8 = 7.8 since one of the operands is real. The value stored, however, is 7 since KX is integer.

3-2-9 The FORTRAN Coding Form

A FORTRAN program consists of a sequence of FORTRAN instructions called *FORTRAN statements*. These FORTRAN statements are punched into specific fields with only one statement allowed per card. The layout for a FORTRAN statement card is shown in Figure 3-4.

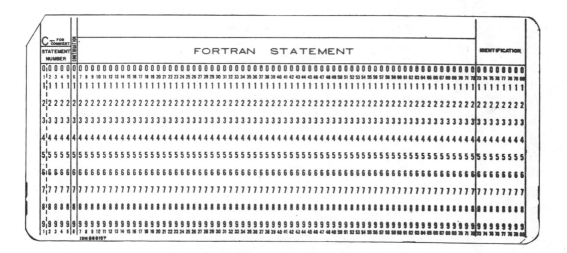

Figure 3-4 FORTRAN statement card.

The following fields are used in punching a FORTRAN statement:

Card columns 1–5	Statement number (optional except for formats).
Card column 6	Continuation (optional) discussed in Chapter 4, Section 4-5-5.
Card columns 7–72	Body of FORTRAN statement (always required).
Card columns 73–80	Identification (optional).

A statement number is an unsigned integer number which identifies a particular FORTRAN statement. It allows one to distinguish one FORTRAN statement from another by giving it a special address if you like. Not all FORTRAN statements need be numbered. The programmer may number all statements if he wants. Statement numbers may be from one to five digits long and are punched anywhere in card columns 1 through 5.[2] The digits should be punched in consecutive card columns. Statement numbers need not be numbered sequentially and are required only when a statement is to be referenced by another FORTRAN statement in the program.

The FORTRAN statement itself may be punched anywhere into card columns 7 through 72. For program readability, the beginning programmer may wish to punch all his statements starting in column 7. If a statement is too long to fit on one card in card columns 7–72, it may be continued onto another card by use of the continuation field (see Chapter 4, Section 4-5-5).

Card columns 73–80 may be used to identify the author and/or for sequencing purposes (see Figure 3-2 and Section 3-5-1 for further discussion), or it may be left blank. FORTRAN coding sheets are available commercially to help the novice identify the various fields in the punched card. The coding sheet simplifies the transcription of the program onto punched cards during the keypunching operation (see Figure 3-5).

In general, FORTRAN statements consist of certain elements, which can be key words, constants, variables and special characters strung together under strict grammatical rules. The most common statements that the reader will use are arithmetic (replacement), decision (control) and input/output statements. The following example illustrates the various grammatical components of a FORTRAN replacement statement and the position of each on the punched card:

---

[2] Some installations require the number to be right-justified in card columns 2–5 because blanks are interpreted as zeros.

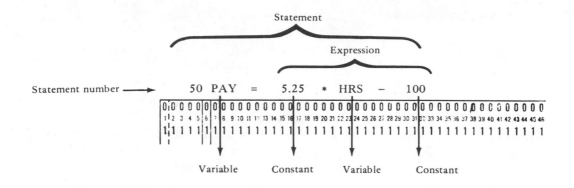

Blanks may be interspersed anywhere in card columns 7–72 within a FORTRAN statement; that is, imbedded blanks are permissible in variables, constants or FORTRAN key words. For example, the above statement could have been punched as follows:

Figure 3-5   A FORTRAN coding form.

3-2-10 The Complete Job

As we have noted in Chapter 1, Section 1-2-3, FORTRAN is an example of a high-level language. FORTRAN allows a user to communicate with a computer in a semi-English-scientific language which hopefully is not too difficult to learn—after all, there are certain easily recognizable words, such as READ, WRITE, FORMAT, STOP, END etc. The FORTRAN programmer can express his problem through mathematical relationships and formulas. The computer, however, does not understand FORTRAN directly; its natural language is machine language. To the computer, FORTRAN is a foreign language (see Figure 3-6), which must be translated into machine language before it can be processed (executed). In the early days of computers, machine language specialists would translate high-level languages into machine language. Today, special language translator programs (*compilers*) are used to perform this translation at extremely high speeds, without human intervention. The compiler reads a FORTRAN program (*source code*) and produces a resulting set of machine instructions (*object code*) that can then be executed by the CPU (see Figure 3-7).

To process a program on a computer requires more than submission of some source code written in a high-level language. The computer system must be told,

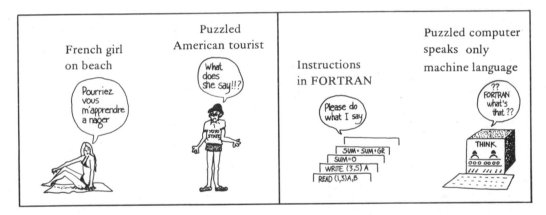

Figure 3-6 Language barrier.

Figure 3-7 Language barrier resolved.

among other things, what high-level language to expect so as to direct the appropriate compiler for the translation process, the name of the user, his password if any and so on. All-in-all the programmer must inform the computer of certain administrative tasks by means of "job control" or "workflow" instructions. A typical FORTRAN job will then generally consist of FORTRAN instructions, data to be processed and control cards telling the computer what to do (see Figure 3-8). These will vary from one system to the other, and the user is advised to check his installation for the particular control cards.

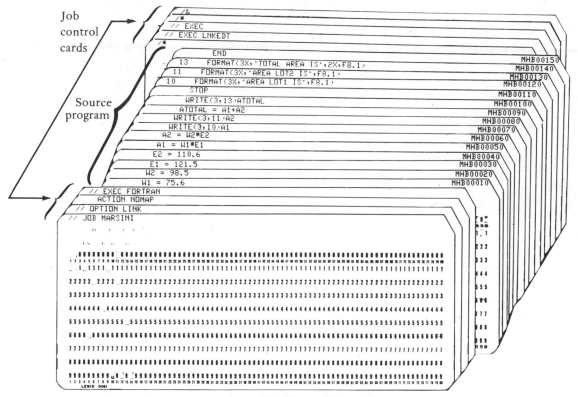

Figure 3-8 Physical job stream.

3-2-11 The WRITE Statement

The general form of the WRITE statement is

WRITE(device-number,format-statement-number)[variable-list]

where device-number is a code (integer constant) representing the output device to be used (printer, tape, disk etc.)

format-statement-number is the number of a FORMAT statement to be used to describe the output operation (layout design)

variable-list is a list of variable names separated by commas. When the WRITE statement is executed the contents of the variables specified in the variable-list are written onto the specified output device according to its specified format

Example

Device-number

Format

List of variable names

WRITE(3,10)PAY,HRS,RATE

The above WRITE statement can be interpreted as follows: Write the contents of memory locations PAY,HRS,RATE onto device number 3 according to the layout description given by the FORMAT labeled 10. Note that even though the content of PAY is written out, the value of PAY in memory is not destroyed. The device-number associated with specific devices is dependent on the computer system being used. A typical assignment might be:

Device-number[3]	Physical device
1	Card reader
2	Card punch
3	Printer
4 or greater	Other devices (magnetic tapes, disks etc.)

In the case of the printer, a typical size for the output page (form) is 132 characters or print positions (see Figure 3-3).

The following are examples of valid WRITE statements:

65 WRITE(3,11)A,IJT	The value contained in A and IJT will be written onto device 3. FORMAT statement 11 will be used to describe the output line.
WRITE(2,15)Q	The value of Q will be written on device number 2 according to FORMAT statement 15.

The following are examples of invalid WRITE statements:

WRITE(3,14)4	The variable-list must consist of variables, not constants.
WRITE(2,16)X + Y	X + Y is an expression and not a variable.

---

[3]The reader is advised to check with his computer center to determine which codes are used at his installation.

WRITE(3,11)THESUMIS,X	Character data cannot be specified in the variable list.
WRITE(3,15.)X,Y	15. is an incorrect statement number, no period.

3-2-12 The FORMAT Statement

It is apparent that the WRITE statement all by itself does not provide the computer sufficient information as to how the write operation is to be carried out; for example,

1. Where on the output line should each result be printed (which print positions?)?

2. How many digits to the right of the decimal point does the programmer want for his results? (In the case of dollars and cents, only two digits should suffice.)

3. How many print positions should be allocated for each result on the line?

A FORMAT statement is needed in conjunction with the WRITE statement to inform the computer precisely how the WRITE operation is to be carried out. Each WRITE statement must specify a format-statement-number, and each FORMAT statement must have a statement number by which it can be referenced. The WRITE instruction is processed according to the specifications described in the FORMAT, i.e., the FORMAT statement is not processed independently of the WRITE instruction, but in conjunction with it at the same time as the WRITE instruction is executed. For that reason the FORMAT statement may be placed anywhere in a program (before the END statement). Some programmers prefer to place all their formats at the end or beginning of their programs, while others like them to immediately follow their associated WRITE statements.

Example

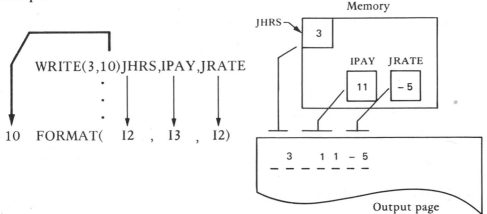

Output page

The above output operation can be interpreted as follows. Write three numbers (three variables are named) on an output page (device-number 3) according to the data layout described by the FORMAT statement labeled 10. The FORMAT may be interpreted as: The first variable (JHRS) will be printed as an integer value (specified by the I format code) in the first two print positions of the output form (I2), the next variable will be printed as an integer in the next 3 print positions (I3), and the last variable (JRATE) will be printed in the next 2 print positions (I2), that is, print positions 6–7.

Temporarily, until discussion of printer carriage control in Section 3-5-2, we shall refrain from printing any data in print position one of an output page, as this position is used to control the printer in terms of vertical page movement.

The general form of the FORMAT statement is

$$\text{statement-number FORMAT}(fd_1, fd_2, \cdots, fd_n)$$

where statement-number is the format label referred to in a WRITE statement.

$fd_1, fd_2, \cdots, fd_n$ are format codes which can be either

1. Data format codes used to identify the mode of the data items (numerical results) to be printed: I for integer and F for real numbers, or
2. Edit codes used to control the placement and editing of the data items in the output record: X for spacing, single quote (') for literal data and T for specifying the beginning print position for an output field. Note that all format codes must be separated by commas.

In this chapter, we shall only consider the I, F, X, literal and T format codes and reserve discussion of other format codes for subsequent chapters.

The X Format Code

The X format code is an edit code used to specify spaces on an output line. It is generally used to provide margins or to separate fields by a certain number of blanks. The general form of the X format code is

$$nX$$

where n is an integer specifying the number of spaces (blanks) desired.

Example The code shown at the top of page 65 can be interpreted as follows: Write the number K on a line with the help of format number 11. Before you print K, give us three blank spaces, and then print an integer (I) using two print positions. Note that the X format code does not have a corresponding item in the variable list of the WRITE statement.

K = 14
WRITE(3,11)K
11   FORMAT(3X,I2)

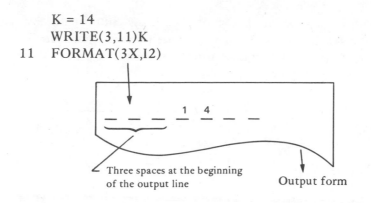

1   4

Three spaces at the beginning
of the output line

Output form

The I Format Code

Integer data is described for an output operation by the I format code. The general form of the I format code is:

Iw

where I specifies that an integer is to be written out.

w specifies the number of spaces to be reserved on the output line for the number (width of output field).

The I format code can be used only to describe integer mode variables. The negative sign occupies one space (print position), which should be included in the total number of spaces allocated for the output field (w).

Example 1

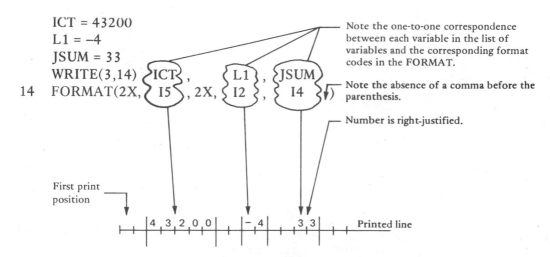

ICT = 43200
L1 = −4
JSUM = 33
WRITE(3,14) ICT , L1 , JSUM
14   FORMAT(2X, I5 , 2X, I2 , I4)

Note the one-to-one correspondence between each variable in the list of variables and the corresponding format codes in the FORMAT.

Note the absence of a comma before the parenthesis.

Number is right-justified.

First print position

| 4 3 2 0 0 | − 4 | 3 3 | Printed line

The first variable, ICT, in the variable-list is associated with the first numeric format code, I5; the second variable, L1, is associated with the second numeric format code, I2, and so on. If the number of digits in the number to be printed is less than the width reserved for it, the number is *right-justified* (the rightmost digit is placed on the rightmost print position of the output field) with blanks inserted to the left in place of leading zeroes.

Example 2

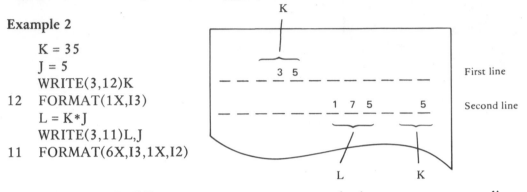

```
     K = 35
     J = 5
     WRITE(3,12)K
12   FORMAT(1X,I3)
     L = K*J
     WRITE(3,11)L,J
11   FORMAT(6X,I3,1X,I2)
```

Note that for each different WRITE statement we obtain a separate output line. In the case of the first WRITE, only one number is printed on one line, whereas in the second WRITE statement two entries are printed on a new line.

Care must be exercised to provide enough space in an I format code for all the digits of the number (including the negative sign "−" if required). If not enough spaces are allocated an error message will be printed. The exact form of the message will differ among systems. In the following example, a set of asterisks indicates insufficient field width.

Example 3

```
     K = 1234
     J = −14
     WRITE(3,15) K ,    J ,    J

15   FORMAT(2X,I3,1X,I2,2X,I4)
```

First print position ⟶ | * * * | * * | | − 1 4 | Printed line

The F Format Code

Real data is described by the F format code. The general form of the F format code is:

$$Fw.d$$

where F specifies that a real number is to be printed out

w specifies the number of spaces (print positions) to be reserved on the output record (line) for the number

d specifies the number of digits to the right of the decimal point that are to be printed for the real number

The decimal point is always printed. It occupies one print position in the output field and hence must be included in the total number of spaces (w) allocated for the real value.

The F format code can only be used to describe real mode variables. The reader may wonder why it is necessary to worry about the number of digits to the right of the decimal point on the output. Internally, the computer carries out computations to many decimal places; for example, the result of 10.12*5.24 is stored internally as 53.0288, and the programmer may only be interested in the first two decimal positions (dollars and cents). Hence it is always the programmer's responsibility to specify the number of digits he wants for the fractional part of the result.

Example 1

```
    A = 63.426
    B = -4.2
    WRITE(3,15)  A ,      A ,            A ,      B ,      B

15  FORMAT(1X,F6.3 ,   F9.5 ,      1X,  F6.1,    F6.1,     F4.0)
```

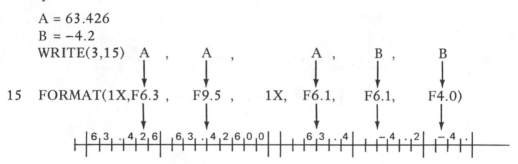

Note that if the number of digits in the number to be printed is less than the width of the field reserved for it, the number is right-justified in the field with blanks inserted to the left instead of leading zeroes.

Depending on the number of digits (d) specified in the format code Fw.d, the data will be rounded as necessary as shown in the following example.

Example 2

```
    A = 12.6534
    B = 13.7
    WRITE(3,16)     A ,        A ,        A ,        B

16  FORMAT(2X,   F9.3,      F6.1,      F5.0,      F7.3)
```

| 1 2 . 6 5 3   1 2 . 7   1 3 .   1 3 . 7 0 0

A is rounded to   A is rounded to   A is rounded to
three decimal places   one decimal place   the nearest whole number

Note that in the case of the variable B the value 13.700 is printed, since the format specifies three fractional positions.

With F format codes care must be exercised to provide enough print columns for all digits to the left of the decimal point, of the real number. If not enough print columns are allocated, an error message will be printed. The exact form of the message differs among systems. In the following example, a row of asterisks will indicate an error specifying insufficient field width.

Example

A = −123.456   If F7.3 is used, then the output field is only seven print
B = 2509.01   columns wide, which cannot accommodate the eight
C = 12.   characters for A.
WRITE(3,12)   A ,   A ,   B ,   C

12 FORMAT(1X, F7.3,   1X, F5.1,   1X, F6.2,   1X, F5.4)

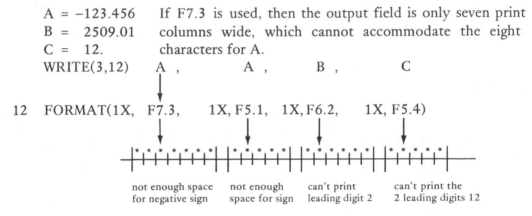

not enough space   not enough   can't print   can't print the
for negative sign   space for sign leading digit 2 2 leading digits 12

To provide a field (w) sufficiently large to represent a real (floating-point) number, the following rule is offered:

$$\text{minimum for } w = d + 1 + (1) + wh$$

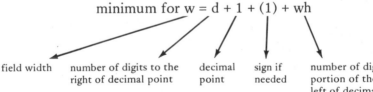

field width   number of digits to the   decimal   sign if   number of digits in the whole
               right of decimal point   point   needed   portion of the number (digits to
                                                                  left of decimal point)

The beginning programmer is warned again that any real variables that are to be printed must be described by F format codes in the FORMAT. For example, the next code segment is invalid:

WRITE(3,11)A,B,C
11 FORMAT(I2,I1,I3)   Should be FORMAT(F2.0,F1.0,F3.0).
        or
WRITE(3,12)J,J,K
12 FORMAT(F1.0,F2.0,F3.0)   Should be FORMAT(I1,I2,I3).

The T Format Code

The T format code is a printer control code used to specify the beginning position on the output line for a data field. The general form of the T format code is:

$$Tn,$$

where n specifies the beginning of the next data field to be processed on the output record.

The T format code can be used to provide margins and act as a tab feature of sorts; it is also extremely convenient when numerous variables must be printed in pre-designated print positions where the data output layout is already specified (business forms, checks, tables, reports etc.).

Example

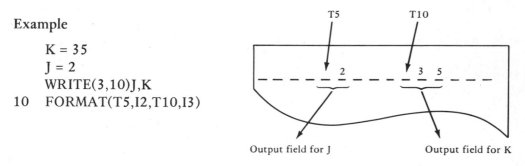

```
    K = 35
    J = 2
    WRITE(3,10)J,K
10  FORMAT(T5,I2,T10,I3)
```

The format code T5 specifies that the output field for J is to start in print position 5 and that the output field for K is to start in print position 10. The T format code arbitrarily allows the programmer to skip to any desired position at will on the line. Note that T4 or 3X would cause the output record to start in print position 4.

The Format Code for Literal Data

The use of single quotes (') in a FORMAT around a string of characters specifies that the string (all characters within the two single quotes) is to be placed on the output line at whatever print position the printer happens to be at that time. Literal strings are generally used to create headings, identify numerical results or provide messages or explanation.

Example 1

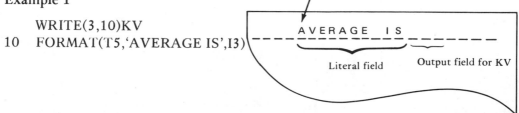

```
    WRITE(3,10)KV
10  FORMAT(T5,'AVERAGE IS',I3)
```

The character string AVERAGE IS, consisting of ten characters (including the blank), is printed starting in print position 5. Immediately following the literal string is the numerical field for KV. Blanks within the single quotes are part of the literal and hence are printed on the output form.

Example 2

```
    IERROR = 999
    WRITE(3,6)IERROR
6   FORMAT(T2,'*** *** ',I3)
```

More than one literal string can be described in a format, as in:

Example 3

```
    K = 35
    J = 3
    WRITE(3,11)J,K
11  FORMAT(T2,'NO-BOYS=',I2,2X,'NO-GIRLS=',I3)
```

Before J is printed, the printer is asked to start in print position 2 (T2) and then write NO-BOYS= then J is printed; but before K is printed the printer is asked to space two print positions and then write NO-GIRLS=. At this point, K is printed.

The reader is warned that literals may not appear in the list of variables of a WRITE instruction. Literals must be specified in the format itself. The following example is invalid:

Example 4

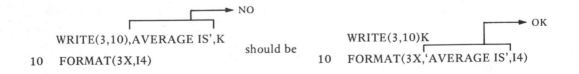

Literals can be used conveniently to provide headings, as follows:

Example 5

```
    M = 5
    ID = 25
    IY = 76
    WRITE(3,5)M,ID,IY
5   FORMAT(T60,'XYZ COMPANY PAYROLL REPORT DATE',1X,I2,'/',I2,'/',I2)
```

Finally, it is possible to have a WRITE statement without any variable-list, as in:

Example 6

```
    WRITE(3,11)
11  FORMAT(3X,'XYZ CORPORATION')
```

The following will be produced on the output line:

Such WRITE statements are generally used to produce headings or page titles.

3-2-13 The STOP Statement

The general form of the STOP statement is

STOP

The STOP statement is used to terminate execution of a program. *At least one* STOP statement should occur in every FORTRAN program; more than one may be used if desired.

3-2-14 The END Statement

The general form of the END statement is

END

The last statement in every FORTRAN program must be the END statement.

Only one END statement may be used in a program. END is a nonexecutable instruction (see Section 3-3, question 7) and should not be assigned a FORTRAN statement number.

3-2-15 Errors

Errors are not uncommon when writing programs. There can be keypunching errors, grammatical errors, logical errors (the program does not solve the intended problem), execution errors, job control or workflow errors. Errors (or bugs as they are commonly called) confront the beginner on all fronts. How good a programmer really is depends to a certain extent on his ability to debug (locate errors) in his program!

There are two distinct classes of errors that are likely to occur in a predefined time sequence during the processing of a FORTRAN program on a computer.

1. *Compile-time errors* (*Syntax errors*). These errors are caught by the compiler during the machine language translation process. Statements are incorrectly structured or grammatical rules are not observed. A list of errors (if any) is generally provided on the printout form within or following the program listing.

   Examples

WRITE(3,15)A	And no FORMAT statement 15 is defined in the program.
X = 3(2 + A)	Multiplication sign missing.
Z = X + (Y − Z	Unpaired parentheses.

   In some systems, depending on the gravity of the syntactical errors, the job will be aborted at the conclusion of the compilation (why execute a set of unsound instructions?).

2. *Execution-time errors* (*Logical errors*). Even though there may be no compile-time errors, the CPU may be incapable of executing certain instructions. The compiler merely translates a FORTRAN statement into machine instructions; it does not execute the machine instructions and hence cannot determine whether the instruction (command) itself is feasible or not. In the cartoon of Figure 3-7, the French girl might ask "Take me to the nearest star"; the translator would dutifully translate the sentence into English, which would severely test the American's ingenuity!

   Examples

I = 0	Since division by 0 is undefined, the CPU could
10 T = J/I	not execute the instruction at 10 and an execution error would result.

WRITE(1,15)X   If 1 is the card reader device, an execution error would occur, since the computer can't write on a card reader!

Certain execution errors can cause immediate cancellation of the job. A list of execution-time errors, their codes and meaning are provided by the system on the printout form. It is recommended that the reader consult the manufacturer's FORTRAN technical reference manual for a complete description and explanation of each of the different types of execution-time errors.

3=3 You Might Want To Know

1. What happens if I insert extra unneeded sets of parentheses in an expression?

   Answer: Extra sets of parentheses have no effect on the evaluation of an expression.

   Example

   $(X + (Y*(Z + W)))$ is equivalent to $X + Y*(Z + W)$

   The important point is that parentheses must occur in matched pairs. For each left parenthesis, there must be a right parenthesis. Too many parentheses may slow down the compilation process, however.

2. How long can a printed line be?

   Answer: This depends on the particular system. Typical lengths vary from 121 to 144 characters.

3. How does the computer represent repeating decimal numbers (rational numbers)? For example, how can the computer represent exactly 1./3. in decimal form?

   Answer: It can't; only the first few digits are retained. For instance, on an IBM 370 computer 1./3. = .3333333 and 8./9. = .8888889 (last digit is rounded off).

4. How many WRITE statements may reference a FORMAT statement?

   Answer: As many as desired. The FORMAT is then shared by many WRITE statements.

5. What happens if I try to divide by zero?

   Answer: An execution-time diagnostic will be printed, and your program will usually be terminated. Division by zero is not a permissible operation.

6. What happens when I multiply (divide, add or subtract) two numbers and the result is too large to be represented as a number on my computer system?

Also, what happens if the number is too small to be represented on the system (less than 10^{-76} for IBM 370)?

Answer: In the first case, an overflow condition will occur, and an execution-time error will appear to that effect. The program will generally not cancel, and execution of the program will continue. The user should check his logic or scale numbers if necessary.

In the second case, an underflow occurs with a corresponding error message. The variable is generally set to 0, and the program will proceed. Check the logic to understand why such a condition would arise.

7. I am confused on the difference between STOP and END. Can you help?

Answer: Perhaps. The END statement is processed at compilation time to inform the compiler that there are no more FORTRAN statements to be translated (no FORTRAN code follows; the physical end of the FORTRAN program has been reached, not the physical end of the complete job, mind you, control cards and all, just the FORTRAN source statements). The END statement is not translated into a machine language instruction. If the END statement is not the last of the FORTRAN statements, the remaining FORTRAN statements will not be read (processed) by the compiler. In the context of the cartoon in Figure 3-6, the French girl could use an END statement to tell the translator that the message preceding the END statement is all she wants translated. The world's shortest FORTRAN program is just an END statement all by itself! The STOP statement on the other hand is translated into a machine language instruction and is therefore executed by the CPU during execution time to inform the system that all machine instructions (corresponding to the program) have been carried out, all results (if any) have been printed out and that as far as this job is concerned there is nothing else to do, i.e., the STOP causes execution to terminate and represents the logical end of the program as opposed to the physical end designated by the END statement. The STOP statement causes control to be turned to the operating system, which will process other programs (if any). As will be seen in Chapter 4, the STOP statement can be placed anywhere in the program (before the END).

8. I am performing some arithmetic computations on some data, and I really don't know how many digits I should reserve for my output field (I,F) in the FORMAT.

Answer: Most of the time you can estimate an upper limit and use that length for your width w. Otherwise, make your field as large as possible I20 or F20.1, for example. The result will be right-justified anyhow, with blanks on the left. If you are working with very large magnitudes, use the E format discussed in Chapter 7.

9. You know, it's really funny, yesterday I visited the computing center and I

overheard someone say, "There's a bug somewhere in my program." I was tempted to tell him to call the local pest control man. What do you think he was really saying?

Answer: A "bug" in the computer science jargon simply refers to an error or a mistake of some kind. To "debug" a program means getting rid of the bugs or errors in a program.

10. Can I use a negative number as a base in exponentiation? For example, is (−3)**2 or (−3.)**2. valid?

Answer: To a certain extent, this depends upon the compiler being used. In many systems, exponentiation involving small integer exponents is implemented by repeated multiplication. For example (−3)**2 is implemented as (−3)*(−3) resulting in no problems. However, for larger integer exponents, and all real exponents, most compilers use logarithms to evaluate the expression. In these cases the use of a negative number as a base in exponentiation will result in an error since the logarithm of a negative number is undefined. For example, (−3.)**2. would result in an execution-time error.

11. Can an exponent be negative?

Answer: Yes. For example, 3.**(−2) is evaluated as $\dfrac{1}{3.^2} = \dfrac{1}{9.}$

12. In everyday life, we don't differentiate between integer and real (floating point) numbers when performing arithmetic operations. Why is it the case in FORTRAN?

Answer: Actually, we do allow for a difference. Sometimes we have to figure the position of the decimal point when multiplying or dividing two real numbers. Obviously, operations involving decimal points are more time consuming than those without a decimal point. When some computers rent for $82 per minute or more and only integer arithmetic is desired, it would be uneconomical and wasteful of time to worry about the position of an unneeded decimal point during computations. On a typical computer, real number operations may be 100 times slower than integer number operations.

In a scientific environment, too, it may be necessary to work with very large numbers requiring the use of exponents and of decimal points. It would be impractical to write 10^{70} as an integer; hence, an alternative arithmetic is required (real arithmetic).

13. Is it possible to reduce the number of operations required to evaluate an expression using nested parentheses?

Answer: Yes. Consider, for example, the evaluation of $2x^3 + 3x^2 − 6x + 1$. A straightforward way to code this expression would be:

$$2*X**3 + 3*X**2 − 6*X + 1$$

Evaluation of this expression will require 2 exponentiations
3 multiplications
3 additions

The above expression can, however, be simplified by factoring as follows:

$$2x^3 + 3x^2 - 6x + 1 = (2x^2 + 3x - 6) x + 1$$
$$= ((2x + 3)x - 6) x + 1$$

This can then be written as

$$((2*X + 3)*X - 6)*X + 1$$

Evaluation of this expression will require 3 multiplications
3 additions

14. How do I cause an apostrophe to be printed as a part of a literal string?

Answer: The difficulty with an apostrophe is that it is used to enclose the literal string; a format code such as 'XYZ'W' would be ambiguous to a compiler. Many compilers use the following rule to avoid ambiguity: In order to print an apostrophe as a part of a literal string, use two apostrophes in succession. The compiler will insert one apostrophe on the output line in place of the two present in the format code.

Example

```
        WRITE(3,16)
   16   FORMAT(3X,'SUSAN''S  GRANDMOTHER')    would produce the
                                              following line:
```

15. What happens as a result of the following code?
```
        X = 23.99
        Y = 567.45
        WRITE(3,11)X,Y
   11   FORMAT(T2,F5.2,T5,F6.2)
```
overlap of two fields due to incorrect use of the Tab feature

Answer: The printed line is constructed in memory as

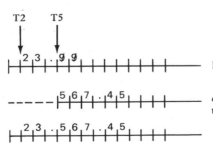

processing F5.2 and then returning to

column 5 to print F6.2 on *same* line. This then results in the following line.

If a Tab number is less than a preceding tab in the same format, this does not cause the printer to skip to the next line but to overlap results on the same line.

3-4 Programming Examples

3-4-1 Finite and Infinite Sums

Consider the sum of the following 1,000 terms:

$$\text{SUM} = \frac{1}{2^0} + \frac{1}{2^1} + \frac{1}{2^2} + \frac{1}{2^3} + \cdots + \frac{1}{2^{999}} = 1 + \frac{1}{2} + \frac{1}{4} + \frac{1}{8} + \cdots + \frac{1}{2^{999}}$$

This is a geometric progression, and its sum can be computed as follows:

$$\text{SUM} = \frac{a(1 - r^n)}{1 - r}$$

where a is the first term of the progression ($a = 1$)

r is the ratio of any two consecutive terms ($r = 1/2$)

n is the number of terms to be added ($n = 1,000$)

The infinite sum

$$1 + \frac{1}{2} + \frac{1}{2^2} + \frac{1}{2^3} + \cdots + \frac{1}{2^{999}} + \cdots$$

and so forth can be computed as

$$\text{SUM} = \frac{a}{1 - r}$$

Let us write a program to compute the sum of the first 1,000 terms, the infinite sum, and the difference between these two sums. See Figure 3-9.

```
      R = .5
      N = 1000
      A = 1.
      SUM1 = A*(1. – R**N)/(1. – R)
      SUM2 = A/(1. – R)
      WRITE(3,10)SUM1,SUM2
      DIF = SUM1 – SUM2
      WRITE(3,11)DIF
      STOP
   10 FORMAT(T5,'THE FINITE SUM IS',F6.3,'THE INFINITE SUM IS',F6.3)
   11 FORMAT(T5,'THE DIFFERENCE IS',F5.3)
      END
```

Figure 3-9 Calculation of the sum of a geometric progression.

3-4-2 Income Calculation

Mr. X. is a widower with three children aged 12, 16 and 19. His monthly salary is $1,023.36. His monthly contribution to a retirement plan is 4.5 percent of his first nine months' salary. For each child under 18, he receives $119.25 in child support from social security. His monthly social security deduction is 5.85 percent of his monthly income, and his federal income tax is 13.6 percent of his yearly gross (deducted on a monthly basis). Monthly payments for life insurance equal 9.6 percent of his monthly salary after social security and federal tax deductions. Write a program to compute Mr. X.'s monthly spendable income after taxes, deductions and supplemental support income. A program to solve this problem is shown in Figure 3-10.

```
        CHILD=119.25
        SALMON=1023.36
        RETIRE=(9.*SALMON*.045)/12.
        SSTAX=.0585*SALMON
        TAXINC=.136*SALMON
        PAYNET=SALMON-(RETIRE+SSTAX+TAXINC)
        PAYLIF=.096*(SALMON-TAXINC-SSTAX)
        PAY=PAYNET-PAYLIF
        PAY=PAY+2.*CHILD
        WRITE(3.14)PAY
14      FORMAT(2X,'SPENDABLE INCOME',F7.2)
        STOP
        END
```

SPENDABLE INCOME 949.14

Figure 3-10 Income tax calculation.

3-5 Probing A Little Deeper

3-5-1 The Identification Field

Card columns 73–80 are listed in the program listing but are not translated by the compiler. This field may be used to identify the program and/or author of the program. In addition, a sequence number may be punched into this field to make it easier to rearrange it in sequence if the deck is dropped. See, for example, the program in Figures 3-2 and 3-3.

3-5-2   Carriage Control Characters

You may have noticed that in all programs written thus far we have purposefully stayed away from print position 1 for the printing of the results on the output form. The reason this is done is to provide one space for a carriage control character to be interpreted by the printer to control the vertical movement of the output form (page). The first character on every line sent to the printer is used as a code to determine the vertical spacing of the paper rather than as a character to appear on the line. In any event the code is not printed. It is just a signal to the printer to tell it to single space, double space, skip to the top of a new page etc. The table shown in Figure 3-11 summarizes permissible codes and the meaning associated with each.

Code	Meaning
1	Skip to the top of a new page.
0	Double space.
+	Do not space, i.e., stay on the same line.
blank	Single space.
other characters	May have special installation printer control effects.

Figure 3-11   Carriage control characters.

The vertical movement of the output form (page) is effected at the very beginning of the WRITE instruction when the printer interprets the carriage control code specified in the FORMAT. The vertical spacing of the form is *not* performed at the end of the WRITE operation.

The X format code or the T format code can be used to provide a blank as the first character on the line and hence cause the printer to single space.

Example 1

```
     :
     AX = 3.2
     WRITE(3,10)AX
10   FORMAT(1X,F6.1)    could have used T2 in the FORMAT instead of 1X.
```

The above code segment will result in the following output.

Last printed line. This is still where the printer is before it encounters WRITE(3,10)AX

auoi bxyo. Pxmxo bzny cmbenl dinsti.

3 · 2

Before printing 3.2, the printer spaces one line since the carriage code is blank.

Example 2

```
     :
     AX = 3.2
     WRITE(3,10)AX
10   FORMAT(F3.1)
```

This would have resulted in the following output.

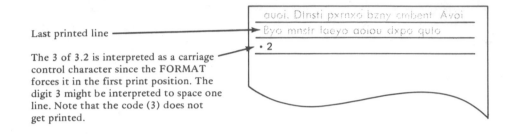

Last printed line ⟶

The 3 of 3.2 is interpreted as a carriage control character since the FORMAT forces it in the first print position. The digit 3 might be interpreted to space one line. Note that the code (3) does not get printed.

Printer control may be achieved by placing the desired carriage control code as a literal in the first position of the output line.

Example 1

```
     I = 423
     WRITE(3,10)I
10   FORMAT( '0' ,I4)
```
                                    note

This code segment would yield the following output:

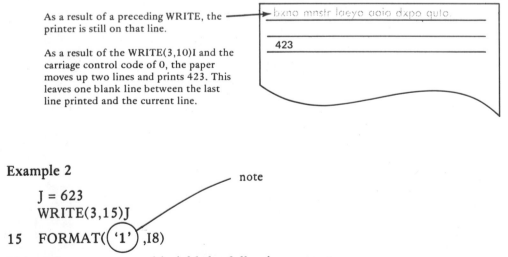

As a result of a preceding WRITE, the printer is still on that line.

As a result of the WRITE(3,10)I and the carriage control code of 0, the paper moves up two lines and prints 423. This leaves one blank line between the last line printed and the current line.

Example 2

```
     J = 623
     WRITE(3,15)J
15   FORMAT( '1' ,I8)
```
                                    note

This code segment would yield the following output:

Last printed line ──────────────▶

The output is printed at top of new page.

```
bxyo  mnstr   Bzny  cmbcnt  dinsti  pxrnxo
mnstr  laeyo.  Dinsti  pxrnxo  bzny  cmbcr
Mnstr  laeyo  aoiou  dxpo  quto
```

```
—o—o—o—o—o—o—o—o—o—o—o—o—o—o—o—o—o—o—o—
           623
```

Example 3

```
10    WRITE(3,11)
11    FORMAT(2X,'THE NUMBER OF GIRLS IS')
      K = 678
15    WRITE(3,12)K                        ── note
12    FORMAT( ('+') ,T28,I3)
```

This code segment yields the output:

Last line printed ──────────────▶

At the conclusion of WRITE(3,11), the literal message is printed and the printer stays put. The next WRITE statement tells the printer not to advance the form (+) but to print data items on that very same line.

```
mnstr  laeyo  aoiou  Pxrnxo  bzny  cmbcnt
it.  Laeyo  aoiou  dxpo  quto  avoi
THE NUMBER OF GIRLS IS    678
```

It is important that a carriage control character be included explicitly in a FORMAT statement used for printed output. The system will use as a carriage control character *whatever* appears as the first character on the line; it does not matter to the system whether this character originated as a literal or a data item from an F or I field.

Example 4

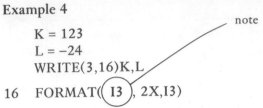

```
    K = 123
    L = -24
    WRITE(3,16)K,L                    note
16  FORMAT( I3 ), 2X,I3)
```

This code will produce the following output:

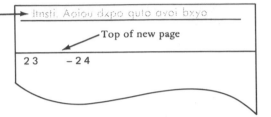

Last line printed ————————————

K has value 123. Since the first character to be printed in the first print position is a 1, that character is interpreted as a "skip to next page" and does *not* get printed.

3-6 Exercises

3-6-1 Self Test

1. What is the difference between an expression and a statement? Between a constant and a variable? Between integer and real data?

2. Define the terms: *source statement, job control cards, execution time* and *compile time*.

3. Characterize each of the following as either an integer constant, a real constant, an integer variable or a real variable. If some of the above are invalid, state reasons.

   a. F   b. I123   c. FORTRAN   d. X1.3
   e. −1234   f. 3ABC   g. XRAY   h. .000000006
   i. +72   j. 4(Y)   k. A1B2C.   l. 234−567−999
   m. 1A2B3C   n. IRAY   o. COUNT   p. KOUNT
   q. 3 + 4   r. I2+1   s. $300.50   t. 3 < 4

4. Translate the following algebraic expressions into FORTRAN:

   a. $x(y + z)$

   b. $\dfrac{a}{b} \cdot c$

   c. $\dfrac{a}{b^5}$

   d. $ax^2 + bx + c$

   e. $\dfrac{a}{bs}$

   f. $y^{1/3}$

   g. πr^2

   h. $\dfrac{a}{x + y} - \dfrac{.5}{xz}$

   i. $2(xy^{-1})$

j. $-x^2$

k. $a^{x+y} + 3.5$

l. $y + a^x$

m. $\dfrac{y - y_0}{y_1 - y_0} \cdot \dfrac{x - x_0}{x_1 - x_0}$

n. $z - 1 + \dfrac{1}{2 + \dfrac{3}{1-x}}$

o. $\dfrac{-b + \sqrt{b^2 - 4ac}}{2a}$

p. u^{2n}

q. $\sqrt{\dfrac{4(x_1{}^2 + x_2{}^2 + x_3{}^2) - (x_1 + x_2 + x_3)^2}{3(3-1)}}$

5. Fill the blanks with the appropriate words:

a. The____ instruction denotes the logical end of a FORTRAN program.

b. Variables not starting with the letters ____ are real variables.

c. ____ statements are used to describe the layout of the data in an I/O operation.

d. Print position 1 of the output form is used as a ____ .

e. ____ can be used to refer to or identify a particular FORTRAN instruction.

f. The____ instruction denotes the physical end of the FORTRAN deck of cards.

g. Integers and real numbers are examples of ____ .

h. Letters of the alphabet and the digits 0 through 9 are referred to as ____ characters.

i. ____ are used to refer symbolically to memory locations.

j. $3*X + 1$ is an example of an ____ .

k. Card columns 73–80 are used for____ .

l. Variable=expression is an example of a FORTRAN____ .

m. ____ cards are generally used to make up a complete job in addition to the FORTRAN program.

n. The output code generated by the FORTRAN compiler is called ____ , while the input to the compiler is called ____ .

o. To identify real and integer numbers in a FORMAT, the format codes ____ are used.

p. A format code used to space data on the output form can be the ____ or ____ format code.

q. Two FORTRAN statements with identical statement numbers would result in a ____ time error, while computing the square root of a negative number would result in a ____ time error.

r. Dividing two integers together results in ____ .

6. Which of the following output instructions are invalid (assume 3 represents the output device)? State reasons.

a. WRITE(3,10),A,B,C
   10 FORMAT(1X,F1.0,F2.0,F3.0)

b. WRITE(3,5)I,J
   5 FORMAT(I1,I4)

c. WRITE(3,11)4,5.23
   11 FORMAT(T5,I2,F4.2)

d. WRITE(3,16)A,I,J
   16 FORMAT(T3,F4.5,I2,I1)

e. WRITE(3,7)A,K,C
   7 FORMAT(F5.2,I3,F4.)

f. WRITE(3,9)'RESULT IS',J
   9 FORMAT(3X,I3)

g. WRITE(3,12.)X,Y
   12 FORMAT(2X,F3.1,F3.1)

h. WRITE(3,15)I,X,K
   15 FORMAT(1X,I2,I3,I1)

i. WRITE(3,11) X – Y
   11 FORMAT(F3.2,F4.0)

j. WRITE(1,9)KL,M1
   9 FORMAT(3X,I3,I3)

7. Which of the following statements are true?

a. Statement numbers must be sequentially numbered.
b. Integer variables must start with one of the letters I, J, K, L, M or N.
c. The statement END denotes the logical end of the program.
d. Statement numbers cannot exceed 99999.
e. Syntax errors are detected at execution time.
f. FORMATs can be located anywhere in the program before the END card.
g. The STOP is used by the compiler to terminate the translation process.
h. SAM. is a valid real variable name.
i. Statement numbers must start in column 1.
j. A FORMAT may be referenced in any number of WRITE statements.
k. X=X+1. is a valid FORTRAN statement.
l. WRITE(3,11) is an invalid output statement.
m. 4./4/5 evaluates to the same as 4./(4/5).
n. 2*J = 3 is a valid replacement statement.
o. The maximum number of characters for a FORTRAN variable name depends on the particular system.
p. Depending on the integer values I and J and the real variable C, I*J*C ≠ I*C*J.

8. For A = 3., B = −2, I = 6 and J = 0, evaluate each of the following expressions.

a. A**2 + B
b. I + 2/3
c. A**B
d. A*3. + B*4
e. A/B
f. A/B*3 + A
g. A/B/2
h. A/B + 2.
i. J/I
j. I/J
k. A**I
l. (A + I)/B
m. A**2**3
n. B**B
o. J**B

9. What value will be stored in X or IX by each of the following statements, assuming that A = 3.2, B = −2., I = 6 and J = 0?

a. X = I

b. IX = A

c. X = (I + 3)/2

d. IX = −A+B

e. X = I**B

f. X = J*I/.1

g. X = J

h. X = B**J

i. IX = J*A

10. As a result of the following program code, indicate what value will be placed in memory locations S, J and JK.

```
I = 4.
A = 1
B = 2
S = (3/I)*3
J = (3./9)*3
JK = (A + 2./B)/2
```

11. Show that depending on the values of the variables I and J integer and C real:

a. $\dfrac{I}{J} \cdot C \neq \dfrac{I \cdot C}{J}$

b. $C \cdot I/J \neq C \cdot (I/J)$

12. Indicate the printed output field (print positions) for A, given the following format specifications:

a. A = 743.25   F10.3

b. A = −643.281   F7.2

c. A = −4768.6   F6.0

d. A = 328.74   F5.3

e. A = .37   F5.2

13. What output will be produced by each of the following program segments?

a.
```
      X = 3.2
      Y = X*.16
      WRITE(3,10)X,Y
  10  FORMAT(3X,F4.0,T10,F9.2,'ALL')
```

b.
```
      I = +1632
      J = −4
      K = I/J
      WRITE(3,11)I,J,K
  11  FORMAT(T8,I4,4X,I1,'+',I5)
```

c.
```
      XXX = 4.3257
      YYY = −.0007
      ZZZ = XXX+YYY
      WRITE(3,12)XXX,YYY,ZZZ
  12  FORMAT(T4,F7.3,F7.3,F7.3)
```

d.
```
      ABC = 19.2
      IJ3 = 4
      WRITE(3,13)ABC,IJ3
  13  FORMAT(2X,I4,3X,F6.0)
```

e.
```
      I = .8
      J = .6
      Z = I+J
      WRITE(3,11)Z
  11  FORMAT(1X,F2.0,'I2,F4.1')
```

f.
```
      I = 11
      WRITE(3,12)I
  12  FORMAT(I2)
      WRITE(3,13)
  13  FORMAT('1','1','ALL')
```

3-6-2 Programming Exercises

1. The lowest temperature ever recorded in the Antarctic is −126.9° Fahrenheit. Write a program to convert this temperature in degrees Centigrade and print result. The formula is $C = \dfrac{5}{9}\,(F - 32)$

2. Write a program to evaluate each of the formulas for the indicated values (use $\pi = 3.1415$) and print the answers with appropriate literal headings.

   a. Simple interest $i = Prt$ for

   $$r = .04$$
   $$t = 3$$
   $$p = 100$$

   b. Volume of a cube $v = c^3$ for $c = 3.1672$

   c. Area of a circle $A = \pi r^2$ for $r = 6.2$

   d. Volume of a cone $v = \dfrac{1}{3}\,\pi r^2 h$ for $r = 9.1$ and $h = 4.932$

3. Write a program segment to interchange the values contained in memory locations S and T.

4. Write the code to produce the fractional remainder (expressed as an integer) of A/B. For example, the fractional remainder of 13/2 is 1; and remainder of 17/3 is 2.

5. Can you write the program in Section 3-4-2 in more compact form?

6. Write a program to compute and print the length of the hypotenuse of a right triangle given its two legs A1 = .0056 and A2 = 135.77.

7. Write a program to compute and print (7/3)*3 and (3*7)/3. Do you expect the result to be 7?

8. Write a program to approximate the Julian date (introduced by Julius Caesar in 46 B.C.) equivalent to the calendar date given in the form: month, day. The Julian date is the day of the year. January 1 has Julian date 1, February 2 has Julian date 33, December 31 has Julian date 365 etc. A formula for approximating the Julian date is (month − 1)*30 + day. Compute the Julian dates for November 7, May 25 and March 21.

9. Write a program to compute and print the area and the length (perimeter) of each of the following:

   a.   b.   c.

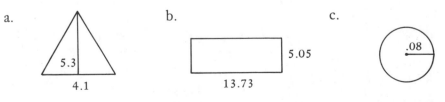

   5.3   4.1   5.05   13.73   .08

10. Write a program to print out your initials by magnifying them as follows:

```
MMM            MMM    BBBBBBB
MMMM          MMMM    BBB    B
MMMMM        MMMMM    BBB    B
MMM  MM    MM  MMM    BBBBBBB
MMM    MMMM    MMM    BBB    B
MMM     MM     MMM    BBBBBBB
```

11. The date for any Easter Sunday can be computed as follows: Let X be the year for which it is desired to compute Easter Sunday.

    Let A be the remainder of the division of X by 19.

    Let B be the remainder of the division of X by 4.

    Let C be the remainder of the division of X by 7.

    Let D be the remainder of the division of (19A + 24) by 30.

    Let E be the remainder of the division of (2B + 4C + 6D + 5) by 7.

    The date for Easter Sunday is then March (22 + D + E). Note that this can give a date in April. To compute the remainder R of the division of I by J, use the statement R = I − J*(I/J). Write a program to assign a year for the variable X and compute the date for Easter Sunday for that year using the formula 22 + D + E.

12. Mr. X. is a brick layer. Last year his gross pay was $23,564.99. After deducting 5.85 percent for social security and 23.5 percent for income tax from his gross pay, was his net income greater than Mr. Y.'s net income? Mr. Y. is a teacher who grossed $19,874 but had $850.45 deducted for his income retirement plan and 16.03 percent of his gross income for income tax purposes.

13. With an interest rate I of 6 percent and a principal P of $1,956.45 deposited for an 11-year period in a savings account, write a program to compute a total principal T given the formula

$$T = P(1 + I)^N$$

where N is the number of years.

Suppose the principal P is compounded daily for the same time period of 11 years. Write a program to compute

a. The total principal given by the formula

$$T = P \left(1 + \frac{I}{J}\right)^{J \cdot N}$$

where J is the number of times the interest is compounded per year.

b. The difference between total amounts when the principal is compounded once and 360 times a year.

14. A wholesaler accepts a $5,000 promissory note at 7 percent in lieu of cash payment for delivered goods. Write a program to compute the maturity value of the note for a 30-, 60- and 90-day short-term loan. The formula to compute the maturity value S is $S = P(1 + I \cdot N)$, where P is the principal, I is the interest rate and N is the number of years (if it is days, expressed as days/360).

15. Mr. X. would like to deposit $1,500 at a savings institution. He considers a local bank and a credit union. The credit union requires an initial nonrefundable fee of $15. Deposits earn 6 1/4 percent at the credit union and 6 percent at the bank. Mr. X. knows he will need the $1,500 in two and a half years from now. Write a program to determine whether he should save at the bank or at the credit union. The formula to compute the amount is $A = P(1 + I)^N$ where P is the principal, I is the interest rate and N is the number of years.

16. A balance sheet showing the financial position of a business has the following format. Assets are generally listed in the order specified. This balance sheet will be referred to repeatedly in later chapters (cc stands for card columns).

CC32 ⟶ XYZ CORPORATION
Balance Sheet
April 30, 1978

CC 5 *Assets*		CC37 *Liabilities and Stockholders' Equity*	
Cash	3500	Liabilities:	
Accounts receivable	500	Accounts payable	3000
Supplies	100		
Land	2000		
Buildings	10000	Stockholders' Equity:	
Machines and equipment	3000	Capital stock	18100
Patents	2000		
		Total Liabilities and	
Total Assets	21100	Stockholders' Equity	21100

a. Write a program to duplicate the above balance sheet. Define each asset and liability by a variable name as in CASH = 3500. Variables for the various entries should appear in the WRITE statements.

b. Write a program to generate a balance sheet as described previously for the Triple Star Corporation for the month of September 1976 given the following data:

Cash = $3,200   Accounts receivable = $1,300
Capital stock = $5,000   Repair supplies = $700
Accounts payable = $2,500   Land = ?

Use variable names to define these entries and let the computer determine the value of the land in such a way that Total Assets = Liabilities + Stockholders' Equity.

17. Fifteen seconds after dropping a stone into a well, the stone hits the surface of the water. Determine the height of the well given the formula $d = \frac{1}{2}gt^2$, where d is the distance, g is the force of gravity (9.81 meter/s) and t is the time in seconds.

18. Write a program to compute the sum of the first 100 terms of the following geometric progressions (use formulas of Section 3-4-1) and their infinite sum whenever possible:

   a. $1 + 2 + 4 + 8 + 16 + \cdots$

   b. $3 - 9 + 27 - 71 + \cdots$

   c. $4 + 2 + 1 + 1/2 + 1/4 + \cdots$

   d. $9/10 + 9/100 + 9/1000 + \cdots$

19. For four resistors R_1, R_2, R_3 and R_4 in parallel, the overall resistance R is given by

$$\frac{1}{R} = \frac{1}{R_1} + \frac{1}{R_2} + \frac{1}{R_3} + \frac{1}{R_4}$$

If R_1, R_2, R_3, and R_4 are respectively 1.5, 3, 4.5 and 6 ohms, write a program to compute R and print the results as follows:

R1 = 1.5   R2 = 3   R3 = 4.5   R4 = 6
THE OVERALL RESISTANCE R = XX.X

20. Determine whether $x = 1.3$ is a root of the polynomial

$$\frac{17}{3} x^{17} + 4x^8 - .76x^2 - 1145$$

3-6-3   Answers to Self Test

1. An expression is a part of a statement. An expression should always be to the right-hand side of the "=" sign. The value of a constant does not change; the value of a variable may change. Integer data may not have a decimal point; real data will have a decimal point.

2. A source statement is a statement written in a compiler language such as FORTRAN. Job control cards are cards required to communicate with the operating system to compile and execute a program. Execution time is the time during which the computer is executing the translated program. Compile time is the time during which the computer is translating a program into machine language.

3. a. Real variable   b. Integer variable   c. Invalid variable: too many characters

   d. Invalid variable: contains special character   e. Integer constant

   f. Invalid variable: numeric first character   g. Real variable

   h. Real constant   i. Integer constant

   j. Invalid variable: numeric first character and special characters

   k. Invalid variable: decimal point   l. Invalid constant: imbedded "−"

   m. Invalid variable   n. Integer variable   o. Real variable

   p. Integer variable   q. Invalid constant: imbedded "+"

   r. Invalid variable: special character   s. Invalid constant: $ must not be used

   t. Invalid constant: imbedded "<"

4. a. $X*(Y + Z)$.   b. $A/B*C$.   c. $A/B**5$.   d. $A*X**2 + B*X + C$.

   e. $A/(B*S)$.   f. $Y**(1./3.)$.   g. $3.14*R**2$.   h. $A/(X + Y) - .5/(X*Z)$.

   i. $2.*(X*Y**(-1))$.   j. $-X**2$.   k. $A**(X + Y) + 3.5$.   l. $Y + A**X$.

   m. $(Y - Y0)/(Y1 - Y0)*(X - X0)/(X1 - X0)$.

   n. $Z - 1 + (1/(2 + 3*(1 - X)))$.   o. $(-B + (B*B - 4.*A*C)**.5)/(2.*A)$.

   p. $U**(2*N)$.

   q. $((4.*(X1*X1 + X2*X2 + X3*X3) - (X1 + X2 + X3)**2)/(3.*(3. - 1.)))**.5$

5. a. STOP   b. I through N.   c. FORMATs.   d. Carriage control.

   e. Statement number   f. END   g. Constants   h. Alphanumeric

   i. Variables   j. Expression   k. Sequencing/identification   l. Statement

   m. Job control   n. Object code, source code   o. F and I   p. X or T

   q. Compilation, execution   r. Truncation of fractional part

6. a. No comma after (3,10), also field for A is too small, should be at least two characters long.

   b. Value of variable I may be used as a carriage control character.

   c. The WRITE statement must contain variables.

   d. F4.5 is an invalid FORMAT code since $5 > 4$.

   e. F4. is invalid: must contain a digit after the decimal point.

   f. The WRITE statement list must not control literal strings.

   g. No "." is used after the format statement number.

   h. The variable X must be described with a real format code.

   i. The WRITE statement list must not contain expressions.

   j. Unit 3 and not unit 1 represents the output device.

7. a. F.   b. T.   c. F.   d. T.   e. F.   f. T.   g. F.   h. F.   i. F.
   j. T.   k. T.   l. F.   m. F.   n. F.   o. F.   p. F.

8. a. 7   b. 6   c. .111111   d. 1   e. −1:5   f. −1.5   g. −.75
   h. 0.5   i. 0   j. error.   k. 729.   l. −4.5   m. 6561.
   n. .25   o. undefined.

9. a. 6.   b. 3   c. 4.   d. −5   e. .0277778   f. 0.   g. 0.
   h. 1.   i. 0.

10. S = 0.   J = 0   JK = 1

11. a. 3/4*4.=0. but (3*4.)/4 = 3.   b. 2.*3/4 = 1.5 but 2.*(3/4) = 0.

12. a. `7 4 3 . 2 5 0`   b. `- 6 4 3 . 2 8`

    c. `- 4 7 6 9 .`   d. `* * * * *`   e. `. 3 7`

13. In this exercise the first print position is not shown.

    a. `3 .            . 5 1 A L L`

    b. `1 6 3 2        * +   - 4 0 8`

    c. `4 . 3 2 6    - 0 . 0 0 1    4 . 3 2 5`

    d. ABC and IJ3 should be defined respectively by F and I format codes.

    e. `0 . 1 2 . F 4 . 1`

    f. `` (blank)   Top of new page.

    `1 A L L`   Top of new page.

INTRODUCTION TO FORTRAN — PART 2

4-1 Problem Example

Mr. Loh is paid at a regular rate of $6.50 per hour for the first 40 hours. The overtime rate for hours in excess of 40 is 1.5 times the regular rate. Write a FORTRAN program to read the number of hours worked and compute and print out Mr. Loh's gross pay.

An example of a FORTRAN program to solve the above problem is shown in Figure 4-1.

New FORTRAN statements used in this program include

1. The READ statement used to read data from punched cards or other input medium.

2. The GO TO statement used to transfer control to a nonsequentially placed instruction.

3. The IF statement used to branch to other program statements depending upon a condition.

4. The COMMENT statement used to document the program.

Note that in the program of Figure 4-1, statements 12, 13, 14 and 15 could have been replaced with just the statement PAY = 40*6.50 + (NHRS − 40)*6.50*1.5.

To make this program more flexible, we could have read a variable rate R and an overtime pay rate factor F so that by changing the above statement to PAY = 40*R + (NHRS − 40)*R*F, the program could have computed any gross pay for any rate R and any overtime rate of F.

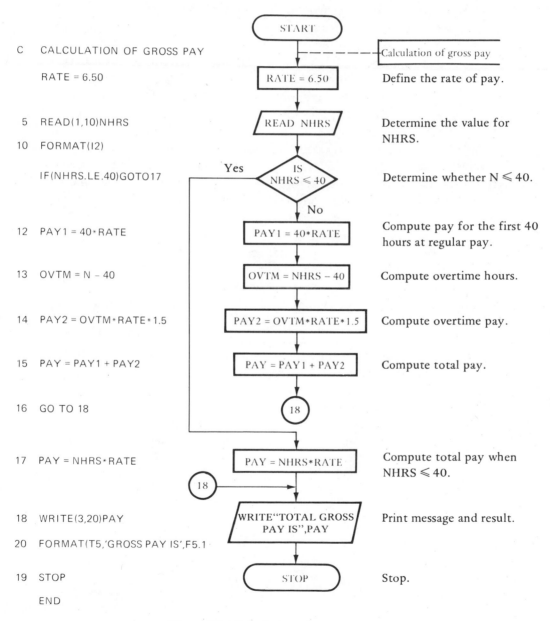

C   CALCULATION OF GROSS PAY

     RATE = 6.50

5   READ(1,10)NHRS

10 FORMAT(I2)

    IF(NHRS.LE.40)GOTO17

12 PAY1 = 40*RATE

13 OVTM = N − 40

14 PAY2 = OVTM*RATE*1.5

15 PAY = PAY1 + PAY2

16 GO TO 18

17 PAY = NHRS*RATE

18 WRITE(3,20)PAY

20 FORMAT(T5,'GROSS PAY IS',F5.1

19 STOP

    END

Figure 4-1 Calculation of gross pay.

4-2   FORTRAN Statements

4-2-1   READ Statement

So far, the only way we have defined variables (given them a value) is by means of the replacement statement; for example, in the problem of Section 4-1 we defined the rate as RATE = 6.50. The problem in defining variables this way is that the program is written too specifically; for example, it computes a pay only for a fixed rate of $6.50. If we wanted to use the same program for different values of RATE, we would have to reset RATE each time to different rates, and every time we did that the entire program would have to be completely recompiled since one statement was changed. This is time consuming, inefficient and inconvenient.

Another way to assign any desired value to a variable is to use the READ statement. The READ statement allows the program to accept data during the execution of the program (after compilation). The data is punched on cards (data cards), and these values can be read by the computer as specified by the FORTRAN READ instructions. For example, a payroll program will be able to compute different salaries depending on the rate of pay punched on each employee's data card.

It is very important to note that even though one program may only consist of one deck of cards, the program deck consists of three separate and distinct parts, all processed differently by the computer system.

The FORTRAN program consists of FORTRAN statements that use FORTRAN key words under strict grammatical rules. Data cards contain numbers that will eventually be read by the FORTRAN READ statements. These two entities are physically separate, as shown in Figure 4-2. Usually the FORTRAN source deck is separated from the data deck by special control cards (workflow or job control cards telling the computer what action to take). These control cards will vary from system to system and will generally be physically located in front of the FORTRAN program, between the program and data deck, and possibly after

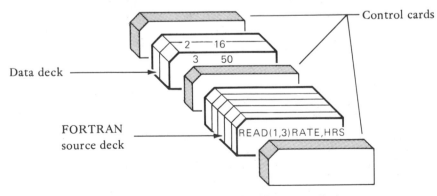

Figure 4-2 Physical job deck before compilation.

the data deck as shown in Figure 4-2. The FORTRAN source deck is first read by the compiler, which translates it into machine language. It is then stored (loaded) into the memory of the computer. This stage is called *compilation and loading*. The data cards still have not been processed.

Once control is passed to the program in memory, the data cards are read by the READ statements in the order these (or their equivalent in machine language) are encountered in the FORTRAN program. See Figure 4-3.

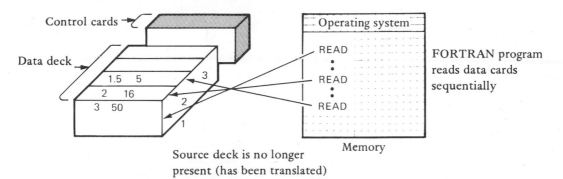

Figure 4-3   Physical job deck during execution.

The general form of the READ statement is

> READ (device-number, format-statement-number) variable-list

where device-number is an integer specifying the input device (address of device), for example card reader, magnetic tape, disk etc.[1]

format-statement-number is a user-selected statement number describing the layout of the data on the input record.

variable-list specifies the names of values to be read from the input medium (cards); each data item on the input record will be stored in the named memory locations.

If cards are used as input, the input data may be punched anywhere in card columns 1–80.

Example

device number   format number   list of variable names

READ(1,10)HRS,RATE,BONUS

The above READ statement can be interpreted as follows: Read three numbers from one or more cards (device number 1 might imply data is read from cards) and store these three numbers in memory location HRS, RATE and BONUS, respectively.

---

[1] These numbers will vary from installation to installation. Throughout this text, the number 1 will be used to refer to the card reader. In many installations, the number 5 is used.

4-2-2   The FORMAT Statement

It is apparent that the READ statement all by itself does not provide the computer sufficient information to know the following:

1. How many items there are per card.

2. In what card column each data item starts.

3. How many card columns are used for each data item (length of data item).

4. The mode of the data item, integer or real.

A FORMAT is needed in conjunction with the READ statement to inform the computer precisely how the READ operation is to be performed; that is, how to process the various data on the input record.

Each READ statement must specify a format-statement-number; each FORMAT statement must have a statement number by which it can be referenced. The READ is an executable statement while the FORMAT is nonexecutable. The READ instruction is carried out according to the specifications described in the FORMAT. For this reason, the FORMAT statement can be placed anywhere in the program (before the END statement).

Some programmers prefer to place all their FORMATs at the beginning or end of their program while others like them to immediately follow the associated READ statements.

Example

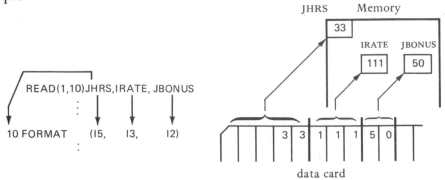

The above input operation can be interpreted as follows:

Read three numbers (three variables are named) from a card (device-number 1) according to the data layout described by the FORMAT labeled 10. FORMAT 10 may be interpreted as follows: The first number (JHRS) will be an integer number (specified by the I format code) found in the first five card columns (1–5). The next number (IRATE) will be an integer number found in the next three card columns (6–8) and the last number (JBONUS) will be an integer found in the following two card columns (9–10).

The general form of the FORMAT statement is

$$\text{statement-number FORMAT}(\text{fd}_1, \text{fd}_2, \cdots, \text{fd}_n)$$

where statement-number is the format label referred to in a READ statement
fd$_1$, fd$_2$, $\cdots$, fd$_n$ are format codes, which can be either:

or

1. Data format codes to identify data on the card as either integer or real numbers

2. Edit codes to control placement or editing of the input record.

Data format codes can be any of the following codes:[2]

F   This code identifies a real number; that is, real data is to be read from the input record (card).

I   This code identifies an integer number.

The I format code

The general form of the I format code is

$$\text{Iw}$$

where I specifies that an integer is to be read.
w specifies the width of the integer field (number of card columns).

One card column must be reserved for the minus sign if the integer is negative. Any blanks within the integer data field whether leading or trailing are interpreted as zeroes; hence the integer number must be right-justified within the field.
Integer data can consist only of the digits 0 through 9 and the + and − sign; any
other character punched in an I field will result in an execution-time error. The
corresponding variable in the READ list must be an integer variable.

Example 1

In Example 1, the READ list specifies three numbers to be read. Since the
FORMAT has three data format codes, this means that three numbers are to be

[2] Other format codes discussed in later chapters are E, D and A.

read from one card. Note that the leading and trailing blanks are read as zeroes. Also note that the plus sign for I in the first data card is not really needed to identify a positive number. Reading starts at the first card column unless otherwise specified (T and X edit format codes) and each new field immediately follows the preceding field on the data card, as long as there are no other control format codes.

The F Format Code

The general form of the F code is

$$Fw.d$$

where F specifies that a real number is to be read.

      w specifies the field width (number of card columns).

      d tells the system where to place the decimal point in the number read in case no decimal point is punched in the number field.

If there is no decimal point punched in the number field on the data card, w columns are read, and then the decimal point is placed automatically by the system d positions to the left of the rightmost position in the field. This results in the number stored in memory with d decimal digits to the right of the decimal point. If a decimal point is punched in the number field, the number is read as is, into memory, and the implied position of the decimal point specified by d is disregarded. The presence of a decimal point on the data card overrides the implied position d, and d can be any number between 0 and w. For grammatical considerations, d must always be specified in the format even though it might not be used.

In all cases, d must be such that $d \leqslant w$. Blanks are treated as zeroes. One card column must be reserved for the minus sign if the real number is negative and another card column must be reserved if the decimal point is to be punched in the number field.

Once again, it should be pointed out that w represents the number of columns to be read. If a decimal point is punched in the field this column is counted as part of the field length w.

Variables in the READ list that are described by an F code in the format *must* be real variables.

Example 1

```
    READ(1,5)A,B,C
  5 FORMAT(F5.5,F3.2,F2.0)
```

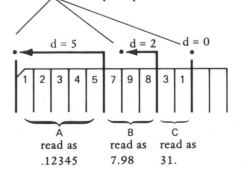

In Example 1, three real numbers are to be read. The first one is located in the first five card columns. Since no decimal point is punched in these five card columns, the decimal point is assumed to be five positions to the left of the rightmost field (d = 5); hence A = .12345, that is, A has five digits to the right of the decimal point. In the case of B, the implied position of the decimal point is at the and hence B = 7.98. For C, the implied position of the decimal point is at the rightmost column of the field (d = 0).

Example 2

```
READ(1,1)X,Y,Z
1   FORMAT(F5.5,F3.2,F2.0)
```

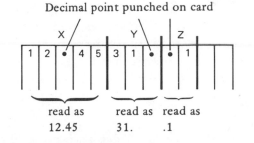

In Example 2, decimal points are punched within each field, hence the values for X, Y and Z are those punched in the three fields. The explicit position of the decimal point overrides the implicit position as defined by d.

Example 3

```
READ(1,5)X,Y,Z,W
5   FORMAT(F1.1,F2.0,F3.2,F4.3)
```

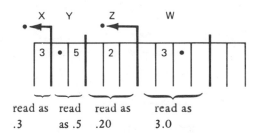

Example 3 illustrates both means of defining the decimal point in the real data: explicitly (Y, W) and implicitly (X, Z).

Example 4

```
READ(1,8)X,Y,Z
8   FORMAT(F4.2,F5.1,F2.0)
```

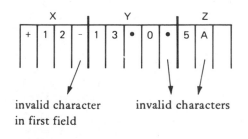

In Example 4, a READ error would occur at execution time as a result of the invalid character (−) in the fourth card column, an invalid decimal point in the Y field and an illegal character (A) in the Z field. In general, the program would stop and an error would be printed. Such READ errors could also occur while reading integer data with invalid characters.

Mixed-Mode Input

It is permissible to combine both real and integer variables in a READ list. The programmer must then make sure that the variable name in the READ list is properly described by a format code of the corresponding type. If a real variable name is read, its corresponding format code should be F; if an integer variable name is read, its corresponding format code should be I. If this is not the case, number conversion will take place, which will change the value of the input data, thereby causing logical errors in the program.

Example

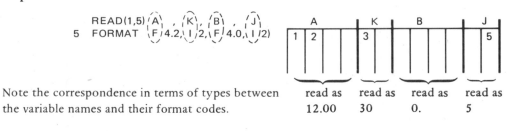

Note the correspondence in terms of types between the variable names and their format codes.

Edit codes allow the programmer to provide spaces between input fields (the X code), to control positioning of each input field (the T code), and to skip records (the / code—see Section 5-2-9).

The T Format Code

The general form of the T format code is

$$Tj$$

where j is an integer specifying the next position in the input record to be processed. The T code causes a data field to be read starting in column j.

Example

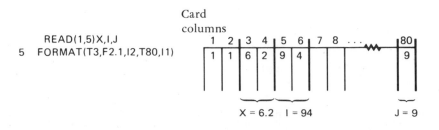

The T feature is generally not used to control the spacing between fields; it only identifies the first position of the field. The above example can be interpreted as follows: Starting in card column 3, find a real number two digits in length (card column 3 and 4); read it and store it in memory location X, then find an integer in the next two card columns (5 and 6) and store it into I. Then go to card column 80 and read one digit into J.

The T feature is extremely useful in the case of prearranged data layouts, where each field is known to start at specific card columns.

The X Format Code

The general form of the X format code is

$$nX$$

where n is an integer specifying the number of positions to be skipped. The effect of the X code is to skip n card columns (positions) between fields.

Example

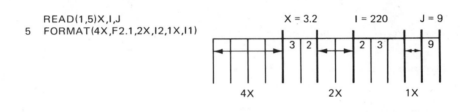

```
        READ(1,5)X,I,J
    5   FORMAT(4X,F2.1,2X,I2,1X,I1)
```

The above example may be interpreted as follows: First skip four card columns and starting in card column 5 find a two-digit real number, then skip two card columns and find a two-digit integer, then skip one card column and find a one-digit integer number. A combination of both T and X can be used in the same format as in

```
    READ(1,7)X,I,J,Z
7   FORMAT(T10,F3.2,2X,I1,3X,I2,T30,F4.1)
```

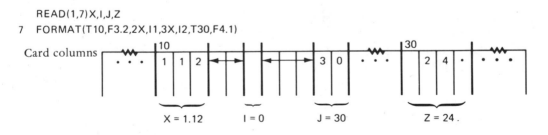

4-2-3 The Unconditional Transfer Statement GO TO

The general form of an unconditional transfer statement GO TO is

$$GO\ TO\ transfer\text{-}statement\text{-}number$$

A FORTRAN program consists of a sequence of FORTRAN statements. FORTRAN will process these statements one after another in sequential order. When FORTRAN encounters a GO TO statement, it will transfer control to the statement specified; that is, processing will continue at the transfer-statement-number. This allows the programmer to bypass certain instructions in his program (in the program of Figure 4-1 statement 17 is bypassed). It also allows the program to branch back to repeat (reprocess) certain instructions or certain procedures; this is called *looping*. (If in the program of Figure 4-1 we replaced statement 19 by the statement GO TO 5, computer would execute the entire program more times with a new value for NHRS each time.)

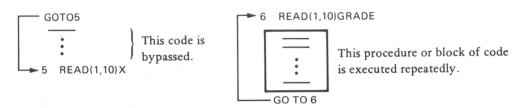

Once again, the reader is reminded that statement numbers need not be in ascending or descending order; statement numbers, however, must be punched in card columns 1 through 5.

4-2-4 The Logical IF Statement

Recall that the central processing unit (CPU) has a unit to carry out logical operations. This hardware feature enables the computer to compare numbers and thereby make decisions. The computer's ability to make decisions is probably one of the most powerful and desirable characteristics of the concept of a stored program. Any computer stripped of its logical capability would be no more than an extremely fast calculator that could only process serial arithmetic and input/output instructions.

The IF statement allows the computer to transfer to a nonsequential instruction in a program depending on whether or not certain conditions are met. In this way, a program can contain several alternate paths that are data dependent. Certain blocks of FORTRAN statements may be bypassed in the program as a result of transferring to a nonsequential instruction.

In Figure 4-1, if NHRS is less than or equal to 40, the block of statements labeled 12–16 will be bypassed, and execution will resume at statement 17. If NHRS is not less than or equal to 40, the next instruction (statement 12) is executed. A very useful form of the logical IF statement is

IF(relational-expression)GO TO statement-number

where relational expression consists of two arithmetic expressions linked together by one of the relational operators shown in Figure 4-4. The reader may think of a relational expression as a proposition, i.e., a statement which is either true or false. For example, the statements "I am 36" or "X is less than 63" are either true or false. The statement-number is the statement transferred to if the relational-expression is true; that is, if the condition specified in the decision statement is met. If the condition is not met (result of the relational expression is false), control is passed to the statement immediately following the IF statement.

FORTRAN relational operators	Mathematical symbols	Meaning
.EQ.	$=$	Equal to
.LT.	$<$	Less than
.GT.	$>$	Greater than
.NE.	$\neq$	Not equal to
.LE.	$\leq$	Less than or equal to
.GE.	$\geq$	Greater than or equal to

Figure 4-4   FORTRAN relational operator.

The logical IF can be flowcharted as follows:

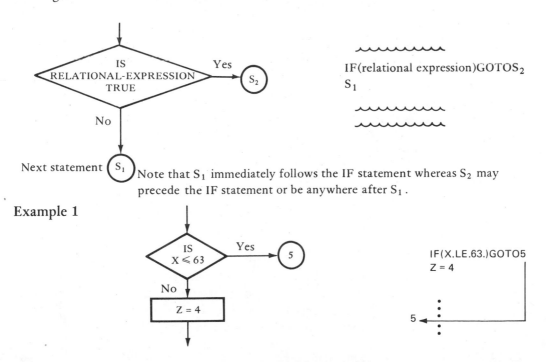

IF(relational expression)GOTOS$_2$
S$_1$

Note that S$_1$ immediately follows the IF statement whereas S$_2$ may precede the IF statement or be anywhere after S$_1$.

Example 1

IF(X.LE.63.)GOTO5
Z = 4

Example 2

Figure 4-5 displays numerous examples of logical IFs and their meaning.

Logical IF statements	Meaning
a. 1 IF(X.EQ.0.)GOTO5 3 A = 4	If X = 0, transfer to statement 5; otherwise process the next statement labeled 3 (meaning X is less than or greater than 0).
b. 4 IF((X – Y)**2.LT.Z)GOTO40 8 IF(Z.GT.2.)GOTO60	If $(X - Y)^2 < Z$, process statement 40; otherwise $(X - Y)^2 \geqslant Z$ fall through and execute statement 8.
c. 5 IF(SQRT(X).GE.2.)GOTO50 7 WRITE(3,11)X	If $\sqrt{X} \geqslant 2$, go to 50. If $\sqrt{X} < 2$ process the next sequential statement 7.
d. 2 IF(X + Y.NE.(J – K))GOTO70 6 READ(1,5)A	If X + Y = J – K, process statement 6; otherwise go to statement 70.

Figure 4-5   Examples of logical IF statements.

To better understand the logical IF statement and its interaction with other FORTRAN statements in a program, consider the following examples:

Example 1

Read an integer number I from a card and determine whether I is even or odd. Since integer division results in the truncation of all digits to the right of the decimal point, the following is true:

If I is even, then 2*(I/2) = I   For example, if I = 4, then 2*(4/2) = 2*2 = 4

If I is odd, then 2*(I/2) ≠ I   For example, if I = 5, then 2*(5/2) = 2*2 = 4 ≠ 5

Example 1 is flowcharted and coded in Figure 4-6.

The reader should analyze the FORTRAN program of Figure 4-6 to understand why the statement GO TO 5 is needed. If this statement were omitted, every time I was odd both messages I IS ODD and I IS EVEN would be printed. The statement GO TO 5 is required to bypass statement number 15.

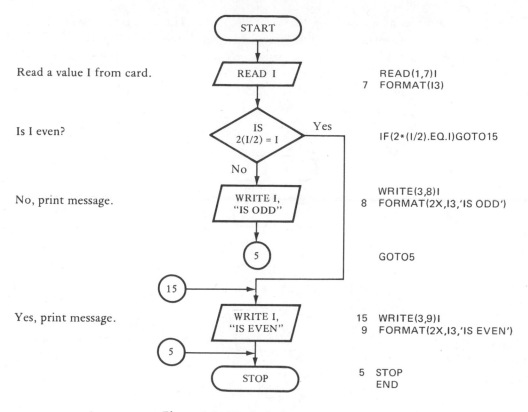

Figure 4-6 The logical IF statement.

FORTRAN logical IF statements allow only for a two-way transfer; that is, either the condition tested for is met or is not met. If a decision involves a three-way outcome, two logical IF statements are required (see Example 2 and Figure 4-7). In that case, it is advantageous to use the arithmetic IF (Section 4-2-6).

Example 2

Read a number N and write a program to do the following:

> If $N > 0$, write the code POS on the output medium.
> If $N = 0$, write the code ZERO on the output medium.
> If $N < 0$, write the code NEG on the output medium.

The flowchart and program are shown in Figure 4-7.

As displayed in Figure 4-7, the sequence of FORTRAN instructions parallels exactly the physical sequence of the flowchart blocks. Note the importance and necessity of the two GO TO 15 statements after the WRITE(3,11) and WRITE(3,22) instructions.

If N were zero and the two GO TO 15s were omitted, the message ZERO would be written as a result of the WRITE(3,11): The computer would execute the next instruction WRITE(3,22), which would write NEG, and finally the WRITE(3,33) would be processed printing the message POS. Altogether, three messages would be printed, when in fact only one should be printed. Note, however, that there is no need for a GO TO 15 after statement 3 since the STOP immediately follows statement 3.

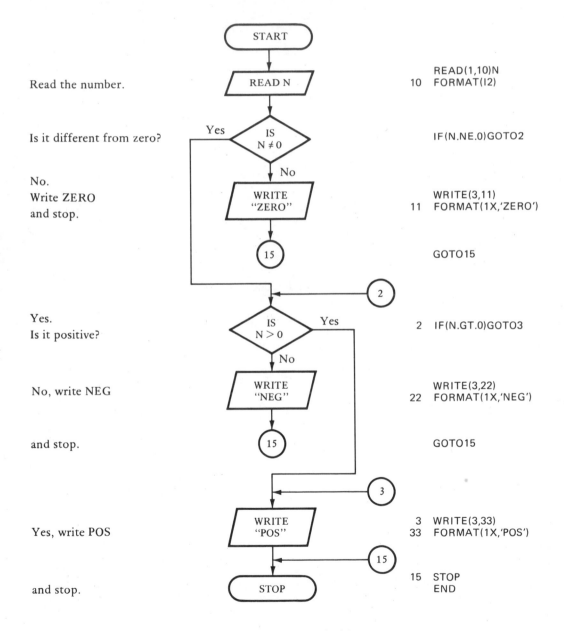

Figure 4-7 A three-way decision.

There are many other ways to code the program in Figure 4-7. An alternative is shown in Figure 4-8, which results in the STOP statement being in the middle of the program.

Note again that the END statement is last in the program, as it should be, since it denotes the physical end of the FORTRAN program. When the compiler encounters the END statement, it knows there are no more FORTRAN instructions to translate into machine language. The STOP statement, on the other hand, is translated by the FORTRAN compiler into a machine language instruction, which when processed by the CPU means that the program has come to its logical

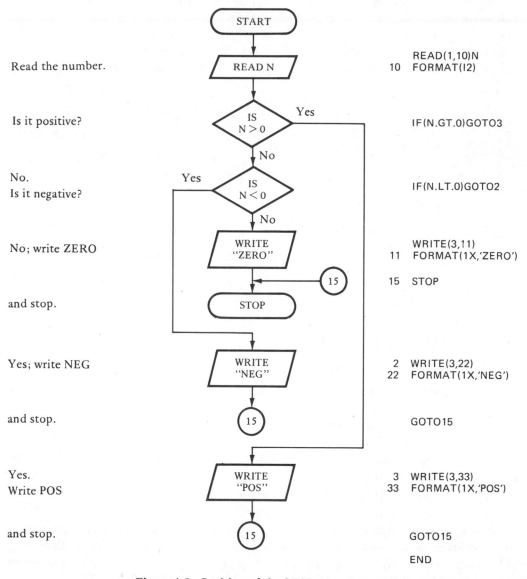

Figure 4-8   Position of the STOP statement.

conclusion; that is, the machine instructions corresponding to the FORTRAN program have been processed and there is nothing more to do in this program. In essence, the END is processed at compilation time, whereas the STOP is processed at execution time—two very distinct times during the life of any FORTRAN program.

Another example will help illustrate the use of more than one IF statement in a FORTRAN program.

Example 3

Read three numbers from a card and print out the largest value. If the three numbers are equal, print either value. The flowchart and program are shown in Figure 4-9. Note that in the case of statement 4 the IF statement transfers control directly to statement 3 whenever N1 < N3. The beginning programmer may be tempted to write the following, which is correct, though awkward:

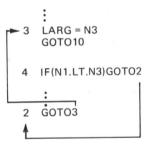

Simpler just to use GOTO3.

4-2-5 The Logical IF Revisited

The logical IF is somewhat more powerful than has been previously shown. The general form of the IF statement is

$$\text{IF(logical-expression)statement}$$

where logical-expression consists of two arithmetic expressions linked together by the logical operators .LE., .GT., .EQ. etc. and statement is any executable statement *except* another IF statement or DO (see Chapter 6).

If the condition described by the logical-expression is met (the value of the logical-expression is true), the statement within the IF statement is executed. If the condition is not met (the value of the logical-expression is false), the statement is not executed. In both cases, control is passed to the statement following the IF. The logical IF can be visualized as shown at the top of page 110.

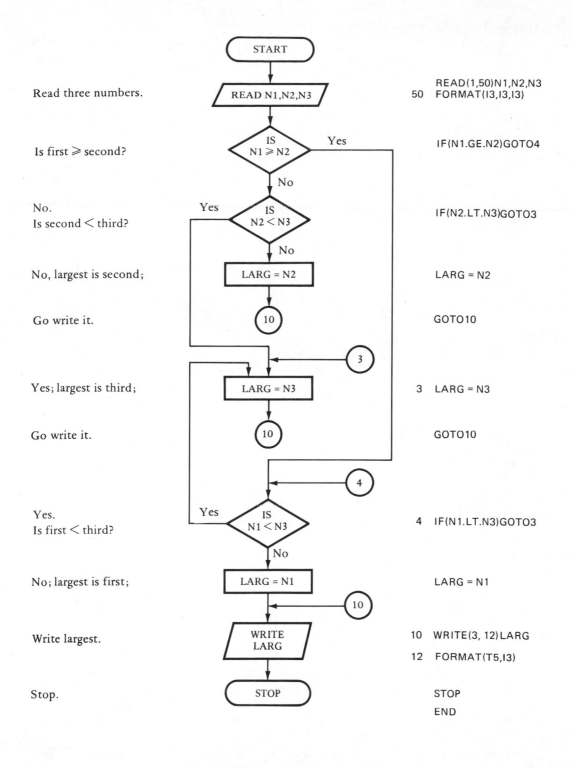

Figure 4-9 Largest of three numbers.

IF (logical-expression) statement

7 ~~~~~~~~~

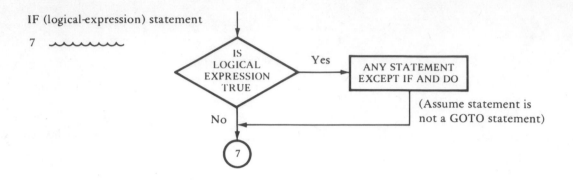

Examples

5	IF(A.LT.B)K = K + 1	If A < B, the statement
10	IF(A.EQ.4)GOTO1	K = K + 1 will be executed. Then statement 10 will be processed. If A ≥ B, statement 10 is processed next.
8	IF(CODE.NE.0.)WRITE(3,1)A	If CODE ≠ 0 A will be printed before terminating.
6	STOP	If CODE = 0 The program is terminated.
7	IF(A.GT.3.1)IF(A.LT.1.)K = K + 1	Example of an invalid logical IF. The statement may not be another IF.
8	Y = 0	

Since only one statement is grammatically permissible on the same line as the logical IF statement, an unusual code is required to account for the following flowchart:

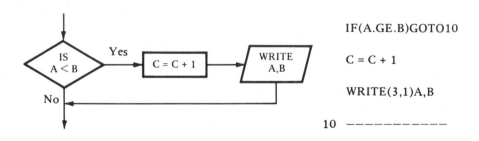

IF(A.GE.B)GOTO10

C = C + 1

WRITE(3,1)A,B

10 — — — — — — —

Another situation where cumbersome code is required to code a particular flowchart is shown as follows:

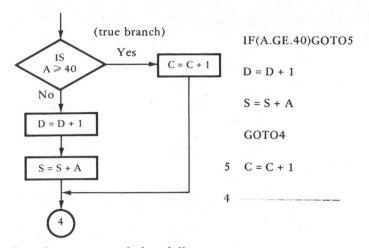

If the above flowchart were coded as follows:

$$IF(A.GE.40)C = C + 1$$
$$D = D + 1$$
$$S = S + A$$

4   ————

then 1 would be added to the variable C, 1 would also be added to the variable D and A would be added to the variable S (in the event $A \geqslant 40$).

4-2-6   The Arithmetic IF Statement

The arithmetic IF allows for a three-way transfer out of a decision block as opposed to a two-way transfer for a logical IF. When comparing, for example, two numbers A and B, the decision block may reflect three exits, one in case A is less than B, a second one in case A equals B and a third one in case A is greater than B. The flowchart symbol for an arithmetic IF is shown as follows:

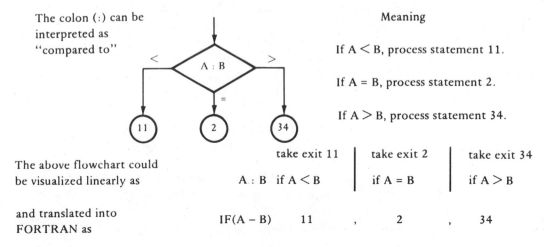

The general form of the arithmetic decision statement is

IF(expression)statement-number-1,statement-number-2,statement-number-3

where expression within parentheses is any FORTRAN expression.

statement-number-1, 2 and 3 are FORTRAN statement numbers defined in the program.

The IF statement can be interpreted as follows:

1. Evaluate the expression.

2. If the result is negative, transfer to statement number 1.
    If the result is equal to zero, transfer to statement number 2.
    If the result is positive, transfer to statement number 3.

It should be noted that the sequence of the three statement numbers in the IF statement always corresponds to the sequence of relational operations: less than 0, equal to 0 and greater than 0 in that order. The reader may visualize this sequence as follows:

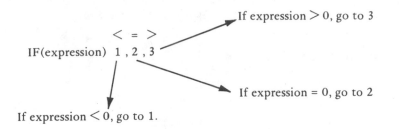

The comparison of two numbers A and B in an IF statement can be made using the expression A − B as follows:

$$\text{IF(A − B)11,2,34} \quad \text{means} \quad \begin{array}{l} \text{if A − B} < 0 \text{ or if A} < \text{B, then go to 11} \\ \text{if A − B} = 0 \text{ or if A} = \text{B, then go to 2} \\ \text{if A − B} > 0 \text{ or if A} > \text{B, then go to 34} \end{array}$$

In some cases, a decision may only require a two-way transfer, in which case appropriate IF statement-numbers may be combined as follows:

$$\begin{array}{l} \text{IF(A − B)1,5,1} \\ \text{IF(A − B)11,11,4} \end{array} \quad \text{meaning} \quad \begin{array}{l} \text{if A} = \text{B, go to 5; otherwise go to 1 (unequal).} \\ \text{if A} \leqslant \text{B, go to 11; otherwise go to 4 (greater).} \end{array}$$

Some valid IF statements and their meanings are shown on page 113.

IF statements	Meaning
IF(X)1,3,5	If X < 0, go to 1; if X = 0, go to 3; if X > 0, go to 5.
IF(X − (−4))1,1,2 IF(X + 4)1,1,2	These two statements are logically the same and could be interpreted as comparing X with −4.
IF(X + Y*Z)3,4,3	If X + Y*Z = 0, go to 4; otherwise go to 3
IF(2*X + (Z − 4)*X**2)1,2,3	Evaluate the expression and transfer to 1, 2 or 3

Some invalid IF statements are shown below:

IF statements	Reason
IF(A*B)1,2	Missing a statement number.
IF(X : 10)1,2,3	Invalid expression. Colon (:) is illegal.
IFA − B2,3,5	Missing both parentheses.
IF(2*(X + 3)1,2,3	Missing right parenthesis.
IFX > 10.GOTO7	Special character > invalid.

To better understand the IF statement and its interaction with other FOR-TRAN statements in a program, let us consider the following example:

Example 1

Read a number N and write a program to accomplish the following:

> if N > 0, write the message POS on the output form.
> if N = 0, write the message ZERO on the output form.
> if N < 0, write the message NEG on the output form.

The flowchart and programs are shown in Figure 4-10.

In method 1, the sequence of FORTRAN instructions parallels exactly the physical sequence of the flowchart blocks. This method is probably the easiest for the beginner to follow. Note the importance and necessity of the two GO TO 15 statements following statements 1 and 2. If N were zero and these two GO TO statements were omitted, the message ZERO would first be written as a result of statement number 1, then the computer would execute the next instruction at 2, which would write NEG, and then statement 3 would be processed, causing the message POS to be printed. Altogether, three messages would be printed, when in fact only one should be printed. Note, however, that a GO TO 15 is not needed after statement 3, since the STOP instruction immediately follows the WRITE statement in the flowchart.

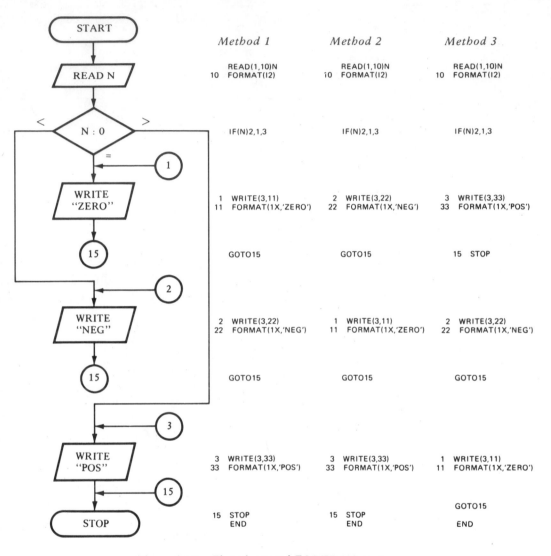

Figure 4-10   Flowchart and FORTRAN programs.

Methods 2 and 3 also illustrate alternative FORTRAN programs. However, these do not reflect a physical matching of FORTRAN statements with the flowchart blocks. Nevertheless, they are correct. The important point to keep in mind is that the logical flowpath in the flowchart be preserved in the FORTRAN program. Whether statement 1 or 2 or 3 follows immediately the IF statement is immaterial as long as the IF statement connects these statements logically (if not physically) as shown in the flowchart.

Method 3 may appear to be incorrect at first glance as a result of the STOP statement being in the middle of the program. This is really not so; the STOP statement in general can be almost anywhere in a program.

Once again, the END denotes the physical end of the FORTRAN program (after the END statement, no more FORTRAN statements) and is used by the compiler to stop translating the program into machine language, while the STOP statement comes into effect at execution time to tell the CPU that processing (execution of the machine instructions corresponding to the FORTRAN program) is completed and that it is the (logical) end of the program.

Another example will help illustrate the use of more than one IF statement in a FORTRAN program.

Example 2

Read three numbers from a card and print out the largest value. If the three numbers are equal, print the value. The program and flowchart are shown in Figure 4-11.

Note that in the case of statement 4, the IF statement transfers control directly to statement 3 if $N1 < N3$. This is perfectly valid, even though the beginner might sometimes be tempted to write the following:

```
         .
         .
         .
  3   LARG = N3

      GOTO10

  4   IF(N1 – N3)2,5,5

  2   GOTO3
         .
         .
         .
```

This statement could be replaced by IF(N1 – N3)3,5,5.

The GOTO statement is not needed.

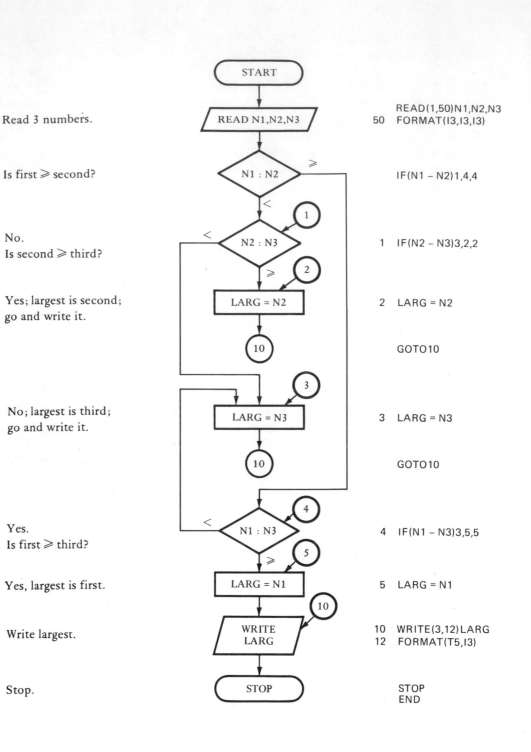

Figure 4-11 Largest of three numbers.

4-3 You Might Want to Know

1. When a data card is read, does the computer only read those fields specified by the data format codes in the FORMAT or does it actually read all 80 card columns?

   Answer: Actually, the computer reads all 80 card columns into memory but only selects and processes those fields described by the data format codes (I, F). By processing, we mean converting each number into its proper internal machine representation and storing it into the corresponding memory location described in the READ list.

2. Do I need to initialize a variable to some value before I can use that variable in a READ-list? For instance:

   $$GR = 0$$
   $$READ(1,10)GR$$

   Answer: No. The fact that GR is in the READ-list implies that a memory location will be reserved for it.

3. If I know ahead of time A can never be greater than B, can I omit the third statement in an arithmetic IF statement as in IF(A − B)1,2?

   Answer: No. For grammatical reasons, the arithmetic IF must always have three statement numbers. Two of these statement numbers can be the same, of course.

4. What happens if during execution, my program is reading data cards, but I forgot to include them in my job deck or I forgot some of them?

   Answer: The computer will read the end-of-file card and cause an execution error. End-of-file checks are discussed in Chapter 5.

5. Suppose that at execution time my program reads numbers from data cards, which have been punched incorrectly. For example, suppose that I punch an alphabetic character in a numeric field, what will happen?

   Answer: A READ error will occur which will cause termination of your program.

6. What happens if I try to read an integer or a real number from a data card and the data card is blank?

   Answer: Blanks are interpreted as zeroes.

7. What happens if I want to read a large number, as follows?

```
    READ(1,10)X
10  FORMAT(F15.0)
```

1	2	3	4	5	6	7	8	9	0	1	2	3	4	5		

Answer: The number of significant digits that can be retained for real numbers varies depending upon the computer in use. Some computers have the capability for 7 significant digits, hence the number X might be stored as 123,456,700,000,000 thereby resulting in an error of 89,012,345. See Chapter 7 for double precision and internal representation of numbers.

8. How can I read imaginary or complex numbers?

Answer: See Chapter 7 for a complete discussion.

9. Can I use the same format for more than one READ statement?

Answer: Yes. For example:

```
      READ(1,5)I,J
      READ(1,5)IPROD
   5  FORMAT(I3,I3)
```

10. What happens if I write the following code?

```
    READ(1,6)I,J,K
6   FORMAT(I3,T2,I3,T1,I1)
```

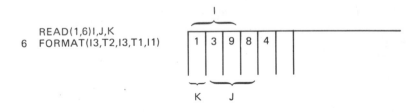

Answer: The T feature allows to restart a READ operation at different positions within a record. In the above case, I = 139,J = 398,K = 1.

11. Can you have more than one STOP statement in a program?

Answer: Yes. For example:

```
         IF(X)16,15,15
   16    WRITE(3,12)
         STOP
   15    WRITE(3,11)
         STOP
   12    FORMAT(3X,'X IS NEGATIVE')
   11    FORMAT(3X,'X IS POSITIVE')
         END
```

Remember, though, you can have *only* one END statement, and it must be the last statement in your program.

12. When you read data from cards is it a good idea to immediately print out that data on the output form?

Answer: Yes. In fact, it is strongly recommended that you print out all the original data that your program is reading. The programmer can then verify the accuracy of the input data, which can then be used for documentation purposes to anyone reading the program who does not have access to the original data cards.

13. Was I surprised the other day! I knew I made a mistake, but the compiler didn't catch it. I punched GOTO51 instead of GO TO 51 and my program still ran. How about that!

Answer: The compiler is smarter than you think. Spaces within FORTRAN statements are ignored by the compiler.

14. Since certain *fractional* numbers may not always be represented exactly in memory due to a binary representation of numbers, would K be set to 3 in the following example?

$$Y = .5$$
$$X = .1 + .1 + .1 + .1 + .1$$
$$IF(X.EQ.Y)K = 3$$

On many systems .1 may be approximated to .09999999; hence X = .4999999. On the other hand, Y can be represented exactly as .5; hence, on some systems X may not equal Y, even though this is the case arithmetically. In such cases, the user may want to ask whether X − Y is close enough to 0, which would mean that X is sufficiently close to Y. This can be expressed as follows:

$$IF(ABS(X − Y).LT.EPS)K = 3$$

where EPS = .01, .001, .0000001 etc., depending on the degree of accuracy needed, and ABS is the symbol to represent the absolute value function.

4-4 Programming Examples

4-4-1 Solution of a Quadratic Equation

Let us write a program to determine the roots of the polynomial $ax^2 + bx + c$. The three constants a, b and c will be read at execution time.

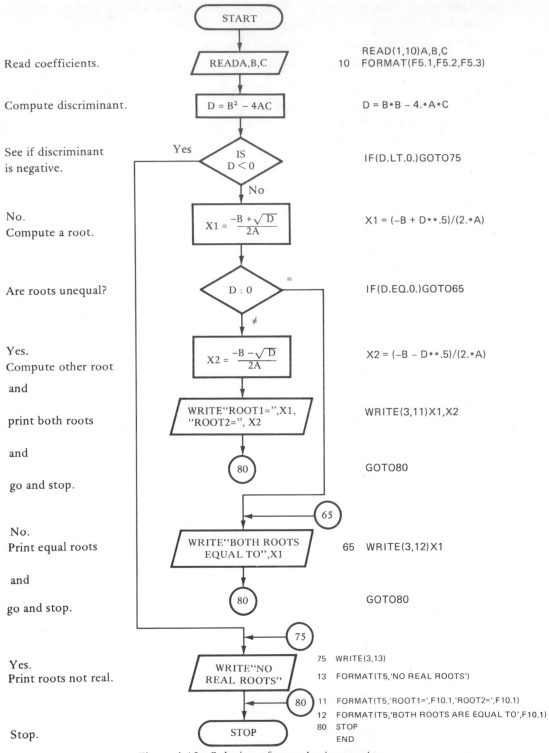

Read coefficients.

Compute discriminant.

See if discriminant is negative.

No.
Compute a root.

Are roots unequal?

Yes.
Compute other root

and

print both roots

and

go and stop.

No.
Print equal roots

and

go and stop.

Yes.
Print roots not real.

Stop.

Figure 4-12 Solution of a quadratic equation.

If there are no real roots, print the message NO REAL ROOTS

If the roots are equal, print the message BOTH ROOTS ARE EQUAL TO XXX.X

If the roots are unequal, print the message ROOT1 = XXX.X ROOT2 = XXX.X

Recall that the formula to compute the roots of a quadratic equation is

$$X_1 = \frac{-b + \sqrt{b^2 - 4ac}}{2a} \qquad\qquad X_2 = \frac{-b - \sqrt{b^2 - 4ac}}{2a}$$

The program to solve this problem is shown in Figure 4-12.

4-4-2 Compound Interest Problem

Write a program to read an interest rate (R), a principal (P) and a number of years (N). If the principal and earned interest are left in the account, compute the total value of the investment after N years. The formula to calculate the total amount is $A = P(1 + R)^N$.

Input considerations:	R = .XX	card columns 1–3	(The decimal may be punched on the card)
	P = XXXX.XX	card columns 10–15	(The decimal point is not to be punched)
	N = XX	card columns 16–17	

Output considerations: The output should be similar to

COMPOUND INTEREST PROBLEM

INTEREST RATE =   0.05
PRINCIPAL AMOUNT = 1000.00
NUMBER OF YEARS   30

PRINCIPAL AMOUNT 1000.00 INVESTED AT 0.05
WILL HAVE A VALUE OF 4321.81

A program to solve this problem is shown in Figure 4-13.

```
      READ(1,10)R,P,N            The decimal point in the R field may be punched.
10    FORMAT(F3.0,T10,F6.2,I2)   The principal P must be right-justified with no
      WRITE(3,11)                decimal point punched (F 6.2).
11    FORMAT('1',T50,'COMPOUND INTEREST PROBLEM')   Skip top new page.
      WRITE(3,12)R
12    FORMAT('0',T40,'INTEREST RATE =',T58,F7.2)        Double space before write.
      WRITE(3,13)P
13    FORMAT(T40,'PRINCIPAL AMOUNT =',T58,F7.2)
      WRITE(3,14)N
14    FORMAT(T40,'NUMBER OF YEARS',T58,I7)
      V=P*(1+R)**N
      WRITE(3,15)P,R
15    FORMAT('0',T40,'PRINCIPAL AMOUNT ',F7.2,' INVESTED AT',F4.2)
      WRITE(3,16)V
16    FORMAT(T40,'WILL HAVE A VALUE OF',1X,F7.2)
      STOP
      END
```

Figure 4-13 Compound interest problem.

4-5 More Fortran Statements

4-5-1 The Comment Statement

Sometimes when a program gets to be lengthy the programmer may find it helpful to explain within the program the purpose of one or more FORTRAN instructions, the usage of a particular variable, or the function of specific program segments. The practice of interspersing comment cards throughout the program can be very helpful when the programmer at a later date decides to review or make revisions to some parts of his program. Comment cards can help him recapture the essence of some of his original thoughts. For another user who wishes to use the program, comment cards will help him understand the overall program structure.

Comment cards may be inserted anywhere in a program by punching a C in card column 1. When the compiler reads the C in card column 1, it realizes that the information on that card is just for the programmer and consequently does not view it as a FORTRAN instruction and does not translate it into machine language. A C in card column 1 causes the content of that card to be listed on the output device with all other FORTRAN instructions. As an example see Figure 4-14. Note the two blank lines in the listing after the heading. Blank cards inserted in a program are translated into blank lines on the program listing.

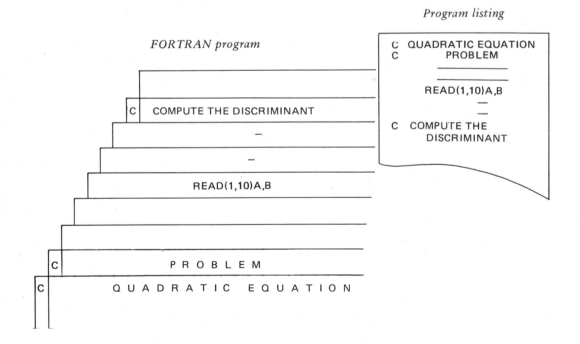

Figure 4-14 Use of the comment card.

4-5-2 Annotation Block

The annotation block ————— is used to indicate a remark or a comment

in a flowchart. The annotation block is placed to the right of flowchart blocks as follows:

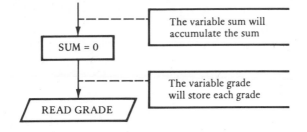

The broken line indicates the placement of the remark in the program. The FORTRAN code for the above flowchart would appear as

        C   THE VARIABLE SUM WILL ACCUMULATE THE SUM
                SUM = 0
        C   THE VARIABLE GRADE WILL STORE EACH GRADE
                READ(1,10)GRADE

4-5-3 The Computed GOTO Statement

A useful and convenient statement which transfers to different points in a program with just one FORTRAN statement is the computed GOTO. The general form of the computed GOTO is

GOTO(statement-number1,statement-number2,· · · statement-number n),variable

where variable must be an *integer* variable name and statement-number 1,2, · · · n are FORTRAN statement numbers defined in the program.

If the value of the integer variable is 1, control is transferred to statement-number 1. If the value of the integer variable is 2, control is transferred to statement-number 2. In general, if the value of the variable is i, control is passed to the ith statement in the list of statements. For example:

            GOTO(3,57,100,4),N   If N = 1, go to 3
                                     N = 2, go to 57
                                     N = 3, go to 100
                                     N = 4, go to 4

If N is less than 1 or exceeds the number of statement numbers within the parenthesis, control is passed to the statement immediately following the computed GOTO.

The reader is cautioned again that an integer variable must be used in the computed GOTO; no expressions are allowed, i.e., GOTO(2,3,4),2∗I is invalid, since 2∗I is not a variable.

Consider, for example, the following problem. It is desired to write out the meaning associated with a class code read from a data card. The possible codes and meanings are shown below:

Class code	Meaning
1	Freshman
2	Sophomore
3	Junior
4	Senior
5	Graduate

The program segment shown below could be used.

```
        GOTO(15,20,25,30,35),KODE
        WRITE(3,100)KODE
100     FORMAT(3X,'INVALID CODE',I3)
        STOP
15      WRITE(3,101)
101     FORMAT(3X,'FRESHMAN')
        GOTO106
20      WRITE(3,102)
102     FORMAT(3X,'SOPHOMORE')
        GOTO106
25      WRITE(3,103)
103     FORMAT(3X,'JUNIOR')
        GOTO106
30      WRITE(3,104)
104     FORMAT(3X,'SENIOR')
        GOTO106
35      WRITE(3,105)
105     FORMAT(3X,'GRADUATE')
106     STOP
        END
```

If KODE is not equal to 1,2,3,4 or 5, then go to the next statement and print an error message.

4-5-4   The Duplication Factor

Many times a sequence of variables is read, each having the same format code description.

Example

    READ(1,101)X,Y,Z
101   FORMAT(F4.0,F4.0,F4.0)

It is possible in such instances to recode the list of the format codes using a duplication factor to specify the repetition of the format code. The following FORMAT statement is equivalent to statement 101 above:

    101   FORMAT(3F4.0)

Any data format code may be duplicated using the duplication factor. A more general form for the I and F format codes is

    nFw.d and nIw

where n is the optional duplication factor; n must be an unsigned integer.

Example

FORTRAN code	Data card	Value stored in memory
READ(1,5)I,J,K,L,M		I = 0
:		J = 10
5 FORMAT(2I2,I1,2I2)		K = 9
		L = 22
		M = 33

Data card values: I | J | K 1 | L 9 2 | M 2 3 3

In the above example, five numbers are to be read. Instead of writing I2,I2,I1, I2,I2, the format list is made more compact by use of duplication factors 2I2, I1,2I2.

Example

    WRITE(1,5)A,J,B,K,L,M,N
5   FORMAT(3X,2(F3.1,I2),3(2X,I1))

The above format is equivalent to (3X,F3.1,I2,F3.1,I2,2X,I1,2X,I1,2X,I1)
                                          2   3

4-5-5 Continuation

A FORTRAN statement often is too long to fit in card columns 7–72. In this event, a statement may be continued onto one or more succeeding cards. If any character other than a blank or zero is punched into card column 6, the statement on that card is treated as a continuation of the preceding line (card). For example, statement 101, shown below, is continued by placing a "*" in card column 6 of the continuation line. Note that statement 101 itself has no continuation in card column 6.

Example

The following two statements are equivalent:

```
        ┌─ card column 6
101│ │FORMAT(3X,'AREA LOT1 IS',2X,F8.1,3X,'AREA LOT2 IS',2X,F8.1)
101│ │FORMAT(3X,'AREA LOT1 IS',2X,F8.1,
   │*│ 3X,'AREA LOT2 IS',2X,F8.1)
```

A statement may be continued onto several successive lines.

Example

The following two statements are equivalent:

```
        ┌ card column 6
100│ │X = Y +
   │1│Z +
   │2│Q
100│ │X = Y + Z + Q
```

Caution must be exercised when continuing a literal string within quotes in a FORMAT.

Example

```
    WRITE(3,11)                                      ┌─ column 72
11  FORMAT(· · ·,'I DREAM OF THINGS THAT─────
  1 NEVER WERE')
```

this example will produce

                                        ┌─ 5 blanks
────────────I DREAM OF THINGS THAT─────NEVER WERE
           ┼

If the following statement had been used,

```
                                            ┌─ card column 72
11  FORMAT(· · ·,'I DREAM OF THINGS THAT NE
  * VER WERE')
```

the following output would be produced:

        I DREAM OF THINGS THAT NEVER WERE
──

4-6 Exercises

4-6-1 Self Test

1. Which of the following coding segments are valid? If invalid, state reasons.

   a.   READ(1,10),A,B,C   b.   READ(1,5)I,J
        10   FORMAT(F1.0,F2.0,F3.0)   FORMAT (I1,I4)

   c.   READ(1,6)A,I,J   d.   READ(1,7)A,B,C
         6   FORMAT(F4.5,I2,I1)   7   FORMAT(F5.2,I3,F4)

   e.   READ(1,8)X,J,Y   f.   READ(1,5)X,I
         8   FORMAT(F3.1,F2.1,I4)   5   FORMAT(T5,F5.1,T2,I2)

2. What values would be read for I,J,K, given the following READ statement with associated data card for the following formats?

   READ(1,5)I,J,K

   ┌─Card column 1 of data card
   ▼

   | 1 | 3 | | 5 | . | 2 | | | | – | 4 | 6 | 7 | . | 1 | 9 | |

   5   FORMAT(T1,I1,I1,I1)   (a)
   5   FORMAT(T2,1X,I1,1X,I2,I5)   (b)
   5   FORMAT(I3,I1,T6,I1)   (c)
   5   FORMAT(I4,I3,I5)   (d)
   5   FORMAT(T8,I1,I4,I1)   (e)
   5   FORMAT(I2,T1,I1,T2,I4)   (f)
   5   FORMAT(2(1X,I1),T10,I3)   (g)

3. What values would be read for A,I,S as a result of the following READ operations?

   READ(1,5)A,I,S

   ┌─Card column 1 of data card
   ▼

   | 1 | . | 3 | | 2 | 5 | . | 1 | . | 5 | | |

   5   FORMAT(F4.0,I2,3X,F1.1)   (a)
   5   FORMAT(T3,F4.3,1X,I1,F3.1)   (b)
   5   FORMAT(2X,F2.1,I3,F3.0)   (c)
   5   FORMAT(T2,F6.1,I1,F2.2)   (d)
   5   FORMAT(T2,F1.1,I2,F2.0)   (e)

4. Simulate the output produced by the following program segments on the printout listing and indicate all print positions and blanks.

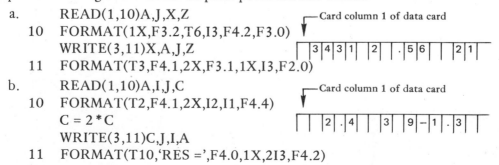

   a.   READ(1,10)A,J,X,Z   ┌─Card column 1 of data card
        10   FORMAT(1X,F3.2,T6,I3,F4.2,F3.0) ▼
             WRITE(3,11)X,A,J,Z | 3 | 4 | 3 | 1 | | 2 | | . | 5 | 6 | | | 2 | 1 |
        11   FORMAT(T3,F4.1,2X,F3.1,1X,I3,F2.0)

   b.   READ(1,10)A,I,J,C   ┌─Card column 1 of data card
        10   FORMAT(T2,F4.1,2X,I2,I1,F4.4)   ▼
             C = 2*C | | | 2 | . | 4 | | 3 | | 9 | – | 1 | . | 3 | |
             WRITE(3,11)C,J,I,A
        11   FORMAT(T10,'RES =',F4.0,1X,2I3,F4.2)

5. Answer the following true or false.

    a. Only one STOP statement is allowed per program.

    b. Card column 1 of a data card is reserved for card control.

    c. A C in card column 6 indicates that what follows on the next card is a continuation of what is punched on this card.

    d. Data may not be punched in card columns 73–80 of a data card.

    e. Data cards are read at compilation time.

    f. FORMATs must immediately follow the READ instruction.

    g. FORMATs are not required to have statement numbers.

    h. The same FORMAT can be used for a READ and WRITE instruction.

    i. A C in card column 1 will cause a compilation error.

    j. FORMATs are nonexecutable statements.

    k. Running out of data cards will cause a compilation error.

    l. The statement 5GOTO5 is grammatically incorrect.

    m. The statement READ(1,10)J,J,J is invalid.

    n. The statement GOTOKODE3 is valid.

    o. In a READ operation, either FORMAT(T2,· · ·), or FORMAT(2X,· · ·) will cause reading to start at the same card column.

    p. Data cards may immediately follow the READ statement within the FORTRAN program deck.

6. What are some execution time errors you could expect as a result of a READ instruction? a WRITE instruction?

7. Write IF statements for the following flowchart blocks.

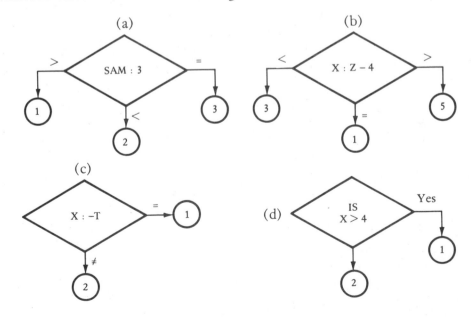

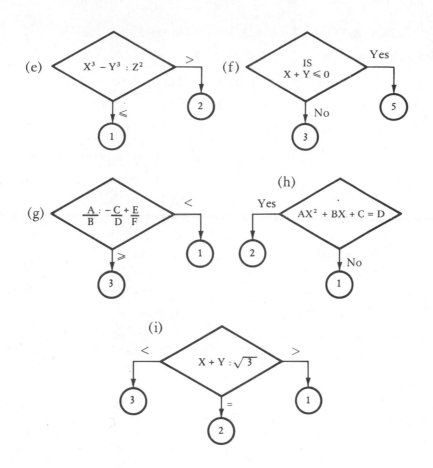

8. Indicate the action taken by each of the following IF statements given the two cases:

$$\text{case 1} \quad A = 3. \quad B = -2. \quad C = 2.$$
$$\text{case 2} \quad A = -4. \quad B = -5. \quad C = 1.$$

a.   IF(B**2.LE.4*A*C)GOTO4
     R = 1
     .
     .
  4 R = 2

b. IF(A.GT.B)WRITE(3,1)A
    GOTO3

c.   IF(A.LE.0)A = −A
     WRITE(3,1)A

d. IF(B.GE.C − 4)STOP
    C=0
    WRITE(3,1)C

e.   IF(A.NE.C*3)WRITE(3,1)C
     WRITE(3,2)A

9. Find errors in the following:

   a. IF(I = N)GOTO15   b. IF(X + Y.GT.3.4)X.EQ.2

c. IFG.GE.3GOTO41   d. IF(X + Y)P = G**(.5)

e. IF(A.LE.(A + B)P = Q   f. 7 IF(17.LE.B)GOTO7

g. IF(A.GE.7),WRITE(3,1)A   h. IF3*A.EQ.B,A = A + 1

i. IF(7.3 + A.GT.2 + B)END   j. IF(A.LT.B)IF(A.EQ.B)STOP

k. IF(A.LT.B)WRITE(3,1)A,GOTO3

10. Write one or more FORTRAN statements to accomplish each of the following:

   a. You have read in three sides of a triangle—the largest side is read last. Write the statements to print the sides of the triangle if the triangle is a right triangle; otherwise, just go to the READ statement (statement 4).
   b. If B is larger than or equal to 60, increase C by 1, and then go to statement 4; otherwise, go to statement 4.
   c. If X is larger than MAX, assign this value to MAX; otherwise continue.
   d. If $B^2 - 4AC$ is negative, set R = 1; otherwise set R = 2.
   e. If HRS is greater than 40, find and print the wage (wage = 1.2*rate*hrs). If HRS is equal to 40, find and print the wage (wage = 1.05*rate*hrs). If HRS is less than 40, print the wage (wage = rate*hrs).

11. For which values of Z will control be passed to statements 1, 2 or 3?

   a. IF(Z – 1.)1,2,2   e. IF(Z*(–2*Z))1,1,4
   b. IF(Z – 6*Z + 1.)1,2,3   f. IF(–Z – 1.)3,2,2
   c. IF(7. + Z)1,2,1   g. IF(Z – 1.)2,2,2
   d. IF(Z**2 – Z)1,2,3

12. Write the necessary IF statements for the following decision blocks:

(a)

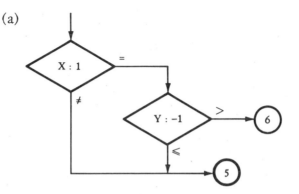

(b)

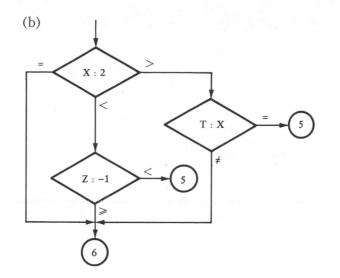

13. Write the necessary IF statements to perform the following:

   a. If X is greater than 0 but less than 3*A, go to 7.
   b. If both A and B lie between 1 and 8 inclusive, go to 8; otherwise go to 4.
   c. If X exceeds 4 while Y is less than 5, or if X is less than 5 while Y is greater than 4, go to 10; otherwise stop.

14. Discuss the following code segment in terms of possible errors:

$$IF(X - 1.)3,3,5$$
$$READ(1,6)A$$
$$\cdot$$
$$\cdot$$
$$\cdot$$
$$3 \quad Y = 2.$$
$$\cdot$$
$$\cdot$$
$$5 \quad Z = 4.$$
$$6 \quad FORMAT$$
$$\cdot$$
$$\cdot$$

15. Will a branch to 15 be taken as a result of the following code? What value is printed for X?

$$X = 1./3. + 1./3. + 1./3.$$
$$IF(X.EQ.1)GOTO15$$
$$WRITE(3,5)X$$
$$5 \quad FORMAT(F4.2)$$

4-6-2 Programming Problems

1. Write a program to read two numbers on a card and print these two numbers and their difference on one output line. The output should be similar to:

NUMBER 1	NUMBER 2	DIFFERENCE
5	2.5	2.5

2. The metric system is upon us! Some simple approximation rules for metric conversions are listed as follows:

   a. Fahrenheit to centigrade: Take half and subtract 15.
   b. Inches to centimeters: Double and add half: 40 inches: $2 \cdot 40 + 20 = 100$cm.
   c. Miles to kilometers: Add 60 percent: 100 miles: $100 + 60\%$ of $100 = 160$ km.
   d. Pounds to kilograms: Take half and then some: 60 lbs: $60/2 = 30 - 10\%$ of $30 = 27$ kg.

   Write a program to read a Fahrenheit temperature, a number of inches, a number of miles and a number of pounds and convert to corresponding metric measures. Identify results with appropriate headers.

3. Write a program to read a value for X and compute X^2, X^3, $\sqrt{X}$ and $\sqrt[3]{X}$.

4. Final grades in a course are determined by adding scores obtained on three tests T1, T2, T3. Students get a PASS if the sum of the three scores is 186 or more and a FAIL otherwise. Write a program to read three scores from one data card and determine the final letter grade. Print the input scores, the average and the final letter grade.

5. Write a program to compute and print the absolute value of a number X read from a data card. Recall that $|X| = X$ if $X \geqslant 0$ and $|X| = -X$ if $X < 0$.

6. A student in DP101 has his account number in card columns 1–4 and three test scores in card columns 11–19. The student's average is based on his two best scores. Starting on a new page, print the student's account number and his average on one line and the three test scores on another line (double space) as follows:

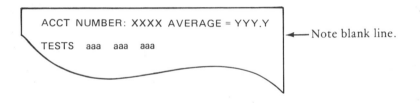

   ACCT NUMBER: XXXX AVERAGE = YYY.Y   ◄— Note blank line.

   TESTS   aaa   aaa   aaa

7. Write a program to read two numbers D and R. D is the balance due for a customer's charge account. R is the amount received from the customer.

Compare these two numbers. If they are equal, print the message "NOTHING OWED." If the amount received is greater than the amount due, the customer is given credit toward his account. Print out his credit balance. If the amount received is less than the amount owed, the new balance is computed by adding a 1.5 percent service charge to the unpaid amount. Print that amount.

8. A salesman is assigned a commission on the following basis:

Sale	Commission
$.00 to $1,000	2.5%
$1,001 to $5,000	6.0
over $5,000	10.5

Write a program to read a sale (real value in card columns 25–29) and compute the commission.

9. Write a program to print a balance sheet as shown in Section 3-6-1 for each of the following three companies for the month of May 1976. The data read for each company should be entered at execution time using the READ statement. Use the following tables for data.

	Company 1	Company 2	Company 3
Cash	$3,900	$2,069	$6,642
Accounts receivable	—	500	517
Supplies	600	3,530	801
Land	3,000	1,000	1,300
Buildings	—	2,400	8,500
Machines and equipment	—	—	9,948
Patents	—	110	1,500
Accounts payable	2,800	470	4,106
Capital stock	7,500	9,127	25,000

Three balance sheets should be printed with respective headings: Company 1, Company 2, Company 3. In case assets do not equal liabilities plus equities, print a message stating that the balance sheet for that company is incorrect.

10. Read a three-digit number N between 100 and 999 and print out each digit as a separate number, i.e., the 100's, the 10's and the unit's digits. (Hint: divide first by 100, then by 10, using real and integer operations.)

11. Read a grade N between 0 and 99 and write a program using the computed GOTO statement to print out appropriate letter grade defined by the following table:

Grades	Letter Grade
0–59	F
60–69	D
70–79	C (Hint: Make use of N/10.)
80–89	B
90–99	A

12. Same problem as 11 except for the grade table and N can be 100.

Grades	Letter Grade
0–60	F
61–70	D
71–80	C
81–90	B
91–100	A

13. Write a program to calculate the area of a right triangle, given the lengths of the three sides. Each data card will contain three integers: the length of the hypotenuse in columns 1–10, the first leg in columns 11–20 and the second leg in columns 21–30. Assume that the last data card will have a zero in the hypotenuse field.

14. Write a program to read three real values and decide whether these represent the sides of a triangle. (Hint: The sum of any two sides must always be greater than the third.)

15. Rewrite the program of problem 13 so that the three numbers on the data card may be in any order. Your program will have to decide which side is the hypotenuse.

16. Change the program in Figure 4-11 to print out a message if all three numbers are equal. Also change the FORTRAN code in Figure 4-11 to ensure that the three IF statements follow one another in the code.

17. John Doe must decide whether to buy a house this year at relatively high interest rates or wait until next year when interest rates are anticipated to be lower, but when inflation will have increased the cost of the house. This year he can buy a $30,000 house with 10 percent down and the balance financed at 9 percent for 30 years. Next year he can buy the same house for $33,000 with 10 percent down and the balance financed at 7½ percent for 30 years. Based on the total cost of the house (principal and interest), should he buy now or wait? The formula to compute the amount of monthly payment M given the principal P, interest rate I and the time in years T is

$$M = \frac{P \cdot \dfrac{I}{12}}{1 - \left(\dfrac{1}{1 + \dfrac{I}{12}}\right)^{T \cdot 12}}$$

Write a program to make the decision for John Doe.

18. A certain metal is graded according to the results of three tests. These tests determine whether the metal satisfies the following specifications:

   a. Carbon content is below 6.7.

   b. Rockwell hardness is no less than 50.

   c. Tensile strength is greater than 70,000 psi.

The metal is graded 1 if it passes all three tests, 9 if it passes tests 1 and 2. If it passes test 1, it is graded 8, and 7 if it passes none of the tests. Write a program to read a carbon content, a Rockwell constant and a tensile strength and determine the grade of the metal.

19. The FHA insures home mortgages up to $45,000. The down payment schedule is as follows:

   a. 3 percent of the amount up to $25,000.

   b. 10 percent of the next $10,000.

   c. 20 percent of the remainder.

The input is a card containing a social security number and the mortgage amount. The output should contain the applicant's social security number and the amount of down payment required. Reject any application over $45,000 and so indicate on the output.

20. Read an amount in cents between 0 and 100. Write a program to break down that amount into the fewest number of quarters, nickels and pennies as is possible. For example:

$$76 \text{ cents} = 3 \text{ quarters and } 1 \text{ penny.}$$

21. The Wastenot Utility Company charges customers for electricity according to the following scale:

Kilowatt-hour

0– 300	5.00
301–1,000	5.00 + .03 for each kwh above 300
1,001–and over	35.00 + .02 for each kwh above 1,000

Write a program to accept as input the old and the new meter readings, and calculate the amount of the customer's bill.

22. Salaries at the XYZ Corporation are based on job classification, years of ser-

vice, education and merit rating. The base pay for all employees is the same; percentage of the base pay is added according to the following schedule:

Job classification	Percentage of base pay	Education	Percentage of base pay
1	0	1 (high school)	0
2	5	2 (junior college)	10
3	15	3 (college)	25
4	25	4 (graduate degree)	50
5	50	5 (special training)	15

Merit rating	Percentage of base pay	Years of service	Percentage of base pay per year
0 (poor)	0	0–10 years	5
1 (good)	10	each additional year	4
2 (excellent)	25		

Write a program to accept numerical codes for each of the four variables and calculate the employee's salary as a percentage of base pay.

23. The square root of a number A can be computed by successive approximations using the iterative formula $x_{n+1} = \frac{1}{2} (x_n + A/x_n)$. This formula can be expressed in FORTRAN as XNEW = .5*(XOLD + A/XOLD). Starting with an initial approximation XOLD = 1, a new approximation XNEW to the square root of A is computed using the above formula. This new approximation, in turn, can be refined by substituting XOLD by XNEW to compute a newer approximation XNEW. This process can be continued until the square of the new approximation XNEW is close to A within a prescribed degree of accuracy ϵ (where ϵ = .1, .01, .001 etc. depending on the accuracy needed); that is,

$$|XNEW^2 - A| < \epsilon.$$

Write a program to read A and EPS (ϵ) to compute $\sqrt{A}$. Write an error message if A < 0.

24. Systems of equations can be solved by iterative techniques. For example, the system

$$\begin{cases} 2x + y = 3 \\ x - 3y = 2 \end{cases}$$

can be solved by solving for x in terms of y in the first equation and for y in terms of x in the second equation to obtain:

$$\begin{cases} x = (3 - y)/2 \\ y = (x - 2)/3 \end{cases}$$

Starting with an initial approximate solution XOLD = YOLD = 1, we refine this approximation by computing XNEW and YNEW as follows:

$$\begin{cases} \text{XNEW} = (3 - \text{YOLD})/2 \\ \text{YNEW} = (\text{XOLD} - 2)/3 \end{cases}$$

This procedure is repeated by letting the old approximations become the new approximations (XOLD = XNEW and YOLD = YNEW) and computing new values for XNEW and YNEW in terms of XOLD and YOLD. The process can be terminated by substituting XNEW and YNEW in the original equation and verifying that:

$$\begin{array}{lll} 2\text{XNEW} + \text{YNEW} \backsim 3 & 2\text{XNEW} + \text{YNEW} - 3 \backsim 0 & |2\text{XNEW} + \text{YNEW} - 3| < \epsilon \\ \text{XNEW} - 3\text{YNEW} \backsim 2 & \text{XNEW} - 3\text{YNEW} - 2 \backsim 0 & |\text{XNEW} - 3\text{YNEW} - 2| < \epsilon \end{array}$$
$$\text{or} \qquad\qquad \text{or}$$

where ϵ is a prescribed degree of accuracy (ϵ = .01, .0001, etc.).

Write a program to solve the following system of equations using the above iterative technique:

$$\begin{array}{l} 2.56x - .034y = -.56 \\ 3.14x + 1.32y = 50.76 \end{array} \qquad \text{and set } \epsilon = .01$$

25. Write a program to read values for a, b, c, d, r, s, and ϵ, to solve the following system of equations:

$$\begin{cases} a \cdot x + b \cdot y = r \\ c \cdot x + d \cdot y = s \end{cases}$$

26. By extending the iterative technique to a system of three or more equations in three unknowns (in the first equation compute x in terms of y and z; in the second equation compute y in terms of x and z, etc.), write a program to solve the following systems of equations:

a. $7x + 2y - 3z = 1$
$\quad x - 5y - 2z = 6$
$\quad -x + y + z = 8$

b. $10x + 3y + 2z - w = -1.5$
$\quad x - 5y + z + w = 3$
$\quad 5x + 5y - 10z = 4.1$
$\quad x - y + z + 5w = 5$

27. Determining the roots of a polynomial $y = P(x)$ implies finding values x_i such that $y = P(x_i) = 0$. A systematic method to determine x_i is presented as follows:

Step 1. Determine by visual inspection two values for X, i.e., XPOS and XNEG such that P(XPOS) > 0 and P(XNEG) < 0. This means that a root of P(X) exists in the interval XPOS, XNEG since polynomials are continuous functions and the graph of $y = P(x)$ must intersect the x axis somewhere between XPOS and XNEG.

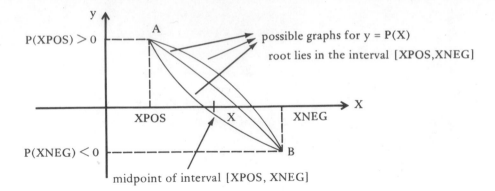

Step 2. For the next approximation X to the root, take the midpoint of the interval XPOS, XNEG:

$$X = \frac{XPOS + XNEG}{2}$$

Step 3. Determine whether P(X) > 0 or P(X) < 0. If P(X) > 0, then the root must lie between X and XNEG. If P(X) < 0, then the root must lie between X and XPOS. Then go back to step 2 and recompute a new (refined) approximation X making sure to replace XPOS or XNEG by X depending on the sign of y = P(X).

The above algorithm can be terminated when y = P(X) is "sufficiently close" to zero; mathematically speaking this means |P(X)| < ϵ where ϵ is a prescribed degree of accuracy.

Using the method described, compute a root of y = x³ − 2x² + x − 16 in the interval [3,4]. Start with XPOS = 4 and XNEG = 3 and stop when ϵ = .1; i.e., |P(X)| < .1.

28. Using the method described in Exercise 27, determine a root of y = x³ + 10x² − 81 in the vicinity of −3.5. Stop when |y| < .001.

4-6-3 Answers to Self Test

1. a. Invalid.   b. Valid.   c. Invalid.   d. Invalid.
    e. Invalid.   f. Valid.

2. a. 1, 3, 0   b. 0, invalid data in field, −4   c. 130, 5, 2
    d. 1305, invalid data, −46   e. 0, −46, 7   f. 13, 1, invalid data.
    g. 3, 5, −46

3. a. 1.3, 25, .5.   b. 3.025, 1, .5.   c. 3.0, Invalid data, 1.5.
    d. Invalid data, 1, .5.   e. 0., 30, 25.

4. a. A = 3.43, J = 20, X = .56, Z = 21.

b. A = 2.4, I = 30, J = 9, C = −1.3

$$\underset{R\ E\ S\ =\ \quad -\ 3\ \cdot\ \qquad\qquad 9\quad 3\ 0\ 2\ \cdot\ 4\ 0}{\vdash\!+\!\dashv}$$

5. a. F.   b. F.   c. F.   d. F.   e. F.   f. F.   g. F.   h. T.
    i. F.   j. T.   k. F.   l. F.   m. F.   n. F.   o. F.   p. F.

6. READ instruction a. Invalid data in a field.   b. No more data cards.
    WRITE instruction a. Format code is wrong mode for variable.   b. Data
    too large for field.

7. a. IF(SAM − 3)2,3,1   IF(SAM.LT.3)GOTO2
                                    IF(SAM.EQ.3)GOTO3
                                    GOTO1

    b. IF(X − (Z − 4))3,1,5   IF(X.LT.Z − 4)GOTO3
                                    IF(X.EQ.Z − 4)GOTO1
                                    GOTO5

    c. IF(X + T)2,1,2   IF(X.NE.(−T))GOTO2
                                    GOTO1

    d. IF(X − 4)2,2,1   IF(X.GT.4)GOTO1
                                    GOTO2

    e. IF(X**3 − Y**3 − Z**2)1,1,2   IF(X**3 − Y**3.GT.Z**2)GOTO2
                                    GOTO1

    f. IF(X + Y)5,5,3   IF(X + Y.LE.0)GOTO5
                                    GOTO3

    g. IF(A/B − (−C/D + E/F))1,3,3   IF(A/B.LT.(−C/D + E/F))GOTO1
                                    GOTO3

8. a. Case 1: R = 2. Case 2: R = 1   b. Case 1: 3 is written.
                                            Case 2: −4 is written.

    c. Case 1: 3 is written. Case 2: 4 is written.   d. Case 1: STOP.
                                                           Case 2: 0 is written.

    e. Case 1: 2 and 3 are written. Case 2: 1 and −4 are written.

9. a. IF(I.EQ.N).   b. X.NE.2 not a statement.   c. Missing parenthesis.
    d. Missing relational operator.   e. Missing right parenthesis.
    f. Infinite loop if 17 ⩽ B.   g. Comma illegal.
    h. Missing parentheses and comma illegal.   i. Illegal END.
    j. IF in YES branch is illegal.   k. Only one statement allowed in YES
                                            branch.

10. a. 4   READ(1,6)A,B,C   b. IF(B.GE.60)C = C + 1
            IF(C**2.EQ.A*A + B*B)WRITE(3,7)A,B,C   GOTO4
            GOTO4

   c.   IF(X.GT.MAX)MAX = X   d.   IF(B*B − 4.*A*C.LT.0)GOTO6

   e.   IF(HRS − 40)1,2,3   R = 2

     3 W = 1.2*R*H   GOTO5

        GOTO6   6 R = 1

     2 W = 1.05*R*H   5 _____

        GOTO6

     1 W = R*H

     6 WRITE(3,5)W

11. a. 1 if $Z < 1$, 2 if $Z \geqslant 1$.   b. 1 if $Z > .2$, 2 if $Z = .2$, 3 if $Z < .2$.

    c. 1 if $Z \neq -7$, 2 if $Z = -7$.   d. 1 if $0 < Z < 1$, 2 if $Z = 1$ or $Z = 0$, 3 if
                                         $Z > 1$ or $Z < 0$.

    e. 1 for all values of Z.   f. 3 if $Z > -1$, 2 otherwise.

    g. 2 for all values of Z.

12. a.   IF(X.NE.1)GOTO5   or   IF(X − 1.)5,3,5

        IF(Y.GT.−1)GOTO6   3 IF(Y + 1.)5,5,6

        GOTO5

    b.   IF(X.EQ.2)GOTO6   or   IF(X − 2)3,6,4

        IF(X.LT.2)GOTO3   3 IF(Z + 1)5,6,6

        IF(T.EQ.X)GOTO5   4 IF(T − X)6,5,6

        GOTO6

     3 IF(Z.LT.−1)GOTO5

        GOTO6

13. a.   IF(X.LE.0.)GOTO5   or   IF(X)5,5,4

        IF(X.LT.3*A)GOTO7   4 IF(X − 3*A)7,5,5

     5 _____   5 _____

    b.   IF(A.LT.1)GOTO4   or   IF(A − 1)4,1,1

        IF(A.GT.8)GOTO4   1 IF(A − 8)2,2,4

        IF(B.LT.1)GOTO4   2 IF(B − 1)4,3,3

        IF(B.GT.8)GOTO4   3 IF(B − 8)8,8,4

        GOTO8

    c.   IF(X.GT.4)GOTO1   or   IF(X − 4)12,12,1

        IF(X.LT.5)GOTO2   12 IF(X − 5)2,11,11

        STOP   11 STOP

     1 IF(Y.LT.5)GOTO10   1 IF(Y − 5)10,11,11

        STOP   2 IF(Y − 4)11,11,10

     2 IF(Y.GT.4)GOTO10

        STOP

14. The statement following an arithmetic IF must have a statement number; otherwise the READ statement will never be processed.

15. No. The value of X will not be exactly 1 due to fractional representation; however, the value of 1.00 will be printed, due to round off.

THE COUNTING PROCESS

5-1 Problem Example

A poll was conducted in a political science class to determine student feelings about isolationism. The code used to record students' opinions was as follows:

Code	Meaning
0	against isolationism
1	neutral
2	for isolationism

All responses were gathered and recorded one per record (card) with the special code 9 as the last data item to indicate the physical end of the results. Write a program to determine the number of students in favor of isolationism. A program to solve the problem is shown in Figure 5-1.

Note the two specification statements used in the program in Figure 5-1:

1. The INTEGER statement.

2. The DATA statement.

Other specification statements will be introduced in this chapter.

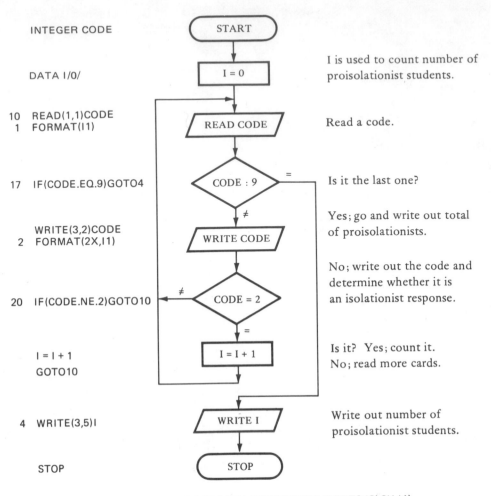

Figure 5-1   Program using counting and end-of-file checking.

5-2   FORTRAN Statements

5-2-1   Specification Statements

There are a number of statements in FORTRAN which are classed as *specification statements* because they specify certain attributes of variables to the FORTRAN compiler. For example, specification statements may be used to specify an initial value for a variable (DATA statement) or the mode of a variable (INTEGER, REAL etc.). Other specification statements will be introduced later.

All specification statements are nonexecutable (see Section 5-3, question 1) and must be placed in the FORTRAN program deck prior to the first executable statement (such as replacement, decision, READ, WRITE etc.).

5-2-2   Explicit Mode Specification

The mode of a variable is implicitly defined by the first character of the name of the variable. If the first character is I, J, K, L, M or N, the variable is normally in integer mode (represents a number without a decimal point); otherwise, it is in real mode. It is possible to explicitly define (change) the mode of a variable by using a specification statement INTEGER or REAL. The general form of these statements is

INTEGER   variable-list
REAL   variable-list

Any variable included in the variable-list of the INTEGER statement automatically becomes an integer wherever it is encountered in the program, even though that variable may not start with I, J, K, L, M or N. Any variable included in the list of the REAL statement becomes a real mode variable.

Examples

INTEGER   X,CODE1,QI,J
REAL   I,J123,SUM

The variables X,CODE1,QI would ordinarily be real but will now become integer. The variables I,J123 would implicitly be integer but are now explicitly defined to be real. In an input/output statement, an INTEGER specified variable should be described in the FORMAT by the format code I and a REAL specified variable should be described by an F format code in the FORMAT.

5-2-3   The DATA Statement

The DATA statement can be used to specify an initial value for a variable. The general form of the DATA statement is

DATA variable-list/constant-list/[, · · ·]

where variable-list is a list of variables separated by commas.
constant-list is a list of constants separated by commas.

The first variable in the variable-list is associated with the first element in the constant-list, the second variable with the second constant etc.

Example

DATA A,B/3.2,0./   The value of A will be 3.2 and the value of B will be 0.

There must be the same number of variables as constants in the associated lists.
Example

The following DATA statement is invalid:

DATA A,J,K/3.2,4/   Only two constants.

The mode of the constant must match the mode of the associated variable. The following DATA statement is invalid because of differences in modes between constant and variable.
Example

DATA CODE,LL/0,3.2/   Mismatch of modes.

More than one variable-list/constant-list/ may be included in a DATA statement. Repetitions must be separated by a comma.
Example

DATA A,B/3.,0./,I,J/1,0/ ——— Note comma required.

The value of A will be 3., B will be 0., I will be 1 and J will be 0

DATA statements *must* be placed after other specification statements.
Example

INTEGER A
REAL   I
DATA   A,I/1,−3.2/

A is an integer variable with value 1; I is a real variable with value −3.2

Finally, the DATA statement may include repetition factors. Suppose we wanted I, J, K to be initialized to 0 and A, B, C, D to be initialized to 4.1. The following statement could be used:

repetition factors

DATA I,J,K/3*0/,A,B,C,D/4*4.1/

In this context,
the * means repetition,
not multiplication.

5-2-4 Counting

Counting is an essential technique in programming. Counting may be used to read a specified number of data records from a file, to repeat a certain procedure a number of times (*loop control*), to count the occurrence of specific events or to generate sequences of numbers for computational uses. In any event, the computer cannot count by itself, and therefore the programmer must resort to certain counting techniques. Consider the problem example in Section 5-1, where it is desired to count the number of occurrences of the code 2. A variable acting as a counter, I in the example, is set (*initialized*) to zero before the counting process starts. A CODE is read and tested to determine whether it is equal to 2. If CODE equals 2, the statement I = I + 1 is processed; that is, the value 1 is added to the counter I; that result then becomes the new value for I, reflecting the fact that another CODE 2 has been found.

The statement I = I + 1 is of such paramount importance that we reemphasize its meaning:

I = I + 1   means   add 1 to I and call this the new value I, or
the new value for I is equal to the old value
plus 1.

Internally, this statement causes the computer to fetch the contents of memory location I, add 1 to it and store the result back into location I. This, of course, causes destruction of the value that was previously stored in I.

Note that in the problem example of Section 5-1, the statement I = I + 1 is bypassed whenever CODE is not equal to 2, which means that for any value other than 2 the counter I will not be incremented by 1. Other examples of counting are discussed in Section 5-4.

5-2-5 Loop Control

An important application of counting is loop control. *Loop control* allows the programmer to repeat a procedure (task) a predetermined number of times by making use of a counter to keep track of the number of times the procedure is being carried out (*loop*). Exiting from the loop is achieved when the counter has reached the designated value. Consider, for example, the following problem: A data file contains six grades (one grade per card). Write a program to read these six grades and print those greater than 90. Also print the number of occurrences of grades over 90.

There are many ways to solve this problem; we offer two methods, shown in Figures 5-2 and 5-4. In Figure 5-2, a counter is used to control the number of times a grade is read and tested. The counter is initially set to zero and incremented by one each time after the READ statement.

In Figure 5-2, the statements 10 through 25 constitute a loop. To better visualize the mechanism of the loop process, we can trace through the loop and, for each cycle through the loop, record the values assumed by the different variables. A table of values can then be constructed. This process is called *tabulation*. The table corresponding to the program in Figure 5-2 is shown in Figure 5-3 with the corresponding data deck.

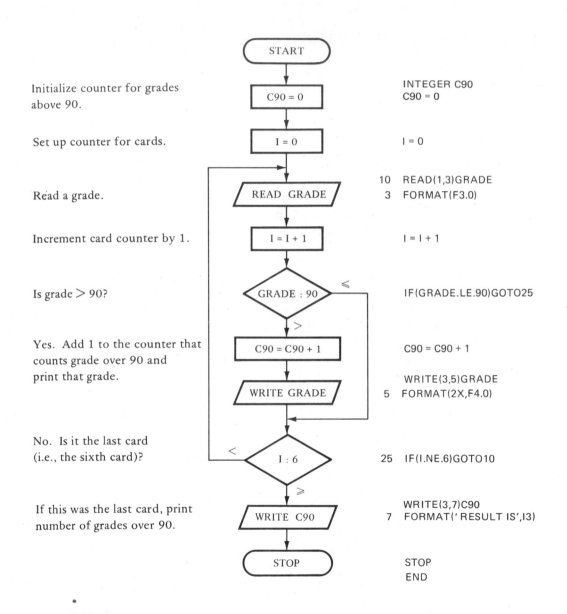

Initialize counter for grades above 90.

Set up counter for cards.

Read a grade.

Increment card counter by 1.

Is grade > 90?

Yes. Add 1 to the counter that counts grade over 90 and print that grade.

No. Is it the last card (i.e., the sixth card)?

If this was the last card, print number of grades over 90.

START

C90 = 0

I = 0

READ GRADE

I = I + 1

GRADE : 90

C90 = C90 + 1

WRITE GRADE

I : 6

WRITE C90

STOP

INTEGER C90
C90 = 0

I = 0

10 READ(1,3)GRADE
3 FORMAT(F3.0)

I = I + 1

IF(GRADE.LE.90)GOTO25

C90 = C90 + 1

WRITE(3,5)GRADE
5 FORMAT(2X,F4.0)

25 IF(I.NE.6)GOTO10

WRITE(3,7)C90
7 FORMAT(' RESULT IS',I3)

STOP
END

Figure 5-2 Counting for loop control.

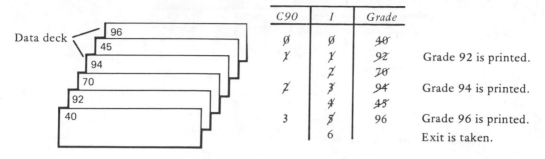

C90	I	Grade	
0̸	0̸	4̶0̶	
1̶	1̶	9̶2̶	Grade 92 is printed.
	2̶	7̶0̶	
2̶	3̶	9̶4̶	Grade 94 is printed.
	4̶	4̶5̶	
3	5̶	96	Grade 96 is printed.
	6		Exit is taken.

Figure 5-3 Tabulation for Figure 5-2.

In Figure 5-4, the counter is initially set to 6 and is decremented by one each time by the statement J = J − 1 after the READ statement. See Figure 5-5 for tabulation.

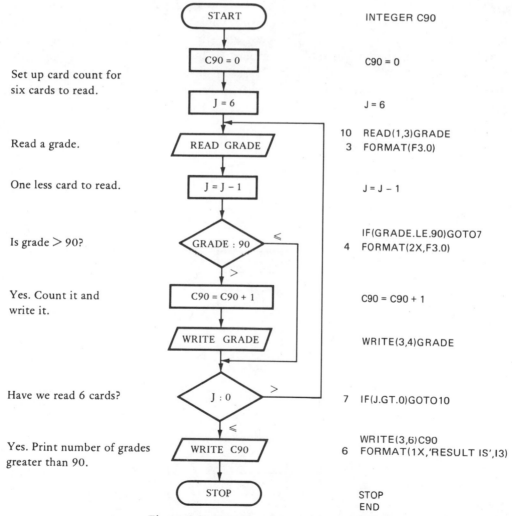

Figure 5-4 Decrementing a counter.

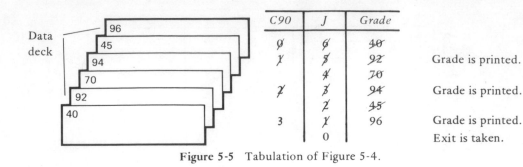

C90	J	Grade
~~0~~	~~0~~	~~40~~
~~1~~	~~1~~	~~92~~	Grade is printed.
	~~4~~	~~70~~
~~2~~	~~3~~	~~94~~	Grade is printed.
	~~2~~	~~45~~
3	~~1~~	96	Grade is printed.
	0		Exit is taken.

Figure 5-5   Tabulation of Figure 5-4.

5-2-6 Number Generation

Another important application of counting is number generation. For example, to generate the even-positive integers the statement I = I + 2 is repeatedly used with I set initially to 0. To generate the odd-positive integers, the same formula could be used, with I initially set to 1. The program shown in Figure 5-6 prints a 12's addition and multiplication table. Numbers 1, 2, 3, · · · , 10 can be generated by the statement I = I + 1, with I initially set to 0. There is no need to read these numbers from cards, since they can be easily generated. Each time a new value is generated for I, it is immediately included in the computational formulas 12*I and 12 + I. The value of I is then compared to 10 to determine the end of the program. A program to solve this problem is shown in Figure 5-6.

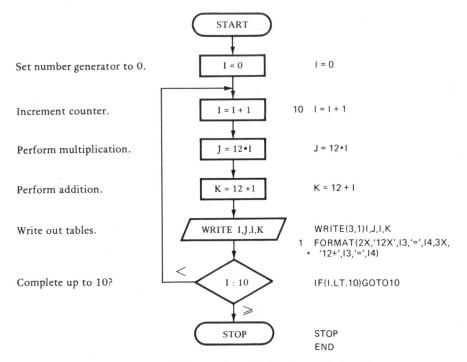

Figure 5-6   Addition and multiplication table for 12.

5-2-7   End-of-File Check

As noted in Chapter 1, computers can read from a variety of devices or mediums: punched card, magnetic tape or terminals. Data on such mediums is generally organized by *fields*; for example, if data cards are used, a field is defined as a group of related card columns. A field identifies a particular fact about an entity; a *record* is a group of related fields and hence describes many characteristics of an entity. An employee record might consist of a social security number field, a name and address field etc., all punched on one card. A *file* is a collection of related records.

When reading a file, it is important that no attempt be made to read more records than are present in the file. The problem of end of file arises when the computer is programmed to read an unknown number of cards (records). Different methods exist to take care of such a situation. This section discusses three end-of-file techniques: the automatic end of file, the trip record and the last-card code techniques.

Automatic End of File

On some systems, the programmer can instruct the computer to keep reading cards until these run out; then, by a special READ statement discussed below, the computer transfers control to a particular statement in the program to continue processing (for example, compute a grade average when all grades have been read). The computer automatically senses the end of file (no more data cards to read) and is told where and what to do when this condition arises (see Figure 5-7). Not

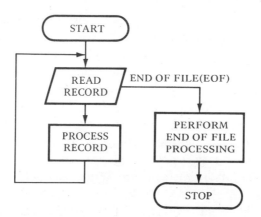

Figure 5-7   Automatic end-of-file processing.

all systems, however, have this automatic end-of-file processing capability, and the reader is advised to check with his computer installation to determine the availability of this feature. Most systems, however, now have the capability to detect an end-of-file condition, which allows the programmer to transfer to a particular statement when there are no more data cards. In such cases, the programmer is relieved of the task of either counting cards or simulating an end-of-file using the last-card code method. The general format for the extended READ is:

READ(device-number,format-statement-number,END=statement-number)variable-list

where END is a key word which identifies the statement number that the programmer wishes to transfer to when an end of file is reached (no more data records).

Consider the following problem example: A deck of cards contains an unknown number of cards, each containing a person's age. Write a program to compute and print the occurrence of age above N where N is an age punched on the very first card of the data deck. A program to solve this problem is shown in Figure 5-8. Note that if the data card containing the age had been left out of the program deck, an error message would be printed out.

Trip-Record Method

If the user's system does not support the automatic end of file, it is the user's responsibility to inform the computer system when it is reading the last data card; otherwise, an error message will be printed by the computer if and when it reads, under control of the user's program, an end-of-file card. An end-of-file card is that card which physically follows all data cards (on some systems it may be a card with /* punched in card columns 1 and 2, or it may be a card with an invalid character punched in card column 1 followed by a blank followed by END JOB or other codes, depending on the system used). In any event, when a *user program* reads such an end of file, the program will be terminated at once.

The program must, therefore, be made to simulate an end-of-file condition. A special end-of-file code, called a *trip code*, purposefully different from any of the data items read, but in the same card columns, may be punched on the very last card of the data deck and tested every time a data item is read. In the program of Figure 5-1, CODE is compared to 9 every time a data item is read. If it is not equal to 9, this means that the physical end of the data deck has not yet been reached and hence more cards can be read. If, on the other hand, CODE equals 9, this means that all the data has been read and an exit is taken from the READ loop. (See statement 17 of Figure 5-1.) Again, this special code is called a *trip* code and is placed on the last record (card). In the case of the program in Figure 5-1, for example, each data item read represents a potential trip code. To select a value for the code is easy; just use a value different than 0, 1 or 2. This may not always be so simple, however. Consider a deck of data cards, each card containing one grade, where the grades range from 0 to 100; the value 9 for trip code is

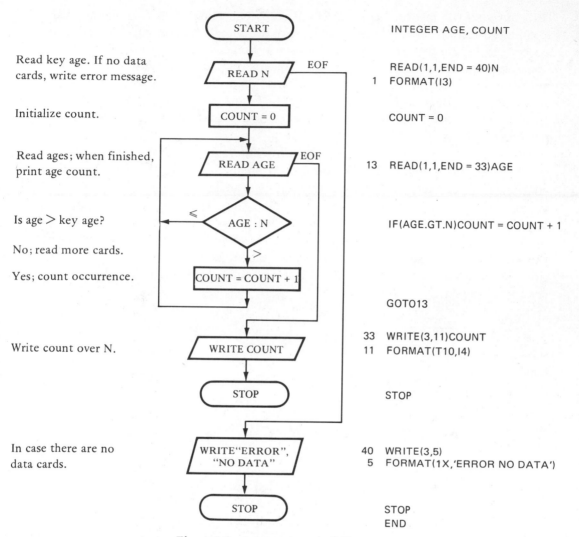

Figure 5-8 Automatic end of file.

unsatisfactory, since it could then be interpreted as a grade. Of course, an out-of-range trip value could be chosen. What about a set of numbers whose range is unknown? In this case, the last-card code technique is used.

Last-Card Code Method

A widely used technique for end of file checking is to add a "last card," on which just one special last-card code (generally a numerical value) has been punched, to the original deck of data cards (see Figure 5-9). This last-card code is punched in different card columns from any of the original data fields that are to be processed, so that it cannot possibly be mistaken as one of the original data fields. Then, every time a card is read not only are all of the original data fields read but also the last-card code (LCC) is read. The value of LCC on all data cards except the last one is zero, since blank fields are interpreted as zeroes by the computer (see Figure 5-9). On the last data card, however, the value of LCC will be nonzero. Hence, if LCC equals zero, this means that the end of the data cards has not been reached and more cards still need to be read; if, on the other hand, LCC equals the user-defined last-card code (99 in Figure 5-9), the end of the deck of data cards has been reached, and a transfer to a predetermined statement in the program is effected.

Consider, for example, the following problem. A deck of data cards (unknown number) contains demographical data on a small midwestern town. Each card consists of three fields: a social security number, an age and a sex field (see Figure 5-9(a)). The town mayor wants to determine the percentage of the total town population of males over 90 including the list of social security numbers of these individuals. A program to solve this problem is shown in Figure 5-9(b). Note that the check for last-card code is performed immediately after the READ instructions lest the three blank fields on the last card (all zeroes) be included in the processing of the data.

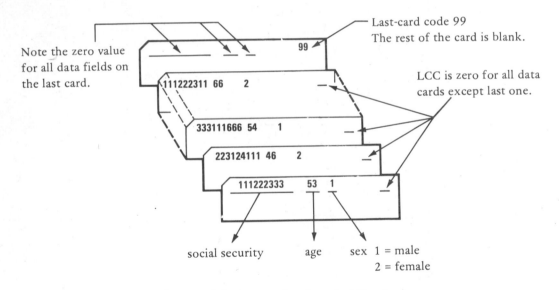

Figure 5-9(a)   Last-card code end-of-file check.

5-2-8   Models of Programs Using Data Cards

There are many different ways to write a program or a flowchart to solve a particular problem. The beginning programmer may be bewildered by all the numerous possibilities and may not know where and how to start. An attempt is made in the following paragraphs to suggest a successful approach to solve a problem that requires reading and processing data cards. Almost all of the problems that you will be asked to solve initially will fit in any one of the following categories.

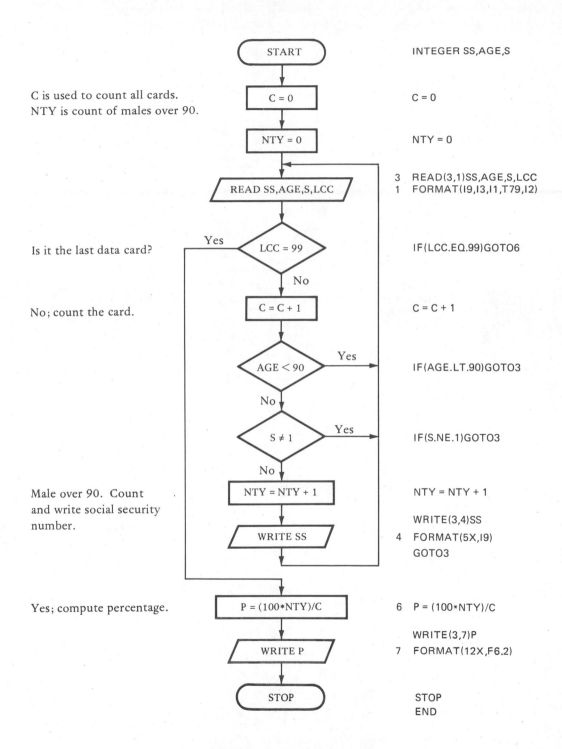

C is used to count all cards.
NTY is count of males over 90.

START   INTEGER SS,AGE,S

C = 0   C = 0

NTY = 0   NTY = 0

READ SS,AGE,S,LCC   3   READ(3,1)SS,AGE,S,LCC
                           1   FORMAT(I9,I3,I1,T79,I2)

Is it the last data card?   Yes   LCC = 99   IF(LCC.EQ.99)GOTO6

                                        No

No; count the card.   C = C + 1   C = C + 1

                                AGE < 90   Yes   IF(AGE.LT.90)GOTO3

                                        No

                                S ≠ 1   Yes   IF(S.NE.1)GOTO3

                                        No

Male over 90. Count   NTY = NTY + 1   NTY = NTY + 1
and write social security
number.   WRITE SS   WRITE(3,4)SS
                                                   4   FORMAT(5X,I9)
                                                        GOTO3

Yes; compute percentage.   P = (100*NTY)/C   6   P = (100*NTY)/C

                                WRITE P   WRITE(3,7)P
                                                   7   FORMAT(12X,F6.2)

                                STOP   STOP
                                                        END

Figure 5-9(b)   Last-card code program.

Case 1. You are asked to process a predetermined number of cards N using the counting method to stop reading cards (see Figure 5-10).

1. Initialize needed counters and variables. Can use the DATA statement. I is used as the card count.

2. Read the data off the card.

3. Increment the card counter.

4. Process the data on the card (count, print, add, make decision etc.).

5. Test to determine whether last card read is really the last. Go back to read on the condition less than.

6. If it is last card, complete last chores, i.e., print results, compute percentage etc.

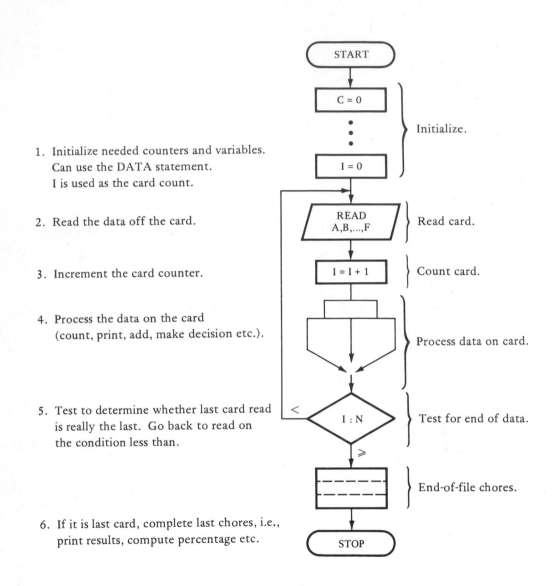

Figure 5-10 Counting data cards.

Case 2. You are to process an unknown number of cards using the last-card code method (last card contains the last-card code and no other data). (See Figure 5-11.)

1. Initialize needed counters used for processing of the data on the data card.

2. Read all the data, including the last-card code.

3. Test if this is the last card.

4. Process the data and then go back to read more cards.

5. Print results and perform general cleanup operations.

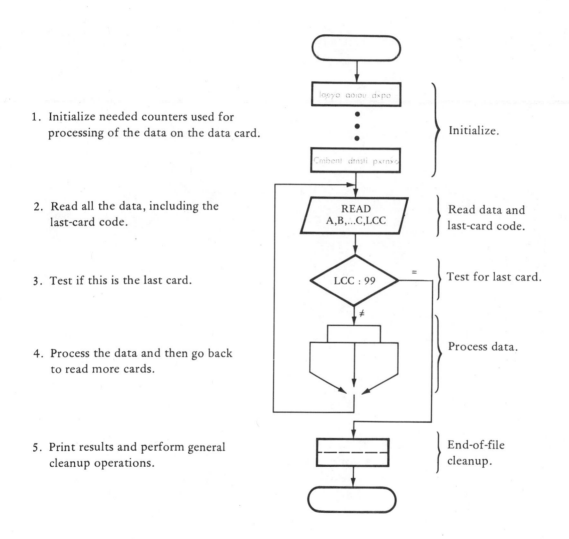

Initialize.

Read data and last-card code.

Test for last card.

Process data.

End-of-file cleanup.

Figure 5-11 Last-card code method.

Case 3. You are to process an unknown number of cards using the automatic end of file. (See Figure 5-12.)

1. Initialize needed counter and variables for program.

2. Read the data.

3. Process the data and go back to read more cards.

4. Print results and perform general cleanup functions.

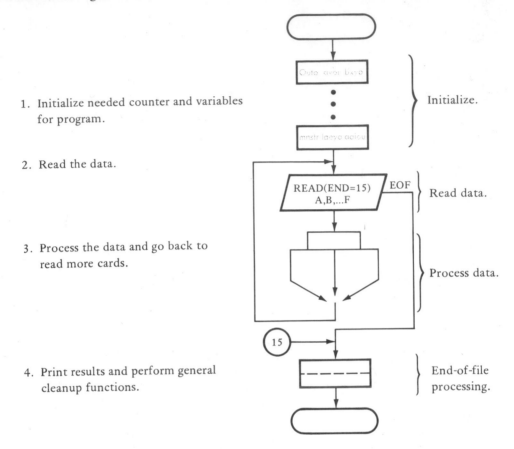

Figure 5-12   Automatic end of file.

Case 4. You are to process an unknown number of data cards using a trip (trigger) record. The trip code is an original data item punched on all data cards which is tested for a value known to be outside the range of the data item (see Figure 5-13).

5-2-9   The Slash (/) Format Code

FORMAT statements written thus far have described one physical input or output record, i.e., one punched card or one line of print. By using the control format code "/" it is possible to describe more than one input or output record with one FORMAT statement. The / format code may be interpreted to mean "end of physical record"; it is used to separate lists of format codes describing different physical records. No comma is required between the / and other format codes,

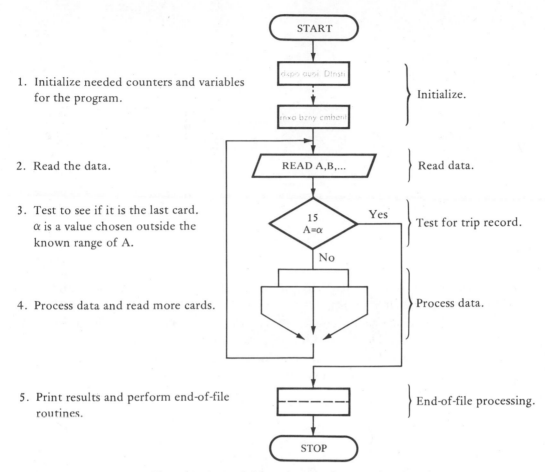

1. Initialize needed counters and variables for the program.

2. Read the data.

3. Test to see if it is the last card. α is a value chosen outside the known range of A.

4. Process data and read more cards.

5. Print results and perform end-of-file routines.

Figure 5-13   Model for trip-record processing.

although a comma may be used. Note that processing will restart at the very beginning of the new record.

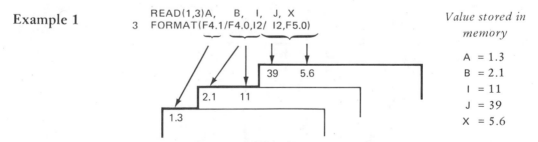

Example 1

```
READ(1,3)A,    B,   I,   J,  X
3   FORMAT(F4.1/F4.0,I2/ I2,F5.0)
```

Value stored in memory

A = 1.3
B = 2.1
I = 11
J = 39
X = 5.6

The READ list specifies that five variables are to be read from three records. The value for A is taken from the first data card. The / means "end of this record, select a new record and continue processing at the beginning of the new record"; hence the values for B and I are captured from the second card, while those for J and X are taken from the third data card.

Example 2

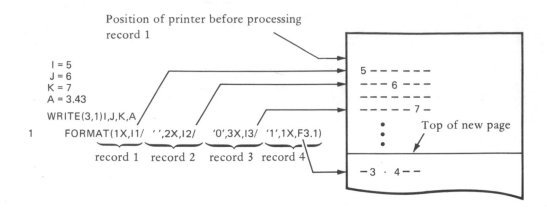

Position of printer before processing record 1

```
I = 5
J = 6
K = 7
A = 3.43
WRITE(3,1)I,J,K,A
1    FORMAT(1X,I1/ ' ',2X,I2/  '0',3X,I3/ '1',1X,F3.1)
```

record 1   record 2   record 3   record 4

Four variables are to be written as four distinct records. The carriage control for the first record is blank as a result of 1X so the printer spaces one line and writes the value for I. The second output record is then processed, a "blank" carriage control character causes the printer to space one line and print the value for J. Record 3 is then processed, the printer double spaces and prints the value for K. Finally, the fourth record is processed, and the value of A is written at the top of a new page.

Example 3

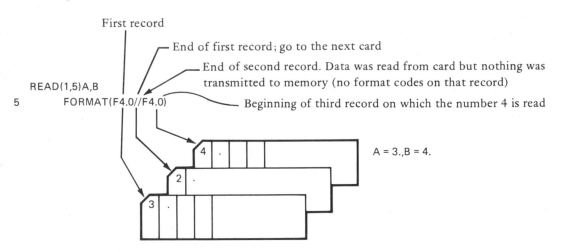

First record

End of first record; go to the next card

End of second record. Data was read from card but nothing was transmitted to memory (no format codes on that record)

```
READ(1,5)A,B
5    FORMAT(F4.0//F4.0)
```

Beginning of third record on which the number 4 is read

A = 3.,B = 4.

In Example 3, three records are read. Any data contained on record 2 is read, but no data on it will be transmitted to memory, since the record has no accompanying data format code. The slash means end of the record and go to the next record.

Example 4

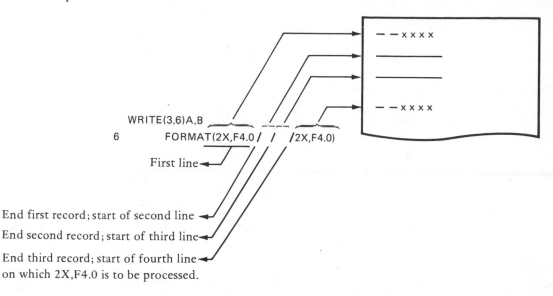

WRITE(3,6)A,B

6   FORMAT(2X,F4.0/ / /2X,F4.0)

First line ◀

End first record; start of second line ◀

End second record; start of third line ◀

End third record; start of fourth line ◀
on which 2X,F4.0 is to be processed.

In Example 4, line 1 will contain the value of A, and the fourth record (line 4) will contain B.

Example 5

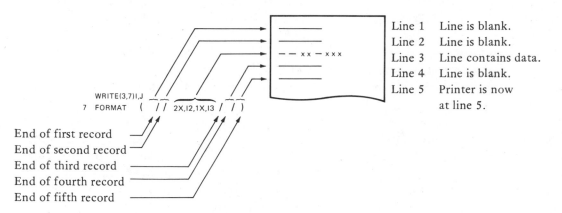

Line 1	Line is blank.
Line 2	Line is blank.
Line 3	Line contains data.
Line 4	Line is blank.
Line 5	Printer is now
	at line 5.

WRITE(3,7)I,J

7   FORMAT   (/ / 2X,I2,1X,I3 / /)

End of first record

End of second record

End of third record

End of fourth record

End of fifth record

In Example 5, if the next WRITE statement contained a '+' carriage control character, data would be printed on the 5th line of Example 5. If, on the other hand, the WRITE statement contained a ' ' (blank) carriage control, then line 5 would be blank, and printing would start on the following line.

Finally, the slash can be extremely useful when creating headings or distributing data items over more than one record with just one WRITE statement.

Example 6

```
    WRITE(3,5)REV,EXP,ANC
  5   FORMAT('1'/T50,'PACIFIC COMPANY'/T49,'INCOME STATEMENT'/T43,
     *'FOR THE MONTH OF JUNE 1979'//T35'REVENUES',T71,F7.2/
     *T35,'EXPENSES',T71,F7.2/T35,'NETINCOME',T71,F7.2)
```

Example 6 would produce the following output:

```
                      PACIFIC COMPANY
                      INCOME STATEMENT
              FOR THE MONTH OF JUNE 1979


          REVENUES                    8800.00
          EXPENSES                    7800.00
          NET INCOME                  1000.00
```

5-3   You Might Want To Know

1. I don't understand the difference between a nonexecutable statement and an executable statement. Could you help?

    Answer: I'll try! The nonexecutable statements that have been encountered so far are END, FORMAT, INTEGER, REAL, DATA, while the executable statements have been READ/WRITE, IF, GOTO, STOP and the replacement statement. Nonexecutable instructions are processed by the compiler and not by the CPU at execution time. Executable instructions are those instructions translated by the compiler into machine language and then executed by the CPU. Essentially, nonexecutable instructions are instructions to the compiler which do not get translated into machine language. The END statement, for instance, is not translated into a machine instruction(s); it merely informs the compiler that there are no more FORTRAN statements to be translated (the physical end of the deck of FORTRAN statements has been reached). The INTEGER specification statement is not translated into machine language but tells the compiler that whenever an INTEGER-specified variable is encountered in the program it is to be processed as an integer. The FORMAT informs the compiler how to complete the translation of the READ/WRITE instructions etc. The statement X = 2. is an executable instruction. It is translated into a set of machine instructions which cause the CPU at execution time to store the number 2. in memory location X.

2. Is it possible to use the DATA statement to reset variables to specified values during execution of a program?

Answer: No. The values of variables specified in a DATA statement are already set at the beginning of execution of a program. The DATA statement is not an executable statement and hence cannot be executed by the program to reset the values of variables. To reset the variable, use a replacement statement.

3. What happens if there are no more records (cards) left to be processed when a READ statement is executed?

   Answer: An error message will be printed. On most systems, the program execution is cancelled at this point. The programmer should recheck his program to determine if
   a. Data cards were included in the job.
   b. The check for last record is in the logically correct place (it should immediately follow a READ statement).
   c. The end-of-file item (code) on the last card is punched correctly and in the card columns specified in the FORMAT.
   d. The FORMAT describing the data record is correct.

4. Yesterday I wrote a program with ten data cards and the computer only read the first five. What happened?

   Answer: Since it read five cards, you instructed it to read only the first five cards, at which time the STOP instruction was encountered in your program. Check the logic of the program. What the computer does with the five remaining cards in the card reader that were unprocessed by your program will vary among systems. The cards expected by the system after your data cards are someone else's job control cards, not your data cards with just numbers on them. Eventually, the excess data cards will be flushed out by the system.

5. If a DATA statement can be replaced by a replacement statement, why use the DATA statement?

   Answer: A primary reason is programmer convenience. A great many variables may be initialized in one DATA statement which otherwise would require many replacement statements. Another reason might be time saving during the execution of a program. The DATA statement is interpreted by the compiler once to accomplish the initialization; replacement statements must be repeated each time the same program is executed. This time saving would apply if the program were to be run a number of times and not recompiled each time.

6. In the example of Figure 5-1, the counter was initialized to zero. Is this necessary?

   Answer: It is necessary to initialize any variable used as a counter before entering the program loop in which that counter is used. The value zero is generally used as the initial value when the counter is used to count occurrences of specific entities (events). Other values may be used when the counter is used for other purposes (see Section 5-4). The counter should not be reset to its initial value within the program loop in which it is used. Note that if a loop is to repeat a procedure 10 times for instance, the counter I could be initialized to 15 and then compared to 25 for loop exiting purposes.

5-4 Programming Examples

5-4-1 Computing a Percentage of Passing Grades

A deck of cards consists of several packets of data decks, each containing grades obtained by different class sections of an Introduction to Business course. Each packet is identified by a header card specifying the section number and the number of grades for the particular section. One student grade (0–100) is punched per card. No section is expected to contain more than 100 students. Write a complete program to determine the percentage of passing grades for each section (passing grades are grades over 60). Provide a listing of grades by section number on different pages with appropriate headings. Both input and output may be visualized as follows:

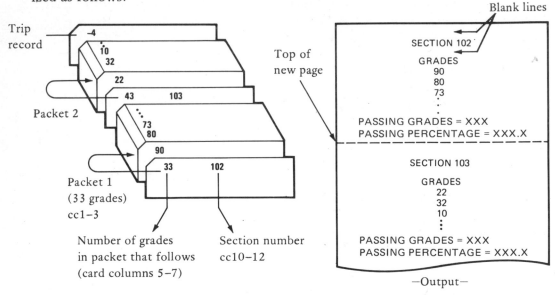

—Output—

The program to solve this problem is shown in Figure 5-14.

Note the position of the FORTRAN STOP statement. It does not immediately precede the END statement.

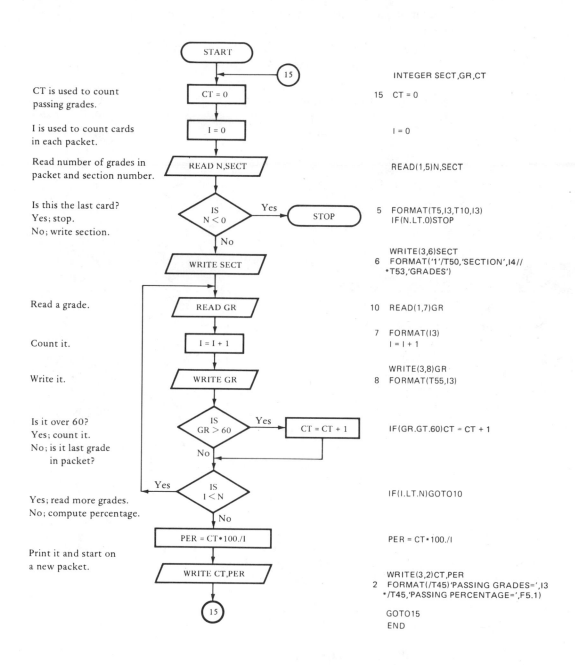

Figure 5-14 Computing percentage of passing grades.

5-4-2 Short-Term Interest

The formula to compute a simple interest INTDUE on a loan of L dollars at an interest rate R for T days is given by:

$$INTDUE = L*R*T/360$$

Write a program to read a dollar amount and an interest rate, and produce a table showing the interest to be paid at the end of each month for a period of 12 months (assume each month is 30 days).

A counter is needed to repeat the computation of the interest due 12 times, while T must be incremented each time by 30. This can be achieved by the statement T = T + 30 with T = 0 or T = 30, depending on whether T = T + 30 precedes or follows the computation for the interest. A program to solve this problem is shown in Figure 5-15.

5-5 Probing Deeper

5-5-1 The IMPLICIT Statement

In programs which make extensive use of integer and/or real variables, it becomes cumbersome to list all such variables in explicit mode declaration statements. For this reason, the IMPLICIT specification statement allows the programmer to formulate his own conventions for implicit mode declaration. For example, the statement IMPLICIT REAL (I) would cause all variables with names beginning with the character I to be real. It is possible to specify a range of letters in alphabetical order in the IMPLICIT statement; for example, the statement IMPLICIT INTEGER(A–D) would cause any variable beginning with A, B, C or D to be an integer variable. The general form of the implicit statement is

$$IMPLICIT\ type\ (a[,a]\cdots)[,type(a[,a]\cdots)]\cdots$$

where type may be INTEGER, REAL or other mode type
$\qquad$ a may be a single letter or a range of letters denoted by $l_1 - l_2$
$\qquad$ l_1 and l_2 are single letters of the alphabet

Example

$$IMPLICIT\ INTEGER(A–F),REAL(I–N)$$

Variables beginning with A, C, D, E and F are implicitly integer; all other variables are real. The IMPLICIT statement must be the *first* statement among other specification statements.

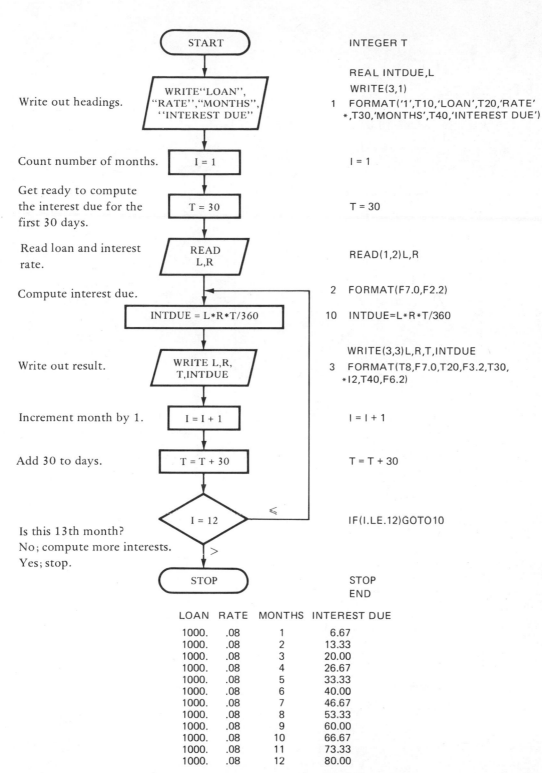

Write out headings.	WRITE"LOAN", "RATE","MONTHS", "INTEREST DUE"	INTEGER T REAL INTDUE,L WRITE(3,1) 1 FORMAT('1',T10,'LOAN',T20,'RATE' *,T30,'MONTHS',T40,'INTEREST DUE')
Count number of months.	I = 1	I = 1
Get ready to compute the interest due for the first 30 days.	T = 30	T = 30
Read loan and interest rate.	READ L,R	READ(1,2)L,R
Compute interest due.	INTDUE = L*R*T/360	2 FORMAT(F7.0,F2.2) 10 INTDUE=L*R*T/360
Write out result.	WRITE L,R, T,INTDUE	WRITE(3,3)L,R,T,INTDUE 3 FORMAT(T8,F7.0,T20,F3.2,T30, *I2,T40,F6.2)
Increment month by 1.	I = I + 1	I = I + 1
Add 30 to days.	T = T + 30	T = T + 30
Is this 13th month? No; compute more interests. Yes; stop.	I = 12	IF(I.LE.12)GOTO10
	STOP	STOP END

LOAN	RATE	MONTHS	INTEREST DUE
1000.	.08	1	6.67
1000.	.08	2	13.33
1000.	.08	3	20.00
1000.	.08	4	26.67
1000.	.08	5	33.33
1000.	.08	6	40.00
1000.	.08	7	46.67
1000.	.08	8	53.33
1000.	.08	9	60.00
1000.	.08	10	66.67
1000.	.08	11	73.33
1000.	.08	12	80.00

Figure 5-15. Calculation of a short-term interest loan.

5-6 Exercises

5-6-1 Self Test

1. How many cards will be read by the following flowcharts?

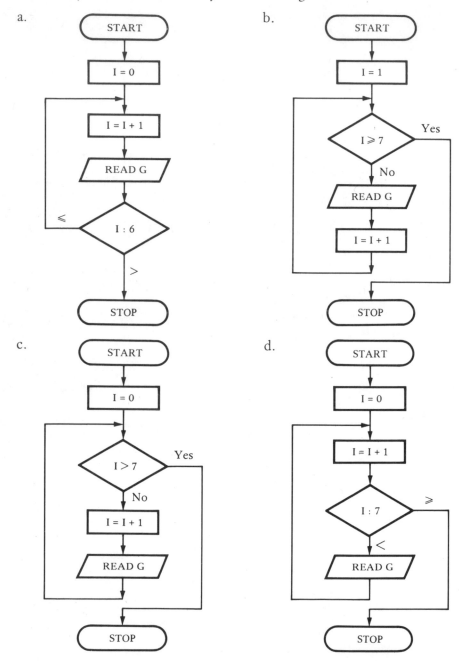

a.

START

I = 0

I = I + 1

READ G

I : 6

≤

>

STOP

b.

START

I = 1

I ⩾ 7

Yes

No

READ G

I = I + 1

STOP

c.

START

I = 0

I > 7

Yes

No

I = I + 1

READ G

STOP

d.

START

I = 0

I = I + 1

I : 7

⩾

<

READ G

STOP

e.

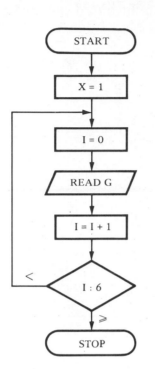

f.

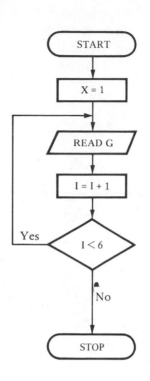

g.

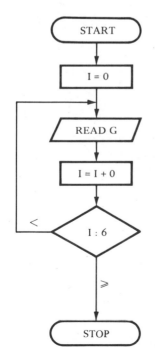

h.

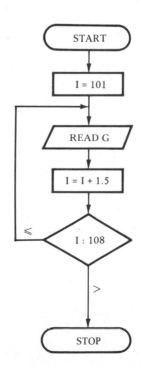

2. Determine the number of cards read, the value printed for I and the last value read for G, given the following flowcharts with data cards as shown. Indicate whether an end-of-file condition will occur (when the computer is instructed to read cards but there are none left).

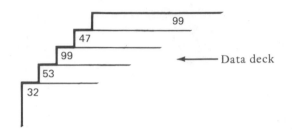

Data deck

a.

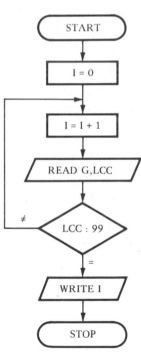

b.

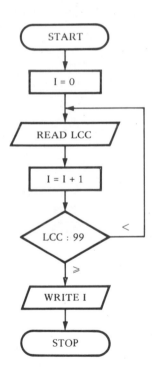

c.

d.

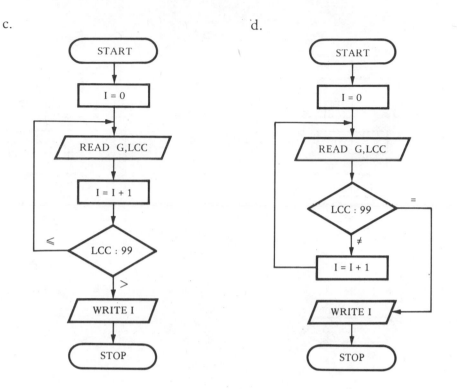

3. A data deck contains ten cards. Which of the following flowcharts will read ten and only ten cards?

a.

b.

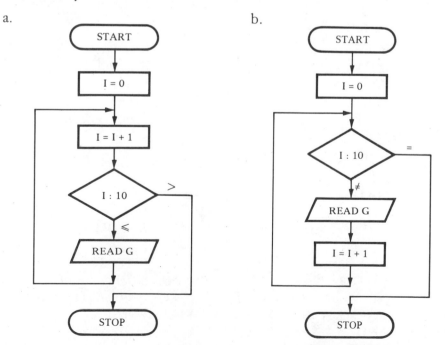

c.

d.

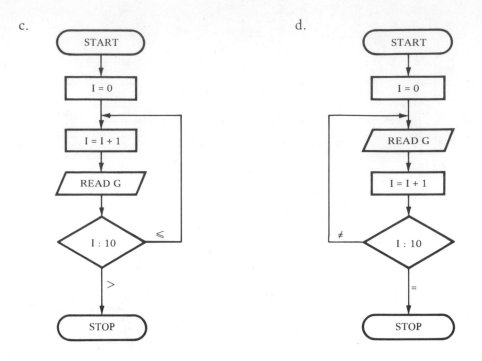

4. Complete each IF statement so that the program will read ten data cards.

a.
```
      I = 0
   2  READ(1,1)J
      IF(I _____ )GOTO6
      I = I + 1
      GOTO2
   6  STOP
   1  FORMAT(I2)
      END
```

b.
```
      I = 0
   2  I = I + 1
      READ(1,1)J
      IF(I _____ )GOTO2
      STOP
   1  FORMAT(I2)
      END
```

c.
```
      DATA I/0/
   2  READ(1,1)J
      IF(I _____ )GOTO5
      GOTO7
   5  I = I + 1
      GOTO2
   7  STOP
   1  FORMAT(I2)
      END
```

d.
```
      I = 0
   2  IF(I _____ )GOTO6
      READ(1,1)J
      I = I + 1
      GOTO2
   6  STOP
   1  FORMAT(I2)
      END
```

e.
```
     I = 10
   2 IF(I [      ])GOTO6
     READ(1,1)J
     I = I − 1
     GOTO2
   6 STOP
   1 FORMAT(I2)
     END
```

f.
```
     DATA I/6/
   2 I = I − 1
     READ(1,1)J
     IF(I [      ])GOTO2
     STOP
   1 FORMAT(I2)
     END
```

5. a. Differentiate between implicit and explicit mode declaration.

   b. Write FORTRAN statements to declare that variables BETA and GAMMA will be integer, while variables KOUNT and MODEM will be real.

   c. What purpose does the DATA statement serve? Is it a statement which is an essential part of the FORTRAN language? Why?

   d. What purpose does the IMPLICIT statement serve? Is it a statement which is an essential part of the FORTRAN language? Why?

   e. Describe at least two methods for processing a file consisting of many records.

6. Given the data cards shown below, indicate the number of cards read by each of the following flowcharts and the terminal value of I.

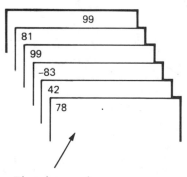

First data card

a.

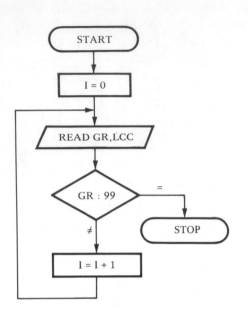

b.

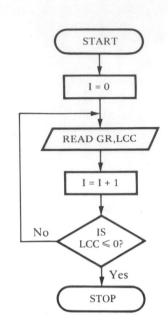

c.

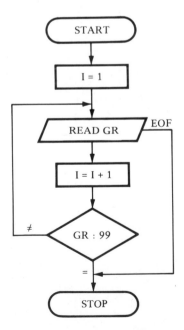

d.

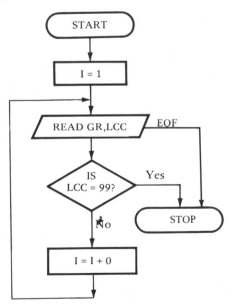

e.

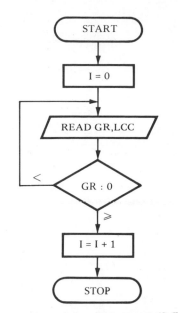

f.

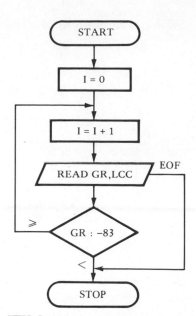

7. Determine the number of lines printed or the number of data cards processed (read) by the following statements, given the various formats:

	READ(1,5)I,J		WRITE(3,6)I,K
a. 5	FORMAT(I4/I3)	f. 6	FORMAT(/1X,I2///1X,I3)
b. 5	FORMAT(/I4,I3)	g. 6	FORMAT('0',I2/1X,I3/)
c. 5	FORMAT(/I4/I3/)	h. 6	FORMAT(//T2,I2/1X,I3)
d. 5	FORMAT(//I4,I3/)	i. 6	FORMAT(//1X,I2/1X/I4///)
e. 5	FORMAT(//I4//I3//)	j. 6	FORMAT(/'0',I2/'0',I3)

8. Which of the following statements are true?

a. Specification statement errors are detected at execution time.

b. DATA statements may be inserted anywhere in a FORTRAN program.

c. Specification statements are nonexecutable statements.

d. The statement INTEGER ISAM,SAM,KKK is valid.

e. Automatic end-of-file may be used in certain cases when printing an unknown number of values.

f. IMPLICIT INTEGER A–Z is an invalid specification statement.

g. Three consecutive slashes at the beginning of an output format (///) mean three blank lines.

h. The statement   READ(1,6)X,I,Y will read three cards.
   6   FORMAT(F5.1/I3/F5.1)

i. The statement   READ(1,7)I,X,K   will read five cards.
   7   FORMAT(I1,F1.1,I2,F2.2,F3.3)

j. The statement   READ(1,6)I,J,K,L,M,N will read six cards.
   6   FORMAT(T5,2X,I4)

5-6-2 Programming Exercises

1. Modify the program of Figure 5-15 so that only one counter (I) is needed in the program instead of both I and T.

2. a. A data deck contains ten pairs of grades (one pair per card). Write a program to compute and print out each pair and its corresponding sum. (Define your own input/output formats.)

   b. Suppose that the first record in the data deck contains the number of records which follow. For example:

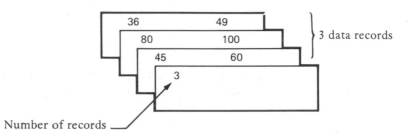

Number of records

   Modify the program written for part (a) above to process this type of data file.

3. A data deck contains an unknown number of positive and negative numbers (one number per card). The value contained on the last card is 999999. Write a program to compute and print out the number of positive, zero and negative values in the file.

4. A data deck contains 30 grades, one per card. Write a program to compute and print out the number of grades greater than 49 and less than or equal to 63.

5. Write a program to read 30 grades, one per card, and determine and print the highest grade. Change the program to print the lowest grade.

6. There are ten data cards, each consisting of two entries. The first entry is a sex code (1 for male, 2 for female). The second entry represents an earnings amount. Write a program to compute the number of females who earned less than $2,500. Use the counting method to stop reading the data records.

7. The radii of circles vary from 2, 7, 12, 17, $\cdots$, 47 inclusive. Print out the radius, circumference and area of each circle.

8. A data deck contains 100 numbers (one number per card). Write a program to read these numbers and stop whenever the number 4 (by itself) has been read three times. Print the total number of items read. (It is conceivable that the number 4 may not occur three times.)

9. Each data record in a file contains two items: an age and a code for marital status (1 = single, 2 = married, 3 = divorced and 4 = widowed). There is an unknown number of data records. A code of 9 in the marital status field signifies that it is the last record. Write a program to compute and print the following:

    a. The percentage of people over 30 years of age.
    b. The number of people who are either widowed or divorced.
    c. The number of people who are over 50 or less than 30 and who are not married.

10. Write a program to read a positive value for J and
    a. Print the even integers that are less than or equal to J starting with −12.
    b. Print the first J odd integers.
    c. Determine if J is a prime number.

11. A data file contains 100 positive or negative numbers (one number per card). Write a program to stop reading the file whenever two numbers of the opposite sign follow one another. Print the total number of items read.

12. A deck of cards consists of an unknown number of cards. Each card contains two integers in card columns 8–9 and 78–79, respectively. Count the occurrence of positive, negative and zero numbers. Print all numbers read and their corresponding counts using the following format; for example:

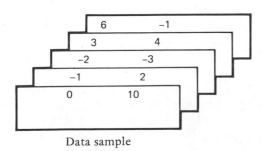

Data sample

Top of new page

0	10
−1	2
−2	−3
3	4
6	−1

Count of positive numbers is 5.
Count of negative numbers is 4.
Count of zero numbers is 1.

13. Write a program to print out multiplication tables from 2 to 12, as follows.

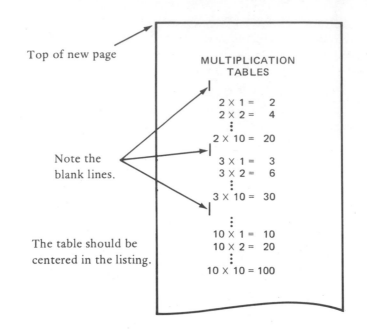

Top of new page

MULTIPLICATION
TABLES

Note the
blank lines.

The table should be
centered in the listing.

```
2 X 1 =   2
2 X 2 =   4
    ⋮
2 X 10 = 20

3 X 1 =   3
3 X 2 =   6
    ⋮
3 X 10 = 30

    ⋮
10 X 1 =  10
10 X 2 =  20
    ⋮
10 X 10 = 100
```

14. Write a program to compute how much a person would weigh on the following planets based on the following table:

Planet	Percentage of Earth Weight
Moon	16
Jupiter	264
Venus	85
Mars	38

Create a table with weights ranging from 50 to 250 pounds in steps of 10 pounds.

15. The number e can be defined as the limit of $(1 + 1/n)^n$ as n gets larger and larger. Write a program to approximate a value for e. Stop when the difference between two successive approximations is less than .001. Print out the values for e and n.

16. Write a program to print out the following board (exactly).

```
*  *  *  *  *  *  *  *  *  *  *  *  *  *  *  *  *  *  *  *  *  *  *  *  *  *  *  *  *  *  *  *
*           *           *           *           *           *           *
*           *           *           *           *           *           *
*           *           *           *           *           *           *
*           *           *           *           *           *           *
*  *  *  *  *  *  *  *  *  *  *  *  *  *  *  *  *  *  *  *  *  *  *  *  *  *  *  *  *  *  *  *
*           *           *           *           *           *           *
*           *           *           *           *           *           *
*           *           *           *           *           *           *
*           *           *           *           *           *           *
*  *  *  *  *  *  *  *  *  *  *  *  *  *  *  *  *  *  *  *  *  *  *  *  *  *  *  *  *  *  *  *
*           *           *           *           *           *           *
*           *           *           *           *           *           *
*           *           *           *           *           *           *
*           *           *           *           *           *           *
*  *  *  *  *  *  *  *  *  *  *  *  *  *  *  *  *  *  *  *  *  *  *  *  *  *  *  *  *  *  *  *
*           *           *           *           *           *           *
*           *           *           *           *           *           *
*           *           *           *           *           *           *
*           *           *           *           *           *           *
*  *  *  *  *  *  *  *  *  *  *  *  *  *  *  *  *  *  *  *  *  *  *  *  *  *  *  *  *  *  *  *
```

17. Compute the monthly payment for a mortgage on a house worth P = $45,000 at an interest I = 9.25 percent for a 10-, 15-, 20-, 25-, 30- and 35-year mortgage. The output should be as follows:

MORTGAGE PAYMENT PLAN
JOHN DOE

PRINCIPAL	INTEREST RATE	DURATION	MONTHLY PAYMENT
45 000	9.25	10	XXXX.XX
45 000	9.25	15	XXXX.XX
.	.	.	.
.	.	.	.
.	.	.	.
45 000	9.25	35	XXXX.XX

The formula to compute the monthly payment is:

$$M = \frac{P \cdot \dfrac{I}{12}}{1 - \left(\dfrac{1}{1 + \dfrac{I}{12}}\right)^{T \cdot 12}}$$

P is the principal.
I is the interest rate.
T is the mortgage duration in years.

18. Same problem as Exercise 17 except that the interest and principal are read from cards.

19. Each employee working at Manpower, Inc., is paid at a regular hourly rate of $5.00 for the first 40 hours. The overtime rate is 1.5 the regular rate. The number of hours worked by each employee is punched into card columns 1–4 on a data card (two decimal positions are assumed, with no decimal point punched in the field.) A card with a zero in the hours field denotes the end of the data deck.

a. Write a program to compute each employee's pay and produce an output similar to the following:

HOURS	RATE	OVERTIME HOURS	PAY
10.00	5.00	0	50.00
50.00	5.00	10	275.00
.	.	.	.
.	.	.	.

b. Same as part a, except that the number of hours and the rate of pay are read from data cards in card columns 1–4 and 7–11. Also 6.1 percent of each employee's pay for the first 30 hours is subtracted from the gross pay. The produced output should be similar to

HOURS	RATE	PENSION PLAN	PAY
50.00	10.00	18.30	531.70
.	.	.	.
.	.	.	.

c. Same as part b, except that a bonus amount is recorded for each employee on the data cards in card columns 15–18 as a three-digit integer number. If the employee's pay exceeds $500, the bonus is added to the employee's pay; if not, the bonus field is left blank on the output, as follows:

HOURS	RATE	PENSION PLAN	BONUS	PAY
50.00	10.00	18.30	100	631.70
10.00	5.00	3.05		46.95
.	.	.		.
.	.	.		.

Note blank field

d. Same as part a, except that overtime hours are converted into corresponding regular hours. For instance, 10 hours of overtime at time-and-a-half rate of $8.00 per hour is equivalent to 15 straight hours (regular hours at $8.00 per hour).

20. Read 30 grades already sorted in ascending order and compute the mode. The mode is defined as the score which occurs most frequently. For example, given the grades 10, 15, 15, 17, 17, 17, 20, 21, the mode is 17.

21. Read N grades (one per card) already sorted in ascending order (N is to be read from the first card) and compute the median. The median is that mark which divides a distribution of scores in two equal parts. For example:

$$10, 11, 12, 13, 14, 15, 16 \qquad \text{The median is 13.}$$

$$10, 11, 12, 13 \qquad \text{The median is } \frac{11 + 12}{2} = 11.5.$$

22. Write a program to make daily weather reports. Each data card should contain nine integer values giving the following information: current month, day and year; high temperature for the day, low temperature for the day; year in which the record high for this day was set, record high temperature; year of record low, record low temperature. After reading a data card, print a message of one of the following four types, depending on the data.

1	10/23/76	HIGH TODAY	52
		LOW TODAY	23
2	10/24/76	HIGH TODAY	71*
		LOW TODAY	38
	*(BEATS RECORD OF 70 SET IN 1906)		
3	10/25/76	HIGH TODAY	73*
		LOW TODAY	−10**
	*(BEATS RECORD OF 68 SET IN 1938)		
	**(BEATS RECORD OF −8 SET IN 1918)		
4	10/26/76	HIGH TODAY	22
		LOW TODAY	−18*
	*(BEATS RECORD OF −5 SET IN 1900)		

Stop reading data cards when you come to one whose month number is zero.

23. Management of any group of people is made more complex by the many types of relationships between the manager and his subordinates and among groups of subordinates. There are three types of relationships.

a. Direct single: the manager relates directly to each subordinate. The number of these relationships is equal to n, the number of subordinates.

b. Direct group: the manager relates to each distinct group of subordinates. The number of these relationships is $2^n - 1$.

c. Cross: each subordinate relates to other subordinates. The number of these relationships is $n(n - 1)$.

The total number of relationships in the group is $2^n + n^2 - 1$. Write a program to calculate the number of direct single, direct group, cross and total number of relationships for 1 to 50 subordinates. Have your program print these in tabular form for each number of subordinates in the range specified. The mode used for the variables in this program will have a significant effect on the results produced. Try using all integer variables, then all real variables. Which results are the most useful?

24. Write a program to perform octal counting up to 27_8, that is, print the numbers 1, 2, $\cdots$, 7, 10, 11, $\cdots$, 17, 20, 21, $\cdots$, 27. Can you generalize your program for counting in octal up to a number N read from a card?

25. A wholesaler accepts a $5,000 promissory note from a retailer at 7 percent in lieu of cash payment for delivered goods. Write a program to compute the maturity value of the note for a 30-, 60- and 90-day short-term loan. (Formula for maturity value is $S = P(1 + I \cdot N)$. S is maturity value, P is principal, I is interest rate and N is the number of years, or, if less than 1 year, number of days/360.)

26. The simple discount is the amount deducted from the maturity value S (see Problem 25 above) of an obligation when the latter is sold before its date of maturity. The formula is $SD = S \cdot D \cdot N$. SD = simple discount, S = maturity value, D = discount rate and N = term of loan, that is, time remaining before maturity.

   A wholesaler receives a $10,500 promissory note for goods sold to a retailer. The note matures in N months and bears an I percent interest rate. One month later, the wholesaler sells his note to a bank at 9 percent discount rate. Write a program to compute:

   a. The maturity value of the note for N = 30, 60 and 90 days with interest rate of I = 4%, 5% and 6%. That is, N = 30 for I = 4%, 5% and 6%. N = 60 for I = 4%, 5%, 6% and so forth.

   b. The proceeds received by the wholesaler as a result of selling the note to the bank for N = 30, 60 and 90 days with interest rate of 4%, 5% and 6%.

27. Mr. Small is thinking of borrowing $5,000 to purchase a new automobile for N months at 8 percent simple discount rate. Write a program to compute the proceeds of this loan for the following values of N: 6 months, 1 year, 2 years and 3 years. The proceeds (P) is the sum remaining after the discount is deducted: $P = S(1 - SD \cdot N)$ (see Problem 26 above).

28. The Kiddie Up Company manufactures toys for adults. The company expects fixed costs for the next year to be around $180,000. With the demand for adult toys increasing, the company is looking for sales of $900,000 in the year to come. The variable costs are expected to run at about 74 percent of sales.

   a. Write a program to determine the break-even point (BEP) (the dollar amount of sales that must be made to neither incur a profit nor a loss) and compute the expected profit. The formula to compute the BEP is

$$BEP = \frac{\text{total fixed costs}}{1 - \dfrac{\text{variable costs}}{\text{sales}}}$$

b. The Kiddie Up Company management is arguing that with the current rate of inflation, variable costs will run higher for the next year—probably, anywhere from 75 to 83 percent of sales. With sales still projected at $900,000, the management directs its DP staff to generate the following report to determine the break-even point and the profits and losses for varying variable costs. Sales and fixed costs remain constant.

KIDDIE UP COMPANY
Operations Forecast 1979

Sales	Fixed costs	Variable cost	% Variable cost of sales	Break-even	Profit	Deficit
900,000	180,000	.	75	.	.	.
.	.	.	76	.	.	.
.	.	.	.	.	.	.
.	.	.	.	.	.	.
900,000	180,000	.	83	.	.	.

Write a program to complete the above report. Place three stars (***) in the profit column if there is no profit. Do the same for deficit.

c. The company employees have just won a new contract. As a result, variable costs are expected to reach 80 percent or 81 percent of next year's projected $900,000 sales. A recent internal study carried out by the company on the various aspects of the manufacturing operations disclosed production inefficiencies. Corrective measures could significantly lower fixed costs. Determine the extent to which present fixed costs could be reduced to satisfy the projected variable costs figures for the coming year.

29. XSTAR is a small company supplying major auto parts companies with a single item. The total fixed costs to run the company amount to $40,000 per year. The company has had a steady dollar break-even point value (BEP) for the last three years, and the president of the company would like to keep his BEP at about the same level of $117,647 for the coming year. To test several options, the president believes the selling price per item could range anywhere from $1.10 to $1.30; however, he feels certain that the variable cost per item should not fall below $.75 nor exceed $.83. To help crystalize the president's thinking, write a program displaying different combinations of selling prices ($1.10 to $1.30 in increments of one cent) and corresponding variable costs all yielding a constant BEP of $117,647, that is, generate a table with headings as follows:

Selling costs	Variable cost/unit	Break-even point	Decision
$1.10	·	117,647	·
1.11	·	117,647	·
·	·	·	·
·	·	·	·
·	·	·	·
1.30	·	117,647	·

If the variable cost per unit falls outside the interval of $.75–$.83, state in the decision column that the variable cost is either too low or too high. The formula to compute the BEP is given by

$$BEP = \frac{\text{total fixed costs}}{1 - \dfrac{\text{variable cost/unit}}{\text{selling price/unit}}}$$

30. G. White & Sons is a ladies' apparel store. The beginning inventory at cost is $100,000, and the ending inventory at cost is $200,000. Generate a table of net sales volume to secure a stock turn of N (N is to vary from 1 to 10 in steps of 1) if the company normally has a gross margin of 30 percent. (The stock turn is a measure of how rapidly an inventory is moving.) The formula to compute the stock turn N is

$$N = \frac{\text{cost of goods sold}}{\text{average inventory at cost}}$$

A gross margin of 30 percent means that the gross margin or gross profit is 30 percent of the net sales where the net sales = gross profit + cost of goods sold. The output should be as follows:

G. WHITE AND SONS

Beginning inventory = $100000
Ending inventory   = 200000
Average inventory   = 150000

Stock turn	Net sales	Gross sales
1	·	·
2	·	·
·	·	·
·	·	·
·	·	·
10	·	·

31. One method for calculating depreciation is to subtract a fixed percentage of the original value of the item each year. Thus a $100 item depreciated at 10

percent would be valued at $90 at the end of the first year, $80 at the end of the second and so forth. Another method for calculating depreciation is to subtract a fixed percentage of the present value of the item. A $100 item depreciated at 10 percent would be valued at $90 at the end of the first year, $90 − .1 x 90 = $81, at the end of the second year and so forth. Write a program to accept as input the original value (V), the depreciation rate (R) and a number of years (N) and produce a table showing the value of the items for the first, second, third, · · · Nth year using both depreciation methods.

32. You have been hired by E. Naddor, Inc., a world-famous firm specializing in inventory control problems, to write a computer program for one of Naddor's largest customers, The Shopping Basket. This firm would like to computerize part of its reordering system to cut down on the cost of replenishing inventories.

   Each Friday at the close of business, the ending inventory of each product is compared to the fixed reorder point for that product. If the ending inventory is equal to or below the reorder point for that product, The Shopping Basket orders enough of the item to bring the amount on hand up to a predetermined order level. Any order placed on Friday is delivered over the weekend so that the company can begin a new week of business with well-stocked shelves. It is possible that the ending inventory could be negative, indicating that demand exceeded supply during the week and some orders were not filled. Shopping Basket policy is to order enough to cover this backordered demand. See inventory summary on page 184.

   Your task is to write a program to read five data cards corresponding to the five different products to determine which products must be ordered and how much of each product to order. The program should also calculate the cost of ordering each item and the total cost for all products ordered. Design the program to make the correct reorder decision for an unknown number of items.

   To aid you in your task, you have been given some old records that illustrate how the reorder system works. You should use the sample data in the *Inventory Summary* to test your program shown below. Note that the only output required from your program is an *Order Report* similar to the one shown below.

   Some helpful formulas and decision rules:

   a. Order an item only if the ending inventory is less than or equal to the reorder point for that item.
   b. Amount to order = order level − ending inventory.
   c. Cost of ordering an item = amount ordered*unit price.

Inventory Summary (week ending October 1, 1979)

Item number Description	15202 Tuna fish	67180 Charcoal lighter fluid	51435 Mouth- wash	49415 Pizza mix	24361 Asparagus
Unit price (per case)	4.27	8.48	12.29	9.27	15.32
Order level (cases)	30	25	55	75	15
Reorder point (cases)	5	8	10	25	2
Ending inventory (cases)	9	5	7	−10	6

Description of Data Cards

Column	Data
1–5	Item number
31–34	Unit price (dollars and cents)
35–37	Order level (cases)
38–40	Reorder point (cases)
41–44	Ending Inventory

For example, the data card corresponding to the tuna fish would be:

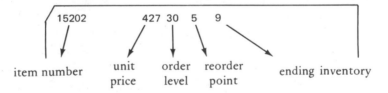

Your output should be similar to the following.

THE SHOPPING BASKET

ORDER REPORT

ITEM NUMBER	UNIT PRICE	ORDER LEVEL	REORDER POINT	ENDING INVENTORY	ORDER	COST
15202	4.27	30	5	9	0	0.00
67180	8.48	25	8	5	20	169.60
51435	12.29	55	10	7	48	589.92
49415	9.27	75	25	−10	85	787.95
24361	15.32	15	2	6	0	0.00
					TOTAL COST	$1547.47

5-6-3   Answers to Self Test

1. a. 7.   b. 6.   c. 8.   d. 6.   e. infinite.   f. I not defined.
   g. infinite.   h. 5.

2. a. End-of-file condition will occur. There are no values of LCC > 99.
   b. I = 5, G = 0.   c. I = 3.   d. I = 4, G = 0.

3. a, b, d

4. a. IF(I.EQ.9)GOTO6   b. IF(I.LT.9)GOTO2   c. IF(I.LT.10)GOTO5
   d. IF(I.EQ.10)GOTO6   e. IF(I.EQ.0)GOTO6   f. IF(I.GT.–4)GOTO2

5. a. Implicit mode specification uses the first character in a variable name to
      define the mode of the data; explicit mode specification uses one of the
      mode specification statements to specify the mode of a variable.
   b. INTEGER   BETA,GAMMA
      REAL   KOUNT,MODEM
   c. The DATA statement is used to specify the initial contents of a variable. It
      is not essential because replacement statements could be used in place of
      the DATA statement.
   d. The IMPLICIT statement allows the programmer to define his own rules for
      implicit mode definition. It is not essential since the explicit specification
      statements can be used.
   e. Trigger and last-card code methods.

6. a. I = 3, four cards read.   b. I = 1, one card read.
   c. I = 5, four cards read.   d. I = 1, six cards read.
   e. I = 1, one card read.   f. I = 6, six cards read.

7. a. 2.   b. 2.   c. 4.   d. 4.   e. 7.   f. 5.   g. 4.   h. 4.   i. 8.   j. 5.

8. a. F.   b. F.   c. T.   d. T.   e. F.   f. F.   g. T.
   h. T.   i. F(1 card).   j. T.

THE ACCUMULATION
PROCESS

6-1 Problem Example

Write a FORTRAN program to compute the sum of the first N integers, where N is an integer read from a data card. A program to solve this problem is shown in Figure 6-1. Note the FORTRAN DO statement used in the program in Figure 6-1 which is used to generate the numbers 1, 2, 3, 4 · · · N.

This chapter also discusses the *accumulation* process (statement 10 of the program in Figure 6-1), which is an extension of the counting concept covered in Chapter 5.

6-2 FORTRAN Statements

6-2-1 The DO Statement

The DO statement represents no new programming concepts; in fact, any FORTRAN program can be written without the DO statement. The purpose of the DO statement is strictly one of convenience to the programmer. It is used primarily for loop control. The usual procedure for loop control is to initialize a counter to a certain value, then increment that counter by a constant and finally compare

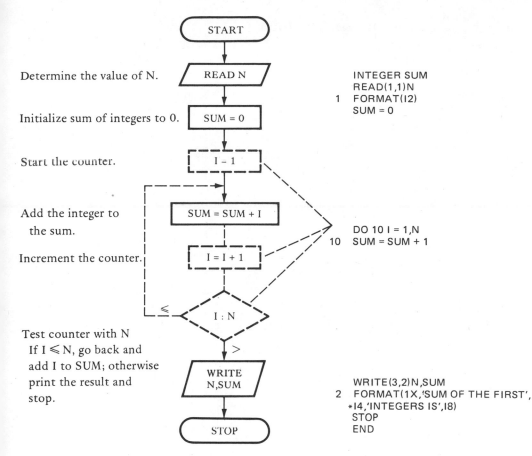

Determine the value of N.

```
INTEGER SUM
READ(1,1)N
1   FORMAT(I2)
SUM = 0
```

Initialize sum of integers to 0.

Start the counter.

Add the integer to
the sum.

Increment the counter.

```
DO 10 I = 1,N
10   SUM = SUM + 1
```

Test counter with N
If I ⩽ N, go back and
add I to SUM; otherwise
print the result and
stop.

```
WRITE(3,2)N,SUM
2   FORMAT(1X,'SUM OF THE FIRST',
   *I4,'INTEGERS IS',I8)
STOP
END
```

Figure 6-1   Sum of N integers.

the counter to a terminal value for loop exiting. With one DO statement, the user specifies the initial, the increment, the terminal value of the counter (index) and the range of the DO within which all statements are to be processed a specific number of times.

The general form of the DO statement is

DO statement-number index = initial, terminal [, increment]

where   *statement-number* is the number of the last statement in the body of the loop; sometimes called the *foot* of the loop;
index is an integer variable name which will assume different values not to exceed the terminal value;
initial is a positive integer constant or integer variable specifying the initial value of the index;
terminal is a positive integer constant or variable against which the index is tested to determine whether or not an exit should be taken from the loop. In some cases the final value of the index may equal this test value;

increment is an optional integer constant or integer variable specifying the increment to be added to the index after each pass through the body of the loop. If omitted, the value of the increment is assumed to be 1.

Following are some examples of valid and invalid DO statements:

Valid DO statements	*Invalid DO statements*	*Comments*
DO 10 I = 1,303	DO 3 X = I,3,4	Index must be integer.
DO 5 J = 4,1000,66	DO 4 I = 1,20,−1	Increment must be positive.
DO 4 KSUM = M1,M2,M3	DO I = 10,3,4	Statement number is missing.
DO 6 LL = NSTAR,MITY	DO 6 K = I,J,TER	Increment is real.
DO 8 K = 10,M,4	DO 8 L = 1.1,10,.1	Should be integer values.
	DO 9 K = I + 1, 10	I + 1 is an expression, not an integer.

The effect of the DO statement can be visualized by a flowchart as follows:

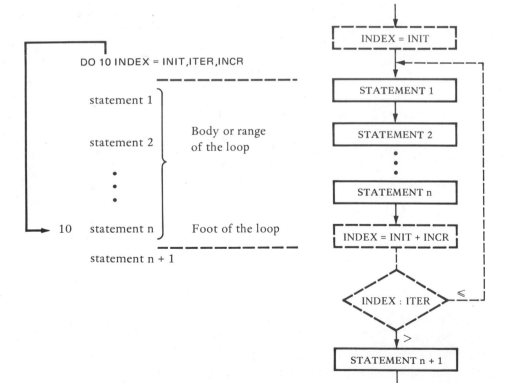

DO statement   *Flowchart representation*

It should be noted that the body of the loop will always be processed at least once.[1] Note also that the DO statement itself is not part of the range but merely identifies the statement following the DO as the first statement of the range. The statements within the body of the loop may be any type of executable statements (IF, GOTO, DO, Input/Output etc.). The foot of the loop may *not* be a STOP, an arithmetic IF, a GOTO, a computed GOTO or another DO statement or END. It may be a logical IF, however.

The statements in the range of the DO loop (statements 1, 2, 3, · · · n) are repeated once for each value of the index starting with the initial value up to the terminal value in steps of the increment specified. Each time the foot of the loop is processed, the variable 'INDEX' is incremented by the incremental value 'INCR' and tested. If INDEX is greater than the terminal value "ITER" the statement following the foot of the loop is processed (the loop has run through its complete cycle). Otherwise, control is transferred to the first statement of the loop (statement 1 in the above diagram). Another interpretation of the DO loop is: Process statement 1, statement 2, statement 3 · · · statement n as many times as the index takes on values ranging from the initial value up to but not beyond the terminal value in steps of the increment.

The DO statement is useful for processing a statement a specific number of times as in Example 1 where it is desired to read a record and write it out 303 times.

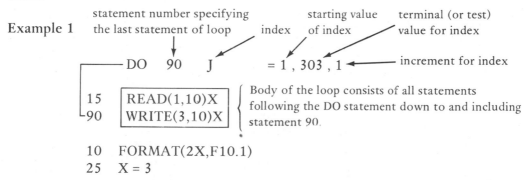

Example 1

All statements in the body of the loop (statements 15 and 90) will be processed 303 times, as J ranges from the starting value of 1 to the terminal value of 303 in steps of 1. Each time the statement at the foot of the loop is encountered the statement is executed and the loop index J is incremented by the increment value (1 in this case) and compared to the terminal value (303 in this case). If it is less than or equal to the terminal value, processing resumes at the beginning of the body of the loop (statement 15); otherwise, the statement following the foot statement is processed (statement 25).

Sometimes it may be convenient to use the index not just as a counting mechanism for loop control but also as a variable (number generator) within the body of the DO loop, as in Example 2.

---

[1] See exceptions in Section 6-3 for new FORTRAN standards.

Example 2

```
┌──DO 15 I = 3,100,2
│    ISQR = I*I
│    SQROOT = I**.5
└15   WRITE(3,1)I,ISQR,SQROOT
 1    FORMAT(2X,I3,I7,F6.2)
```

This code will generate a table of the square root and the square of the numbers 3, 5, 7 · · · 99.

It is often convenient to express the terminal value of a DO loop as a variable as in Example 3.

Example 3

```
     READ(1,1)N
┌── DO 15 K = 1,N
│   ┌─────────────┐
└15 │             │
    └─────────────┘
```

The increment part of the DO is omitted. The increment value is assumed to be 1.

The body of the loop will be repeated N times.

The initial, terminal and increment values may all be expressed with variables (see Example 4).

Example 4

```
     READ(1,1)N,M,INC
     DO 16 L = N,M,INC
    ┌─────────────┐
16  │             │
    └─────────────┘
```

See Section 6-3 for the number of times the body of the loop will be executed.

6-2-2   DO Dont's

A. The last statement of a DO loop must *not* be:

- an arithmetic IF statement.
- another DO statement.
- a STOP statement.
- a computed or unconditional GOTO.
- a nonexecutable statement.[2]

---

[2] Some compilers may accept a FORMAT statement at the foot of a loop.

Thus the following code would be invalid:

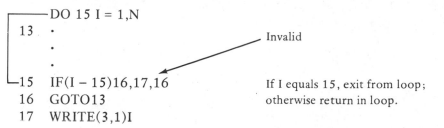

```
        ┌──────DO 15 I = 1,N
   13   │      ·                              Invalid
        │      ·
        │      ·
        └─15   IF(I – 15)16,17,16            If I equals 15, exit from loop;
          16   GOTO13                         otherwise return in loop.
          17   WRITE(3,1)I
```

B. The index, the beginning value, the terminal value and the incremental value may *not* be changed within the DO loop. If these are changed, unpredictable results will occur. For example:

```
   ┌──────DO 15 J = 1,10,3        Invalid
   │      J = T + 1 ◄─────────    The value of the index is changed.
   └─15   S = S*J
```

C. Don't count on the last value of the index to be equal to the test value specified in the DO statement, upon normal exit from a loop ("normal" meaning not transferring prematurely out of the DO loop before it has completed its full cycle). The value of I in that case is undefined. Consider the following, for example:

```
   ┌──────DO 5 I = 1,10            Undetermined.
   └─5    WRITE(1,6)I              The loop will print 1,2,3, ··· 10.
          WRITE(1,6)I ◄─────       I is not defined in this case, since the loop has completed
              ·                    its full cycle.
```

This does *not* mean that if an exit is made out of the loop before the loop has completed its full cycle then the value of the index is *undetermined*. The index will have whatever value it had at the time of the exit. Consider the following example:

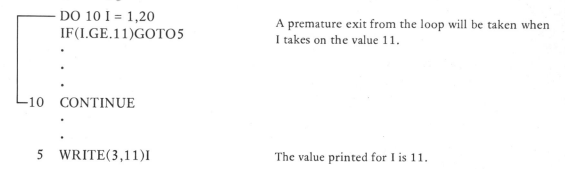

```
   ┌──────DO 10 I = 1,20           A premature exit from the loop will be taken when
   │      IF(I.GE.11)GOTO5         I takes on the value 11.
   │      ·
   │      ·
   │      ·
   └─10   CONTINUE
          ·
          ·
     5    WRITE(3,11)I             The value printed for I is 11.
```

6-2-3 The CONTINUE Statement

Many non-DO controlled loops often terminate with an IF or GOTO statement. Coding these loops with a DO statement becomes difficult, since the last statement of a DO loop may not be a transfer or decision statement. The dummy statement CONTINUE provides the programmer with a grammatical way out. Consider the problem of reading 100 grades and counting those greater than 90.

Incorrect code	*Correct code*

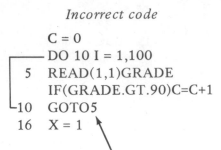

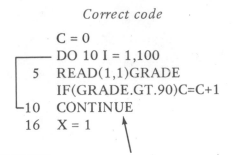

Incorrect code even though logically it makes sense. A GOTO is not allowed at the foot of the loop.

The CONTINUE statement causes loop processing to continue if I does not exceed 100 (i.e., go back to first statement of the body of the loop). If I exceeds 100, the CONTINUE causes the next sequential statement to be processed (statement 16).

The general form of a CONTINUE statement is

statement-number   CONTINUE

The CONTINUE statement used at the foot of the DO loop acts as a "visual bracket" to denote the end of a DO range. It helps delineate the range of the loop while not causing any operation to take place. Many programmers will always use a CONTINUE statement as the terminal statement of the body of a DO loop; for example:

```
       DO 10 I = 1,10
       READ(1,1)X
       WRITE(3,1)X
   10  CONTINUE
```

The following three examples are invalid but are shown as common mistakes made by most beginning programmers. Study them carefully and understand why they will not "work."

Example 1

```
       C = 0.
       DO 10 I = 1,100
   5   READ(5,1)GRADE
       IF(GRADE.LE.90)GOTO5
   10  C = C + 1.
```

In order to increment the index I of the DO loop, the foot of the loop must be processed. In this case, every time a grade $\leqslant 90$ is encountered the index I will not change. The foot of the loop is bypassed.

Example 2

```
      C = 0.
  1   DO 10 I = 1,100
      READ(5,1)GRADE
      IF(GRADE.LE.90)GOTO1
 10   C = C + 1.
```

Every time the grade is ≤ 90, transfer is made to statement 1, which means that the index I is reset to 1. This would cause an infinite loop.

Example 3

```
      C = 0.
      DO 10 I = 1,100
      READ(5,1)GRADE
      IF(GRADE.GT.90)GOTO5
 10   CONTINUE
  5   C = C + 1.
      GOTO10
```

There is no need to transfer out of the DO loop to "do" something and then "come back" into the DO loop. If a task is to be processed, then perform that task within the DO loop.

6-2-4 Transfer Into and Out of Loops

Case 1. It is not permissible to transfer from a statement outside of a loop to a statement within the body of a loop.

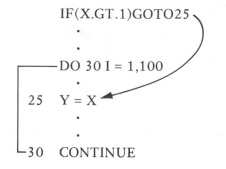

```
      IF(X.GT.1)GOTO25
          .
          .
      DO 30 I = 1,100
          .
 25   Y = X
          .
          .
 30   CONTINUE
```

Not permissible

This would not make sense, since the value of I would be unknown.

Case 2. Transfer can be made to a loop as long as the transfer target is the DO statement.

```
      IF(X.GT.1)GOTO10
          .
 10   DO 30 I = 1,100
          .
          .
          .
 30   CONTINUE
```

Permissible

In this case, I is properly initialized.

Case 3. Transfer can be made from one statement to another within the same loop.

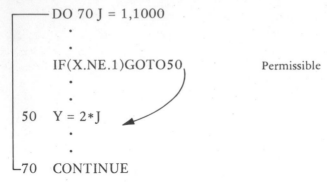

```
    ┌──── DO 70 J = 1,1000
    │        .
    │        .
    │        .
    │     IF(X.NE.1)GOTO50          Permissible
    │        .
    │        .
    │ 50   Y = 2*J
    │        .
    │        .
    └─70   CONTINUE
```

Case 4. Transfer can be made from a statement in the loop to the foot of the loop.

```
    ┌──── DO 100 K = 1,66
    │        .
    │        .
    │        .
    │     IF(X.NE.1)GOTO100          Permissible
    │        .
    │        .
    └─100   CONTINUE
```

Case 5. Transfer from a statement within a loop to a statement outside the loop is permissible.

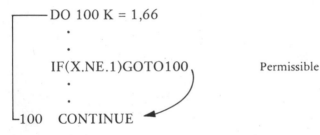

```
    ┌──── DO 10 JOE = 1,10
    │        .
    │        .
    │        .
    │     IF(Y.EQ.6.)GOTO70          Permissible
    │        .
    │        .
    └─10   CONTINUE
      70   DO 15 I = 1,JOE
```

The value assumed by JOE will be the value assumed by the index at the time the exit was taken from the loop. (JOE is undefined if body of loop is processed ten times.)

Case 6. A transfer from within a DO loop to the DO statement itself will cause a reinitialization of the index rather than a continuation of the loop process. The following code will result in an infinite loop:

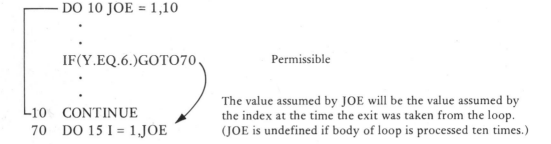

```
  4 ┌─DO 10 I = 1,10
    │  X = I**2 − 7*I + 12          Not permissible
    │  IF(X.NE.0.)GOTO4
    │  WRITE(3,1)I
 10 └─CONTINUE
```

I	X
1	6
1	6
1	6	X ≠ 0 : back to 4
.	.
.	.
.	.

6-2-5 Nested Loops

Many times, when writing programs, it is necessary to repeat a loop a certain number of times. This is an example of a loop within a loop, or more exactly, a complete loop is part of the body of another loop. In such cases, each pass in the outer loop causes the inner loop to run through its complete cycle. The code shown below illustrates the mechanism of the so-called *nested* loop.

Outer loop   DO 20 I = 1,3   Inner loop

Since I varies from
1 to 3, the inner loop
will be processed 3 times.

```
         DO 20 I = 1,3

         DO 10 J = 1,4
         WRITE(3,6)I,J
10       CONTINUE

20   CONTINUE
```

The inner loop will cause the WRITE statement to be processed 4 times. Since the outer loop is processed three times, the WRITE statement will be processed altogether 12 times.

The result produced by the above code is

I	J	
1	1	
1	2	First time through the inner loop
1	3	(outer loop index I = 1)
1	4	
2	1	
2	2	Second time through the inner loop
2	3	(outer loop index I = 2)
2	4	
3	1	
3	2	Third time through the inner loop
3	3	(outer loop index I = 3)
3	4	

In nested loops, the innermost loop will always cycle the fastest while the outer loop will cycle slowest.

Any number of DO statements may share the same foot or the same CONTINUE statement. The above program segment could be coded as follows:

```
         DO 20 I = 1,3
         DO 20 J = 1,4
20   WRITE(3,10)I,J
         .
         .
         .
```

The inner loop is repeated four times for each cycle of the three cycles of the outer loop.

When using nested loops, it is important to keep in mind that each nested loop must lie totally within the body of an outer loop. Consider, for example, the following graphical illustrations of valid and invalid loops:

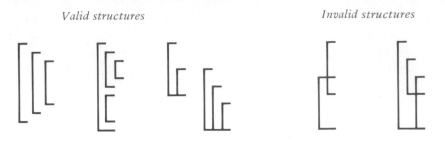

6-2-6   The Accumulation Process

We have already seen how counting in FORTRAN is made possible by repeated execution of such statements as I = I + 1 where I is initially set to a beginning value. Each time I = I + 1 is executed, the value 1 is added to the counter I, which then takes on successive values 1, 2, 3, 4 and so on, if I is set initially to zero. Counting can be thought of as "accumulating a count." The main difference between "counting" and "accumulating" is that instead of adding repetitively a constant (1 for example) to a counter, a variable is added[3] repetitively to an accumulator (a special variable used to keep track of running sums of partial sums, products, etc.). See Figure 6-2.

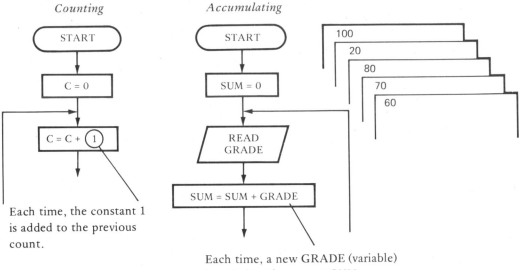

Figure 6-2   Comparison between counting and accumulating.

---

[3]Multiplication and other arithmetic operations can also be part of the accumulation process.

A complete program will help clarify the accumulation process. Five test grades are punched on cards, one grade per card. The program shown in Figure 6-3 computes and prints out the average of the five grades.

SUM = 0	Initialize SUM to 0. SUM is used as an accumulator to accumulate all grades.
DO 25 I = 1,5	Process statements 15 through 25 five times.
15 READ(1,1)GRADE	Read a GRADE.
	The new SUM is equal to the old SUM plus the GRADE just read.
SUM = SUM + GRADE	
1 FORMAT(F3.0)	The first time around the loop SUM + GRADE = 0 + 60 = 60, hence new SUM = 60.
	The second time around SUM + GRADE = 60 + 70 = 130, hence the new SUM = 130. Each time through the loop, we are adding the grade just read to form a running or partial sum of grades. When five grades have been read, the sum of five grades will have been computed.
25 CONTINUE	Go back to statement 15 until the loop has been
AV = SUM/5.	processed five times. Now that all the grades have been
WRITE(3,2)AV	read, i.e., the loop has gone through its full cycle, we
STOP	can compute the average and print it out.
2 FORMAT(2X,'AVERAGE=',F5.1)	
END	

Figure 6-3   Average of five grades.

Note the importance of setting SUM initially to 0 outside of the loop, and note how the partial sums of grades are formed each time a GRADE is read, using the statement SUM = SUM + GRADE. The statement Y = SUM + GRADE would *not* accumulate a sum.

The accumulation process in the program of Figure 6-3 can be better understood or visualized if we tabulate the values of SUM and I given sample grades as follows:

	Sequence of partial sums	Counter	Grades read
	SUM	I	GRADE
100.	0̸	1̸	6̸0̸
20.	6̸0̸ (0 + 60)	2̸	7̸0̸
80.	1̸3̸0̸ (60 + 70)	3̸	8̸0̸
70.	2̸1̸0̸ (130 + 80)	4̸	2̸0̸
60.	2̸3̸0̸ (210 + 20)	5	100
Input data	330 (230 + 100)		

$6\text{-}3$ You Might Want To Know

1. What happens if the initial value of the index exceeds the terminal value in a DO statement?

Answer: This depends on the version of FORTRAN used. In most present compilers, it results in the execution of all the statements in the loop once. The 1976 standards for ANSI[4] FORTRAN specify that the index is to be tested prior to execution of any statements in the body of the loop; control is passed to the statement following the foot of the loop.

2. Given the initial value (INIT), the increment (INC) and the terminal value (ITER) for a DO statement, how many times will the following loop be executed?

$$\text{DO 10 I INIT,ITER,INC}$$

Answer: The number of times the loop is executed is given by the formula:

$$NT = \frac{ITER - INIT}{INC} + 1$$

where only the integer result of the division is kept.

Example

$$\text{DO 10 K} = 3,10,2$$

The number of times through the loop is

$$NT = \frac{10 - 3}{2} + 1 = \frac{7}{2} + 1 = 3 + 1 = 4$$

The values assumed by K will be 3,5,7,9.

3. Can the CONTINUE statement appear anywhere other than at the foot of a DO loop?

Answer: Yes, if it is not used at the foot of a DO loop, the CONTINUE statement passes control to the next statement in the program.

6-4 Programming Examples

6-4-1 Transfer Inside and Outside a Loop

A deck of cards contains an unknown number of cards, each containing a grade (a maximum of 100 cards including trip record). Passing grades are those grades above 73. Print each passing grade and compute the percentage of passing grades. A negative grade signifies end of data. A program to solve this problem is shown in Figure 6-4. Note how the DO index I is used to keep track of the number of grades read. In computing the percentage note the division by $I - 1$ since the last

---

[4]ANSI is short for American National Standards Institute, which attempts to establish standards for many commercially available products, among them programming languages.

```
        KOUNT = 0                        Initialize sum of grades above 73 to zero.
        DO 10 I = 1,100                  Process at most 100 cards.
        READ(1,1)GRADE                   Read a grade.
        IF(GRADE.LT.0.)GOTO15            Is this the end of the data?
        IF(GRADE.LE.73.)GOTO10           If grade ⩽ 73, read more cards.
        WRITE(3,3)GRADE                  Otherwise, write out passing grade
        KOUNT = KOUNT + 1                and count it.
   10   CONTINUE

   15   PERCEN = 1.*KOUNT/(I – 1)*100    Compute percentage of passing grades.
        WRITE(3,1)PERCEN,KOUNT           Write results.
    1   FORMAT(1X,F5.1,2X,I3)
        STOP
    3   FORMAT(2X,F6.1)
        END
```

Figure 6-4   Average of passing grades.

grade read is a trip record, not a grade to be averaged out. Exit from the loop is made by transfer and not through the CONTINUE statement, hence value of I is well defined. Also note that in order to avoid truncation in the calculation of the percentage, KOUNT is multiplied by 1. to force a real division.

If no trip record or last-card code were used in the program of Figure 6-4 and there happened to be fewer than 100 cards, an end-of-file error condition would occur at the READ statement, since the DO loop would instruct the computer to read 100 cards.

6-4-2   Calculation of N!

N! is read as N factorial. The factorial function N!, where N is a positive integer, represents the product of the first N positive integers starting with one. For instance $15! = 1 \cdot 2 \cdot 3 \cdot 4 \cdots 14 \cdot 15$. The program in Figure 6-5 computes N! where N is a number read from a data card. Note that in this case the numbers $1,2,3 \cdots$, N are not read from data cards but are generated internally by the DO statement $I = I + 1$. Every time a new value is generated for I, it is immediately multiplied to the current product in PROD.

```
    INTEGER PROD
    PROD = 1
    READ(1,5)N
 5  FORMAT(I2)
    DO 2 I = 1,N
    PROD = PROD*I
 2  CONTINUE
    WRITE(3,4)N,PROD
 4  FORMAT(1X,'FACTORIAL',I3,'IS',I16)
    STOP
    END
```

Set PROD initially to 1. This variable is used as the accumulator for the product. It should not be set to 0 since this would cause the product to remain 0.

Read a value for N and use the DO index I to generate the values $1,2,3, \cdots$ N while at the same time forming the product of these numbers.

The factorial function produces rapidly growing results in terms of magnitudes. Most systems cannot express 17! as an integer result.

Figure 6-5   Calculation of N factorial.

6-4-3 Multiplication Tables

The program in Figure 6-6 uses nested DO loops to generate vertically the five partial multiplication tables (6 through 10) up to 10.

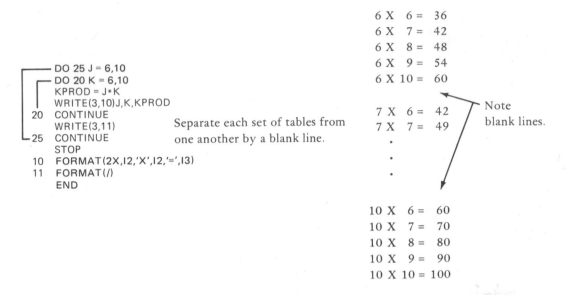

Figure 6-6 shows the following:

```
        DO 25 J = 6,10
        DO 20 K = 6,10
        KPROD = J*K
        WRITE(3,10)J,K,KPROD
20      CONTINUE
        WRITE(3,11)
25      CONTINUE
        STOP
10      FORMAT(2X,I2,'X',I2,'=',I3)
11      FORMAT(/)
        END
```

```
6 X  6 =  36
6 X  7 =  42
6 X  8 =  48
6 X  9 =  54
6 X 10 =  60

7 X  6 =  42     Note
7 X  7 =  49     blank lines.
     .
     .
     .

10 X  6 =  60
10 X  7 =  70
10 X  8 =  80
10 X  9 =  90
10 X 10 = 100
```

Separate each set of tables from one another by a blank line.

Figure 6-6 Multiplication tables.

6-4-4 Standard Deviation

The general formula to compute the standard deviation for n grades x_1, x_2, x_3, $\cdots$, x_n is given by

$$SD = \sqrt{\frac{n(x_1^2 + x_2^2 + x_3^2 + \cdots + x_n^2) - (x_1 + x_2 + x_3 + \cdots + x_n)^2}{n(n-1)}}$$

Write a program to read 30 grades from data cards (one grade per card) and compute the average and the standard deviation. In this particular case, n is 30. To compute the standard deviation, it is necessary to

1. Accumulate the sum of the grades $(x_1 + x_2 + \cdots + x_{30})$, and call it S.

2. Accumulate the sum of the square of each grade $(x_1^2 + x_2^2 + \cdots + x_{30}^2)$ and call this sum Q.

The program shown in Figure 6-7 could be used.

```
       DATA N,Q,S/30,0.,0/              Set counter of grades to 0, and initialize both
                                        accumulators S and Q to 0.
       DO 35 K = 1,N                    Start the loop.
       READ(1,1)GRADE
       S = S + GRADE                    Accumulate the sum of the grades.
       Q = Q + GRADE*GRADE              Accumulate the sum of the square of each grade.
   35  CONTINUE
       D = ((N*Q – S*S)/(N*(N – 1.)))**.5    Compute the standard deviation.
       AV = S/N
       WRITE(3,2)D,AV
       STOP
    2  FORMAT(T10,'STANDARD DEVIATION=',F5.2,//T10,'AVERAGE=',F5.2)
    1  FORMAT(F5.1)
       END
```

Figure 6-7   Calculation of standard deviation.

6-5 Probing Deeper

6-5-1 Flowchart Symbol for the DO Statement

There exists a variety of flowchart symbols to represent the DO statement. The symbol presented in this section is conceptually in accordance with the new standards proposed for ANSI FORTRAN. The main difference between the existing standards in terms of the DO loop processing and the proposed standards is that the DO index is set to the initial value and tested immediately with the terminal value. If the initial value is greater than the terminal value the body of the loop is bypassed and processing resumes with the statement following the foot of the loop. Consider, for example, the following statement:

$$DO\ 80\ J = 3,10,2$$

The corresponding flowchart symbol is depicted in Figure 6-8.

The sequence of activities in the DO flowchart symbol can be visualized as follows:

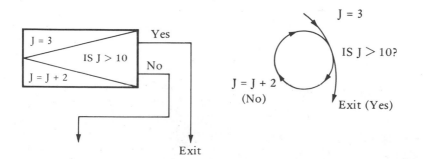

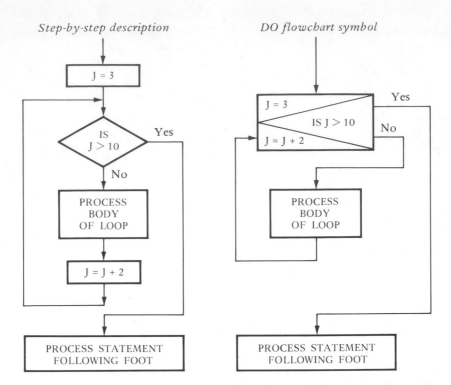

Figure 6-8 The DO flowchart symbol.

Consider the following problem: The principal P left in a savings account for T years at interest rate R compounded yearly, yields a total amount A given by the formula $A = P(1 + R)^T$. Write a program to compute a total amount A given a principal of \$1,000 at different interest rates varying from 5 to 8 percent in steps of 1 percent for a time period of 1 to 3 years. Document your program with an appropriate flowchart (see Figure 6-9).

6-5-2 Relationship Between the List of Variables and List of Format Codes

If there are more data format codes in a FORMAT statement than there are variables in the corresponding list of variables in the READ/WRITE statement, the unused data format codes are ignored.

Example 1

```
    READ(1,5)IX,IY
        .
        .
        .
  5 FORMAT(I3,I2,I4,I5)
```

	IX			IY		
1	2	3	4	5	6	7

IX = 123
IY = 45

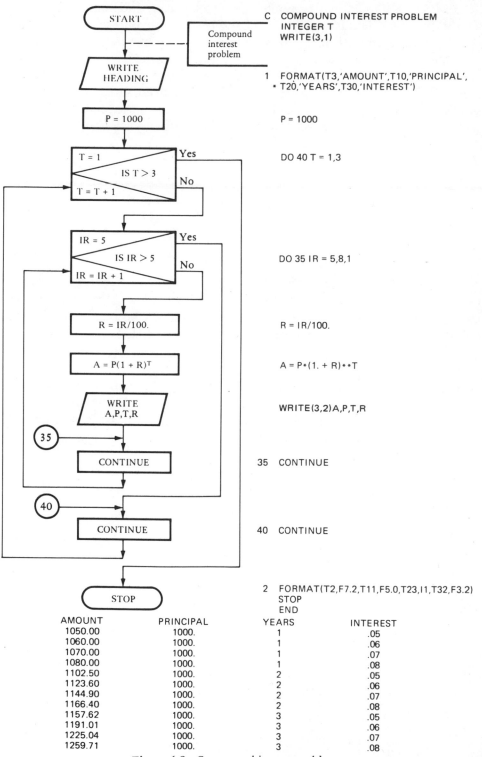

```
C   COMPOUND INTEREST PROBLEM
    INTEGER T
    WRITE(3,1)

1   FORMAT(T3,'AMOUNT',T10,'PRINCIPAL',
  * T20,'YEARS',T30,'INTEREST')

    P = 1000

    DO 40 T = 1,3

    DO 35 IR = 5,8,1

    R = IR/100.

    A = P*(1. + R)**T

    WRITE(3,2)A,P,T,R

35  CONTINUE

40  CONTINUE

2   FORMAT(T2,F7.2,T11,F5.0,T23,I1,T32,F3.2)
    STOP
    END
```

AMOUNT	PRINCIPAL	YEARS	INTEREST
1050.00	1000.	1	.05
1060.00	1000.	1	.06
1070.00	1000.	1	.07
1080.00	1000.	1	.08
1102.50	1000.	2	.05
1123.60	1000.	2	.06
1144.90	1000.	2	.07
1166.40	1000.	2	.08
1157.62	1000.	3	.05
1191.01	1000.	3	.06
1225.04	1000.	3	.07
1259.71	1000.	3	.08

Figure 6-9 Compound interest table.

In Example 1, only two numbers are to be read, and these will be described by the first two data format codes I3 and I2. The remaining format codes (I4 and I5) are not processed, since only two numbers are to be read.

If on the other hand, there are more variables in the list of variables than there are data format codes, the sequence of format codes is reused (start at the beginning of the FORMAT) until all variables have been satisfied. Each FORMAT statement describes one record; hence any reuse of the sequence of format codes will cause a new input record to be selected or output record to be produced.

Example 2

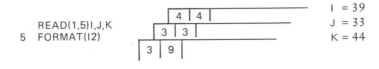

```
        READ(1,5)I,J,K
     5  FORMAT(I2)
```

I = 39
J = 33
K = 44

In Example 2, the READ list specifies that three numbers are to be read. Since the FORMAT has only one data format code, only one number will be read per card. Hence to satisfy the READ list three cards will be read. The three integers will be read from the first two card columns of the three data cards.

The list of variables in the READ statement tells the computer how many variables it *must* read; the number of data format codes (I,F etc.) in the FORMAT specifies how many items are to be read per record (card). For example, if there are three data format codes in the FORMAT and the READ list specifies eight variables, three cards will be read with only two items read on the third card, assuming the control code / is not used. Consider the following examples:

Number of variables in the READ list	Number of data format codes in FORMAT	Number of cards read	Number of items read from last card
6	8	1	6
6	7	1	6
6	6	1	6
6	5	2	1
6	4	2	2
6	3	2	3
6	2	3	2
6	1	6	1

Example 3

```
        A = 3.2
        B = -6.0
        C = 4.9
        D = 0.
        WRITE(3,10)A,B,C,D
    10  FORMAT(2X,2F6.1)
```

```
  3 . 2      - 6 . 0
  4 . 9        0 . 0
```

In Example 3, the WRITE list contains four variables; however, using FOR-MAT statement 10, only two items are to be placed on one line of output. The sequence of format codes is re-used to complete the output of the four variables. Each re-use of the format codes results in a separate output line.

6-5-3 Random Numbers

Random numbers are introduced in this section as some exercises starting with this chapter will require the use of random numbers to simulate certain real-life events. Such exercises can be most interesting and fun, since in many instances the outcome cannot be predicted (unless user has knowledge of statistics). Random numbers are often used in writing programs which must simulate events which are probabilistic in nature. For example, consider the throwing of a die. The outcome of the event can be 1, 2, 3, 4, 5 or 6; each outcome is equally likely to occur. A program can use random numbers in the range 1 to 6 to simulate the outcome of a single throw of a die.

There is no standard method for generating random numbers from a FOR-TRAN program. However, most computer installations have random number routines stored in their libraries that can be accessed by the user. Typically there is a function (which might be called RANDOM, or RAND) which returns a random number in some range. A function is a special program which accepts one or more values as arguments and returns a single value to the calling program.[5] For example, Y = RANDOM(I) might result in a random value for Y in the range 0 to 1, that is, $0 < Y < 1$, while I might return a random integer value. Thus X = RAND(I) might return a value for X such that $0 < X < 1$. Thus to simulate the throwing of a die we might use

$$IDIE = RAND(I)*6. + 1.$$

The value returned by RAND(I)*6. will be in the range of 0. to 6. (not including 0. or 6.). Adding 1 will yield a value in the range 1. to 6.9999. Placing this real value in the integer location IDIE will result in the truncation of all fractional digits so that the value of IDIE will be 1, 2, 3, 4, 5 or 6.

The reader must determine the specifics of random number generation for his installation before attempting any programming exercises using random number generation.

Example

Write a program to simulate the throwing of a die 1,000 times and determine the frequency with which each of the results appears. In theory, if the experiment

---

[5]See Chapter 10 for a complete discussion of functions. The random number generator program presented in Section 10-5-1 can be used here.

is repeated a sufficiently large number of times, each result should occur an equal number of times; but since the events are random in nature, we can only expect that the frequencies will be nearly equal. A program to solve this problem is shown in Figure 6-10.

```
    DATA K1,K2,K3,K4,K5,K6/6*0/
    DO 10 I = 1,100
    IDIE = RANDOM(L)*6+1        Determine the throw.
    GOTO(1,2,3,4,5,6),IDIE      Increment appropriate counter.
 1  K1 = K1 + 1
    GOTO10
 2  K2 = K2 + 1
    GOTO10
 3  K3 = K3 + 1
    GOTO10
 4  K4 = K4 + 1
    GOTO10
 5  K5 = K5 + 1
    GOTO10
 6  K6 = K6 + 1
10  CONTINUE
    WRITE(3,11)K1,K2,K3,K4,K5,K6
11  FORMAT(3X,6I5)
    STOP
    END
```

Figure 6-10   Program using random number generator.

6-6   Exercises

6-6-1 Self Test

1. Which of the following are valid DO loops? State the reason if loop is invalid.

a.	DO 10 I = 1,5	b.	DO 20 IJ = 2,6.5
	.		.
	.		.
	10 CONTINUE		20 CONTINUE

c.	DO 30 K = 1,10	d.	DO 15 I = I,6
	DO 40 K = 1,40		.
	.		.
	.		15 CONTINUE
	40 CONTINUE		
	30 CONTINUE		

e.
```
        DO 50 I – 1 = 2,6
              .
              .
   50   CONTINUE
```

f.
```
        DO 60 I = 1,5
        DO 70 J = 1,10,–1
              .
              .
   70   CONTINUE
   60   CONTINUE
```

g.
```
        DO 60 I = 1,5
        DO 70 J = 1,10
              .
              .
   60   CONTINUE
              .
              .
   70   X = 1
```

h.
```
        DO 80 A = 1,N
              .
              .
   80   CONTINUE
```

i.
```
        DO 90 L = 1,5
        DO 91 K = 2,8
        S = S+G
   90   CONTINUE
```

j.
```
        DO 21 M = 10,6,1
              .
              .
        CONTINUE
   21   CONTINUE
```

k.
```
        DO 5 K = 1,5
              .
              .
    5   IF(L – 80)3,3,2
```

l.
```
        DO 20 L = 8,1
        DO 30 K = 1,3
        L = L + 1
   30   CONTINUE
   20   CONTINUE
```

m.
```
        DO 5 I = 1,3
              .
              .
        IF(Q.EQ.6)GOTO5
        DO 5 K = 1,10
        SUM = SUM + J
    5   CONTINUE
```

n.
```
        DO 6 I = 1,10
        J = I*I + 1
    6   CONTINUE
```

o.
```
        DO 8 K = 1,6
        READ(1,5)K1,K
        SUM 1 = SUM 1 + K1
    8   SUM 2 = SUM 2 + K
```

p.
```
        DO 10 I = 1,17
   15   X = X + SUM
        IF(X.GT.10)GOTO17
   10   CONTINUE
   17   IF(SUM.NE.J)GOTO15
```

q.   DO 8 K = 1,110,5
                .
                .
      8   SUM = SUM + X
            DO 9 K = 1,15
                .
                .
      9   CONTINUE

r.   DO 9 J = 40,60
            DO 9 K = 1,3
                .
                .
      9   CONTINUE

s.   DO 85 I = 1,4
                .
                .
            CONTINUE
    85   DO 90 J = 3,6,1
                .
                .
    90   X = 10.3

2. What output will be produced by each of the following coding segments?

a.   DO 5 I = 1,10,2
      5   WRITE(3,1)I
      1   FORMAT(2X,I3)

b.   DO 7 J = 6,18,3
      2   FORMAT(2X,I3)
      7   WRITE(3,2)J

c.   DO 8 K = 4,1
      8   WRITE(3,3)K
      3   FORMAT(2X,I3)

3. Assuming all loops go through their complete cycle how many times will statement 3 be processed?

a.   DO 20 I = 1,3
            DO 20 J = 1,4
            DO 20 K = 1,10
      3   X = 1
    20   CONTINUE

b.   DO 33 I = 2,20,3
            DO 33 J = 3,17,5
                .
                .
      3   X = 1
    33   CONTINUE

c.   DO 10 IO = 2,8,2
            DO 10 IM = IO,2,1
            DO 10 II = 1,4,2
      3   X = 1
    10   CONTINUE

4. Determine whether the following code will result in a compilation or execution-time error.

```
15    DO 10 I = 1,5
      WRITE(3,1)I
      IF(I.GT.5)GOTO15
10    CONTINUE
```

5. Will the following code compute the average of ten grades?

a.
```
      SUM = 0
      DO 10 I = 1,10
      READ(1,1)GRADE
10    SUM = SUM + GRADE
      AVERAG = SUM/I
 1    FORMAT(F5.1)
```

b.
```
      SUM = 0
      DO 15 I = 1,10
      READ(1,1)GRADE
      SUM = SUM + GRADE
15    AVE = SUM/I
      WRITE(3,6)AVE
```

6. What will the final value of J be?

```
      J = 0
      DO 4 I = 1,10
 4    J = J + .1
```

7. How many cards will be processed by the following READ instructions?

a. READ(1,5)A,B,C with FORMATS
$$\begin{cases} 5 & \text{FORMAT(F5.1,F5.1,F5.1)} \\ 5 & \text{FORMAT(F5.1,F5.1)} \\ 5 & \text{FORMAT(4F5.1)} \end{cases}$$

b. READ(1,6)I,J,K,L,M,N with FORMATS
$$\begin{cases} 6 & \text{FORMAT(I1,I2,I2)} \\ 6 & \text{FORMAT(I1,I2,I3,I4)} \end{cases}$$

c. READ(1,7)A,I,D with FORMATS
$$\begin{cases} 7 & \text{FORMAT(F5.1,I3,F4.1)} \\ 7 & \text{FORMAT(F5.1/I2)} \\ 7 & \text{FORMAT(F5.1)} \end{cases}$$

8. Which of the following statements are true? If false, state the reason.

a. DO 10 IX2 = N, N + 1 is a valid statement.

b. In some special cases, the index of a DO loop may be a floating point variable.

c. If the initial value of the index of a DO loop is not specified, it is assumed to be 1.

d. The CONTINUE statement may only be used as the last statement in the range of a DO loop.

e. New ANSI FORTRAN standards state that the body of a loop will always be processed at least once.

f. A nonexecutable statement in the body of a DO loop may be processed more than once at execution time.

g. The value of the index of a DO loop having completed its full cycle becomes undefined.

h. A DO loop should always be entered at the DO statement.

i. Accumulating and counting are synonymous terms.

j. One comment card in the range of a DO loop will cause a listing of at least one comment and probably more, depending on the number of times the body of the loop is executed.

6-6-2 Programming Problems

1. Write a program to compute $3 + 5 + 7 + 9 + \cdots + 225 + 227$. Do not read cards.

2. Write a program to compute $1 - 2 + 3 - 4 + 5 \cdots - 100$. Do not read cards.

3. Write a program to read a value for N and compute the sum of the squares of the first N even integers. For example if $N = 4$, the sum is $2^2 + 4^2 + 6^2 + 8^2$.

4. Write a program to compute $1 + (1 \cdot 2) + 1 \cdot 2 \cdot 3) + (1 \cdot 2 \cdot 3 \cdot 4) + \cdots + (1 \cdot 2 \cdot 3 \cdot 4 \cdot \ldots \cdot 11)$

5. Write a program to read a value for N and compute $1 \cdot N + 2 \cdot N + 3 \cdot N + \cdots + 40 \cdot N$. For example, if $N = 3$, compute $1 \cdot 3 + 2 \cdot 3 + 3 \cdot 3 + \cdots + 40 \cdot 3$.

6. A data deck contains positive and negative numbers varying from -100 to 100. Using the last-card code method, write a program (using the DO statement) to compute the sum of the positive numbers and the sum of negative values. Print both sums. (Maximum number of cards is 100.)

7. Grades are recorded on cards, two grades per card. The first negative number indicates the end of the data deck. Write a program to determine the largest and smallest grade, and the average of the grades. Make use of the DO loop. (Maximum number of cards is 100.)

8. Mr. X. is hired for 30 days' work. The first day he earns $.01; the second day, $.02; the third day, $.04; in general double the previous day. Print out a table showing the day and the amount earned for each of the 30 days. Don't ask for the name of the company for which Mr. X. works. The last line of the output should read

TOTAL WAGES ARE $10737418.23 FOR 30 DAYS WORK

9. You work in a diner. Every time a meal is sold, a card is punched with the cost of the order and then a 1, 2 or 3. A 1 means breakfast meal, a 2 means lunch and a 3 means dinner. Write a program to compute:

   a. The total sales.

   b. The average cost of a breakfast meal.

   c. The minimum cost of a dinner meal.

10. A file containing numbers thought to be in ascending sequence is contained on cards (one number per card). Write a program to perform a sequence check, i.e., make sure that no numbers are out of order. If one is out of sequence, print it and print its position in the list (was it the fourth, seventh etc.). Stop at the first out of sequence number.

    Example

3,9,15,14,17	14 is out of sequence.
10,1,4,5,6	1 is out of sequence.

11. Same problem as Exercise 10, except that all numbers out of sequence are to be printed.

    Example

3,9,15,14,17,20,13,16,23	14,13,16 are out of sequence.
10,1,2,3,6,9,10,11	1,2,3,6,9 are out of sequence.

12. Using a DO loop, write a program to determine whether a number N read from card is prime. A prime number is any number which can only be divided by itself and 1.

13. Write a program to compute the following sequences of sums:

    $$S_1 = 1$$
    $$S_2 = 1 + \frac{1}{2}$$
    $$S_3 = 1 + \frac{1}{2} + \frac{1}{3}$$
    $$S_4 = 1 + \frac{1}{2} + \frac{1}{3} + \frac{1}{4}$$
    $$\cdot$$
    $$\cdot$$
    $$\cdot$$

    How many different sums would you have to compute before the sum exceeds 3.5?

14. A data file consists of records each containing the following information about items produced at a manufacturing plant: department number, item number, quantity and cost per item. Assume the data has been sorted into order by ascending department number. Write a report to summarize the inventory in the following manner:

DEPARTMENT	ITEM NO.	QUANTITY	COST/ITEM	VALUE	TOTALS
15	376	4	3.20	12.80	
15	476	2	7.00	14.00	
					26.80
16	276	8	2.00	16.00	
					16.00
19	376	100	.03	3.00	
19	476	20	4.00	80.00	
19	576	4	16.00	64.00	
					147.00
TOTAL					189.80

(Use your own data to test your program.)

15. The first card in a data deck contains the current date. Each succeeding card contains (among other items) the date of the last time an item was sold, the number of items on hand, the cost per item and the regular selling price. A store plans a sale to try to sell slow-moving items. The purpose of the program is to produce a report showing recommended sale price as follows:

> If item has not been sold in last 30 days, discount is 10 percent.
> If item has not been sold in last 60 days, discount is 20 percent.
> If item has not been sold in last 90 days, discount is 40 percent.

However, any item which has sold in last 30 days is not to be placed on sale. If there is only one (1) of an item left in stock, it is not to be placed on sale no matter when the last date of sale was. The amount of discount allowed is also subject to the following rule: Sale prices may not be lower than cost.

The report should have page headings at the top of each page of output; assume any reasonable number of lines as the page length.

16. You would like to buy a new car on credit. You make monthly payments at the beginning of the month. The interest is also calculated monthly and added to the balance each month. Compute and print a formatted table containing (1) the number of months the loan has been in effect, (2) the remaining balance after adding the interest and subtracting the payment and (3) the total amount paid to your loan company so far. The interest is calculated on the balance *before* the payment is subtracted. Be sure that you don't overpay on the last payment.

Input: Read values of cost, interest and payment from data cards.

Cost: the total cost for the car at purchase time.

Interest: the monthly interest that you are paying on the balance.

Payment: the *maximum* that you are able to pay towards the balance every month.

Output: Use the description below to format your output beginning on a new page.

THE BALANCE OF A CAR LOAN

COST OF CAR = $xxxxx.xx   INTEREST = xx.xx%   PAYMENT = $xxx.xx

MONTH	BALANCE	TOTAL
xx	xxxxx.xx	xxxxx.xx
xx	xxxxx.xx	xxxxx.xx
xx	xxxxx.xx	xxxxx.xx
.	.	.
.	.	.

Note 1: If the value stored for interest is, for example, .1060, you are to print it out *on this line* as 10.60.

Note 2: A schedule such as that described above is called an *amortization schedule.*

17. The Meals on Wheels Company operates a fleet of vans used for the delivery of cold foods at various local plants and construction sites. The management is thinking of purchasing a specially built $18,000 van equipped to deliver hot foods. This new addition to the fleet is expected to generate after-tax earnings E_1, E_2, $\cdots$, E_6 (as displayed below) over the next six years, at which time the van's resale value will be zero. Projected repair and maintenance costs C_0, C_1, C_2, $\cdots$, C_6 over the six years are shown below.

Projected earnings   *Projected costs*

		C_0	$18,000 (purchase cost of the van)
E_1	$2,500	C_1	610
E_2	2,500	C_2	745
E_3	3,000	C_3	820
E_4	4,500	C_4	900
E_5	6,000	C_5	950
E_6	6,000	C_6	1,000

a. Write a program to determine whether or not the company should acquire the van. The decision depends on the benefit cost ratio (*BCR*) (grossly speaking, earnings/expenditures) given by the formula

$$BCR = \frac{E_1(1 + i)^1 + E_2(1 + i)^2 + \cdots + E_6(1 + i)^6}{C_0 + C_1(1 + i)^1 + C_2(1 + i)^2 + \cdots + C_6(1 + i)^6}$$

where i is the rate of investment of earnings by the company (6 percent in this problem). If $BCR < 1$, then the company should not accquire the van. Use the accumulation process to compute the *BCR*. The first data card contains E_1 and C_1, the second data card contains E_2 and C_2 etc.

b. When shown the projected maintenance costs for the next six years, the repair and maintenance shop foreman argues that these cost figures are unrealistic and proposes instead the following costs starting with the first year: 1,000, 1,500, 2,000, 2,000, 2,100, 2,400. Using these figures, determine whether the company should purchase the van.

c. Having found out that the *BCR* is less than 1 with the projected maintenance costs shown in part b the management decides to recompute the *BCR* with the same figures as in part b except for a resale value of the van set at $1,000.00 (note that the sale of the van represents an earning).

The following Exercises 18–25 require the use of random numbers and are probably the most "fun" problems. Determine what random function your system library has; if it has none, use the function described in Section 10-5-1. Let us assume that your random function returns a real number between 0 and 1 and that the name of the function is RANDOM; that is, when you write Y = RANDOM(1.),Y will contain any number between 0. and 1. To see how to make use of such a function, suppose that we are able to simulate the toss of a coin. We might agree that 1 would represent heads while 2 would represent tails. To generate the random numbers 1 and 2, we would use the statement:

K = 2*RANDOM(1.) + I   and K would either have the value 1 or 2.

If we wrote K = 6*RANDOM(I.) + 1, then K would take on one of the values 1, 2, 3, 4, 5 or 6. To determine the probable outcome of a particular event, a program would just need to simulate that event a great number of times and count the different outcomes. The greater the number of simulations, the more accurate the projection of the frequency of the different outcomes. For example, to determine the probability of Johnnie tossing a five with an "honest" die, we would simulate 1,000 tosses and count the number of times a five came out; 1,000 tosses would probably result in an answer close to 167 representing 1/6 of the time.

18. Write a program to generate 100 random numbers in the range 0–10. Determine the average of the numbers. What would you expect the result to be?

19. Marc and Laura each toss a die. What is the probability that each toss the same number?

20. Sue Ellen and Anabelle each toss a pair of dice. What is the chance that both toss out a 2 (i.e., each tosses two ones)? a 3? a 4? a 12?

21. Charlie tosses a pair of dice. What number (sum of the face values of both dice) is more likely to be thrown; i.e., a two is face value of one and one, a 7 is a combination of 4, 3; 5, 2; 6, 1 etc.

22. On a multiple-choice test consisting of ten questions, each question has five answers to choose from—A, B, C, D or F. Margie doesn't know the answer to

questions 3 and 7. What is the probability that she guesses both 3 and 7 correctly? that she guesses exactly one of them? that she guesses none of them?

23. a. A dog is lost in a tunnel at node 0 (see diagram below). It can move one node at a time in either direction forwards and backwards with equal probability. When the dog hits node B_2; however, a force of nature always propels him directly to node B_4. The dog escapes from the tunnel when he either hits B_5 or F_4. Does the dog have a better chance to exit forwards or backwards? What is the chance that the dog could stay in the tunnel forever? How long, on the average, does the dog stay in the tunnel (each node takes one minute to cover)? Restart the dog at node 0, 1,000 times and count the number of times he escapes through F_4 or B_5. Kick the dog out if he stays in tunnel more than 30 moves.

node 0

B_5 B_4 B_3 B_2 B_1 F_1 F_2 F_3 F_4

b. Same as part a, except that node B_2 propels the dog to node B_4 only when traveling in a left direction. If node B_2 is reached when traveling to the right, the node B_2 has no effect.

24. Let us define a string of numbers as either an ascending sequence of numbers (e.g., 1, 5, 9, 17, 17, 18; each value is greater than or equal to its predecessor) or as a descending sequence of numbers (e.g., 17, 16, 9, 9, 0; each value is less than or equal to its predecessor). The length of a string is the number of numbers in the sequence. For example, the following sequence contains six strings:

$$\text{String 2} \qquad \text{String 4} \qquad \text{String 6}$$
$$\text{length} = 4 \qquad \text{length} = 2 \qquad \text{length} = 1$$

$$6, 8, 10, 4, 2, 0, 1, 7, 8, 1, 2, 1$$

$$\text{String 1} \qquad\qquad \text{String 3} \qquad \text{String 5}$$
$$\text{length} = 3 \qquad \text{length} = 4 \qquad \text{length} = 2$$

Write a program to generate 100 random numbers in the range 0 to 10 and determine the average length of the strings encountered. A "good" random number generator should generate a low average string length.

25. John Jones has $200,000 to invest in speculative gold stock. The gold mines are of such a nature that they either go broke leaving stock worthless or strike gold and make the stock owners wealthy. Mr. Jones's goal is to retire with $2,000,000. He plans to invest $100,000 at a time. He estimates that the probability of losing each $100,000 investment is 75 percent while the

probability of making $1,000,000 from the same investment is 25 percent. In either case, he will sell the stock and make further $100,000 investments of the same nature. What is the probability of Mr. Jones retiring with $2,000,000?

Write a FORTRAN program to simulate the behavior of the investment scheme, using a random generator to determine whether the stock (the initial investment of $100,000) becomes worthless or valuable. Simulate 100 such investments, count the wins (makes $2,000,000) and losses (goes broke) and from these figures determine the probability for a successful retirement.

26. You are the owner of a bookstore that sells both paperback and hardback books. For every book you sell, you have a card punched with two numbers:

   • The amount the book cost.
   • Either a 0 or a 1 (0 if the book is a paperback; 1 if the book is hardback).

   You want to know the following information:

a. total amount taken in	(TOT)	real variable
b. total number of books sold	(NUM)	integer variable
c. average price per book	(AVG)	real variable
d. minimum price of a hardback book	(XMIN)	real variable
e. average price of a paperback book	(PAP)	real variable

   Input: 1. Set of prices and codes; one set per card; all prices are between 0.00 and 1000.00 (real number); all codes are either 0 or 1 (integer number).
   　　　　2. Trip card (last-card code) contains −1.0, −1.

   Output: Print TOT, NUM, AVG, XMIN, PAP on one line in this order.

   Test data:

5.00	1
.99	0
3.25	1
1.75	0
1.25	0
5.65	1
−1.0	−1

27. Write a program to compute the value of $\pi/4$ using the formula:

   $$\frac{\pi}{4} = 1 - \frac{1}{3} + \frac{1}{5} - \frac{1}{7} + \frac{1}{9} - \cdots$$

   First approximation is $\pi/4 = 1$.
   Second approximation is $\pi/4 = 1 - 1/3$.
   Third approximation is $\pi/4 = 1 - 1/3 + 1/5$.
   etc.

   Stop when the difference between two successive approximations is less than .01.

28. The sine of an angle can be computed from its series expansion:

$$\sin x = x - \frac{x^3}{3!} + \frac{x^5}{5!} - \frac{x^7}{7!} \ldots \qquad \text{where } x \text{ is expressed in radians.}$$

If $x = 1$, compute the number of terms required to produce $\sin 1$ with a truncation error less than 5.10^{-5}. The truncation error is equal to the first term neglected. For example, if the first two terms are used to compute $\sin x$, the truncation error is $x^5/5!$ (the first term not used).

29. The number e can be approximated by the formula

$$e_4 \simeq 1 + \frac{1}{1}(1 + \frac{1}{2}(1 + \frac{1}{3}(1 + \frac{1}{4})))$$

However, a better approximation would be

$$e_{100} \simeq = + \frac{1}{1}(1 + \frac{1}{2}(1 + \frac{1}{3}(1 + \frac{1}{4}(1 + \frac{1}{5}(1 + \frac{1}{6}(\ldots \frac{1}{99}(1 + \frac{1}{100})) \ldots)$$

Write a program to compute e_{100}.

30. A study was conducted to determine whether different communication modes to computers could affect a student's attitude towards programming. In a computer-related course, 13 students used batch-processing mode to solve problems on the computer, while 12 other students used conversational mode to solve the same problems. The following entries reflect the average score obtained by each student across all the 20 questions of the Attitude Test Toward Programming (ATTP) given at the end of the semester:

Mode of communication

Batch-processing	*Conversational*
2.75	4.15
2.95	3.70
3.00	3.55
3.10	4.45
4.50	4.20
4.75	3.95
2.50	3.80
3.35	4.00
4.00	3.00
3.05	3.65
2.00	4.00
3.35	4.35
4.10	

Conversational students had a higher average score than batch-processing students. Write a program to determine if this difference is significant. The difference is significant if $t > 2.069$, where t is given by the following formula:

$$t = \frac{\overline{X_c} - \overline{X_b}}{\sqrt{\dfrac{[(N_c - 1)S_c^2 + (N_b - 1)S_b^2]}{(N_c + N_b - 2)} \cdot \dfrac{(N_c + N_b)}{N_c \cdot N_b}}}$$

where $\overline{X_c}$ and $\overline{X_b}$ are the averages of the conversational and batch scores respectively.

S_c and S_b are the standard deviations for conversational and batch modes respectively. (See Section 6-4-2 for the programming example of a standard deviation.)

N_c and N_b are the number of scores for conversational and batch processing respectively.

31. Write a program to compute the area under a curve $y = f(x)$:

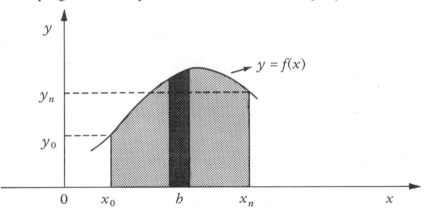

The darkened area under a curve $y = f(x)$ can be approximated by breaking the interval (x_0, x_n) into n equal intervals of size

$$h = \frac{x_n - x_0}{n}$$

and computing the sum of the n areas of the trapezoids with base h. The smaller the interval h the closer the approximation is to the exact area. The formula to compute the sum of the areas of the n trapezoids is

$$A = \frac{h}{2}(y_0 + 2y_1 + 2y_2 + \cdots + 2y_{n-1} + y_n)$$

where $y_0, y_1, y_2, \cdots, y_n$ are the values of the function at the points $x_0, x_1, x_2, \cdots, x_n$.

Your program should approximate the area under the curve $y = e^{-x^2/2}$ for x between 1 and 2 for three different values of h: .1, .01, .001. (This is equivalent to obtaining an approximation for $\int_1^2 e^{-x^2/2}$.)

32. A *perfect* number is a number which is the sum of all its divisors except itself. Six is the first perfect number; the only numbers which divide 6 evenly are 1, 2, 3, 6 and $6 = 1 + 2 + 3$. An *abundant* number is one which is less than the sum of its divisors (e.g., $12 < 1 + 2 + 3 + 4 + 6$); a *deficient* number is greater than the sum of its divisors (e.g., $9 > 1 + 3$). Write a program to generate a table of the first N integers (N is read from a card) and classify each as perfect, abundant or deficient.

33. Write a program to determine a five-digit number $d_1 d_2 d_3 d_4 d_5$ which when multiplied by a digit k between 2 and 9 will give a result of $d_5 d_4 d_3 d_2 d_1$. For instance:

$$\begin{array}{r} d_1 \ d_2 \ d_3 \ d_4 \ d_5 \\ \times \ k \\ \hline d_5 \ d_4 \ d_3 \ d_2 \ d_1 \end{array}$$

6-6-3 Answers to Self Test

1. a. Valid. b. Limit must be an integer. c. Index must not be changed. d. Inconsistent use of I. e. Expression not allowed for index. f. Increment must be positive. g. Body of interior loop overlaps body of outer loop. h. Index must be integer mode. i. Limit must be integer mode. j. Valid. k. Foot of loop cannot be IF. l. Foot of loop 91 is missing. m. Valid. n. Valid. o. Index cannot be modified within loop. p. Cannot branch into body of loop after normal exit from loop. q. Valid. r. Valid. s. Foot of loop cannot be a DO statement.

2. a. 1,3,5,7,9. b. 6,9,12,15,18. c. 4.

3. a. 120. b. 21. c. 8.

4. Neither. The value of I will never be greater than 5.

5. a. The value of the index I should not be used after normal/complete exit from loop. The value of I is indeterminate. b. Yes.

6. J = 0.

7. a. 1,2,1. b. 2,2. c. 1,3, error I is integer, and described by F type.

8. a. F: limit on a DO statement may not be an expression. b. F: index must be integer. c. F: Initial value must always be specified. d. F: the CONTINUE statement may be used anywhere in a program. e. F: New standards provide that if the initial value exceeds the limit the body of the loop is not processed at all. f. F: Nonexecutable statements are processed at compilation time, not execution time. g. T. h. T. i. F: Counting is a special kind of the accumulation process. j. F: The comment will be listed once at compilation time.

DATA REPRESENTATION

7-1 Problem Example

Each card of a deck of cards contains a student's name and the student's final score. Write a program to assign each student a letter grade, as shown below. The output should be similar to the following:

Grade	Letter grade
score $\geqslant 90$	A
$80 \leqslant$ score < 90	B
$60 \leqslant$ score < 80	C
$50 \leqslant$ score < 60	D
score < 50	F

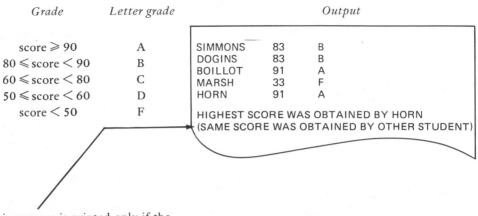

Output

```
SIMMONS     83     B
DOGINS      83     B
BOILLOT     91     A
MARSH       33     F
HORN        91     A

HIGHEST SCORE WAS OBTAINED BY HORN
(SAME SCORE WAS OBTAINED BY OTHER STUDENT)
```

This message is printed only if the highest score is obtained by at least two students; otherwise, it is not printed.

```
       DOUBLE PRECISION NAME,IHOLD

       LOGICAL P

       DATA A,B,C/'A','B','C'/
       DATA D,F/'D','F'/
       P = .TRUE.

       AMAX = 0.

15     READ(1,5,END = 6)NAME,SCORE
       K = SCORE/10. + 1.


       K1 = K – 5

       GOTO(1,2,2,3,4,4),K1
       GRADE = F
       GOTO10
 1     GRADE = D
       GOTO10
 2     GRADE = C
       GOTO10
 3     GRADE = B
       GOTO10
 4     GRADE = A
10     WRITE(3,11)NAME,SCORE,GRADE
       IF(AMAX – SCORE)13,14,15




14     P = .FALSE.
       GOTO17
13     AMAX = SCORE
       P = .TRUE.
17     IHOLD = NAME
       GOTO15

 6     WRITE(3,7)IHOLD

       IF(P)GOTO9

       WRITE(3,8)
 9     STOP
 5     FORMAT(A8,F5.1)
11     FORMAT(T10,A8,3X,F6.1,2X,A1)
 7     FORMAT(T10,'HIGHEST GRADE WAS OBTAINED BY',1X,A8)
 8     FORMAT(T10,'SCORE WAS OBTAINED BY OTHER STUDENT(S)')
       END
```

NAME is used to store the student's name and IHOLD is used to identify the student name with highest current score.

The proposition that there is one and only one highest score is either true or false. The logical variable P is used for this purpose.

The variables A, B, C, D and F now contain the alphabetic characters A, B, C, D and F, respectively. The logical variable P is initially set to .TRUE., stating that there is only one highest score. If two or more highest scores exist, P will be changed to .FALSE. by statement 14.

AMAX is the current highest grade and is used to keep track of the student's name with highest grade so far. It is initially 0 but will be reset to the first grade by statement 13.

For A grades K = 10,11; for B grades K = 9; for C grades K = 8,7; for D grades K = 6 and for F grades K = 1,2,3,4 or 5. For A grades K1 = 6,5; for B grades K1 = 4; for C grades K1 = 3,2,; for D grades K1 = 1 and for F grades K1 is negative. The reason for using K1 instead of K is to list only 6 statements in the computed GOTO statement, versus 11 statements if K had been used.

If K1 is negative or zero, the statement following the GOTO is taken.

Note that if K1 = is 3 or 2, transfer will be made only to statement 2.

If current highest score is larger than grade, just go back and read more cards. If current highest score is equal to the grade read, then it is no longer true that there is only one highest score. Set P to false and keep track of the name at 17. A highest grade has been found and hence the proposition that only one highest grade exists is (temporarily) true. Keep track of name and score and read more cards.

Write the name of last student with highest score.

If P is true, then only one student obtained highest score.

If P is false, print message that highest score was shared by other student(s).

Figure 7-1 Letter grades.

A program to solve this problem is shown in Figure 7-1. Note the three new FORTRAN features:

1. The DOUBLE PRECISION statement.

2. The LOGICAL statement.

3. The A (alphabetic) FORMAT code.

7-2 Number Representation

7-2-1 Internal Data Representation

Integer Data

The internal form for integer data differs from that used for real or alpha-numeric data. On most computers, integer data is represented in binary form (also called *fixed point*—the decimal point is assumed fixed to the right of the right-most digit). Each integer in memory occupies a computer word consisting of a fixed number of *Binary digITs* (BITs). Integer variable names then, are just names for computer words. Word lengths on different computers vary from 8 to 60 bits; some typical lengths for specific computers are shown in Figure 7-2. The range of values that can be represented in integer mode is directly proportional to the word length used. Maximum integer values for some computers are shown in Figure 7-2.

Real data

Real data is represented internally in a form called *floating-point form* (the decimal point is allowed to move or float anywhere in the number). Floating-point notation permits the representation of numbers with decimal points and exponents. A floating-point number may be expressed as follows:

mantissa $\times$ base^{exponent} (mantissa = number expressed in fractional form)

For example, in base 10 the number 6325.3 might be expressed as

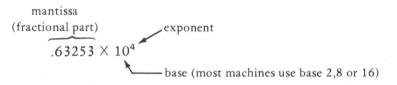

It should be noted that a real number occupies one computer word, which consists of a fixed number of bits (see Figure 7-3). Internally, this means that the

Computer	Word length (bits)	Maximum integer value	Number of decimal digits
IBM 1130	16	$2^{15}-1$	5
IBM 360/370	32	$2^{31}-1$	10
Burroughs 6700	48	$2^{38}-1$	15
CDC Cyber 72	60	$2^{59}-1$	18

Figure 7-2 Word length and maximum integer values.

computer word is broken down into two parts: an exponent and a mantissa (fractional part).

Example

The number 6325.3 might be expressed as

$.63253 \times 10^{4}$

and its internal representation might be

| 04 | 6 3 2 5 3 0 | one word

exponent (base 10 assumed)   implied position of decimal point   fractional part (mantissa)

The range of values that can be represented using floating-point representation is dependent on the number of bits (digits 0 or 1) allowed for the exponent, and the number of bits allocated to the mantissa in each computer word. Some typical ranges are shown in Figure 7-3.

Computer	Word length (bits)	Exponent range	Number of digits in mantissa (significant digits)
IBM 1130	32	$10^{38}-10^{-39}$	7
IBM 360/370	32	$10^{76}-10^{-76}$	7
Burroughs B6700	48	$10^{67}-10^{-47}$	11
CDC Cyber 72	60	$10^{308}-10^{-308}$	15

Figure 7-3 Word length and range of real values.

7-2-2 Alphanumeric Data and the A Format

All data processed so far has been numeric in nature. Many times it may be convenient or necessary to process alphabetic or alphanumeric information. Alphanumeric data is defined as a sequence of letters, digits and special characters. For example, "1201 NORTH 12 AVE" is a string of 17 characters consisting of 6 digits, 3 blanks and 8 letters; it is commonly referred to as a *character string* or a *literal string*. Zip codes, telephone numbers, social security numbers, names and addresses are examples of character strings. Character strings are not generally processed numerically; that is, they do not participate in additions, subtractions, etc.

The internal form used to represent alphanumeric (character) data differs from that used to represent integer or real data. Each computer word can "hold" a limited number of characters. The number of characters depends on the particular computer. The number of characters per word on various computers is shown in Figure 7-4. Hence many words (variables) will be needed to store long character strings. For example, the character string 173 FIR DR. would require three words on an IBM/360/370:

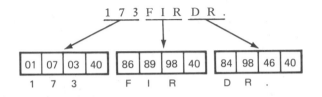

The code used might be, for instance:

$$01 = 1 \quad 86 = F \quad 84 = D \quad 40 = \text{blank}$$
$$07 = 7 \quad 89 = I$$
$$03 = 3 \quad 98 = R \quad 46 = .$$

(A common code to represent characters is called the EBCDIC code and is discussed in Section 7-3.)

Computer	Word length (bits)	Number characters per word	Double precision
IBM 360/370	32	4	8
Burroughs 6700	48	6	12
CDC Cyber 72	60	12	24

Figure 7-4 Number of characters per word.

Thus far we have encountered three distinct types of data: integer, real and alphanumeric. A variable (word) can thus contain an integer, a real number or a character string. Each of these data types uses a different code for its internal memory representation and hence the integer constant 1, the real constant 1. and the character 1 will all have different memory representations. The internal code used by the computer to represent each type depends on the way a variable is assigned a value.

Example

I = 1234   Tells the computer to use an integer internal representation for 1234, since I is an integer.

X = 1234 Tells the computer to use a real number representation for 1234, since that constant is to be stored in a real variable.

DATA Y/'1234'/ Tells the computer to use a character code to represent the individual digits, 1, 2, 3 and 4 in the memory word Y. The quotes (' ') are used to identify alphanumeric data.

Of course, the mode of the data can also be defined by an input FORMAT code. If the data is to be read from cards, an I code tells the computer to represent the data in integer code, an F code in real number code and an A code in character code.

To better understand the alphanumeric A format code and the way in which character data is used in a program, it is helpful to visualize the differences in the internal representation of the three data modes. The following discussion is purely conceptual but serves to illustrate the three different data representations.

Consider the collection of digits 1234. This group of digits can be thought to represent a signed *integer* number 1234 or a signed *real* number 1234. or a string of *characters* 1, 2, 3 and 4 (as in an address 1234 North 12th Ave.). These three different data modes can be visualized as follows:

Integer code 1234	*Real* number code 1234.	*Character* code 1234
00 00 12 34	04| 12 34 00	01|02|03|04

straight integer representation	exponent fractional part	code used to represent each
	$1234 = .1234 \times 10^4$	digit or character is
	exponent = 04	01 = 1 03 = 3
	fractional part = 123400	02 = 2 04 = 4

From the above, then, we could conceivably look at the *character* string 01 02 03 04 and interpret it as the *integer* number 1,020,304 or we could interpret it as the *real* number $020304 \times 10^1 = 203040$ if we don't know the mode used. Conversely, the *real* number 04123400 could be interpreted as the *character* string 4BZ0 if 12 is the code for the letter B and 34 the code for the letter Z. Even though we can give different interpretations to the memory contents of a variable, the computer does not get confused when it processes the variable, since it knows in what mode the variable is to be processed (from the definition of the variable).

Alphanumeric data may be stored in variables of any mode, but no arithmetic operations should be performed on these variables (it does not make any sense to compute an average of telephone numbers, or divide one name by another name!). To avoid errors, the programmer should be careful not to use mixed-mode alphanumeric variables in IF statements or across the equal sign in a replacement statement. Consider the following example: Suppose the variable L contains the alphanumeric string 01020304 and it is desired to store that character string in X. If the statement X = L is used, then X will not contain 01020304. Before storing L in X, the computer will convert L to real mode, since X is real and hence X will contain 07102030 (01020304 = 1,020,304 = .1020304 × 10^7 = 07102030).

However, if the statement M = L is used, then the mode is preserved across the equal sign and no conversion takes place and M will contain 01020304. Similarly, if X contains the string 01020304 and L contains the string 01020304 the statement: IF(X.EQ.L)GOTO5 will not result in a transfer to statement 5, since L will be converted to real mode before the comparison is made (07102030) and the two numbers (variables) will be unequal.

Initialization of Alphanumeric Variables

The DATA statement can be used to initialize variables to alphanumeric data. Most systems allow the programmer to define alphanumeric variables as follows:

1. Count the number (n) of characters in the constant and precede the character string by nH as follows:

$$DATA\ SAM,STAR,J/3HTHE,1H*,4HHHHH$$

The results (on IBM 360/370) in memory is: SAM = T H E ♭
where ♭ is the character "space"   STAR = * ♭ ♭ ♭
                                       J   = H H H H

2. Enclose the character string within single quote marks. For example:

$$DATA\ SUE,SAM,JSUM/'A♭CA','+','♭♭T.'$$

                                                  └——Note two blanks.

Assuming four characters per word, this results in SUE A ♭ C A
                                                    SAM + ♭ ♭ ♭
                                                    JSUM ♭ ♭ T .

The A Format Code

The A data format code is used to describe alphanumeric data fields for both input and output. The general form of the A format code is

$$nAw$$

where w is the field width and n is a duplication factor. Alphanumeric data may be stored in either integer or real variables. On input, if w is less than the maximum number of characters which can be stored in a word, blanks are inserted to the right in the word in memory.

Example 1

Assume each variable can contain four characters:

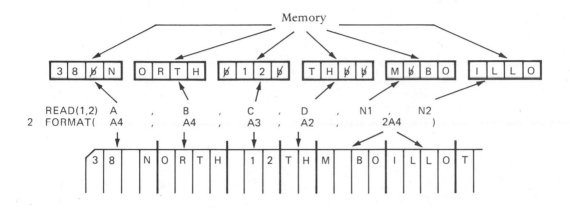

The variable A stores the first four characters, B stores the next four; three characters are read for C and the system automatically provides one filler blank to the right. Two filler blanks are provided for D and four characters are stored in each of the variables N1 and N2.

If the field w exceeds the maximum number of characters l that can be stored in a word (see Figure 7-4), the rightmost l characters in the field are read and stored in the variable.

Example 2

Assume each variable can contain four characters:

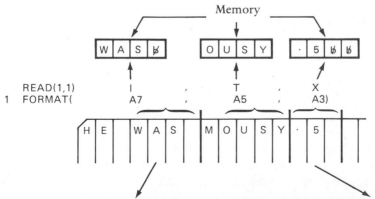

The first 7 columns are read. Since I is used to read characters only the rightmost 4 characters are stored in I.

The next 5 columns are read but only the rightmost 4 characters are stored in T.

The characters . and 5 and 2 blanks are stored into X.

On output, the same rules as above are observed.

Example 3

Assume each variable contains six characters ($l = 6$, Burroughs 6700).

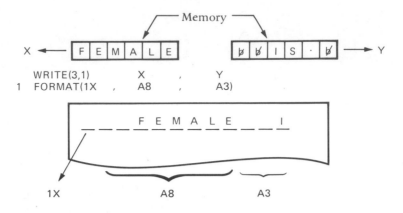

As noted previously, one computer word can contain a limited number of characters. This, then, means that many words are required to store even the smallest of character strings. It is possible to double the number of characters per variable by declaring such a variable a DOUBLE PRECISION variable. In effect, this results in two contiguous memory words being allocated to the variable. (The DOUBLE PRECISION statement is discussed in Section 7-2-4.) For example, with $l = 8$ (IBM 370 double precision):

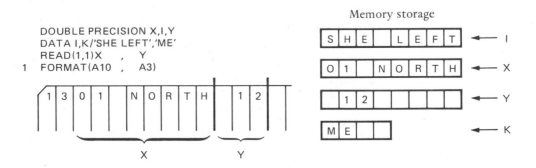

Ten columns are read but only the rightmost eight characters (columns) are stored in X.

Variables containing alphanumeric data may be tested by IF statements. To avoid potential problems on certain computers, the programmer is advised to test only alphanumeric data stored in *integer variable names.* When alphanumeric data is compared, the following ordering of characters is observed:

$$\text{blank} < A < B < C \cdots < Y < Z < 0 < 1 < 2 \cdots < 9$$

Example

Suppose J = <u>B</u> <u>E</u> <u>T</u> <u>A</u>   then J > K since blank < A
        K = <u>B</u> <u>E</u> <u>T</u> <u> </u>   and K < L since B < 1
        L = <u>1</u> <u>A</u> <u>B</u> <u>C</u>

Alphanumeric strings are compared one character at a time. Even with the DOUBLE PRECISION statement, it is difficult and inconvenient to process alphanumeric strings, since individual variable names are required to identify character substrings. Alphanumeric data can best be manipulated with arrays, which are discussed in Chapter 8.

7-2-3 Real Constants in Exponential Form and the E Format Code

A real constant in a FORTRAN program can be represented in two forms: a basic form and an exponential form. A real constant in basic form is a sequence of digits with a decimal point. The maximum number of significant digits is shown in Figure 7-3. For example:

   X = –999.9901   is a valid real constant on the IBM/370.
   Y = 1.00000000000099   is a valid real constant on the CDC cyber.

If more than the allowed number of significant digits is used, the system will generally represent the constant in double precision mode, as discussed in Section 7-2-4.

The exponential form for a real constant has the general form

$$\text{basic–real–constant E integer–exponent}^1$$

The value of a constant in this form is computed as

$$\text{basic–real–constant} \times 10^{\text{integer–exponent}}$$

Examples

FORTRAN exponential form	Value
6.2E + 4	$6.2 \times 10^4 = 62000.$
–4.32E14	$-4.32 \times 10^{14} = -432000000000000.$
.034E – 2	$.034 \times 10^{-2} = .00034$
–1.2E – 7	$-1.2 \times 10^{-7} = -.00000012$

Exponential form for real constants is typically used in place of the basic form for numbers with large or small magnitudes. The exponential form may be used in lieu of the basic form in any arithmetic expression.

---

[1] The number of digits in the basic–real–constant and in the integer–exponent will vary depending on the system used.

Examples

Exponential form	Basic form
X = −.01E3*Y	X = −10.*Y
Y = 16.2E − 4*Z + W	Y = .00162*Z + W
Z = 4.2E + 20**2 − Z*.5E − 21	Only exponential form is practical.

The E Format Code

Input of exponential numbers. Numbers in exponential form may be read from data cards using the E format code. Recall that an exponential number can be written as

basic-real-constant E integer-exponent

For example:

$$\underbrace{-2134}_{\text{basic-real-constant}} \text{E} \underbrace{+ 30}_{\text{integer-exponent}}$$

The general form of the E format code is

$$Ew.d$$

where w represents the number of card columns reserved for the data field. d informs the system where to place the decimal point in the basic-real-constant in case no decimal point is punched on the card.

If there is no decimal point punched in the basic-real-constant, the basic-real-constant is adjusted (read) with d fractional digits (the decimal point is assumed d positions to the left of the character E punched in the field). This adjusted value is then raised to the specified integer-exponent. If the decimal point is punched in the basic-real-constant, d is ignored and the basic-real-constant is raised to the specified integer power; d nevertheless must be included in the E format description.

Example 1

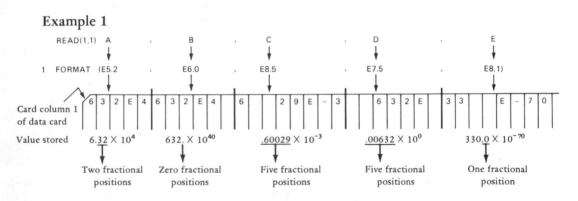

Note that blanks are read as zeroes.

Example 2

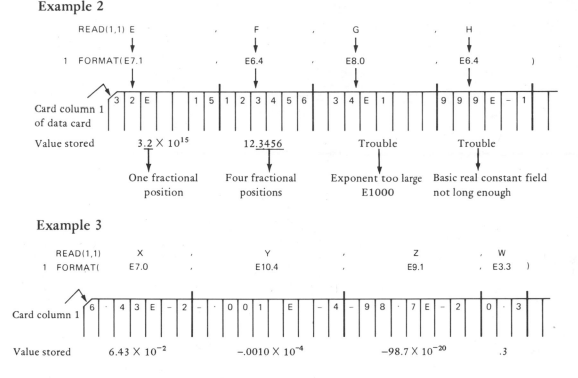

Example 3

To avoid errors, the programmer should always try to right-justify numbers in their input fields. This also includes the digits of the exponent.

Output of exponential numbers. Any exponential number printed by E$w.d$ will generally have the following standardized output form:

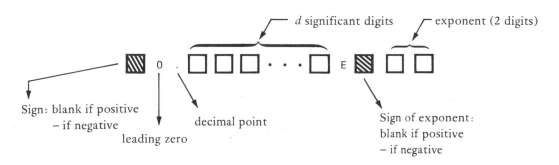

Hence the generally considered minimum of print positions to print any negative number with no digits of significance is − 0 . E − ☐ ☐ which means that

Seven print positions

right from the start w must be greater than or equal to 7 if it is to print the sign, the leading 0, the decimal point, the E, the sign of the exponent and the two digits for the exponent. (If w is not large enough some systems will not print the leading zero.) Consider the following examples:

Value of data item in memory	Output format code	Printed value	Comments
632000.	E10.3	ƀ0.632Eƀ06	Leading blank.
632000.	E8.3	.632Eƀ06	No room for leading 0.
632999.	E9.3	0.633Eƀ06	Round off.
−.83247	E12.5	−0.83247Eƀ00	Leading blanks and
−.83247	E13.4	ƀƀ−0.8325Eƀ00	round off.
−.000004269	E10.3	−0.427E−05	Round off.
−.000004269	E10.1	ƀƀ−0.4E−05	Leading blanks.
−98.5678	E8.1	−0.1Eƀ03	Round off.
−98.5678	E8.0	ƀ−0.Eƀ03	No significant digits.
123.4567	E15.9	ƀ.123456721Eƀ03	The digits 21 are not significant if significancy of digits is 7.
3.256	E8.4	********	Missing at least one space.

7-2-4 Double Precision Numbers and the D Format Code

For some applications, the number of significant digits which can be maintained using real mode data may be unsatisfactory. Many computers offer an extended version of floating-point data representation allowing for the retention of more significant digits. Figure 7-5 displays the number of significant digits available in double precision on certain computers.

Computer	Word length (bits)	Exponent range	Number of significant decimal digits
IBM 1130	48	10^{38} to 10^{-39}	10
IBM 360/370	64	10^{76} to 10^{-76}	16
Burroughs B6700	96	10^{29603} to 10^{-29581}	24
CDC Cyber 72	120	10^{308} to 10^{-308}	33

Figure 7-5 Double precision characteristics.

Usually, the magnitude (exponent) of a real constant does not increase with double precision representation.[2] Only the number of digits in the fractional part (mantissa) is affected. The only way to specify that a variable is in double precision mode is to declare the variable in a DOUBLE PRECISION statement. There

---

[2] An exception is found in the Burroughs B6700/7700 systems, in which both the number of significant digits and the size of the exponent increase.

is no implicit mode specification for double precision variables. The general form of the DOUBLE PRECISION statement is:

DOUBLE PRECISION   list-of-variables

Each variable in the list-of-variables is assigned double precision mode. It should be noted that DOUBLE PRECISION affects *only real numbers, not* integer numbers. The double precision feature does not exist for integers. This does not mean that a variable name starting with I through M cannot be declared in a DOUBLE PRECISION list. Such a variable would just represent a double precision real number.

Example

    DOUBLE PRECISION X,I
    X = 123456789012345.   Both X and I are now double precision real
    I = .123456789012345D40   constants.

DOUBLE PRECISION is a nonexecutable specification statement subject to the same restrictions as other specification statements (see Section 5-2-1).

Double precision constants may be represented in a basic form similar to the basic-real-constants except that double precision constants will have more significant digits than can be stored in an ordinary floating-point word. For example on the IBM 360/370 the constant 63217869.2, which contains more than seven significant digits, automatically becomes a double precision constant.

There is also an exponential form for double precision constants which is analogous to the exponential form for real constants, except that the character D is used in place of E.

Example

    6.2D + 4 has value 62000
    −.0326798432156D − 4 has value −.00000326798432156

Double precision constants and variables may be mixed with real and integer constants and variables in any arithmetic expression. When any double precision operand and a nondouble precision operand are involved in an arithmetic operation, the nondouble precision is converted to double precision; the operation is then carried out using double precision arithmetic. The final result of the expression is a double precision number.

Example

$$\text{DOUBLE PRECISION T,X}$$
$$X = I*J/C**K + T$$

First C**K is performed in real mode.
Then I*J is performed in integer mode.
Then (I*J)/(C**K) is performed in real mode.
Then (I*J)/(C**K) + T is performed in double precision.
Finally, the double precision result is stored in the double precision variable X.

If, in a replacement statement, a double precision value is to be placed into a real variable, significant digits may be lost. Consider the following example, assuming a real variable can hold at most seven significant digits:

	Results
DOUBLE PRECISION X,Y	
REAL A,B	
X = 1.23456789D3	X will contain 1234.56789
A = X	A will contain 1234.567
Y = 999999999	Y will contain 999999999.
B = Y	B will contain 999999900.
I = 1.29456789D1	I will contain 12 (no round off).
J = Y	J will contain 999999999

The D format code[3] may be used for input/output of double precision data. The general form of the D format code is D*w.d*. Details of the way the D format code is used are exactly the same as for the E format code discussed in Section 7-2-3.

Double precision data occupies more memory space than real data. Operations performed on double precision operands take longer than the same operations with real arithmetic.

7-2-5 Logical Type Data and the L Format Code

Without being aware of it, we have already made extensive use of logical expressions. A logical expression can be thought of as a proposition (a proposition is a statement that is either true or false). For example, the statement "I am 36 years old" is either true or false; similarly, the statement "X is greater than 63" is either true or false. Such expressions have been used in logical IF statements. Syntacti-

---

[3]The F format code may also be used for double precision input and output, as in the following:

```
         DOUBLE PRECISION X,Y
         READ(1,1)X,Y
    1    FORMAT(F8.0,F10.4)
         WRITE(3,2)X,Y
    2    FORMAT(2X,F9.0,3X,D18.5)
```

cally speaking, a FORTRAN logical expression can be defined as two arithmetic expressions linked together by a relational operator (.GT.,.GE.,.LT. etc.). Consider, for example, the following elementary logical expressions:

valid   X.LT.1.3   invalid   X + 23*Z   No logical operator.
        XAM.NE.Y   .LE.100   Missing arithmetic expression.
        (X + Y)**2.EQ.4   (X.LT.Y) + Z   Logical values cannot
        2.*Y.GT.X − Y   participate in arithmetic
        −1..LE.SQRT(Z)   operations.

Logical expressions, just like arithmetic expressions, can be processed in replacement statements and in logical IF statements. In either case, the logical expression is first evaluated and the result of this evaluation takes on the logical values .TRUE. or .FALSE. (these values are called *logical constants*), just as the evaluation of 3. + 5. takes on the numerical value 8. These logical values, .TRUE. and .FALSE., can be stored in logical variables in the same way as arithmetic constants can be stored in variables. However, logical variables must be declared in a LOGICAL statement. The LOGICAL statement has the general form:

LOGICAL   variable-list

where   variable-list is a list of any variable names (integer or real).

Example

LOGICAL   X,I,A

The following are now logical variables: X,I,A. Once a variable is declared LOGICAL, it can be assigned the values .TRUE. or .FALSE. through replacement statements. It cannot, however, be assigned numeric values. The general form for logical replacement statements is

logical-variable = logical-expression

The following are valid examples of logical replacement statements:

    LOGICAL A,B,C
    X = 4
    Y = −2
    A = .TRUE.   A is true
    C = A   C is true
    B = X.LT.Y   B is false since   4 ≮ −2
    C = Y.NE.SQRT(X)   C is true since −2 ≠ 2
    B = (X + Y)**2.EQ.4   B is true since   4 = 4
    C = 2.*Y.GT.X − Y   C is false since −4 ≯ 6

The following are examples of invalid logical replacement statements:

```
LOGICAL A,B,C
A = 2.1*X            Invalid logical expression, no logical operators.
B = 2.*C             Invalid logical expression, C is logical, 2. is numeric.
C = A + B            Cannot add two logical variables.
A = B.EQ.TRUE.       Cannot compare two logical values.
C = A.LT.X           A is not numeric.
A = IF(X.LT.4)       Invalid logical expression, IF key word not allowed.
Z = .FALSE.          Z is not declared logical.
C = X.LT.Y + Z.GT.3  Cannot add logical values.
```

Sometimes it may be practical to create a more complex proposition by combining (*conjuncting*) elementary logical expressions. For example, it might be desirable to know whether "SEX is 1 and STATUS is 4" or "AGE is less than 18 or AGE is greater than 65" etc. Such a combination of elementary logical expressions is called a *compound logical expression.* A compound logical expression can be defined as elementary logical expressions linked to one another by the logical operators .AND., .OR. and .NOT. .

The effect of the logical operators on two logical expressions e_1 and e_2 can be described as follows:

e_1 .AND. e_2 is .TRUE. if and only if e_1 and e_2 are both .TRUE. .
e_1 .OR. e_2 is .TRUE. if either e_1 or e_2 (or both) are .TRUE. .
.NOT. e_2 is .TRUE. if e_2 is .FALSE. (evaluate e_2 and negate it).

The above can be illustrated in table form, as shown in Figure 7-6. Note that the .NOT. operator can only be connected to one logical expression.

e_1	e_2	e_1.AND.e_2	e_1.OR.e_2	.NOT.e_1
.True.	.True.	.True.	.True.	.False.
.True.	.False.	.False.	.True.	.False.
.False.	.True.	.False.	.True.	.True.
.False.	.False.	.False.	.False.	.True.

Figure 7-6   Truth tables for logical operators.

Some examples of compound logical expressions and their outcomes are shown in the following table with X = 4, Y = 2 and Z = 2.

e_1	Logical Operator	e_2	e_1	e_2	Outcome
X.GT.SQRT(Y)	.AND.	Y.EQ.Z	.True.	.True.	.True.
X.LT.Z	.OR.	Y.NE.Z	.False.	.False.	.False.
Y.LE.X	.OR.	Y+Z.LT.X	.True.	.False.	.True.
X.GT.5.1	.AND.	X.EQ.2*Z	.False.	.True.	.False.
	.NOT.	X.LT.Y+Z		.False.	.True.

The values of compound logical expressions can be stored in logical variables. Consider the following examples:

LOGICAL A,B,C,D,E,F   *Logical value outcomes*

X = 3.
Y = −2.3
A = X.LT.Y   A = .FALSE. 3 ≮ −2.3.
B = Y.LE.20.   B = .TRUE.   −2.3 < 20.
C = A.AND.B   C = .FALSE. .FALSE..AND..TRUE. = .FALSE.
D = A.OR.X.LT.6   D = .TRUE.   since A is .FALSE. but X < 6 is .TRUE.
E = .NOT.C   E = .TRUE.   since C is .FALSE. .
F = A.AND..NOT.B   F = .FALSE. Both A and .NOT.B are .FALSE. .
E = (.TRUE..OR..FALSE.).AND..TRUE.   The expression is evaluated as .TRUE. .

Some examples of invalid compound expressions are

LOGICAL A,B,C
A = .NOT.X   X is not logical.
B = X + 1.OR.Y + 6   X + 1 and Y + 6 are not logical expressions.
C = X.LT.Y + Z.GT.3   No logical operator.
A = B.OR. C + 1   C + 1 is an invalid logical expression.

If more than one logical operator is used in a compound logical expression, parentheses may be used to specify which expression is to be evaluated first. Consider the logical expression e_1.AND.e_2.OR.e_3 with e_1 = .FALSE. and e_2 = e_3 = .TRUE. . Depending on the placement of positions, the above logical expression could be interpreted two ways:

$$e_1.AND.(e_2.OR.e_3) = .FALSE.$$

or

$$(e_1.AND.e_2).OR.e_3 = .TRUE.$$

Since all of the arithmetic operations, arithmetic relation operations and logical operations may appear in one expression, it becomes important to know the relative precedence (in the absence of parentheses) of the operations. This precedence or hierarchy of operations is summarized in the following table:

Operation	Comment	Precedence
arithmetic operations	according to usual rules of precedence	highest
arithmetic relations	in order from left to right	
(.LT.,.LE.,.GT.,.EQ. · · ·)		
.NOT.	operates on expression to immediate right	
.AND.		
.OR.		lowest

Parentheses may be used as necessary to change the implied precedence.

Example 1

Suppose X = 30, Y = 40, A = .TRUE.

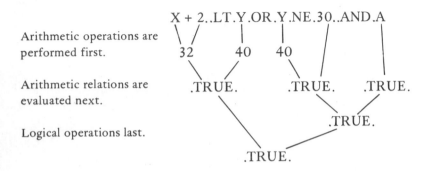

Arithmetic operations are performed first.

Arithmetic relations are evaluated next.

Logical operations last.

The above expression is evaluated as ((X + 2.).LT.Y).OR.((Y.NE.30.).AND.A).

Example 2

Suppose X = 30, Y = 40, A = .TRUE. and B = .FALSE. .

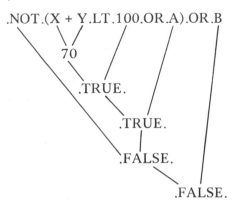

Any logical expression may be used in a logical IF statement, the general form of which is

$$\text{IF(logical-expression) statement}$$

If the value of the logical-expression is .TRUE., the statement is executed; if the value of the logical expression is .FALSE., the statement following the IF is executed.

Example

Suppose X = 30, Y = 40 and B = .TRUE. .

```
        LOGICAL A,B,C
          .
          .
          .
        IF(B)GOTO30                      B is .TRUE., hence the branch to 30 is taken.
          .
          .
          .
  30    A = X.LT.Y                       A is .TRUE.; A.AND.B is .TRUE.;
        IF(A.AND.B)C = .TRUE.            therefore C = .TRUE. is processed.
          .
          .
          .
        IF(X.GT.100.OR..NOT.B)GOTO7      X.GT.100 is .FALSE.; .NOT.B is .FALSE.;
          .                              therefore the next statement is executed.
          .
          .
```

The L Format Code

Logical variables may participate in input/output statements. In order to assign value to a logical variable via the READ or WRITE statements, the L format code must be used. The general form of the L code is:

$$Lw$$

where w represents the field width.

When reading a logical variable, the input field is scanned from left to right. If the first nonblank character is T the value stored for the logical variable is .TRUE.; if the first nonblank character is F or if the entire field is blank, the value stored is .FALSE. . Remaining characters in the field are ignored. On output, a T or an F is printed, depending on whether the variable is .TRUE. or .FALSE. . The character T or F is right-justified in the output field with $w - 1$ blanks to the left.

Example

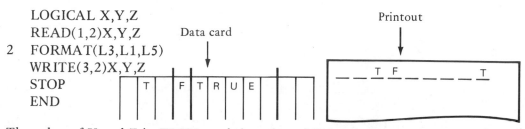

```
        LOGICAL X,Y,Z                                    Printout
        READ(1,2)X,Y,Z          Data card
  2     FORMAT(L3,L1,L5)
        WRITE(3,2)X,Y,Z
        STOP
        END
```

The value of X and Z is .TRUE. and the value of Y is .FALSE. .

7-2-6 Complex Data

A complex number is a number of the form

$$a + bi \qquad \text{where } i = \sqrt{-1} \text{ and } a,b \text{ are real numbers.}$$

real part   imaginary part

For example, the following are complex numbers:

$$4 + 3i$$
$$3.2 + (-4)i$$
$$-.6 + 70.i$$
$$3.$$

Some versions of FORTRAN allow processing of complex data. A FORTRAN complex constant is a number of the form:

$$(A,B) \longleftarrow \text{parentheses required}$$

where A and B are real constants with A representing the real part of the constant and B the imaginary part. Note the *enclosing* parentheses.

Examples

Constants	Value
(4.,3.)	$4 + 3i$
(3.2,−4)	$3.2 - 4i$
(24.3E − 2,79.)	$.243 + 79i$
(1.1E+10,.2E − 3)	$11000000000 + .0002i$

Following are invalid examples of complex constants:

(0. + 1.*I)	I is not a constant.
1.,1.	No parentheses.
(3115,3.4)	The real part is an integer.
(.004E + 4,5.1D10)	The parts differ in mode.

Before a complex variable can be processed, it *must* be declared in the COMPLEX statement, which has the form:

$$\text{COMPLEX} \qquad \text{list-of-variable-names}$$

For example, COMPLEX A,B,X(10) specifies that A,B and an array X of length 10 are complex variables.

Internally, each complex variable consists of two memory locations; the first for the real part and the second for the imaginary part of the number. Complex expressions can be formed in much the same way as real and integer constants. The result of evaluating an expression where a term is complex is always a complex value.

Examples

COMPLEX A,B,C

A = (2.,2.) + (0.,1)	A = 2. + $3i$
B = (5.,−1.)*2.	B = 10.−$2i$
C = A + B − 5.	C = 7 + i
X = A − B	X = − 8 (Since X is real, the imaginary part is discarded.)
C = A*B	C = 26 + $26i$
C = (3.,5.) − A	C = 1 + $2i$
C = (A*B)/2.*(0.,1.)	C = −13 + $13i$
C = A**2 − (2.,3.4)**3	C = −66.36 + 64.904i
C = (X,Z)	Invalid (X,Z not constants).
C = A + 2	C = 4 + $3i$

It should be noted that the exponent in a ** (exponentiation) operation cannot be complex. For example, 3.14**(1.,3.) is invalid. Additionally, complex numbers may *not* be raised to a real power. Thus C = A**2. is invalid, while C = A**2 is valid.

Most FORTRAN libraries have complex functions available to the user to carry out COMPLEX operations. Following is a list of usually available COMPLEX functions:

FUNCTIONS	*Meaning*
REAL	Real (a,b) = a (a,b real constants)
AIMAG	Imaginary (a,b) = b
CONJG	Conjugate (a,b) = (a,−b)
CABS	Absolute value (a,b) = $\sqrt{a^2 + b^2}$
CSQRT	Principal square root of a + bi (positive real part)
CLOG	Logarithm
CSIN	Trigonometric functions
CCOS	
CMPLX	If z is complex and a,b real, z = cmplx(a,b) means z = a + bi.

A well-documented description of these functions is generally available in the FORTRAN technical reference manual for the particular computer system.

Input/Output of Complex Variables

Input/output of complex variables requires two data descriptor format codes for each complex variable. The first format code describes the real part, and the second describes the imaginary part of the number.

Example

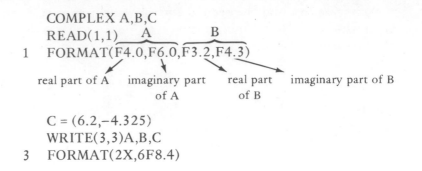

COMPLEX A,B,C
READ(1,1)
1   FORMAT(F4.0,F6.0,F3.2,F4.3)

C = (6.2,−4.325)
WRITE(3,3)A,B,C
3   FORMAT(2X,6F8.4)

7-3   You Might Want To Know

1.   What does "significant" digits really mean?

Answer: Generally speaking, significant digits are those digits used to represent any number; leading zeroes as well as zeroes immediately following the decimal point are not significant. For example:

1001.56 has six significant digits

0012.4
.000315 } have three significant digits (.000315 = .315 $\times 10^{-3}$)

Trailing zeroes may or may not be significant, depending on what context they are used in. For example, in the following set of measurements, 10.5, 13.6 and 10.0, the number 10.0 has three significant digits; in a different set of measurements, 11.356, 12.555 and 10.000, the number 10.000 has five significant digits, yet 10.0 = 10.000.

Computers represent numbers and carry out operations using a fixed number of significant digits n, which is dependent on the computer's hardware. Any number or any result of an operation must then be expressed as accurately as possible with those n digits.

Since computers cannot, in general, represent nonterminating decimal numbers exactly, those numbers are rounded off. Rounding off a number to *n* significant digits amounts to finding the closest approximation to that number with *n* or fewer nonzero digits. More technically, this means discarding all digits to the right of the *n*th significant digit. If the first discarded digit is 5 or greater, add 1 to the *n*th digit; otherwise, leave the *n*th digit unchanged.

Example

The following numbers are rounded off to seven significant digits (IBM 360/370):

41.239824	rounded to 41.23982	$= .4123982 \times 10^2$
.0011145678	rounded to .001114568	$= .1114568 \times 10^{-2}$
315.00075	rounded to 315.0008	$= .3150008 \times 10^3$
1000001499999.98	rounded to 1000001000000.00	$= .1000001 \times 10^{13}$

Note in the last example the loss of precision in the final number representation (499,999!).

2. Does "significance" of digits imply accuracy of result? That is, if the computed result of an operation is carried out to seven significant digits, does this mean that the computer result represents the first seven digits of the true answer?

Answer: No. Significance and precision or accuracy of results are not synonymous. Consider the following example: Two carpenters must saw a board in seven equal parts. Assume they use a computer for their calculations which carries out operations to seven significant digits. Both carpenters feel very satisfied with the accuracy of their measurement of the board—40.01 and 39.89 inches respectively. A computer printout yields an answer of 5.715714 (40.01/7) and 5.698541 (39.89/7) for one-seventh of the board. The very presence of seven digits on the computer printout form might so overwhelm the carpenters that each might think his seven digits must be "right" or correct. Yet both results have only one digit in common! How many of these digits are then truly meaningful? one? two? Precision depends on the accuracy of the measurements, not on the seven significant digits. Many programmers have blind faith in computer printouts, yet much of a computer's input data in real life deals with approximate measurements of weights, distances, temperatures, forces etc.; significant digits themselves will not affect the precision of results to any great extent. Hence results should always be interpreted with the greatest of care even if 15 digits are used to express a result and even if DOUBLE PRECISION is used.

If it is known that the input data is 100 percent accurate, then of course the number of significant digits used in carrying operations can affect the precision of the results. The reader might be interested in the subject of error analysis, which treats the effects of significant digits or roundoff on numerical operations.

3. Is it true that most decimal numbers don't have an exact internal representation on the computer?

Answer: Yes. In fact 99.999... percent of the numbers that we can manipulate in everyday life are not represented exactly on a computer, which is not surprising when we stop and realize that the set of real numbers on a computer is finite. Numbers with small magnitudes have the best chance of being the most accurately represented in a computer. There are literally thousands and thousands more computer real numbers in the interval [0,1] than there are, say, in the interval between 100,000 and 100,001 and the interval or gap between any two successive computer real numbers widens dramatically as the numbers grow in magnitude. For example, on the 360/370 the real number following 3,000,000,000 is 3,000,001,000, not 3,000,000,001 (using single precision).

It should be noted however that all *integers* are represented exactly in memory up to the number of significant digits allowed by the computer system (see Figure 7-2). Note also the difference in significant digits for real versus integer numbers (see Figures 7-2 and 7-3). Integers are represented exactly in memory because the integer conversion to binary is exact. In the case of floating-point number conversion, the fractional part generally does not convert exactly in binary; for example, $.1_{10} = .00011001100_2 \cdots$ which must be rounded off.

4. Does the DOUBLE PRECISION statement give me more significant digits for integer numbers?

Answer: No. The DOUBLE PRECISION statement affects only real numbers. There is no double precision for integers. If an integer variable is declared in a DOUBLE PRECISION statement, that variable becomes automatically a real variable and should be described by an F edit code in a READ/WRITE format.

5. I need more significant digits than DOUBLE PRECISION can give me on the system that I use. What can I do?

Answer: You will have to write your own code. See Exercise 40 Section 8-6-2 for some thoughts on this matter.

6. Was I surprised the other day when a result of −0. was printed for my answer! I didn't know the computer used negative zeroes!

Answer: Some do and some don't! But your result wasn't really −0. anyhow. Your FORMAT just didn't leave enough places to print additional fractional digits. For example:

        X = −.04
        WRITE(3,1)X   This statement would cause −0.0 to be printed.
    1   FORMAT(2X,F4.1)

7. What characters can be processed by the alphanumeric A format code?

Answer: Any valid FORTRAN characters. The FORTRAN character set consists of 26 letters, 10 digits and 13 special characters, as follows:

Graphic symbol	Punched card code	Hexadecimal representation
Blank	None	40
. Decimal point	12–8–3	4B
(Left parenthesis	12–8–5	4E
+ Plus	12–8–6	50
$ Currency symbol	12	5B
* Asterisk	11–8–4	5C
) Right parenthesis	11–8–5	5D
: Colon	11–8–6	5E
– Minus	11	60
/ Slash	0–1	61
, Comma	8–3–0	6B
' Apostrophe	8–5	7D
= Equals	8–6	7E

The numeric code representing the FORTRAN character set is called EBCDIC (Extended Binary Coded Decimal Interchange Code). The collating (ordering) sequence is

special characters < letters of the alphabet < digits (0 through 9)

The ordering of the special characters is shown in ascending order above. Some FORTRAN compilers may accept source programs punched in the ASCII code (similar code to EBCDIC).[1]

8. Is there any way to process a variable-length character string using just one variable name for that string?

Answer: Some systems allow the use of the CHARACTER type statement, which may be used as follows:

```
      CHARACTER*36MESS1,MESS2,JOE
            .
            .
      READ(1,1)MESS1
    1 FORMAT(A36)
      IF(JOE.EQ.MESS1)MESS2 = MESS1
      WRITE(3,5)MESS2
    5 FORMAT(T5,A36)
```

Each string variable is defined to be 36 characters long. A string of a maximum of 256 characters could be declared as CHARACTER*256.

Compare all 36 characters.

Write out 36 characters at one go.

9. Can I initialize an alphanumeric string through a replacement statement; for example, X = 'DOG'?

Answer: Not usually. WATIV systems will permit it, however, if X has been declared a character variable.

10. What is the advantage of using logical variables and logic processing?

---

[1] ASCII stands for *A*merican *S*tandard *C*ode for *I*nformation *I*nterchange.

Answer: Decisions can be expressed in a straightforward fashion. Also, logical variables can be employed in Boolean algebra, which can be used as a mathematical tool or model in the study of sets, in the study of switching circuits and in applications which make use of truth or decision tables.

11. Can I define a logical variable in a DATA statement?

    Answer: Yes.

    Example

    > LOGICAL X
    > DATA X/.TRUE./

12. Can I use the SQRT function or **.5 to compute the square root of a complex number?

    Answer: No, use the CSQRT function. A list of functions that can operate on complex numbers is shown in Chapter 10, Figure 10-3. Complex numbers may, however, be raised to an integer exponent, i.e., (3.,−4.)**4 is valid.

7-4 Programming Examples

7-4-1   Logical Problem Example

Each card of a deck of cards contains the following fields:

Student name	(eight characters at most)	cc1–8
Age	An age of 0 terminates the data deck.	cc9–10
Sex	1 = male, 2 = female	cc11
Class	1 = freshman, 2 = sophomore	cc12

Write a program to list the names of students who are over 21 years of age and compute the number of male freshmen, female freshmen, male sophomores and female sophomores. A program to solve this problem is shown in Figure 7-7. Note the simplicity of using the logical IF.

7-4-2   Switching Circuits

Consider an electrical circuit consisting of a power source and switches such as:

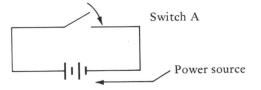

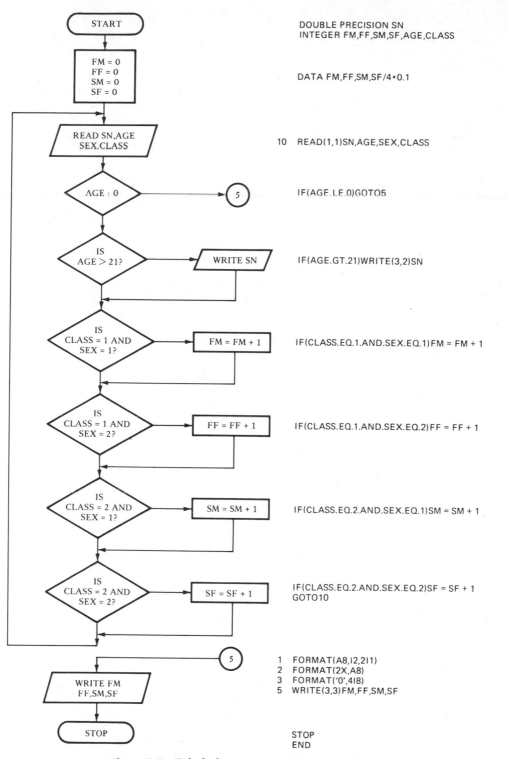

START

FM = 0
FF = 0
SM = 0
SF = 0

READ SN,AGE
SEX,CLASS

AGE : 0 → 5

IS
AGE > 21? → WRITE SN

IS
CLASS = 1 AND
SEX = 1? → FM = FM + 1

IS
CLASS = 1 AND
SEX = 2? → FF = FF + 1

IS
CLASS = 2 AND
SEX = 1? → SM = SM + 1

IS
CLASS = 2 AND
SEX = 2? → SF = SF + 1

5

WRITE FM
FF,SM,SF

STOP

DOUBLE PRECISION SN
INTEGER FM,FF,SM,SF,AGE,CLASS

DATA FM,FF,SM,SF/4*0.1

10   READ(1,1)SN,AGE,SEX,CLASS

IF(AGE.LE.0)GOTO5

IF(AGE.GT.21)WRITE(3,2)SN

IF(CLASS.EQ.1.AND.SEX.EQ.1)FM = FM + 1

IF(CLASS.EQ.1.AND.SEX.EQ.2)FF = FF + 1

IF(CLASS.EQ.2.AND.SEX.EQ.1)SM = SM + 1

IF(CLASS.EQ.2.AND.SEX.EQ.2)SF = SF + 1
GOTO10

1   FORMAT(A8,I2,2I1)
2   FORMAT(2X,A8)
3   FORMAT('0',4I8)
5   WRITE(3,3)FM,FF,SM,SF

STOP
END

Figure 7-7   Tabulation program with logical IFs.

If the switch is up, no current travels through the circuit; if the switch is down, current flows through the circuit. Let us represent the switch A with a logical variable having value .TRUE. if the switch is down and .FALSE. if the switch is up.

Two switches can be arranged in series as:

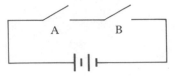

In this case, current travels through the circuit only when both A and B are down. The expression A.AND.B represents the series circuit.

Two switches can also be arranged in parallel:

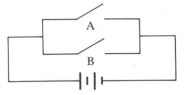

In this case, current travels through the circuit when A or B (or both) are down. The expression A.OR.B represents the parallel circuit.

It is possible to write logical expressions for any switching circuits:

Examples

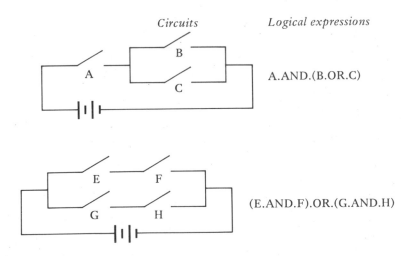

The program shown in Figure 7-8 can be used to evaluate the above circuits for various values of the switches.

```
     LOGICAL A,B,C,E,F,G,H,X,Y
 2   READ(1,1,END = 10)A,B,C,E,F,G,H
 1   FORMAT(7L1)
     X = A.AND.(B.OR.C)
     Y = (E.AND.F).OR.(G.AND.H)
     WRITE(3,3)A,B,C,X
 3   FORMAT(3X,'CIRCUIT1',3L2,'IS',L2)
     WRITE(3,4)E,F,G,H,Y
 4   FORMAT(3X,'CIRCUIT2',4L2,'IS',L2)
     GOTO2
10   STOP
     END
```

Figure 7-8   Evaluation of circuit expressions.

7-4-3   Complex Roots of a Quadratic

The roots of $ax^2 + bx + c = 0$ are given by

$$x_1 = \frac{-b + \sqrt{b^2 - 4ac}}{2a} \qquad x_2 = \frac{-b - \sqrt{b^2 - 4ac}}{2a}$$

If $b^2 - 4ac \geqslant 0$, the values of x_1 and x_2 are real; otherwise, they are complex. The program shown in Figure 7-9 will determine roots of the quadratic equation. If the solutions are real, the imaginary part of the roots will be zero (assume A1 $\neq$ 0).

```
     COMPLEX X1,X2,A1,B1,C1,D
 2   READ(1,1,END = 10)A,B,C
 1   FORMAT(3F4.0)
     A1 = A
     B1 = B
     C1 = C
     D = CSQRT(B1**2 - 4A1*C1)          CSQRT required complex arguments.
     X1 = (-B1 + D)/(2.*A1)
     X2 = (-B1 - D)/(2.*A1)
     WRITE(3,3)A,B,C,X1,X2
 3   FORMAT(2X,'A=',F5.0, 'B=',F5.0,'C=',F5.0,
   * 'X1=',2F7.3,'X2=',2F7.3)
     GOTO2
10   STOP
     END
```

Figure 7-9   Complex roots of a quadratic.

7-5 Probing Deeper

7-5-1   More on Floating-Point Numbers and Integers

Operations on floating-point data are performed using both the exponent and mantissa in much the same way as hand operations are performed using numbers represented in scientific notation.

Examples

$$4.2 \times .003 = .42 \times 10^1 \times .3 \times 10^{-2} = (.42 \times .3) \times (10^1 \times 10^{-2}) = .126 \times 10^{-1}$$
$$4.2 + .003 = .42 \times 10^1 + .3 \times 10^{-2} = .42 \times 10^1 + .0003 \times 10^1 = .4203 \times 10^1$$

Much larger and much smaller numbers can be represented with floating-point than with fixed-point numbers. However, the number of significant digits is limited with floating-point representation. For example, on the IBM 360/370, 1000000999999999 is internally stored as 1000000000000000 since the computer can only retain seven significant digits. This really means that $10^{15} + 999,999,999 = 10^{15}$. Any operations performed on large magnitudes result in large errors called *absolute errors*. For example, $10^{60} + 10^{52} = 10^{60}$ which means that 10^{52} is totally ignored. On the real line, there are gigantic gaps between numbers as these become larger and larger. The number that immediately follows 10^{75} on the IBM 360/370 is $10^{75} + 10^{69}$, not $10^{75} + 1$ or even $10^{75} + 1,000,000,000,000$! The gap is worth 10^{69}! Comparatively speaking, the numbers between 0 and 1 are extremely dense and well stocked.

The absolute error, such as the one above, is not as horrendous as one might suppose. After all, if the computer represents 1,000,000,400 as 1,000,000,000, the absolute error may be 400, but, relatively speaking, what is 400 compared to 1,000,000,400? Very little. Also, suppose the computer represented .6 as .5; then the absolute error would be .1, which is small, but, relatively speaking, to commit an error of .1 to represent .6 is horrendous even though the absolute error is small. Hence another measure of error is introduced, called the *relative error,* which may be more meaningful than the notion of absolute error.

The relative error of a computer-generated number is the absolute error divided by the computer approximation for that number. For example, if we have a true value of .00006 and a computer approximation of .00005, the absolute error is only 10^{-5} but the relative error is .00001/.00005 = .2 or 20 percent. If, on the other hand, we have a true value of 1,000,000,400 and an approximation 1,000,000,000, the absolute error is 400 but the relative error is 400/1,000,000,000 = $.4 \times 10^{-8}$ or nearly zero, percentagewise.

Fixed-point arithmetic is much faster than floating-point arithmetic, hence if execution time is critical it may be wise to use integer mode data and arithmetic whenever possible. There is some inherent error in the representation of data in floating-point schemes. During the number conversion process, some decimal numbers cannot be translated exactly in binary; for example: $.1_{10}$ has no exact binary representation. The resulting binary value is an approximation of $.1_{10}$ to within seven digits of accuracy (IBM 370). There are also other rational numbers that have no finite decimal representation, such as 1./3. = .3333333.

After any calculation, only a given number of digits are stored for the result. In a program with many calculations, this error (called *round-off error*) may encroach on one or more of the digits of the calculated result causing fewer than the anticipated number of digits to be correct. For example, on the IBM 370:

$$1.0007*1.007 = 1.007705$$
while in real life
$$1.0007*1.007 = 1.0077049$$

This is only one digit off in the sixth fractional position. However, if the result were to be multiplied by 10^{10}, this would result in an error of 1,000.

7-6   Exercises

7-6-1   Self Test

1. What advantage is there in using double precision mode variables and constants? What is the price that you pay for double precision mode, however?

2. What restrictions are there on the placement of specification statements in FORTRAN programs?

3. Express each of the following exponential constants in basic form:
    a. 3.2E − 4
    b. .0034E10
    c. −132.4E6
    d. −132.4E − 6
    e. 432.4D2
    f. −163.94872D − 10
    g. 1632543.11D − 8
    h. .0000324D15

4. What value will be stored in each of the following examples as a result of a READ operation? The result should be expressed as $0.ddddddd \times 10^{ee}$, where d and e are the significant digits and the digit exponent respectively.

Punched data	READ FORMAT code	Value stored
a. 632E4	E5.2	
b. −.623E14	E8.2	
c. 1234E − 2	E7.0	
d. −1234E − 5	E8.2	
e. 69.52D4	D7.2	
f. 000003241	E9.3	
g. −00002561E4	E11.4	
h. 333.447E − 50	E12.0	

5. What output will be produced in each of the following examples?

Value in memory	Output FORMAT code	Output results
a. .0032456	E8.2	
b. −98.9437	E15.1	
c. .0032456	E11.4	
d. 31245.E − 31	E15.2	
e. −12340000.	E13.4	
f. −12340000.	D16.7	
g. −.0000006972	E8.1	
h. +212.E + 26	E7.1	
i. 212.E26	E6.1	
j. 123.4567891	E17.10	
k. 123.4567891	D16.8	

6. Which of the following statements are TRUE?
   a. Specification statement errors are detected at execution time.
   b. DATA statements must be the first statements in a FORTRAN program.
   c. Specification statements are nonexecutable statements.
   d. The statement INTEGERISAM,SAM,KKK is valid.
   e. Double precision numbers imply twice as many significant digits as ordinary real constants.
   f. A real constant has the same internal representation as an exponential real constant.
   g. Double precision numbers also exist for integers.
   h. The statement DOUBLE PRECISION I,J,K is valid.
   i. The REAL statement may be used to define a double precision constant.
   j. The statement X = 12345678901134.56 causes X to become a double precision variable.
   k. Integers are always fixed in length in terms of memory representation. For instance, the constant 1 uses the same number of bits as 1234567.
   l. Double precision always implies greater number of significant digits and a greater range for the exponent.
   m. The F, E and D format codes can be used to read real numbers in non-exponential form.
   n. The A format code can be used to read any data that can be read by an I,F,E,D format code.

7. Which of the following statements are correct?
   a. A + B could be a valid logical expression, depending on how A and B are specified.

b. X + Y.LT.5. is an elementary logical expression.

c. B.OR.10 is a compound logical expression.

d. A.NOT.B is an invalid compound logical expression.

e. The value of A.AND.(.NOT.A) is .FALSE. .

f. Y.AND.SQR(X) is a valid logical expression.

8. Evaluate each of the following logical expressions if A = 3.0, B = −4 and C = 0.

a. A.LT.B

b. .NOT.A.GT.0.

c. B.LT.C.OR.A.LT.B

d. B.LE.C.AND.A.LT.B

e. C.GT.B.AND.(A.LE.16.0.OR.B.EQ.4.)

f. .NOT.(A.GT.B.OR.C.EQ.0)

g. .NOT.A.GT.B.OR.C.EQ.0

h. A.EQ.B.AND.B.LT.C.OR.(.NOT.A.LT.B)

9. Determine the value of the following expressions, given A = .TRUE., B = .TRUE., C = .FALSE. .

a. A.OR.B

b. .NOT.C

c. (A.OR.B).AND.C

d. .TRUE..OR.C

e. .TRUE..AND.C (read it quickly!)

f. .NOT.C.OR.B

10. Write one IF-statement which will have the same effect as the statements below.

```
a.       IF(X.GT.0)GOTO20
         GOTO30
     20  IF(X.LT.10)STOP
     30  · · ·
b.       IF(X.GT.10)GOTO20
         IF(X.LT.0)GOTO20
         GOTO30
     20  STOP
     30  · · ·
```

11. Write a LOGICAL expression involving two LOGICAL variables A and B, which has the value .TRUE. if only A is .TRUE. or if only B is .TRUE.; and is .FALSE. if both A and B are .TRUE. or both are .FALSE. . (This expression is called the *exclusive-or*.)

12. Represent each of the following circuits by means of a logical expression.

a.

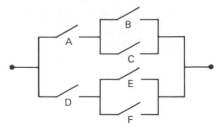

b.

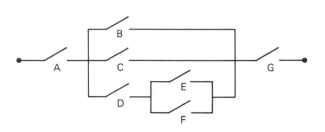

c.

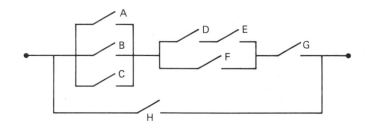

d.

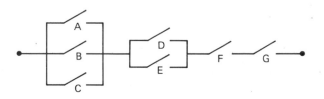

e.

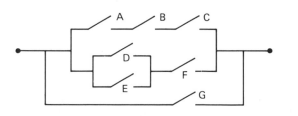

13. Which of the following are valid complex constants:

   a. (0.0).   b. (6,4).   c. (12.3,−1.2E−3).   d. (X,Y).

14. Determine the values of the following expressions:
    a. 2.*(1.4,−3.7)
    b. (0.,1.)**2
    c. C*(1.,0.) + D*(0.,+1) where C = 2., D = −3.
    d. A*(1.,−1.) where A = (2.,−3.)

7-6-2 Programming Problems

1. Write a program to print and/or punch the content of a deck of data cards.

2. A deck of cards contains two fields per card: A name and a marital status code (1 = single, 2 = married, 3 = divorced, 4 = widowed). Produce a listing (using just one WRITE statement) of the names and their corresponding alphabetic marital status.

   Example

   $$\begin{array}{ll} \text{JONES} & \text{MARRIED} \\ \text{SALEM} & \text{SINGLE} \end{array}$$

3. In a physical education class, students either get a pass or fail for the course. If the average of the student's three test scores is below 70, the student fails the course. The student's three test scores are recorded on cards as follows (assume no more than 30 cards):

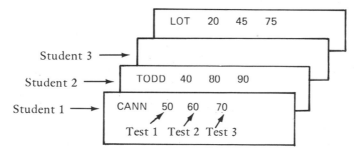

   Write a program to produce the following output:

STUDENT	TEST1	TEST2	TEST3	AVERAGE	FINAL GRADE
CANN	50	60	70	60	FAIL
TODD	40	80	90	70	PASS
.	.	.	.	.	.
.	.	.	.	.	.
LOT	20	45	75	46.6	FAIL

   THE PERCENTAGE OF STUDENTS WHO FAILED IS XX.

4. Omega Triple Pooh sorority girls are very selective about their blind dates. The housemother keeps a card file of male characteristics of the local fraternities. Each card contains a code describing the following attributes:

Complexion	Height	Trait	Age
fair	tall	handsome	
dark	medium	timid	
whitish	small	aggressive	

All dates must satisfy the following conditions:
Tall and handsome, but not dark, and between the ages of 20 and 30
or
Medium height, timid, but not whitish, either under 22 or over 28
but under no condition
Small and aggressive and over 65, or timid and tall and under 16
Write a program to compute the number of lucky dates.

5. Each data card consists of six items described as follows:

Item		Description/code
1	Marital status	1 = single 2 = married 3 = divorced 4 = widowed
2	Sex	1 = female 2 = male
3	Age	1 = over 30 2 = under 30
4	Contentment	1 = happy 2 = unhappy
5	Family name	
6	First name	

Write a program to transcribe this data into English sentences having the following structure:

$$\text{first-name family-name IS} \begin{Bmatrix} \text{OVER 30} \\ \text{UNDER 30} \end{Bmatrix} . \begin{Bmatrix} \text{SHE} \\ \text{HE} \end{Bmatrix} \text{IS} \begin{Bmatrix} \text{SINGLE} \\ \text{MARRIED} \\ \text{DIVORCED} \\ \text{WIDOWED} \end{Bmatrix} \text{AND} \begin{Bmatrix} \text{HAPPY} \\ \text{UNHAPPY} \end{Bmatrix} .$$

For example, the data card ⌈2 2 1 2 OAKS ZAN⌉ should produce the following sentence:

ZAN OAKS IS OVER 30. HE IS MARRIED AND UNHAPPY.

6. To be eligible for promotion, teachers at Franzia College must have taught at Franzia College for at least five years or, if not, at least seven years in the state. Teachers are not eligible for promotion after 25 years of teaching. To be eligible for promotion to:

Assistant professor: teacher must have at least a master's degree in the field in which he teaches.
Associate professor: teacher must have at least a master's degree plus 30 hours in his teaching field.
Full professor: teacher must have a doctorate in any field.

In addition, no teacher is eligible for promotion if he has not served three full years in his rank. The rank below assistant professor is Instructor. Only four ranks exist at Franzia College. Design a card layout form for personnel to record all faculty data and write a program to determine the number of faculty eligible for promotion.

7. Write a program for the IRS to determine who should file income tax returns (use current IRS data forms).

8. Write a FORTRAN program to determine whether the following logical equations are always satisfied regardless of the values of A, B and C.
   a. .NOT.(A.AND.B) = .NOT.A.OR.(.NOT.B)
   b. A.OR.(B.AND.C) = (A.OR.B).OR.(A.OR.C)
   c. .NOT.(A.AND.B).OR.A = True
   d. A.AND.B.OR.(.NOT.A.AND.C) = .NOT.A.AND.(.NOT.B).AND.C.OR.A
   $$.AND.B.AND.(.NOT.C).OR.B.AND.C$$

   Problem 8a can be partially verified by observing that:

   $$\overset{?}{.NOT.(.TRUE..AND..FALSE.)} = .NOT..TRUE..OR.(.NOT..FALSE.)$$

   $$
   \begin{array}{lcl}
   \overset{?}{.NOT.(.FALSE.)} & = & .FALSE..OR..TRUE. \\
   .TRUE. & = & .TRUE.
   \end{array}
   $$

   Hence when A = T B = F, the equation holds. It remains to be proved what happens for other combinations of A and B. A table of all possible values that A, B and C can assume is constructed as follows:

A	B	C
.FALSE.	.FALSE.	.FALSE.
.FALSE.	.FALSE.	.TRUE.
.FALSE.	.TRUE.	.FALSE.
.FALSE.	.TRUE.	.TRUE.
.TRUE.	.FALSE.	.FALSE.
.TRUE.	.FALSE.	.TRUE.
.TRUE.	.TRUE.	.FALSE.
.TRUE.	.TRUE.	.TRUE.

   Punch eight data cards with three items on each (first card contains F,F,F; second card contains F,F,T etc.) and write the code to determine whether part of a,b,c,d of Exercise 8 is true. If any equation does not hold true, write the values of A, B and C for which the equation does not hold true.

9. The effect of round-off using floating-point arithmetic can be demonstrated as follows: Suppose we are working with a decimal machine capable of storing four significant digits. Suppose, further, we wish to perform the following computation:

$$2000 + .1 = .2000 \times 10^4 + .1000 \times 10^0$$

When an addition is to be performed and the exponents are not equal, the mantissa of the variable having the smaller exponent is shifted to the right and the exponent is increased until it is equal to the larger exponent. Thus:

$.1000 \times 10^0 = .00001 \times 10^4$

and

$.2000 \times 10^4 + .00001 \times 10^4 = (.2000 + .00001) \times 10^4 = .200001 \times 10^4$

However, the machine can only store four digits; hence the digits calculated must either be rounded or truncated (some machines do it one way, some another) to four digits. In either case, the value stored for this example will be $.2000 \times 10^4$. Devise an experiment to show this effect using your computer. Can you determine whether your machine rounds or truncates when storing a floating-point value?

10. Floating-point arithmetic may not obey all of the usual rules of real numbers. In particular, the associative property does not hold. For example, consider the four-digit based floating-point machine described in Exercise 9, and suppose that truncation is performed. Let us evaluate $(2000. + .4) + .6$ and $2000. + (.4 + .6)$.

$$
\begin{aligned}
(2000. + .4) + .6 &= (.2000 \times 10^4 + .4000 \times 10^0) + .6000 \times 10^0 \\
&= (.2000 \times 10^4 + .00004 \times 10^4 + .6000 \times 10^0 \\
&= (.20004 \times 10^4) + .6000 \times 10^0 \\
&= (.2000 \times 10^4) + .6000 \times 10^0 \qquad \text{Truncation occurs.} \\
&= (.2000 + .00006) \times 10^4 \\
&= .20006 \times 10^4 \\
&= .2000 \times 10^4 \qquad\qquad\qquad \text{Truncation occurs.}
\end{aligned}
$$

$$
\begin{aligned}
2000. + (.4 + .6) &= .2000 \times 10^4 + (.4000 \times 10^0 + .6000 \times 10^0) \\
&= .2000 \times 10^4 + (.1000 \times 10^1) \\
&= .2000 \times 10^4 + .0001 \times 10^4 \\
&= (.2000 + .0001) \times 10^4 \\
&= .2001 \times 10^4
\end{aligned}
$$

Devise an experiment to show that the associative property does not hold for floating-point arithmetic on your machine.

11. Another source of error when using floating-point data representation is the change in base that is performed in storing a decimal value. Consider, for example, the decimal value .1. There is no exact representation of this value in base 2,8 or 16. The value stored for .1 is only an approximation of .1. Consider the following code:

```
X = .1
Y = X + X + X + X + X + X + X + X + X + X
WRITE(3,5)Y
```

If a sufficient number of significant digits are written out the value of Y will be .9999999999...

Test the above program with appropriate format codes (F20.15 etc.) to determine the approximate accuracy of your computer.

7-6-3 Answers to Self Test

1. Double precision mode data allows more significant digits to be computed but takes more space to store each value.

2. Specification statements must precede executable statements.

3. a. 0.00032.   b. 34000000.   c. −132400000.   d. −.0001324.
   e. 43240.   f. −.000000016394872.   g. 0.0163254311.
   h. 32400000000.

4. a. 0.6320000×10^5.   b. $-0.6230000 \times 10^{14}$.   c. 0.1234000×10^2.
   d. $-0.1234000 \times 10^{-3}$.   e. 0.6952000×10^6.   f. 0.3241000×10^1.
   g. -0.2561000×10^4.   h. $0.3334470 \times 10^{-47}$.

5. a. $\underline{0.32E-02}$ b. $\underline{\qquad\qquad -0.1E\ \ 03}$
   c. $\underline{\ 0.3246E-02}$ d. $\underline{\qquad\qquad 0.31E-26}$
   e. $\underline{\qquad -0.1234E\ \ 08}$ f. $\underline{\ \ -0.1234000D\ \ 08}$
   g. $\underline{-0.7E-06}$ h. $\underline{0.2E\ \ 29}$ i. $\underline{.2E\ \ 29}$
   j. $\underline{\ 0.123456789 1E\ \ 03}$ k. $\underline{\qquad 0.12345679D\ \ 03}$

6. a. F.   b. F.   c. T.   d. T.   e. F.   f. T.   g. F.   h. T.   i. F.
   j. F.   k. T.   l. F.   m. T.   n. T.

7. a. F.   b. T.   c. F.   d. T.   e. T.   f. F.

8. a. F.   b. F.   c. T.   d. F.   e. T.   f. F.   g. T.   h. T.

9. a. T.   b. T.   c. F.   d. T.   e. F.   f. T.

10. a. IF(X.GT.0.AND.X.LT.10)STOP   b. IF(X.GT.10.OR.X.LT.0)STOP

11. (A.AND.(.NOT.B)).OR.((.NOT.A).AND.B)

12. a. A.AND.(B.OR.C).OR.D.AND.(E.OR.F)
    b. A.AND.(B.OR.C.OR.(D.AND.(E.OR.F))).AND.G
    c. (A.OR.B.OR.C).AND.((D.AND.E).OR.F).AND.G).OR.H
    d. (A.OR.B.OR.C).AND.(D.OR.E).AND.F.AND.G
    e. (A.AND.B.AND.C).OR.((D.OR.E).AND.F).OR.G

13. a. Invalid.   b. Invalid.   c. Valid.   d. Invalid.

14. a. (2.8, −7.4).   b. (−1.0,0.0).   c. (2.0,−3.0).   d. (−1.0,−5.0).

ONE-DIMENSIONAL ARRAYS

8-1 Problem Example

Let us write a program to calculate the average of five grades read from cards, one grade per card, and print the difference between each grade and the average. Up until this time, it has been possible to compute an average of grades simply by reading each grade in just one variable name, using the statement READ(1,3)GRADE and accumulating these grades as they are read. This procedure cannot be used in this case, however, since each new grade destroys the previous value in GRADE, thereby making it impossible to compare each grade with the average once the average has been computed. Each grade must therefore be preserved, and for that reason five distinct memory locations (variables) are needed, as shown in Figure 8-1.

One method for solving this problem is shown in Figure 8-2. This code is somewhat cumbersome, due to the individual labeling of the five different variable names.

Another approach to the problem is to use an *array* to store the grades. An array is a sequence of consecutive memory locations in which data (*elements*) are stored. Any element in an array can be referenced by specifying the name of the array and a position number (*subscript*) indicating the position of the desired element with respect to the first position of the array; for example, first, fourth,

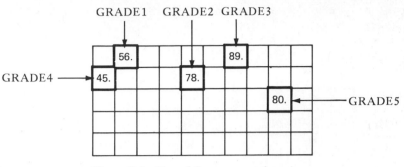

Figure 8-1   Use of five memory locations.

```
C DEVIATION OF 5 GRADES WITHOUT ARRAYS
      READ(1,5)GRADE1,GRADE2,GRADE3,GRADE4,GRADE5
   5  FORMAT(F5.1)
      AVE=(GRADE1+GRADE2+GRADE3+GRADE4+GRADE5)/5
      DIF=GRADE1−AVE
      WRITE(3,10)GRADE1,DIF
      DIF=GRADE2−AVE
      WRITE(3,10)GRADE2,DIF
      DIF=GRADE3−AVE
      WRITE(3,10)GRADE3,DIF
      DIF=GRADE4−AVE
      WRITE(3,10)GRADE4,DIF
      DIF=GRADE5−AVE
      WRITE(3,10)GRADE5,DIF
  10  FORMAT(T10,F5.1,3X,F5.1)
      STOP
      END
```

```
            56.0   −13.6
            78.0     8.4
            89.0    19.4
            45.0   −24.6
            80.0    10.4
```

Figure 8-2   Average and deviation without an array.

fifth position etc. The name for the array of grades might be called GRADE and would consist of five memory locations, as shown in Figure 8-3.

Allocation of the five memory locations to the array GRADE is made through the DIMENSION statement (see Figure 8-4), which tells the compiler to reserve five memory locations for the array GRADE. Both of the methods described to solve the problem of Section 8-1 make use of the same amount of memory locations. In the case of the array GRADE, a block of five sequential memory locations is reserved for the five grades. Five memory locations are also used in the case of the individualized labeling of each grade GRADE1,GRADE2,... . What makes the array concept different and powerful is that elements within the array can be indexed with a subscript thereby considerably simplifying the task of manipulating array elements for processing and for input/output considerations (see Figure 8-4).

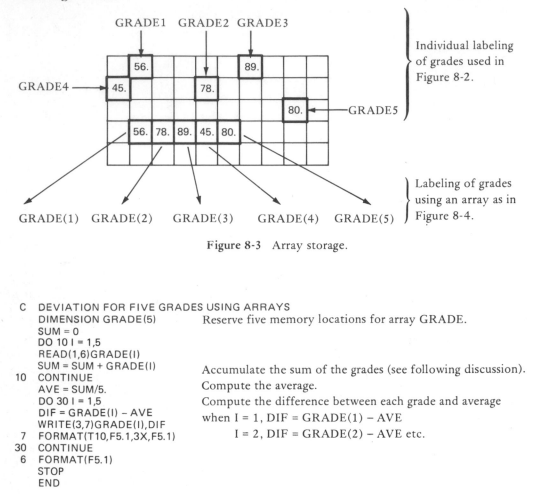

Figure 8-3   Array storage.

```
C    DEVIATION FOR FIVE GRADES USING ARRAYS
     DIMENSION GRADE(5)              Reserve five memory locations for array GRADE.
     SUM = 0
     DO 10 I = 1,5
     READ(1,6)GRADE(I)
     SUM = SUM + GRADE(I)            Accumulate the sum of the grades (see following discussion).
10   CONTINUE
     AVE = SUM/5.                    Compute the average.
     DO 30 I = 1,5                   Compute the difference between each grade and average
     DIF = GRADE(I) – AVE            when I = 1, DIF = GRADE(1) – AVE
     WRITE(3,7)GRADE(I),DIF               I = 2, DIF = GRADE(2) – AVE etc.
7    FORMAT(T10,F5.1,3X,F5.1)
30   CONTINUE
6    FORMAT(F5.1)
     STOP
     END
```

Figure 8-4   Average and deviation with arrays.

For example, to read the five grades into the array GRADE (storing them into GRADE(1),GRADE(2),...,GRADE(5), the program in Figure 8-4 repeatedly processes the statement READ(1,6)GRADE(I) for values of I ranging from 1 to 5. I is called a *subscript* or an *index*. It is initially set to 1... so that the first time the statement READ(1,6)GRADE(I) is executed GRADE(I) will refer to GRADE(1) and hence the value read from the data card will be stored in GRADE(1). The second time I is 2 and GRADE(I) will identify GRADE(2); a new value will be stored in GRADE(2). Eventually I will be 5 and GRADE(I) refers to GRADE(5) and the last value read will be stored in GRADE(5). For example, if the five following data cards were read, the array GRADE could be visualized as

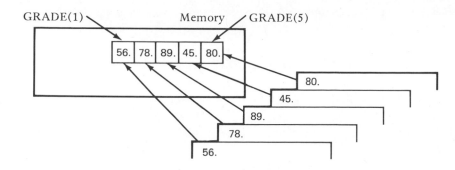

Through the use of indexing, accumulation logic can be used to calculate the sum of grades. The statement SUM = SUM + GRADE(I) (see Figure 8-4) accomplishes this accumulation process. The first time through the loop, I = 1 and SUM = SUM + GRADE(I) = 0 + GRADE(1) = 56; the first grade in the array is added to SUM, which is initially zero. The second time through the loop, I = 2 and SUM = SUM + GRADE(I) = 56 + GRADE(2) = 56 + 78 = 134. Finally, when I = 5, the fifth grade in the array will have been added to the sum of the four previous grades. Output also can be handled in a loop by using a variable subscript on the array GRADE, in much the same way as for input. In this example, the use of an array may not result in a significantly shorter program, but the array technique can be used for many more grades with no increase in the number of statements required and no explicit use of additional variable names.

8-2 Fortran Statements

8-2-1 DIMENSION Statement

The general form of the DIMENSION statement is

DIMENSION variable$_1$ (limit$_1$) [, variable$_2$ (limit$_2$) . . .]

where   DIMENSION is a FORTRAN key word.

variable$_1$, variable$_2$, . . . are names of the various arrays (any valid variable name). The type of the array (integer or real) is implicitly determined by the name of the array. If the name starts with I through N, the array elements are integer; otherwise, they are real.

limit$_1$, limit$_2$, . . . are unsigned integer constants representing the maximum number of memory locations reserved for each array.

This does not mean that all reserved locations must be used when processing the array. Array subscripts may vary from 1 to the limit declared in the DIMENSION statement and may not exceed that limit. Any array used in a program must first be declared in a DIMENSION statement. Any number of arrays may be declared in a DIMENSION list. For example, the statement

DIMENSION X(6),Z(20),JSUM(107)

declares X and Y as real arrays and JSUM as an integer array. In this case, the array X may contain up to 6 elements, the array Z up to 20 elements and the array JSUM up to 107 integer values. One might visualize the elements of X, Y and JSUM as shown in Figure 8-5.

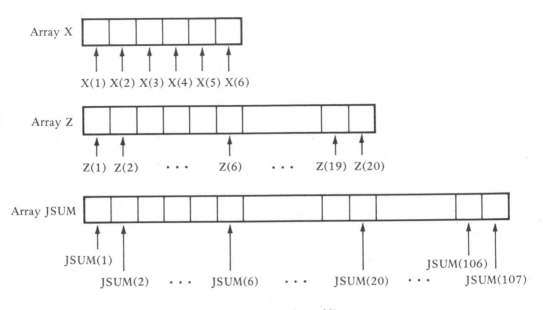

Figure 8-5 Representation of linear arrays.

The following DIMENSION statements are invalid:

DIMENSION (A3.) Invalid limit—should be an integer constant.
DIMENSION A(N) N is not an integer constant.

DIMENSION statements must appear in the program prior to the first executable statement (Replacement statement, I/O statement, IF and GOTO statements). A simple practice is to place the DIMENSION statement at the very beginning of the program. Array names are ordinary variable names that must be declared in a DIMENSION statement. The maximum value that can be specified as a limit to an array size may depend on the size of the memory of the particular computer used.

Arrays may also be declared using FORTRAN-type statements such as

INTEGER, REAL, DOUBLE PRECISION

For instance, the following are all valid array declaration statements:

INTEGER GRADE(30),JSUM(30)	All 30 elements of GRADE are integer values.
REAL A(336),K(32)	The elements of K are treated as real values.
DOUBLE PRECISION B(5),LT(6),M	Both B and LT are double precision (real) arrays. M becomes a double precision variable.

The following declaration would be invalid, however:

INTEGER A(100)
DIMENSION A(100)

8-2-2 Subscripts

Subscripts are used with array names to locate specific elements within an array. The subscript is enclosed within parentheses following the array name and can be an integer constant, an integer variable or certain expression forms shown in the following table.

Subscript expression form[1]	Example	Meaning
c	A(3)	Third element of array A
V	B(J)	refers to jth element of B.
k*V	COST(3*K)	If K is initially 1, the subscript spans every third element of COST.
k*V ± c	L(10*ISUM − 7)	Evaluate 10*ISUM − 7 and look at the corresponding entry in array L.

V is an unsubscripted integer variable name.
c and k are unsigned integer constants.

It is important to differentiate between the subscript value and the corresponding array element value. The value of A(3) generally has nothing to do with the number 3, for instance A(3) = .0076. Also the same subscript can be used to reference two different array elements, for example A(I) and B(I).

Note that the subscript expression must be an integer expression. Since subscripts identify the position of an element in an array, it is important that no subscripts evaluate to zero or a negative number. Following are some examples of invalid subscripts:

A(−3)	Negative subscript.
E(2*A(1) + 1)	Expression contains a subscripted array name.
G(LOG(K) − 1)	Illegal function reference.
Z(3.)	Real constant as a subscript.

---

[1] See Section 8-3 for generalization of subscripts.

Subscripted variables may be used in any FORTRAN statement in the same way as nonsubscripted variables. For example:

$$X(4) = 2.1*(X(1)*X(3) - LOG(Y)/X(4))$$ is perfectly valid.

It should be emphasized again that no array subscript should ever exceed the length or size of the array declared in the DIMENSION statement; that is, if 50 memory locations have been reserved for an array A, the subscript used for A should not exceed 50. Consider the following examples assuming that values for arrays A and B have already been established:

```
      DIMENSION A(100),B(10)
      I = 101
      Y = A(I)                Invalid use of A(I), since I = 101, which exceeds 100.
      B(11) = 3.              Maximum subscript for B is 10.
      DO 10 I = 1,11          On the last pass of the DO loop, I will be eleven,
   10 B(I) = 0.               causing an invalid reference to B(11).
```

8-2-3   Array Manipulation

When working with arrays it is often necessary to initialize arrays to certain values, to create duplicate arrays, to interchange elements within arrays, to merge two or more arrays into one, to search or accumulate array entries, to sort arrays etc. This section illustrates certain commonly used array manipulation techniques so that the reader may get a better grasp of the array index mechanism. In the following discussions, it is assumed that arrays have been dimensioned and values have been read in.

Array Initialization and Duplication

The following code sets all elements of the array A to zeroes, sets each element of B equal to X and creates a duplicate copy of the array D in array SAVE.

```
      READ(1,5)N            Read a value for N. That value must not exceed the size of arrays
      DO 10 I = 1,N         A,B,SAVE and D as declared in the DIMENSION statement.
      A(I) = 0              A(1),A(2), · · · ,A(N) are set to 0, one entry at a time as I ranges
      B(I) = X              from 1 to N. Similarly B(1),B(2), · · · ,B(N) are set to the value in X.
   10 SAVE(I) = D(I)        SAVE(1) = D(1),SAVE(2) = D(2), · · · ,SAVE(N) = D(N).
```

Sometimes it might be required to set an array C to the sum of two other arrays A and B in such a way that $C(1) = A(1) + B(1)$, $C(2) = A(2) + B(2)$, · · · , $C(100) = A(100) + B(100)$. The following code might be used (assume A and B have already been loaded):

DO 15 I = 1,100
15   C(I) = A(I) + B(I)

For example:

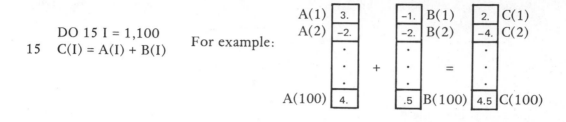

Suppose it is desired to initialize two arrays A and B as follows:

$$A(1) = B(10) = 1$$
$$A(2) = B(9) = 2$$
$$A(3) = B(8) = 3$$
.
.
.
$$A(10) = B(1) = 10$$

The numbers $1,2,3, \cdots ,10$ can be generated by the index of a DO loop as follows:

```
     DO 20 I = 1,10
     A(I) = I
     K = 10 – I + 1          K generates the numbers 10,9,8, · · · ,1 as I ranges from 1 to 10.
20   B(K) = I                If I ranged from 1 to N, the formula K = N – I + 1 would generate
                             the numbers N,N – 1,N – 2, · · · ,3,2,1.
```

Reversing Arrays

Suppose A is an array of size N where N has been previously defined and it is desired to interchange A(1) with A(N), A(2) with A(N – 1), A(3) with A(N – 2) etc. The following code could be used:

```
     L = N/2              Since each interchange step involves a pair of array elements
     DO 10 I = 1,L        (A₁,A_N), (A₂,A_N–1) etc., the interchange process need only be
     TEMP = A(I)          repeated N/2 times. If N is odd, the median element stays the same
     K = N – I + 1        and the interchange procedure does not affect it.
     A(I) = A(K)          K generates the numbers N,N – 1, · · · ,3,2,1.
10   A(K) = TEMP          TEMP is a temporary storage area needed to save A(1) before the
                          statement A(1) = A(N) is executed; otherwise A(1) would be
                          destroyed.
```

If L were N instead of N/2, the array would "re-reverse" itself and end up as it began.

Assume each element of an array K of size 20 contains a character string such as

$$K(1) = \boxed{C}$$
$$K(2) = \boxed{A}$$
$$K(3) = \boxed{T}$$
$$\vdots \qquad \vdots$$

The following code will write it out in reverse order.

```
       DO 10 I = 1,20
       J = 21 − I          J generates the numbers 20,19,18, · · · ,2,1.
  10   L(J) = K(I)
       WRITE(3,1)(L,J)
```

Accumulation of Array Elements

To compute the sum of the elements of the array A = $\boxed{10.\ |\ 20.\ |\ 30.\ |\ 40.\ |\ 50.}$, the
following code could be used:

```
       SUM = 0          SUM is set to 0 before the loop is entered.
       DO 10 I = 1,5    The first time through the loop SUM = SUM + A(1) = 0. + 10. = 10.
  10   SUM = SUM + A(I) The second time through the loop SUM = SUM + A(2) = 10. + 20.
                        = 30 etc.
```

The accumulation process can be visualized as follows:

I	SUM
	0.
1	10. (0 + 10)
2	30. (10 + 20)
3	60. (30 + 30)
4	100. (60 + 40)
5	150. (100 + 50)

Suppose it is desired to compute the sum of two arrays A and B both of size
N. The following code could be used:

```
       SUM = 0                SUM is used to accumulate the sum and is set to 0.
       DO 10 I = 1,N          The first time through the loop SUM = 0 + A(1) + B(1).
  10   SUM = SUM + A(I) + B(I) The second time through the loop SUM = A(1) + B(1) +
                              A(2) + B(2) and so on.
                                                          SUM
```

Array Merge

A and B are both arrays of size 10. It is desired to create a third array C whose entries are arranged in the order $A_1, B_1, A_2, B_2, \cdots, A_{10}, B_{10}$. The following codes could be used:

```
    K = 1                                                      K = 1
    DO 10 I = 1,10        DO 10 I = 1,10                DO 10 I = 1,20,2
    C(K) = A(I)           C(2*I − 1) = A(I)             C(I) = A(K)
    K = K + 1         10  C(2*I) = B(I)                 C(I + 1) = B(K)
    C(K) = B(I)                                     10  K = K + 1
10  K = K + 1
```

Array Search

Assume array A contains 100 grades and it is desired to determine the number of grades over 53. The following code could be used:

```
    K = 0
    DO 10 I = 1,100
    IF(A(I).GT.53)K = K + 1    If A(I) > 53 increment counter K by one. Otherwise compare
10  CONTINUE                   next grade with 53.
```

8-2-4 Input and Output of Arrays

There are essentially two methods for loading (reading) and writing out arrays. The first method uses the *explicit* form of the DO loop as illustrated in Figure 8-4. The second method uses an implied form of the DO loop, which is equivalent to listing all array entries individually in the READ list. This method is called the *implied DO list*. The selection of the method for inputting or outputting arrays depends on the arrangement of the data which may preclude one method from being used. If the exact number of array elements to be processed is known ahead of time, then the implied DO list can always be used. The two methods are discussed in more detail as follows:

Explicit Use of the DO Loop

The READ statement is part of the DO loop where the array subscript is also used as the index of the DO loop. For example, to read ten data items from cards (one data item per card), the following code might be used:

Example 1

```
    DIMENSION A(10)
    DO 10 I = 1,10
10  READ(1,5)A(I)
 5  FORMAT(F5.0)
```

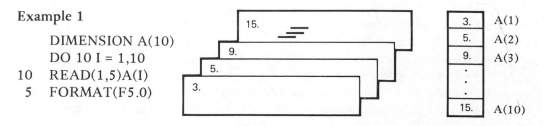

The first time through the loop I is 1, and A(1) is read from the data card. The second time through the loop I is 2, and the data item on the second card is stored into A(2). Finally, I is 10, and the tenth data item on the tenth card is read into A(10). Because there is only one variable in the READ list the corresponding format should only specify one data format code.

To read two numbers per card into two different arrays IHR and RATE, the following code could be used:

Example 2

```
      DIMENSION IHR(10),RATE(10)
      DO 10 I = 1,10
      READ(1,5)IHR(I),RATE(I)
10    CONTINUE
5     FORMAT(I3,2X,F4.0)
```

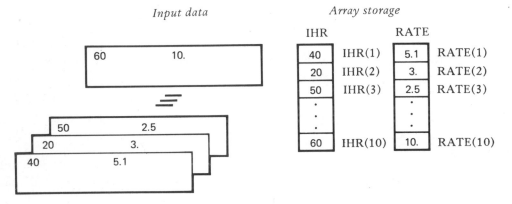

Assume each element of array SALES contains a daily sales amount and it is desired to print the daily sales with each corresponding day; the following code could be used:

```
      DIMENSION SALES(7)
      DO 10 I = 1,7
15    WRITE(3,11)I,SALES(I)
10    CONTINUE
11    FORMAT(2X,I2,3X,F5.1)
```

Output

```
1    101.0
2    200.0
3    150.2
4    300.0
5    400.8
6    500.4
7     50.0
```

Note the relationship between I and SALES(I) in statement 15. I is the day number and SALES(I) is the sales for that day, i.e., for the Ith day.

Data may sometimes have to be read into arrays, from an unknown number of cards. For example, someone may give us a large deck of cards with one number per card and ask us to read this data into an array A. Since the DIMENSION statement must specify an integer constant for the size of the array, the programmer must decide ahead of time what he thinks is the maximum number of entries he will need for the array. Of course, he may never use that many array locations. The programmer may *not* proceed as follows: declare the array DIMENSION A(N) and then read a value for N. This may sound logical, but the practice is syntactically incorrect.

Consider the following problem: Each card of an unknown deck of cards contains a student's name and two test scores. Read into an array NAME the name of each student (eight characters maximum) and store in array SCORE the average of each student's score. Print the number of records processed. Assume a maximum of 100 student records. The following two methods are presented:

Last-card code method. An additional card containing a last-card code is appended to the data deck. Conceivably, 101 cards may have to be read, if there are exactly 100 student records.

```
       DOUBLE PRECISION NAME(101)
       DIMENSION SCORE(100)
       DO 10 I = 1,101
       READ(1,11)NAME(I),T1,T2,LCC
       IF(LCC − 99)9,8,9
  9    SCORE(I) = (T1 + T2)/2.
 10    CONTINUE
  8    I = I − 1
       WRITE(3,1)I
 11    FORMAT(A8,2F5.0,I2)
  1    FORMAT(I4)
```

For example: NAME(1) = JOHN _ _ _ _
             NAME(2) = MICHAEL _
             NAME(3) = SANDRA _ _

If 101 cards are read, NAME(101) will contain blanks and T1,T2 will be zero.

The number of student records processed is one less than the last value of the index, since I includes the count for the last-card code.

Automatic end-of-file method.

```
       DIMENSION SCORE(100)
       DOUBLE PRECISION NAME(100)
       DO 10 I = 1,100
       READ(1,11,END = 8)NAME(I),T1,T2
       SCORE(I) = (T1 + T2)/2.
 10    CONTINUE
       I = 101
  8    I = I − 1
       WRITE(3,5)I
 11    FORMAT(A8,2F5.0)
```

Process a maximum of 100 student records. If there are 100 records, the end-of-file card will not be read.

If the loop goes through its complete cycle, the index I will be undefined after the CONTINUE statement and hence I must be reset to 100. If the end of file is reached before 100 records have been read, then the value for I will include the count for the end-of-file card, and hence 1 must be subtracted from the index.

If it is desired to read into an array A more than one number per card (two, for instance), the following code might be used:

```
       DIMENSION A(10)
       DO 10 I = 1,5,2
       READ(1,5)A(I),A(I + 1)
10     CONTINUE
 5     FORMAT(2F5.0)
```

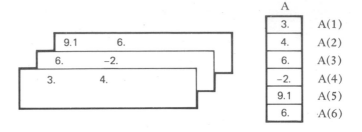

Note that only the first six elements of the array will be initialized. In the event six numbers were to be read per card, the READ list within the DO loop would have to specify A(I),A(I + 1),A(I + 2),A(I + 3), A(I + 4), A(I + 5), which proves somewhat inconvenient. In such a case, the implied DO list is advantageous.

Implied DO List

The implied DO list is essentially a short-form notation to list subscripted variables in a READ/WRITE list. Instead of writing

$$READ(1,5)A(1),A(2),A(3),A(4),A(5),A(6)$$

the more compact and convenient notation is used:

$$READ(1,5)(A(I),I = 1,6,1)$$

The above statement can be interpreted as follows: Read the numbers A(I) as I ranges from 1 to 6 in steps of 1. The incremental step 1 can be omitted, which results in an automatic incremental value of 1. Six values will then be read from one or more cards as specified by the number of data format codes in the format. Once again, the implied DO list specifies the total number of values to be read into memory or written out, and the format specifies how many of these values will be read per card (or written per line). In the case of the implied DO, there is no one-to-one correspondence between the number of variables in the READ/WRITE list and the data format codes in the corresponding formats. Consider the following examples:

Example 1

    READ(1,10)(A(I),I = 1,5)   WRITE(3,10)(B(I),I = 1,5)
10 FORMAT(F5.0)   10 FORMAT(2X,2F6.0)

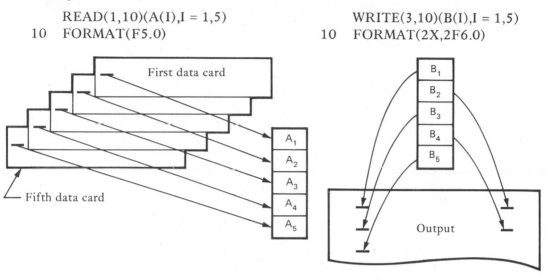

In both cases, five elements are to be read or written. The format specifies the number of records to be processed. For the READ operation, there is one item per card; hence five cards will be read. For the WRITE operation, there are two items (2F6.0) per line; hence three lines will be printed, with only one item printed on the last line.

Example 2

    READ(1,10)(A(I),I = 1,13)   WRITE(3,10)(A(I),I = 1,13)
10 FORMAT(3F5.0)   10 FORMAT(12F6.0)

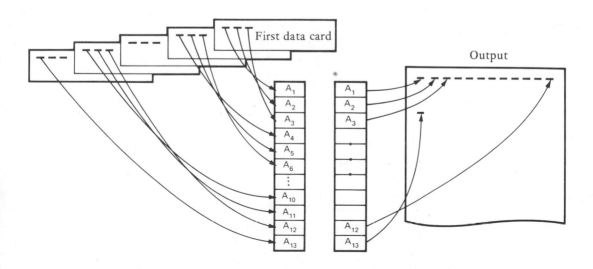

In both cases above, 13 elements are processed. For the READ operation, there are three items per card (3F5.0); hence five cards will be read, with only the first entry on the fifth card read. For the WRITE operation, 12 items are printed per line (12F6.0); hence two lines will be printed, with only one field printed on the second line.

Example 3

READ(1,10)(A(I),B(I),I = 1,5)	WRITE(3,10)(A(I),B(I),I = 1,5)
10 FORMAT(2F5.0)	10 FORMAT(3F6.0)

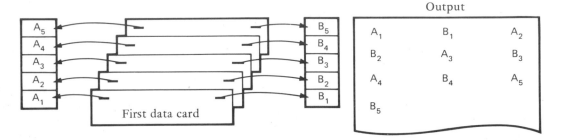

In both examples above, the elements A(I),B(I) are read as I varies from 1 to 5. This is equivalent to the list of variables A(1),B(1),A(2),B(2),A(3) · · · A(5),B(5). In the case of the READ operation, a pair of A and B are read; hence five data cards are needed. In the case of the WRITE operation, three numbers are written per line (3F6.0).

Example 4

To process long strings of alphanumeric data, arrays can be used to great advantage. For example, to read 80 card columns of data a double precision array might be used to store eight character substrings into each of its array elements (assuming a double precision word can contain eight characters). For example:

```
      DOUBLE PRECISION A(10)    A(1) = S O M E _ _ P E O
      READ(1,1)(A(I),I = 1,10)  A(2) = P L E _ _ S E E _
    1 FORMAT(10A8)              A(3) = T H I N G S _ _ A
         .                      A(4) = S _ _ T H E Y _ A
         .                      etc.
         .
```

SOME PEOPLE SEE THINGS AS THEY ARE AND SAY WHY. I DREAM OF . . .

Example 5

Suppose that for a particular problem the following heading at the top of a new page is required:

```
┌─────────────────────────────────────────────────────────┐
│                                                         │
│   PARTNO.    MACHINE 1  MACHINE 2  MACHINE 3 · · · MACHINE 9   │
│                                                         │
└─────────────────────────────────────────────────────────┘
```

The literal "MACHINE" is repeated 10 times, and the numbers 1,2,3, · · · 8,9 can be generated by the implied DO list, as follows:

```
        WRITE(3,1)(I,I = 1,9)      Write I as I varies from 1 to 9.
    1   FORMAT('1',T50,'PARTNO.',4X,9('MACHINE',I2,2X))
```

It should be noted that with the implied DO list, the last-card code method cannot be used to read an unknown number of cards, since it is not possible to test array elements as they are read within the DO list. The automatic end of file in the READ statement can be used, however. The last value of the index used in the DO list will reflect the count of logical records read plus one (because of the end of file). For example, if the array A is to be loaded from a deck of unknown number of cards (no more than 100 cards), with three data items per card, the following code might be used:

```
        DIMENSION A(300)
        READ(1,5,END = 15)(A(I),I = 300)
    5   FORMAT(3F5.0)
        I = 301                      Reset I to 300 if all 100 cards were read (since
   15   I = I – 1                    index is undefined if the implied DO list is
        DO 10 K = 1,I                terminated normally).
                                     Process the I elements read.
```

In conclusion, the implied DO list is a convenient method to load or write out arrays. The implied DO list cannot be used if it is desired to analyze or test data items as they are read into memory or written out. For example, if one wishes to load an array with numbers from data cards and stop loading when a specific number is encountered in the input file, an explicit DO loop must be used, since the implied DO list does not allow the testing while reading.

The DATA Statement

The DATA statement was used earlier (see Chapter 5, Section 5-2-3) to establish initial values for nonsubscripted variables. It can also be used to initialize arrays. Recall that the DATA statement should be placed after the DIMENSION statement. Initialization of an array can be done by listing explicitly the named array elements and their corresponding values or by defining the array elements through the DO list (see Example 1):

Example 1

DIMENSION A(5)
DATA (A(I),I = 1,5)/1.,2.1,−3.,4.,5.6/   Implied DO list.

or   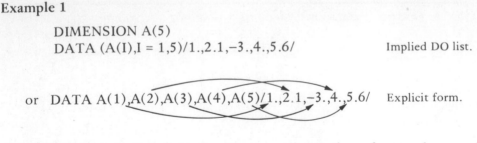 Explicit form.

or DATA A/1.,2.1,−3.,4.,5.6/   In this case, the number of array elements initialized is equal to the size of the array declared in the DIMENSION statement.

The duplication factor "*" in the list of constants may be used to simplify the constant list.

Example 2

To initialize 100 elements of array A to zeroes, we write:

DIMENSION A(200)
DATA (A(I),I = 1,100)/100*0./

Note that A(101,A(102), · · · ,A(200) still remain undefined. Note that the "*" in the constant list means repetition of a constant, not multiplication.

8-3 You Might Want to Know

1. Can you have more than one DIMENSION statement?

    Answer: Yes, as many as you want. For example:

    DIMENSION A(10),B(3)
    DIMENSION SAM(4)   is equivalent to DIMENSION A(10),B(3),SAM(4),JP(10)
    DIMENSION JP(10)

2. Are subscripts limited to the form $k*V \pm c$ as shown in Section 8-2-2?

    Answer: Many systems will allow any integer expressions having a value of 1 or more; however, the subscript expression may not contain array or function references.

3. What happens if I have dimensioned PRICE as an array and I use PRICE in a statement such as Y = PRICE*QUAN(J)?

    Answer: On a few systems, PRICE will be interpreted as PRICE(1). On most systems, however, this is an error. PRICE should be subscripted, i.e., provided with an index.

4. What can I do to change the implicitly defined mode of an array, i.e., store integer values in a floating-point array or store floating-point values in an integer array?

Answer: Declare the array using the INTEGER or REAL type statement, as in:

DIMENSION A(100),B(60),I(45),C(50)
INTEGER A,B   The array elements of A and B will be processed as integers in the program.
REAL I   The array elements of I are processed as real numbers.

An equivalent method to dimension and define the mode for the arrays is

INTEGERA(100),B(60)
REALI(45)

5. Is there any limit to the size of an array?

Answer: No, the maximum size for an array is a function of the memory size of the system in use.

6. Does a DIMENSION statement initialize array elements to any specific values?

Answer: No, it is the programmer's responsibility to initialize arrays.

7. What happens if I write WRITE(3,10)A or READ(1,10)A, where A is the name of an array?

Answer: The entire array as specified in the DIMENSION statement will be processed. If A has been dimensioned A(79), all 79 entries will be written or read.

Example

DIMENSION A(10)
READ(1,10)A
10   FORMAT(F6.0)

The above code is equivalent to READ(1,10)A(1),A(2),A(3),A(4),A(5),A(6), A(7),A(8),A(9),A(10) or READ(1,10)(A(I),I = 1,10).

Care must be exercised when just using names of arrays without subscripts in an input/output operation. Consider the following example:

DIMENSION HRS(3),RATE(3)
READ(1,3)HRS,RATE
3   FORMAT(F3.0,2X,F5.2)

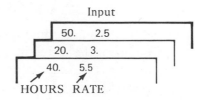

The above code would load arrays HRS and RATE as follows:

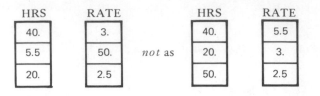

8. Can you dimension an array for 50 elements and use only the first 30 elements?

    Answer: Yes, there will just be 20 memory locations that will not be used.

9. What differentiates a FORTRAN function from a subscripted variable? For instance, when I write Y = SIN(X), is SIN(X) a subscripted variable?

    Answer: Unless you dimension an array called SIN in your program, SIN(X) is not a subscripted variable name but a function name.

10. Can I use an implied DO list in an arithmetic statement to process an array? For example, (A(I),I = 1,10) = 0?

    Answer: Implied DO lists are valid only in input/output and DATA statements.

11. Can I use arrays to store logical values?

    Answer: Yes. For example:

    > DIMENSION A(30)
    > LOGICAL I(20),A

    The following are now logical variables: I(1),I(2), $\cdots$,I(20),A(1),A(2), $\cdots$, A(30).

12. What if I use a subscripted variable name in my program and I forget to dimension it?

    Answer: No compilation error will occur, since the compiler will think that it is a function. A logical or execution error will occur later on, however.

13. Can the same index be used more than once in implied DO lists as follows:

    > READ(1,5)((A(I),I = 1,5),SAM,I = 1,9)

    Answer: No, the inner implied DO list A(I),I = 1,5 will change the value of I used to control the outer implied DO list, i.e., I = 1,9. Note, however, that the following is permissible READ(1,6)(A(I),I = 1,4),(B(I),I = 1,6),I. In this case, I is used to control three independent entities.

8-4 Programming Examples

8-4-1 An Array Search

Suppose array G contains ten grades and it is desired to determine the largest grade. Searching an array for a particular item is a frequent activity while working with arrays. The following partial code illustrates a method for finding the largest value of G. The grades have already been read into G.

DIMENSION G(10)	Assume grades have already been read.
XLARG = G(1)	Set XLARG initially to the first grade.
DO 5 I = 2,10	
14 IF(XLARG.LT.G(I))XLARG = G(I)	If the largest grade so far is less than the new grade G(I), replace XLARG by the new grade G(I).
5 CONTINUE	Otherwise, keep on searching.
WRITE(3,4)XLARG	Write largest grade.

The variable XLARG is initialized to G(1) before searching the remaining elements of the array. Any element that is larger than XLARG becomes the new value of XLARG at statement 14. This method, however, does not indicate the position of the largest element within the array G. It just identifies XLARG as the largest element.

Another method which indicates the position of the largest element within the array makes use of an index or pointer to locate the largest element. Initially, this index is set to the position of the first element (generally position one). Then, as array elements are compared to one another, the index or pointer is changed appropriately to reflect the new location of the largest number found so far. Thus if K is the pointer to the largest element found so far and G(K) < G(I), then I is now obviously the position of the largest element and K is set to I and the comparison of G(K) with G(I) for different values of I is continued.

This search method is illustrated by the following example given the array G with elements 6,4,7,2 and 8.

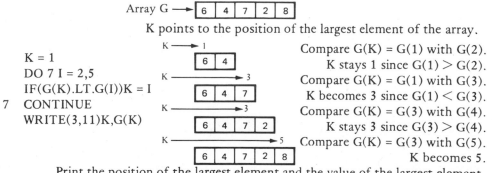

Array G → | 6 | 4 | 7 | 2 | 8 |

K points to the position of the largest element of the array.

```
         K = 1
         DO 7 I = 2,5
         IF(G(K).LT.G(I))K = I
7        CONTINUE
         WRITE(3,11)K,G(K)
```

K → 1 | 6 | 4 | Compare G(K) = G(1) with G(2). K stays 1 since G(1) > G(2).

K → 3 | 6 | 4 | 7 | Compare G(K) = G(1) with G(3). K becomes 3 since G(1) < G(3).

K → 3 | 6 | 4 | 7 | 2 | Compare G(K) = G(3) with G(4). K stays 3 since G(3) > G(4).

K → 5 | 6 | 4 | 7 | 2 | 8 | Compare G(K) = G(3) with G(5). K becomes 5.

Print the position of the largest element and the value of the largest element.

8-4-2 Table Look-Up

The table look-up process is a fast and efficient method to access data directly in an array (table) without any search of the array elements. Consider the following example: To transport their merchandise, Widgets, Inc., manufacturers of widgets of all types, contracts with a trucking company that charges a fixed amount per pound based on a shipping zone. The rate table per pound is as follows:

Zone code	Cost per pound	Meaning
1	.50	The cost to ship one pound of merchandise
2	.75	to zone 1 is $.50.
3	1.05	
4	1.25	
5	1.40	The cost to ship one pound of merchandise
6	1.70	to zone 6 is $1.70.

Write a program that will read a destination zone and a weight of shipment and print the corresponding shipping cost. A program for this task is shown in Figure 8-6.

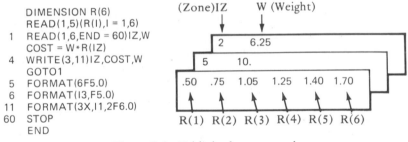

```
     DIMENSION R(6)
     READ(1,5)(R(I),I = 1,6)
   1 READ(1,6,END = 60)IZ,W
     COST = W*R(IZ)
   4 WRITE(3,11)IZ,COST,W
     GOTO1
   5 FORMAT(6F5.0)
   6 FORMAT(I3,F5.0)
  11 FORMAT(3X,I1,2F6.0)
  60 STOP
     END
```

Figure 8-6   Table look-up example

The table of constants is stored in the array R via the READ statement. If a zone (IZ) and weight (W) are read with values 5 and 10 respectively, the corresponding shipping rate is $R(IZ) = R(5) = 1.40$. The total cost of shipping a package of $W = 10$ pounds is then $R(IZ)*W = 1.40*10 = 14$. More generally, the cost per pound to send a package to a zone IZ is $R(IZ)$. The total cost for sending a package of W pounds to a zone IZ then becomes $W*R(IZ)$.

8-4-3 Frequency Distribution

Write a program to produce a frequency distribution of test grades. Given a list of grades, we must find how many times a grade of 1 appears, how many times a grade of 2 appears, a grade of 3,4,5, · · · 100. The grades range from 1 to 100 and are read from data cards (one per card). For example, suppose you can get 1 to 10 on a quiz and you have a list of scores in any order; if you wanted to find out the number of each different score by hand, you might draw a chart and count each score as follows:

Scores   *Count of different grades*

1,5,6,8,1,2,3,3,5,3,3, · · ·

II	I	IIII		III	JHT I	JHT	JHT II	I	
1	2	3	4	5	6	7	8	9	10

Input of grades will be terminated when a value outside the permissible range of grades is encountered. A program to solve this problem for grades ranging from 1 to 100 is shown in Figure 8-7. Since there are 100 possible grades, 100 counters will be required to record all occurrences of grades. The array K will be used for that purpose with K(1),K(2), · · · ,K(100) serving the 100 counters.

In the first DO loop, the array of counters K is initialized to zero. As each grade is read, it is tested for proper range. If the grade IG satisfies the test, the IGth counter is incremented by 1, i.e., K(IG) = K(IG) + 1. The value of IG is used to designate which of the counters should be incremented. Thus, if IG has a value of 65, the statement K(IG) = K(IG) + 1 is the same as K(65) = K(65) + 1, and hence K(65) is incremented by 1 (K(65) is the counter used to record occurrences of the grade 65). When a value outside the range is encountered, a listing of all the nonzero grades and their corresponding frequency count is produced. (See Figure 8-7.) On output, only the counters with nonzero values are printed. In statement 75 WRITE(3,6)I,K(I), the variable I represents the grade, while K(I) represents the corresponding grade count (the one counting the grade I). If K(I) = 0, this means that there was no grade I read.

8-4-4 Bar Graphs

It is often very desirable to produce graphic output from a computer program. A scientific problem may require the graph of a function; a business problem might require a bar graph. Consider, for example, the following problem. Data regarding company sales for a week has been tabulated as shown:

Day	Sales		DAY	SALES
1	3	To visualize graphically the sales trend,	1	***
2	7	we can represent the daily sales by a	2	*******
3	10	corresponding equivalent number of	3	**********
4	6	geometric symbols "*" per line. The fol-	4	******
5	8	lowing output might be desired.	5	*******
6	2		6	**
7	0		7	

```
C    FREQUENCY DISTRIBUTION
     DIMENSION K(100)
     DO 1 I = 1,100
     K(I) = 0                          Initialize the 100 counters to zeroes.
 1   CONTINUE
 4   READ(1,5)IG
 5   FORMAT(I5)
     WRITE(3,5)IG
     IF(IG.LE.0)GOTO70                 Test for value outside grade range.
     IF(IG.GT.100)GOTO70               Increment the counter corresponding to the grade IG.
55   K(IG) = K(IG) + 1
     GOTO4
70   WRITE(3,7)
     DO 80 I = 1,100                   If the count of grades for grade I is 0, do not print it.
     IF(K(I).EQ.0)GOTO80
75   WRITE(3,6)I,K(I)                  Write these grades and their corresponding frequency
80   CONTINUE                          count.
     STOP
 6   FORMAT(I5,I9)
 7   FORMAT(/' GRADES  FREQUENCY')
     END
```

Sample output

```
        23
        45
        23
        12
       100
       100
       100
         0

GRADES  FREQUENCY
    12         1
    23         2
    45         1
   100         3
```

Figure 8-7 Frequency distribution.

The solution to this problem is shown in Figure 8-8. Note that the variable STAR is initialized to the character "*" and every time a sale is read (KSALES), only the number of stars (*) equal to KSALES is printed by the implied DO list in statement 15.

```
     DATA STAR/'*'/
     WRITE(3,1)
 1   FORMAT('1DAY',T8,'SALES')
     DO 20 IDAY = 1,7
     READ(1,2)KSALES
     IF(KSALES.NE.0)GOTO15
     WRITE(3,3)IDAY
     GOTO20                            Print the day and number of stars
15   WRITE(3,3)IDAY,(STAR,J = 1,KSALES)   corresponding to the sales for that day.
20   CONTINUE
 3   FORMAT(T3,I2,T8,20A1)
 2   FORMAT(I2)
     STOP
     END
```

Figure 8-8 Example of a bar graph.

8-4-5 Array Input/Output

To be admitted to the MENSA club, candidates must score a minimum of 74 points on an intelligence test. Each candidate's name and test score are recorded on punched cards, as shown below. Write a program to read a deck of cards to produce the following information:

1. Two separate paragraph listings of names of successful and unsuccessful candidates. Each line should contain four names.
2. Two consecutive tables listed vertically of names and scores of successful and unsuccessful candidates (one name and corresponding score per line). The input and output may be visualized as follows:

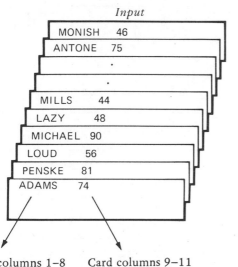

Input

MONISH	46
ANTONE	75
	.
	.
MILLS	44
LAZY	48
MICHAEL	90
LOUD	56
PENSKE	81
ADAMS	74

Card columns 1–8   Card columns 9–11

No more than 100 data cards

Output

SUCCESSFUL CANDIDATES ARE

ADAMS,PENSKE,MICHAEL,SALAAM
JONES,CLARK,WILLS,BROWN
EMMA,BRYARS,ANTONE

UNSUCCESSFUL CANDIDATES ARE

LOUD,LAZY,MILLS,GAMBINO
BOILLOT,MONISH

RESULTS	NAMES	SCORES
PASSING	ADAMS	74
	PENSKE	81
	MICHAEL	90
	⋮	
	ANTONE	75
FAILING	LOUD	56
	LAZY	48
	MILLS	44
	⋮	
	MONISH	46

A program to solve this problem is shown in Figure 8-9. Since the names of the candidates must be printed by group (success/failure), two arrays are needed to store the names of successful candidates and those of the unsuccessful candidates.

A name and a score are both read from a card. If the score is not greater than 74, the name is stored in the array IFAIL and its corresponding grade in array

```
      INTEGER SCPASS(100),SCFAIL(100),SCORE
      DOUBLE PRECISION IFAIL(100),IPASS(100),NAME
      DATA KP,KF/0,0/
10    READ(1,1,END = 70)NAME,SCORE
1     FORMAT(A8,I3)




      IF(SCORE.GE.74)GO TO 60



      KF = KF + 1


      IFAIL(KF) = NAME


      SCFAIL(KF) = SCORE


      GO TO 10


60    KP = KP + 1


      IPASS(KP) = NAME


      SCPASS(KP) = SCORE



      GO TO 10

70    WRITE(3,11)(IPASS(I),I = 1,KP)

11    FORMAT('1',T50,'SUCCESSFUL CANDIDATES ARE',
     */(T50,4(A8,',')))
      WRITE(3,12)(IFAIL(I),I = 1,KF)



12    FORMAT(T50,'UNSUCCESSFUL CANDIDATES ARE',
     */(T50,4(A8,',')))
      WRITE(3,13)(IPASS(I),SCPASS(I),I = 1,KP)


13    FORMAT(/T50,'RESULTS',T60,'NAMES',T70,'SCORES',
     *//T50,'PASSING',(T60,A8,T70,I3))
      WRITE(3,14)(IFAIL(I),SCFAIL(I),I = 1,KF)


14    FORMAT(//T50,'FAILING',(T60,A8,T70,I3))
      STOP
      END
```

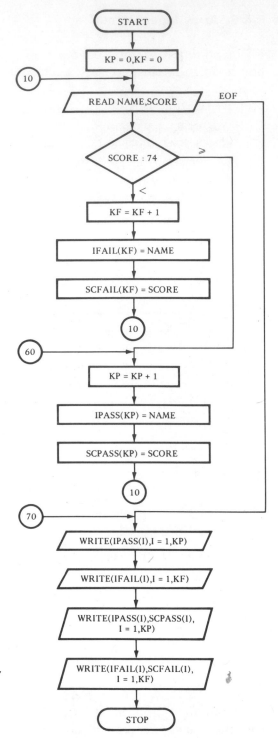

Figure 8-9 I/O with arrays.

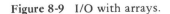

SCFAIL. The index KF is used to place each name and score in successive array locations. Arrays IPASS, SCPASS and index KP are used similarly to record the passing candidates' data. When the end of file (EOF) is reached, KP reflects the number of passing candidates, while KF reflects the number of failing candidates.

The implied DO list WRITE(3,11)(IPASS(I),I = 1,KP) specifies the list of all passing candidates, while FORMAT11 tells the computer to print first a heading with four names per line under the heading. Similarly the names of passing candidates and their scores are specified by the statement WRITE(3,13)(IPASS(I), SCPASS(I),I = 1,KP). Format 13 specifies that one name and one score are to be printed per line. Note the position of the literals 'PASSING' and 'FAILING' in formats 13 and 14 and note the use of the parentheses in (T60,A8,T70,F6.1)) to force format control to restart at the rightmost open parenthesis in the format to print all remaining names and scores. (See Section 8-5-2 for a complete discussion of this feature.)

8-4-6 Sorting

Two methods for sorting are discussed. One method is called the Bubble sort and the other the Interchange maximum or minimum.

Bubble Sort

Write a program to sort a group of grades into descending sequence. A maximum of 100 cards, each containing a grade, will be read. The program to perform this sort is shown in Figure 8-11.

The method used to sort the five numbers in the program of Figure 8-11 is illustrated graphically in Figure 8-10. This method shifts the smallest value to the fifth position of array G, then shifts the next smallest value to the fourth position, then to the third and so on. The shifting is accomplished by comparing pairs of contiguous array elements, one pair at a time and interchanging the two numbers whenever necessary to ensure that the smallest value is continuously moved to the right. For instance, the first and second numbers are compared; if the second is less than the first, the second is compared to the third. If the second is larger than the first, these two numbers are interchanged, and the second number (the smallest now) is then compared to the third. Ultimately the smallest value is moved into the fifth position (see Figure 8-10).

The sorting algorithm requires two loops. An outer loop (statement 90) to control the positioning of the smallest element in the rightmost position of the ever-shrinking array (positions 5,4,3 · · · 2) and an inner loop (statement 100) to control the movement of the smallest element to the rightmost position of the shrinking array through the interchange procedure (statements 120,130,140). Once again, the outer loop controls the number of passes (see Figure 8-10). If an array has N elements, then N − 1 passes will be required.

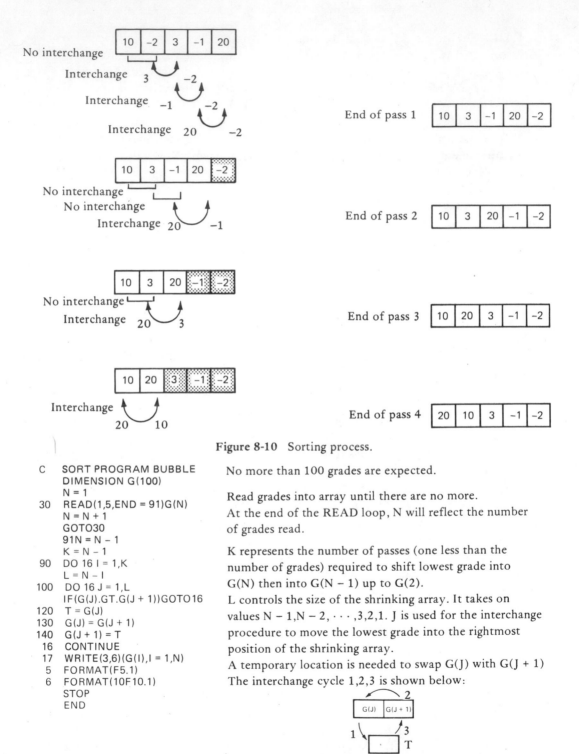

Figure 8-10 Sorting process.

```
C    SORT PROGRAM BUBBLE
     DIMENSION G(100)
     N = 1
30   READ(1,5,END = 91)G(N)
     N = N + 1
     GOTO30
91N = N - 1
     K = N - 1
90   DO 16 I = 1,K
     L = N - I
100  DO 16 J = 1,L
     IF(G(J).GT.G(J + 1))GOTO16
120  T = G(J)
130  G(J) = G(J + 1)
140  G(J + 1) = T
16   CONTINUE
17   WRITE(3,6)(G(I),I = 1,N)
5    FORMAT(F5.1)
6    FORMAT(10F10.1)
     STOP
     END
```

No more than 100 grades are expected.

Read grades into array until there are no more.
At the end of the READ loop, N will reflect the number of grades read.

K represents the number of passes (one less than the number of grades) required to shift lowest grade into G(N) then into G(N − 1) up to G(2).

L controls the size of the shrinking array. It takes on values N − 1, N − 2, · · · ,3,2,1. J is used for the interchange procedure to move the lowest grade into the rightmost position of the shrinking array.

A temporary location is needed to swap G(J) with G(J + 1)
The interchange cycle 1,2,3 is shown below:

Statement 17 prints out the N grades ten per line.

Figure 8-11 Descending order bubble sort.

Interchange Maximum/Minimum

Another method which can be used to sort an array of numbers in ascending (or descending) order is to determine the location (position) of the smallest element in the array and interchange that element with the first element of the array. At the end of this first search pass, the smallest element is in the first position. The array is then searched for the next smallest element, with the search starting at position 2 of the array; the smallest element is then swapped with the number in position 2 of the array. At the end of this second search pass, the first two elements of the array are already in ascending sequence order. The search for the next smallest number starts in position 3, and the same search and interchange process is repeated until the last two rightmost array elements are processed. Using this sorting procedure, an array of N elements will require N − 1 passes for the search and interchange procedure. The search for the smallest number itself will involve comparing N numbers during the last pass. This sort process can be constrasted with the bubble sort of Figure 8-10 as follows:

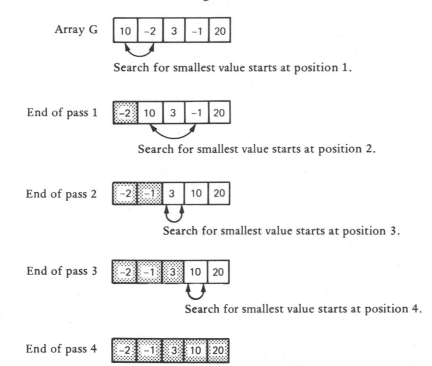

To better understand the complete FORTRAN sort program, let us initially write the code for the first pass, which determines the position of the smallest element of the array and which performs the interchange of the smallest number with the number in the first position of the array. Assume the array G contains N elements:

```
   K = 1                    Initially the pointer to the smallest element is 1, that is, G(K) or G(1)
                            is assumed to be the smallest number before entering the loop.
   L = K + 1                L is 2, since there is no reason to compare G(1) with G(1) if the first
                            value of I in the DO loop was 1 initially.
   DO 10 I = L,N            Compare N numbers to determine smallest value.



   IF(G(K).LE.G(I))GOTO10   If G(K) ⩽ G(I), then G(K) is still the smallest element and K still
                            points to the location of the smallest element.
   K = I                    If G(K) > G(I), then the smallest element so far is at position I, and so
                            we reset K to I to keep track of the smallest number, keeping in
                            mind, of course, that G(K) is the current smallest number.
10 CONTINUE                 At the completion of the loop, K identifies the location of the smallest
                            element and G(K) is the smallest number in the array.
   T = G(1)                 Save the value of G(1).
   G(1) = G(K)              Store the smallest number in G(1).
   G(K) = T                 Store G(1) in the location that used to contain the smallest number.
```

To generalize the above code for the complete sort program, K must take on values, 1,2,3, $\cdots$ N − 1 (for N − 1 passes). The interchange process will require that T = G(2) on the second pass, T = G(3) on the third pass etc. Hence an additional loop is required to control K and the positioning of the succeeding smallest values into locations G(1),G(2),G(3), $\cdots$,G(N − 1). The complete code is shown in Figure 8-12, assuming the array G has been loaded.

```
      DIMENSION G(100)
      READ(1,1)N
 1    FORMAT(I3)
      N1 = N − 1
      DO 15 J = 1,N1          N − 1 passes.
      K = J                   K = 1,2,3, ··· ,N − 1.
      L = K + 1
      DO 10 I = L,N           L = 2,3, ··· ,N − 1,N.
      IF(G(K).LE.G(I))GOTO10
      K = I                   On the last pass G(N − 1) is compared to G(N).
10    CONTINUE
      T = G(J)
      G(J) = G(K)             Interchange procedure.
15    G(K) = T
```

Figure 8-12   Interchange maximum/minimum.

8-4-7 Graph

Plotting the graph of a function $y = f(x)$ can be accomplished by computing integer values for y for successive values of x, i.e., $J = f(x)$ and placing a graphic symbol such as "*" at position J on each output line. To better understand the graphing process, let us plot the functions $y = x^2 + x - 6$ and $y = \sin x$ in the interval $(-4, 3.6)$:

1. Fill in an array ILINE with blanks.

2. Compute a value $J = x^2 + x - 6$ for $x = -4$ and insert the symbol "$*$" in position J of the array (ILINE(J) = '*') and print the array ILINE.

3. Repeat steps 1 and 2 for values of $x = -3.6, -3.2, \cdots 3.6$ (incremental value is arbitrary).

There is one minor problem, though: For some values of x, J is negative (see Figure 8-13); J cannot be negative, since it is used as a subscript of ILINE to indi-

`      DIMENSION ILINE(28),JLINE(28)`	
`      DATA IBLANK,ISTAR/' ','*'/`	Initialize graphic symbol "$*$".
`      WRITE(6,9)`	
`    9 FORMAT('1',T4,'X',T9,'Y',T35,'X',T40,'Y')`	
`      XP = -4`	
`      XS = 0`	
`   18 YP = XP*XP + XP - 6`	To compute $Y = X^2 + X - 6$.
`      YS = SIN(XS)`	To compute $Y = SIN(X)$.
`      DO 15 I = 1,2,8`	
`      ILINE(I) = IBLANK`	Blank out array for the parabola.
`   15 JLINE(I) = IBLANK`	Blank out array for the sine curve.
`      JP  = YP + 7.25`	Compute the integer value of the function JP,
`      JS = (YS + 2.)*8`	and place a '$*$' in position JP of the array,
`      ILINE(JP) = ISTAR`	and print the array.
`      JLINE(JS) = ISTAR`	
`      WRITE(6,11)XP,YP,ILINE,XS,YS,JLINE`	
`   11 FORMAT(2F5.1,2X,22A1,T32,2F5.1,28A1)`	
`      XP = XP + .4`	
`      XS = XS + .4`	
`      IF(XP - 3.6)18,18,20`	
`   20 STOP`	
`      END`	

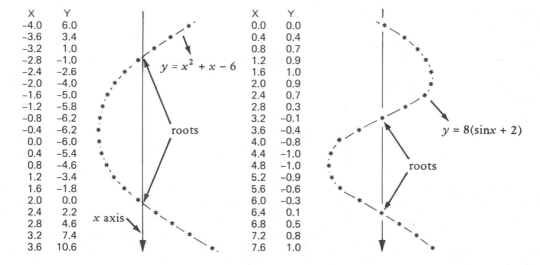

Figure 8-13 Plotting.

cate the position of the symbol "*" on the output line. This problem can be taken care of by adding to $x^2 + x - 6$ a constant C, which will neutralize the largest negative value of $x^2 + x - 6$ in the given interval and ensure that J $\geqslant$ 1. Adding such a constant does not change the shape of the graph but results in the translation of the x axis by C. In the above example, a constant C = 7.25 could be used, since the largest negative value for J is −6.25 (x = −.5). With J = $x^2 + x - 6$ + 7.25, the smallest and largest value for J in the interval is J = 1 (x = −.5) and J = 18 (x = 3.6). Hence the array ILINE must be dimensioned to a size at least 18.

In the case of the sine function, a constant of 2 is added to J = SIN(X) to ensure that J $\geqslant$ 1 (SIN(X) = −1 for some values of x). Plotting J = SIN(X) + 2 is somewhat difficult, since most of the values taken by J will be 1 or 2 (J truncates fractional digits). To magnify or stretch the graph over a wider area of print columns, we can multiply SIN(X) + 2 by a factor—let us say 8 in this case— which will spread out J from a minimum of 1*8 (SIN(X) = −1) to a maximum of 3*8 = 24 (SIN(X) = 1). An array of size at least 24 must be reserved for the array to print the sine function. Multiplying the function by 8 does not plot the original function exactly but gives a fairly good idea of the shape of the curve while preserving the roots (see Figure 8-13).

8-5   Probing a Little Deeper

8-5-1   Errors and Arrays

The FORTRAN programmer should realize that arrays, when used improperly, can represent a potential source of execution-time errors that may be very difficult to trace. By means of the DIMENSION statement, the programmer informs the compiler on the maximum number of memory locations he needs for the array. If the user inadvertently, at execution time, refers to an array element A(J) where J is outside the range specified in the DIMENSION statement (exceeds the size declared in the DIMENSION statement), some systems may not inform the user that he has exceeded the array dimension, but will actually process A(J) as that element J positions away from the first element of A. This can result in destruction of data or machine instructions representing FORTRAN instructions, depending on the value of J and depending on whether A(J) is to the left or to the right of the equal sign in a replacement statement. The following example illustrates conceptually the problems that arise as a result of exceeding the dimension of an array.

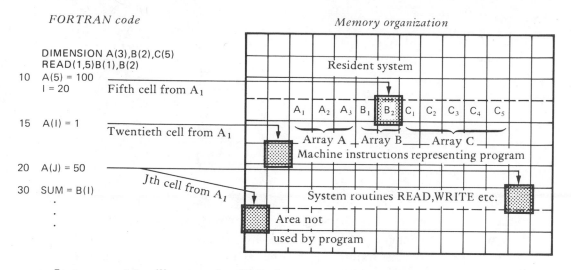

FORTRAN code   *Memory organization*

```
      DIMENSION A(3),B(2),C(5)
      READ(1,5)B(1),B(2)
10    A(5) = 100
      I = 20          Fifth cell from A₁
15    A(I) = 1
                      Twentieth cell from A₁
20    A(J) = 50
                      Jth cell from A₁
30    SUM = B(I)
      .
      .
      .
```

Statement 10 will cause the fifth element starting at A_1, i.e., B_2 to be replaced by 100, thereby destroying whatever value was in B_2. The error in this case is that we should never have referred to A(5), since we only reserved three locations for A. Note, though, that the system does not give out any error message.

Statement 15 will cause the twentieth element, starting at A_1, to be replaced by 1. This could well result in the destruction of some machine instructions representing the FORTRAN program.

Statement 20 can result in the destruction of some memory location depending on the value of J. If J is large enough, A(J) could refer to a memory location in an area of system routines used by the FORTRAN program or possibly to an area of memory not used by the program.

Statement 30 does not cause destruction of any memory location (since B(I) is not to the left of the equal sign). SUM is set to whatever the twentieth element, starting at B_1 is—which could be anything.

In conclusion, when writing a program with references to arrays that have variable names as subscripts, always make sure that the values of the subscripts do not exceed the array size specified in the DIMENSION statement. Otherwise, unusual execution-time error messages are likely to appear (as a result of random destruction of cells) that are difficult to track down.

8-5-2 Special Cases: Format Reuse and (/)

In general, if *n* variables are specified in a READ/WRITE list, the system scans the format for *n* corresponding data format codes (I,F,A). If there are *m* data format codes in the format and *m* is less than *n* (fewer format codes than variables), reading or writing will start at the beginning of a new record (card or line) and scanning for data format codes will resume at the rightmost *open* (left) parenthesis in the format, to complete processing the *n−m* variables left in the READ/WRITE list.

Example 1

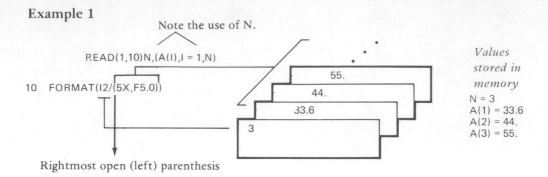

In Example 1, N is first read, and then N is used as the terminal value in the implied DO list to control the number of variables to be read. All values for the array A will be read under the format 5X,F5.0, since after encountering the rightmost parenthesis format scanning will resume at the rightmost *open* parenthesis.

Example 2

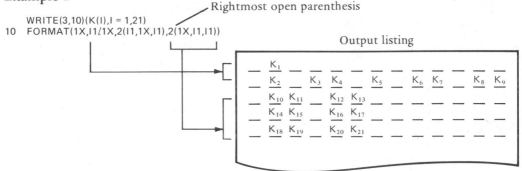

After the rightmost parenthesis has been encountered the first time, FORMAT control will resume scanning at 2(1X,I1,I1) which is equivalent to 1X,I1,I1,1X,I1, I1, and from then on all the variables in the WRITE list will be processed according to this latest format, each time beginning a new line. Note the importance of having 1X for carriage control.

Example 3

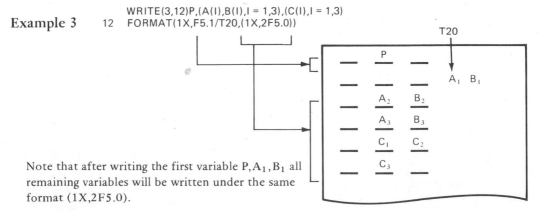

Note that after writing the first variable P, A_1, B_1 all remaining variables will be written under the same format (1X,2F5.0).

Example 4

```
    WRITE(3,5)A,B,C,D,E,F,G,H,S,T,V,W,X
5   FORMAT(F5.0/2(3X,F3.0),2(1X,F3.0),F3.0)
```

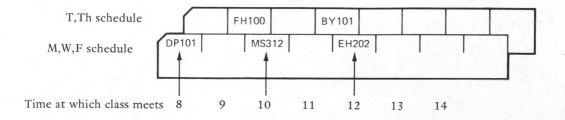

Output

Once the rightmost parenthesis has been encountered
in the format, a new line is started and format control
starts at the rightmost open parenthesis, i.e.,
2(1X,F3.0),F3.0) and all remaining variables in the
WRITE list are written according to this partial format code.

Consider, for example, the following problem, which requires the reuse of the format. Each pair of cards of a deck of cards contains a student's class schedule for the week. The first card contains the student's Monday schedule (identical to Wednesday and Friday) and the second card contains the student's Tuesday schedule (same as Thursday). Write a program to produce a weekly class schedule comparable to the following.

TIME	M	T	W	TH	F
8	DP101		DP101		DP101
9		FH100		FH100	
10	MS312		MS312		MS312
11		BY101		BY101	
12	EH202		EH202		EH202
13					
14					

TOTAL CLASS HOURS IS 13

Each data card is divided into seven fields reflecting the time offering of each course:

T,Th schedule

M,W,F schedule

Time at which class meets   8   9   10   11   12   13   14

A program to solve this problem is shown in Figure 8-14.

```
      DOUBLE PRECISION WFM(7),TTH(7),BLANK
      DATA BLANK/' '/
    5 READ(1,1,END = 8)(WFM(I),I = 1,7),(TTH(I),I = 1,7)
      I = 0
      DO 10 J = 1,7
      IF(WFM(J).NE.BLANK) I = I + 3
      IF(TTH(J).NE.BLANK) I = I + 2
   10 CONTINUE
      WRITE(3,2)(J,(WFM(J – 7), TTH(J – 7), L = 1,2),WFM(J – 7),J = 8,14),I
      GOTO5
    8 STOP
    1 FORMAT(7A6)
    2 FORMAT('1',//T8,'TIME',T20,'M',T30,'T',T40,'W',T50,'TH',T60,'F'//
     *7(T9,I2,T13,5A10/),T25,'TOTAL CLASS HOURS IS',I3)

      END
```

Read M,W,F schedule first and then the T,Th schedule.

M,W,F meets three times a week.
T,TH meets twice a week.

J prints the time at which courses are offered.

Seven lines, with each line containing a time (I2) and five course descriptions (5A10). Note the use of the end slash (/) to cause skipping to the next line for each logical record.

Figure 8-14   Class schedule.

To print the student's class schedule without the end statement "TOTAL HOURS WORKED IS", the reuse of the format should be used; that is, statement 2 in Figure 8-13 should be changed to:

    2   FORMAT('1'//T8,'TIME',T20,'M',T30,'T',T40,'W',T50,'TH',T60,'F'//
       *(T9,I2,T13,5A10))

Each line following the header line is printed according to the format starting at the rightmost open parenthesis.

8-6   Exercises

8-6-1   Self Test

1. Which of the following are legal array declarations for arrays A and B?
   a. INTEGER B(3)
   b. DIMENSION A(100),B(N)
   c. REAL A
   d. INTEGER(2*100)

2. In terms of memory arrangement, what is the difference between a three-element array and any three variable names?

3. In the context of subscript expressions discussed in Section 8-2-2, which of the following are invalid subscripts?
   a. B(3.)
   b. C(–3)
   c. B(J + K)
   d. C(2 + 3*K)
   e. D(K*3 – 4)
   f. F(3/J + 4)
   g. E(–3*K)
   h. A(I + 3.4)
   i. SAM(5 – 3)

4. State whether the following statements are true or false:
   a. The DIMENSION statement is an executable statement.
   b. An implied DO list is an executable statement.
   c. A FORMAT is an executable statement.
   d. END is a nonexecutable statement.
   e. The DATA statement is an executable statement.
   f. If A is an array, then READ(1,1)A will cause reading of just A(1).
   g. Subscripted variables can be used in any FORTRAN statement in the same way as nonsubscripted variables.
   h. The INTEGER and REAL statements can be placed anywhere in the program.

5. Determine the number of cards read by the following code:

   a.　　DO 10 I = 1,5　　　　　　　b.　　DO 10 J = 1,9
   　　　　READ(1,6)A(I)　　　　　　　　　READ(1,6)A(J),B(J)
   　 6　FORMAT(3F5.0)　　　　　　 6　FORMAT(F5.3)
   　10　CONTINUE　　　　　　　　10　CONTINUE

   c.　　DO 10 K = 1,6,2
   　　　　READ(1,7)(A(I),I = 1,K)
   　 7　FORMAT(3F5.0)
   　10　CONTINUE

6. Convert the following implied DO lists to the explicit DO loop form:

   a.　　READ(1,5)(A(I),I = 1,6)　　b.　　READ(1,6)(A(I),K(I),I = 2,9,2)
   　 5　FORMAT(2F5.0)　　　　　　 6　FORMAT(2(F5.1,I2))

7. Specify the exact output (print positions etc.) for the WRITE operations given the arrays A,B and K, defined as follows:

   array A　　| 1.5 | −3.2 | 3. | 4.8 | .34 |

   array B　　| −1. | 2. | 3. |

   constant K = 3

   　　　　　　　　　　　　　　　　FORMAT(I1)
   a. WRITE(3,11)(I,I = 1,5)⎯⎯ FORMAT(I2,I2)
   　　　　　　　　　　　　　　　　FORMAT(1X,20I1)

   　　　　　　　　　　　　　　　　FORMAT(I2,5F5.0)
   b. WRITE(3,11)(K,I,I = 1,4)⎯⎯ FORMAT(I3,1X,I1)
   　　　　　　　　　　　　　　　　FORMAT(5I2)

   　　　　　　　　　　　　　　　　　　FORMAT(I2,5F4.0)
   c. WRITE(3,11)(J,(A(I),I = 1,5),J = 1,2)⎯⎯FORMAT(I1/5F4.0,I2/5F4.0)
   　　　　　　　　　　　　　　　　　　FORMAT(I2/(5F4.0))

FORMAT(2F4.0,3F3.1)

d. WRITE(3,11)((A(I),I = 1,2),(B(I),I = 1,2),L = 1,2) FORMAT(1X,F4.1)

FORMAT(12F3.0)

8. Write possible formats for the following input/output statements.

   a. READ(1,5)(A(I),I = 1,5),(K(I),I = 1,1000)

   b. WRITE(1,5)(A(I),B(I),I,I = 1,500)

   c. WRITE(3,5)(A(I),I = 1,3),(JPAY(I),I = 1,1000),COST,K

9. Which of the following DO lists are invalid? In the event the implied DO list is valid, specify the number of cards read or lines written. If the implied DO list is invalid, state the reason, and state whether an error will occur at compilation or execution time.

   a.   READ(1,5)(A(I),I = 1,5),(B(J),J = 1,3)
        5 FORMAT(3F5.2)

   b.   WRITE(3,6)(K,A(I),B(I),I,I = 1,5)
        6 FORMAT(I2,2F3.0,I3)

   c.   READ(1,5)(A(J),B(J),I = 1,9)
        5 FORMAT(F5.1)

   d.   WRITE(3,8)(A(J),J = 1,N,K – 1)
        8 FORMAT(F10.1)

   e.   READ(1,7)A,(A(J),J = 1,7),B,KK
        7 FORMAT(4F3.0)

   f.   READ(1,8)(A(I),(B(J),J = 1,5),I = 1,5)
        8 FORMAT(F5.1)

   g.   WRITE(3,11)(PAY(J),J = 1,3)
       11 FORMAT(2F6.1)

   h.   WRITE(3,4)(I,(A(I),I = 1,3),B,I = 1,5)
        4 FORMAT(1X,I1,3F5.0,F3.0)

10. Given an array A of size 100, write the code to generate the following output, using both the implied DO list and explicit DO loop for the WRITE statement.

   a.   b.

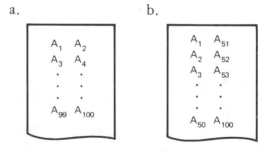

c.   d.

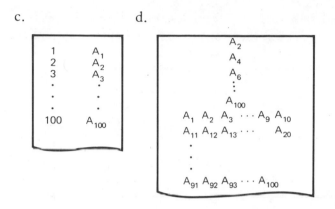

11. Given the following complete programs, infer potential execution-time errors:

   a. DIMENSION A (100)
      I = 1
      X = 4
      A(J) = X**2+2*X+I
      STOP
      END

   b. DIMENSION A(100)
      I = 1
      X = 4
      A(I) = X**A(J)
      STOP
      END

   c.   DIMENSION A (100)
              WRITE(3,5)A
              READ(1,5)(A(I),I = 1,110)
      5   FORMAT(10F5.0)
              STOP
              END

   d.   DIMENSION A(6)
              DO 10 I = 1,5
              READ(1,7)A(I),A(I + 1)
      7   FORMAT(2F5.0)
      10   CONTINUE
              STOP
              END

12. As a result of the following code segment, which type error would you expect? Discuss.

   I = −3   a. Compilation error
   X = A(I) + 4   b. Execution error
                            c. Neither a or b

8-6-2 Programming Problems

1. Write the code to fill successive elements of an array with the values 5,7,9, 11, · · · ,225. Do not use a READ statement.

2. Assume array A with 50 elements has already been loaded. Write the code to compute the sum of the squares of the elements of array A.

3. Input two vectors A and B with five coordinates and compute $A_1 B_1 + A_2 B_2 + \cdots A_5 B_5$.

4. Write a program to read 16 grades (one grade per card) and compute the number of grades less than the average. The output should be as follows:

5. Same problem as 4, except that it is not known how many data cards there are. Any grade outside the range 0–100 indicates the end of the input file. Assume no more than 1,000 cards. Could you print the message "AVERAGE IS" on the same line as the last grade?

6. The Miles Furniture Store is going out of business. All different store items have been labeled 1,2,3, · · · ,100 (100 different items in all). The cost per item and the number of items in stock have been recorded as follows: COST(I) is the cost of item I and QUAN(I) is the number of items I. Assume the COST and QUAN arrays have already been read in. Write a program segment to compute Miles inventory in dollars.

7. A deck of 60 cards contains three numbers per card. Write the code to read the first 20 numbers into array A, the next 30 in array B and the next 10 in array C.

8. An array A supposedly contains 20 elements already sorted in ascending order. Write the code to perform a sequence check. Print YES if the array is in sequence; otherwise, print NO.

9. Array A (10 elements) and array B (16 elements) have already been loaded. Write the code to determine the number of identical elements in both arrays.

10. Read into an array A of size 11 ten numbers in ascending order from one card; read another number R from another card and insert it in proper sequence in array A.

11. A and B are arrays of size 100 and 50 respectively. Write the code to store the numbers 1,2,3, · · · ,100 into array A, and the first 50 odd integers starting at 101 into array B. Then store arrays A and B in ascending order in array C. Do not read data from cards.

12. A deck of cards (no more than 100 cards) contains one grade per card. These grades are already in ascending order. Compute and print the median. The

median is that score which divides a distribution of scores into two equal parts. For example:

10,12,20,87   The median is (12 + 20)/2 = 11.
16,53,99   The median is 53.

To determine whether N is even or odd, evaluate $2*(N/2) - N$

13. A deck of 100 cards contains numbers ranging from –100 to 100, one number per card. These numbers are already in ascending sequence. Store the positive numbers in array A and the negative numbers in array B.

14. An array A contains 31 numbers that can be either positive, zero or negative. Write a program to print the negative numbers, the count of zero numbers and the positive numbers, three per line, as follows:

```
NEGATIVE NUMBERS        -XX.  -XX.  -XX.
                        -XX.  -XX.  -XX.
                          .
                          .
                        -XX.
COUNT OF ZERO NUMBERS    X
POSITIVE NUMBERS         XX.   XX.   XX.
                         XX.   XX.   XX.
                          .
                          .
                         XX.
```

Don't print the positive numbers if none exist. Same holds for zero or negative numbers.

15. A deck of cards contains one real number per card. Read the positive numbers in array A and the negative numbers in array B, in the order they are encountered in the input deck. Can you print them out as follows:

```
 2  -1
 3  -4
56
74
```

16. Read in a group of saving account numbers and amount deposited (ranging from 0.00 to 99999.99). There will be a maximum of 15 accounts and deposits.

   Output: 1. Print all the account numbers of those persons who have 50000.00 or more deposited.

   2. *Then* print all the account numbers of those persons who have *between* 10000.00 and 50000.00 deposited.

Input: 1. Set of saving account numbers and amount deposited; one set per card(= 15 cards); all saving account numbers range from 1 to 5000 (integer numbers); all amounts deposited range from 0.00 to 99999.99 (real number).
2. Trip record card (last-card codes) containing an integer and a real number less than zero.

17. At the beginning and at the end of each month, members of the U-WATCH-UR-WEIGHT club are weighed in. Each member's name and initial and terminal weights are punched onto one card. The first card of the deck has the exact number of club members (no more than 1,000) whose weights are recorded on the following cards. Write a program to print out each member's name, including the initial and terminal weight as well as the weight loss. Also print the number of members whose weight loss is above the average weight loss. For example:

HUBIT	200	180	20
FARAH	130	120	10
TODINI	160	154	6

AVERAGE WEIGHT LOSS IS 12 POUNDS
ONE MEMBER HAS A WEIGHT LOSS OVER 12 POUNDS

18. Same problem as 17, except that a "*" is to be printed beside each member's name whose weight loss is over the average. Hint: Use the carriage control character + to print the star (*).

19. An encyclopedia company has hired 20 girls. On cards, for each girl, they have the girl's name and the number of sets of encyclopedias she sold. Each girl gets paid $9.00 commission for each set sold but she also gets $2.00 extra for each set (and fraction) sold over the *average* of sets sold. Print out each girl's name, amount sold and amount earned.

xxxxxxxx SOLD xxx SETS. COMMISSION IS $xxxxx.xx

20. A deck contains an unknown number of cards, with three positive numbers per card. The first negative number encountered in the input deck signifies the end of the data. Write a program to read the first 20 numbers into array A, the next 30 into array B and the remaining elements into array C. Note that it is possible that there may only be ten numbers in all in which case only array A gets partially filled, or there might be enough to fill array B but not C etc. Assume no more than 90 data items in all and print out any array that has been either fully or partially filled.

21. Same as Exercise 8, except that the output will list each element out of sequence. For example, assume array A contains 15,5,6,20,30,4,70. Then:

5 is out of sequence since $15 > 5$.
6 is out of sequence since $15 > 6$.
4 is out of sequence since $30 > 4$.

22. The Meals on Wheels Company operates a fleet of vans used for the delivery of cold foods at various local plants and construction sites. The management is thinking of purchasing a specially built $18,000 van equipped to deliver hot foods. This new addition to the fleet is expected to generate after-tax earnings $E_1, E_2, \cdots, E_6$ (as displayed below) over the next six years, at which time the van's resale value will be zero. Projected repair and maintenance costs $C_0, C_1, C_2, \cdots, C_6$ over the six years are shown below.

Projected earnings		Projected costs		
E_1	$2,500	C_0	$18,000	(purchase cost
E_2	2,500	C_1	1,000	of the van)
E_3	3,000	C_2	1,500	
E_4	4,500	C_3	2,000	
E_5	6,000	C_4	2,000	
E_6	6,000	C_5	2,100	
		C_6	2,400	

The decision to purchase the van depends on the benefit/cost ratio (BCR) (grossly speaking, earnings/expenditures) given by the formula

$$BCR = \frac{E_1(1+i)^1 + E_2(1+i)^2 + \cdots + E_6(1+i)^6}{C_0 + C_1(1+i)^1 + C_2(1+i)^2 + \cdots + C_6(1+i)^6}$$

where i is the rate of investment of earnings by the company. If $BCR > 1$, then the company should acquire the van.
Write a program to determine how high the investment rate (i) would have to be raised to permit the purchase of the vehicle. Write a program to compute the BCR for investment rates starting at 6 percent and increasing in amounts of .1 percent. The output should be as follows:

Benefit/Cost ratio	Investment rate
.	6%
.	6.1
.	.
.	.
.	.

Stop when the BCR is greater than 1 and print the message

PURCHASE OF THE VAN REQUIRES AN INVESTMENT RATE OF XX.XX

23. Read a line of text from a card and determine the number of words in the line. Words may be defined as character strings separated by commas, periods or blanks.

24. Read a line of text and write the code to count the number of vowels (A,E,I,O,U) occurring in that line. Then determine the number of words and the number of vowels in each word.

25. Write a program to calculate the exact Julian date equivalent to the date specified in the form: month, day, year. The Julian date is the day of the year. January 1 has Julian date 1, February 2 has Julian date 33, December 31 has Julian date 365 etc. Use a table showing the number of days which have occurred since the beginning of the year for each month. For example:

Month	Days	
1	0	Remember that leap years have
2	31	one more day in February!
3	59	
4	90	

26. Write a program to convert dates given in the form month-number, day, year to the form month-name, day, 19year. For example, input in the form 11 18 78 should produce output NOVEMBER 18, 1978.

27. An interesting alternative to problem 26 is to allow input in the form month name, day, 19year and convert the date to the form month number, day, year.

28. To minimize transmission errors, words in telegrams are usually separated by slashes (/). Read a telegraphic line of text and regenerate it to its original form by substituting blanks wherever slashes appear.

29. Addresses in telegrams are transmitted serially. A double slash indicates a new line. For example: 1308/NORTH/20TH/AVE//ATLANTA//GEORGIA/ 75603//. Read five such addresses and recreate them as envelope addresses.

30. Using the bar graph method discussed in Section 8-4-4, produce abstract computer art as follows. Fill an array S of size 60 with random numbers between 1 and 100 and graph the corresponding bar graph for each element of S.

31. Using the bar graph method discussed in Section 8-4-4, write the code to graph the function $y = x^2$ and $y = 10|\sin x|$ to obtain a graph similar to:

```
 *       ↑ y    *       ↑ y
 *       |      *       |
 *       |      *       |
 *       |      *       |
 * *     |    * *       |
 * *     |    * *       |       * * *              * * *
 * * *   |    * * *      |     * * * * *          * * * * *
 * * * * | * * * *  x    |   * * * * * * *      * * * * * * *
 *+*+*+*+|+*+*+*+*+→     | * * * * * * * * *  * * * * * * * * *   x
                        +*+*+*+*+*+*+*+*+*+*+*+*+*+*+*+*+*+*+*+→
```

32. Write the code to produce the following outputs using a combination of DO and implied DO lists.

a.

1	2	3	4	5	6	7	8	9	10
1	2	3	4	5	6	7	8	9	
1	2	3	4	5	6	7	8		
1	2	3	4	5	6	7			
1	2	3	4	5	6				
1	2	3	4	5					
1	2	3	4						
1	2	3							
1	2								
1									

b.

1									
1	2								
1	2	3							
1	2	3	4						
1	2	3	4	5					
1	2	3	4	5	6				
1	2	3	4	5	6	7			
1	2	3	4	5	6	7	8		
1	2	3	4	5	6	7	8	9	
1	2	3	4	5	6	7	8	9	10

c.

10									
10	9								
10	9	8							
10	9	8	7						
10	9	8	7	6					
10	9	8	7	6	5				
10	9	8	7	6	5	4			
10	9	8	7	6	5	4	3		
10	9	8	7	6	5	4	3	2	
10	9	8	7	6	5	4	3	2	1

d.

10	9	8	7	6	5	4	3	2	1
10	9	8	7	6	5	4	3	2	
10	9	8	7	6	5	4	3		
10	9	8	7	6	5	4			
10	9	8	7	6	5				
10	9	8	7	6					
10	9	8	7						
10	9	8							
10	9								
10									

33. The following 12 integers are punched on one card:

$$36,27,43,18,5,6,9,33,45,34,22,42$$

Read these 12 numbers in ARRAY and write a program to accomplish the following:

a. Compute the average (mean) of these 12 numbers rounded to the nearest whole number.

b. Compute the difference between each of these 12 numbers and the mean (let the subtraction be in the order: number–mean) and store each of these deviations in an array called DEV.

c. Determine which of the 12 numbers starting at ARRAY deviates the most from the mean (this corresponds to the deviation having the largest absolute value) and print that number (not the deviation).

The output should be as follows:

```
ARRAY          DEV
  36            XX
  27            XX
  43            XX
   .             .
   .             .
   .             .
  38            XX
NUMBER DEVIATING MOST FROM MEAN IS XX
```

34. A deck of cards contains two fields per card: A name and a code representing a marital status: 1 = single; 2 = married; 3 = divorced; 4 = widowed. Read the deck of cards and produce a listing of the names with their corresponding marital status (in word form). Use only one write statement in the program.

35. Write a program to generate 1,000 random integer numbers between 1 and 100 and print their frequency. Compare the observed frequency with the expected frequency for randomly selected numbers.

36. Write a program to read 30 grades (ten per card) and compute and print the number of grades falling in the following intervals:

    1–9
    10–19   Hint: Use A(1),A(2), · · · ,A(10) as counters and
    20–29   evaluate A(IG/10 + 1) where IG is the grade read.
       .
       .
       .
    90–99

37. Write a program to read n grades ($n > 10$) and calculate the standard deviation of these n grades. The standard deviation may be computed by the following formula.

$$sd = \sqrt{\frac{(x_1 - \bar{x})^2 + (x_2 - \bar{x})^2 + (x_3 - \bar{x})^2 + \cdots + (x_n - \bar{x})^2}{n - 1}}$$

    where n = number of grades.
           $\bar{x}$ = average of grades.
           $x_1, x_2, x_3, \cdots x_n$ are the grades.

38. For each student in a class, you have one card with his account number in card colums 1–4 and ten test scores in card columns 11–40 (3 columns each). A blank card is used to indicate the end. The student's average is based on his nine best scores. Write a program to produce the following output at the top of a new page:

GRADING REPORT
ACCOUNT NUMBER: XXXX   AVERAGE = YYY.Y
TESTS   :   aaa aaa aaa aaa aaa aaa aaa aaa aaa aaa

ACCOUNT NUMBER: XXXX   AVERAGE = YYY.Y
TESTS   :   aaa aaa aaa aaa aaa aaa aaa aaa aaa aaa
.
.
.

39. Two arrays A and B contain numbers already sorted in numerical ascending order. Write a program to merge these two arrays in ascending sequence in C. (Do not sort the array C.) For example, if A = 1,3,7 and B = −1,3, then C = −1,1,3,3,7.

40. Using the bubble sort method described in Section 8-4-6, sort an array in ascending order.

41. Read into an alphanumeric array a list of names. Fix the length of each name to the double precision word length on your system.
    a. Sort the names alphabetically.
    b. Write the program in such a way that you can update the name list by accepting names at execution time and inserting them in their proper sorted sequence in the original array of names.

42. A variant to the sort described in Section 8-4-6 is to identify (i.e., locate) the largest array element and interchange it with the rightmost element of the array. On the next pass, only the first N − 1 array elements are searched for the largest (assume array has N elements). That largest number is then stored in the N − 1 position of the array; the same procedure is repeated till the search for the largest elements ends up with the first two elements. Write a program to accomplish this sort.

43. In the sorting process (bubble sort process) discussed in Section 8-4-6, it is possible that all numbers be sorted before the Nth pass. This would happen if no interchange occurred during any one pass. How can this condition be tested? Write a program to include this feature in the sort process.

44. Read a three-digit number N and store each individual digit of N in three consecutive array locations. For example, if N = 193, then $J(3) = 1$, $J(2) = 9$, $J(1) = 3$. Hint: Divide N by 100 to get 1 ($J(3) = 1$); then divide $N − J(3)*100$ (93) by 10 to obtain 9 ($J(2)$) and so on.

45. Write a program to compute $n! = n*(n − 1)*(n − 2)* \cdots *2*1$ for values of n that are so large that the result can't fit in a single integer memory location. For example, 25! = 15,511,210,043,330,985,984,000,000. A method to solve the problem is to use an array to store the answer (and partial results)

using one memory location in the array per digit. Thus 12! = 479,001,600 would be stored as follows:

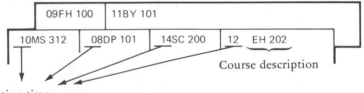

to compute 13! multiply each memory location by 13 (taking care to move the carries) to obtain

6	2	2	7	0	2	0	8	0	0

46. The program in Figure 8-14 read a student's schedule and arranged it in an easy to read format. Write a program to read two cards: the first one containing the student's Monday schedule (same as Wednesday and Friday) and the second one containing his Tuesday schedule (identical to Thursday). The course description and meeting time are punched in any order on the data cards. For example:

> 09FH 100 11BY 101
>
> 10MS 312 08DP 101 14SC 200 12 EH 202
>
> Course description
>
> Course meeting time

Each data field occupies eight card columns, with the first two card columns reserved for the meeting time. The program should produce the following output.

TIME	M	T	W	TH	F
8	DP101		DP101		DP101
9		FH100		FH100	
10	MS312		MS312		MS312
11		BY101		BY101	
12	EH202		EH202		EH202
13					
14	SC200		SC200		SC200

TOTAL HOURS IS 16

47. Dr X. is an information-science teacher. A file consisting of his students' names and their respective grades is stored in memory as follows:

Student	Grade 1	Grade 2	Total
MARGULIES	91	56	147
GLEASON	40	50	90
HORN	50	65	115
MONISH	70	70	140
.	.	.	.
.	.	.	.
.	.	.	.

END$

The last entry in the list of names is specified by END$.

a. Write a program to create such a file consisting of some ten or so students.

b. Add the necessary code to allow Dr. X. to correct his file in the event grades are listed incorrectly. Change of grades are read according to the following format:

> STUDENT NAME   GRADE 1,   GRADE 2

For grades that need not be changed, enter in their place a negative number. For example, HORN −1,98 means change HORN's second grade to 98 and compute new total.

48. A deck of cards contains the inventory for ten items sold by PARTS Ltd. as of the close of the November 17, 1978 business day. Each card contains the item number in card columns 1–4 and the number of items in stock in card columns 7–9. During November 18, some of the ten items are sold and shipped out; at the close of the November 18 business day, transaction cards are appended to the original ten cards, each reflecting the item number (card columns 1–4) and the number of items shipped that day (card columns 7–9). Not all items will have been shipped out, and a blank card will indicate the end of the transaction cards. Write a program to punch on cards an updated inventory (ten new punched cards) with the same format as the original inventory deck, and print out the total inventory at the closing of the November 18 business day. For example:

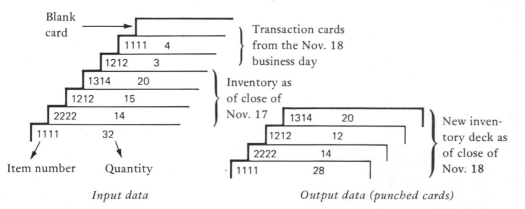

Input data   Output data (punched cards)

The printed output should be structured as follows:

```
                    NOV. 17 INVENTORY
          UNIT                        QUANTITY

          1111                           32
          2222                           14
          1212                           15
          1314                           20

                  NOV. 18 TRANSACTIONS
          UNIT                        QUANTITY
          1212                            3
          1111                            4

                    NOV. 18 INVENTORY
          UNIT                        QUANTITY
          1111                           28
          2222                           14
          1212                           12
          1314                           20

TOTAL INVENTORY IS 74.
```

49. At the Kilpatrick Community College, General Mathematics MS101 has always been offered in the traditional teacher/lecture format. This year, for the first time, students may take MS101 using a self-paced approach to instruction through a Computer Assisted Instructional (CAI) method. Because of the novelty of the CAI approach, the mathematics faculty has formulated the following policies concerning grades and tests for those taking MS101 in the CAI mode.

1. Students may take one or two or three tests during the semester.

2. The final score is based on the student's average score scaled as follows. If the CAI class average AV is less than 80 (the standardized average for traditional teacher/lecture form), then the difference 80 − AV should be added to each student's average score; otherwise, the difference AV − 80 is subtracted from each student's average. The input data is formatted as follows:

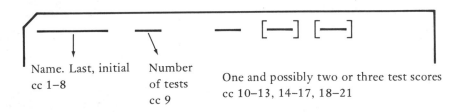

Name. Last, initial   Number
cc 1–8   of tests   One and possibly two or three test scores
                        cc 9   cc 10–13, 14–17, 18–21

Write a program to produce the following class/student/score information. For example, the following input data would produce the following output data:

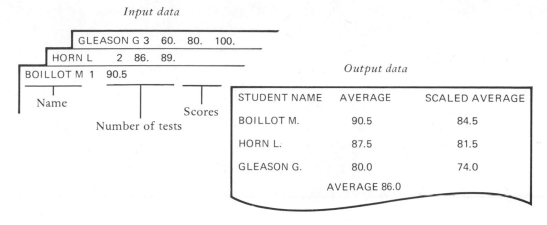

Input data

GLEASON G 3	60.	80.	100.
HORN L	2	86.	89.
BOILLOT M 1	90.5		

Name Number of tests Scores

Output data

STUDENT NAME	AVERAGE	SCALED AVERAGE
BOILLOT M.	90.5	84.5
HORN L.	87.5	81.5
GLEASON G.	80.0	74.0
	AVERAGE 86.0	

Can you rewrite the code for the above exercise in such a way that each student's grade is printed across each line of the output form after the student name but before the average? After the scaled average as shown in the output of the above exercise?

50. On NBC's *Today* show weather report, temperatures from various cities in the United States are listed by geographical areas. Temperature readings are collected from various weather-measuring stations and punched on cards in no special sequence order. Each card contains the following data:

| City | Temperature | Section code | 1 = East Coast | 2 = Midwest |
| cc 1–8 | cc 10–12 | cc–13 | 3 = South | 4 = Pacific |

a. Write a program segment to provide the weatherman with a list of cities and corresponding temperatures by geographical area in the order the cities are encountered in the input deck. The output should identify each of the geographical areas by name rather than by numeric code, using the A format for each geographical area. The output should be as follows:

Input data						
BOSTON	45	1		EAST COAST		
FRESNO	66	4		BOSTON	45	
NEW YORK	51	1		NEW YORK	51	
MOBILE	73	3		MID WEST		
MADISON	–5	2		MADISON	–5	
CHICAGO	57	2		CHICAGO	57	
MIAMI	88	3		SOUTHERN STATES		
				MOBILE	73	
				MIAMI	88	
				PACIFIC COAST		
				FRESNO	66	

.
.

THE HIGHEST TEMPERATURE RECORDED WAS IN MIAMI WITH 88 DEGREES.

b. Write another program segment to list cities by ascending temperature order (four cities per printed line) as follows:

MADISON −5   BOSTON 45   NEW YORK 51   CHICAGO 57
FRESNO   66   MOBILE 73   MIAMI   88

51. The Boihorn Company employs a variable number of salesmen. Records of sales by each salesman are transcribed on cards. These cards are already sorted in ascending order by salesman number. For example, a typical data deck might appear as follows:

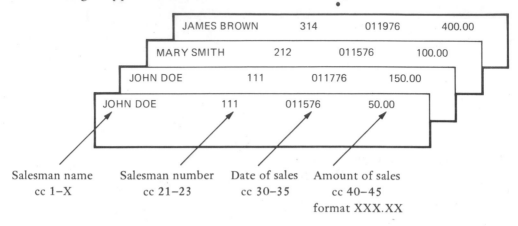

Salesman name   Salesman number   Date of sales   Amount of sales
    cc 1–X   cc 21–23   cc 30–35   cc 40–45
                                                      format XXX.XX

Fix the salesman-name field to the size of your double precision word character format.

The director wishes to print out a monthly sales report to summarize the total sales for each salesman and the total amount of all sales. Also, a salesman-of-the-month award will go to the salesman with highest sales for the month. Entries are to be listed in ascending order by salesman number. Observe the following output for your data.

SALESMAN NAME	SALESMAN NUMBER	DATE SALES	AMOUNT SALES	TOTAL SALES
JOHN DOE	111	011576	50.00	
		011776	150.00	250.00
MARY SMITH	212	011576	100.00	100.00
JAMES BROWN	314	011976	400.00	400.00
		TOTAL SALES		750.00

AWARD GOES TO JAMES BROWN

Write a program to read a deck of cards, each containing a transaction, and produce a summary report as shown above. Be sure you include more than one transaction for some of the salesmen and note that in such a case you only print the number of the salesman once.

52. a. Without reading any data cards (initialize arrays to the constants specified) create and print the following inventory file for an auto parts dealer:

PART NUMBER	QUANTITY	COST/PART
115	50	90
120	60	91
125	70	92
130	80	93
.	.	.
.	.	.
.	.	.
160	140	99

For example, there are 50 parts item 115 at a cost of 90 cents each. During the day, sales transactions are recorded on punched cards (or simulated by a random number generator) as follows:

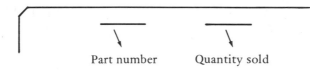

Part number   Quantity sold

b. Write a program to read the day's transaction deck to produce a parts inventory and to:
1. Print a "reorder" message whenever less than 20 items are in stock.
2. Discount the price on any unsold part by 10 percent of its original cost (rounded to nearest digit).

The inventory report, for example, might be drawn as follows:

PART NUMBER	QTY. STOCK	NUMBER SOLD	COST PART	
115	40	10	90	
120	0	60	91	**REORDER**
125	70	0	83	DISCOUNT
130	15	5	93	**REORDER**
.	.	.		
.	.	.		
.	.	.		
160	70	70	99	

c. In the event a parts number is incorrectly punched in the transaction data deck, generate the **same report as in part** b **with a** list of the incorrect part numbers at the **bottom of (following) the** inventory report. For example:

PART NUMBER	QTY. STOCK	NUMBER SOLD	COST PART
115	40	10	90
.	.	.	.
.	.	.	.
.	.	.	.
160	70	70	99

117 ***NO SUCH EXISTING PART. CHECK RECORD.***
126 ***NO SUCH EXISTING PART. CHECK RECORD.***

d. To prepare for the following day, recreate a new inventory file by deleting all part numbers with exhausted stock, and print the new inventory table as follows:

PART NUMBER	QUANTITY	COST/PART	
115	40	90	
125	70	83	Note absence of
130	5	93	part number 120.
.	.	.	
.	.	.	
.	.	.	
160	70	99	

e. During the day, a parts salesman persuades the manager to add three new parts to his current line of parts. The parts numbers are numbers between 100 and 170, excluding those already in use. The manager decides to purchase 300 of each of those new parts. Read three cards with a part number and corresponding cost on each card and produce a new inventory table by inserting the new records in their appropriate ascending position in the file as follows:

PART NUMBER	QUANTITY	COST/PART	
100	300	60	Note new
115	40	90	inserts.
130	5	93	
132	300	95	
.	.	.	
.	.	.	
.	.	.	

53. Read into a double precision array named WORD eight of each of the following: nouns, pronouns, verbs, adverbs, adjectives and articles (repeated if necessary) and store their corresponding numerical word code in an integer array called KODE. The word codes are: 1 = pronoun, 2 = verb, 3 = adverb,

4 = adjective, 5 = noun, 6 = article. Both the words and their corresponding numerical codes are recorded randomly on cards, as follows:

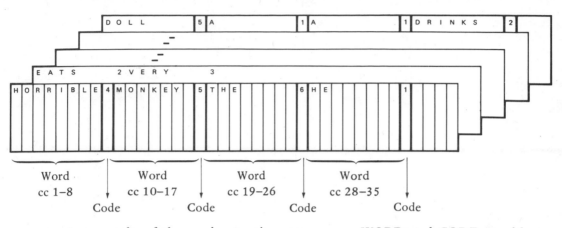

As a result of the read operation, two arrays WORD and CODE would appear as follows

WORD	HORRIBLE	MONKEY	THE	HE	EATS	VERY	...	DOLL	A	A	DRINKS

KODE	4	5	6	1	2	3	...	5	1	1	2

KODE(1) KODE(2)   KODE(48)

a. Write a program to search the word code array to print out all the words of the word array using the following format:

PRONOUNS	VERBS	ADVERBS	ADJECTIVES	NOUNS	ARTICLES
HE	EATS	VERY	HORRIBLE	MONKEY	THE
.	.	.	.	.	.
.	.	.	.	.	.
.	.	.	.	.	A
	DRINKS			DOLL	A

b. Using the random number generator routine to extract entries from the 48-word array (not from the six above sorted word arrays), construct two English sentences to fit the following grammatical structure:

Article,noun,verb,adjective. Pronoun,verb,article,adverb,adjective,noun.

For example, the following sentence might be generated:

THE BOY IS TALL. HE IS A VERY BEAUTIFUL MONKEY.

Analyze the selected numerical codes to keep rejecting words until they satisfy the desired grammatical structure. Hint: You might want to store the numerical word codes for the sentence in an array where NUM(1) = 6,NUM(2) = 5,NUM(3) = 2, · · · ,NUM(10) = 5, and compare NUM(I) with KODE(J), where I varies from 1 to 10 and J is a random number between 1 and 48.

54.   You work in the library and want to show your boss what you can do with the computer. This library uses the Dewey decimal notation for categorizing books. You are provided with a number of cards with the following format:

> columns
>   1–8   author of a book
>   10–16 Dewey decimal number for the book
>   20–39 title of the book
>   51–55 cost of the book

Since you do not know how many books you have, the last data record is followed by a record containing "$" in column 1 to indicate the end of the data. You have *at most* 15 books to survey.

You are to read in a set of these cards and answer the following:

a.   What is the total cost of all books surveyed?

b.   How many books are in the Humanities (those books with Dewey decimal numbers between 100 and 300 inclusive)?

c.   How many books are in the Sciences (600–699.999)?

d.   How many books are by SHELLY and what is their total cost?

e.   Provide an alphabetic listing of all the *authors* in this survey. (If an author appears more than once, his name should be printed in this alphabetic listing more than once).

f.   Print everything according to the coding form below.

LIBRARY SURVEY
TOTAL COST OF BOOKS IS $xxxx.xx.
xx BOOKS IN THE HUMANITIES (100–300).
xx BOOKS IN THE SCIENCES (600–699.999).
xx BOOKS BY SHELLY WORTH $xxx.xx.
THE AUTHORS SURVEYED
aaaaaaaa
.
.
.

8-6-2   Answers to Self Test

1.   a. Valid.   b. Invalid.   c. Invalid.   d. Invalid.

2.   The three-element array is stored in consecutive memory locations; three variables may or may not be assigned to consecutive locations.

3. a. B(3).   b. Invalid.   c. Invalid.   d. C(3*K + 2).   e. Valid.
    f. Invalid.   g. Invalid.   h. Invalid.   i. Invalid.

4. a. F.   b. T.   c. F.   d. T.   e. F.   f. F.   g. T (except for sub-
    scripts).   h. F.

5. a. 5.   b. 18.   c. 4.

6. a.   DO 1 I = 1,6,2   b.   DO 2 I = 2,9,4
        1   READ(1,5)A(I),A(I + 1)   2   READ(1,6)A(I),K(I),A(I + 2),
                                                 *K(I + 2)

7. a. (1.) Skip to the top of a new page, space down 4 lines
        (2.) 1 _ 2   (3.) 1 2 3 4 5
             3 _ 4
             5 _ _

    b. (1.) Invalid; mixed modes.   (2.) _ 3 _ 1
                                                _ 3 _ 2
                                                _ 3 _ 3
                                                _ 3 _ 4

        (3.) 3 _ 1 _ 3 _ 2 _ 3
             3 _ 3 _ 4 _ _

    c. (1.) 1 _ _ 2 . _ _ – 3 . _ _ _ 3 . _ _ 5 . _ _ _ 0 .
             2 _ _ 2 . _ _ – 3 . _ _ _ 3 . _ _ 5 . _ _ _ 0 .

        (2.) _ 2 . _ _ – 3 . _ _ _ 3 . _ _ 5 . _ _ _ 0 . _ _ 2 Top of page
             _ 2 . _ _ – 3 . _ _ _ 3 . _ _ 5 . _ _ _ 0 . _ _ 2

        (3.) 1
             _ 2 . _ _ – 3 . _ _ 3 . _ _ _ 5 . _ _ _ 0 . _ _
        J cannot be described by an F format.

    d. (1.) _ 2 . _ _ – 3 . * * * 2 . 0
             _ – 3 . _ _ – 1 . 2 . 0 _ _ _

(2.) $\underline{1}$. $\underline{5}$
$\underline{-\ 3}$. $\underline{2}$
$\underline{-\ 1}$. $\underline{0}$
$\underline{2}$. $\underline{0}$
$\underline{1}$. $\underline{5}$
$\underline{-\ 3}$. $\underline{2}$
$\underline{-\ 1}$. $\underline{0}$
$\underline{2}$. $\underline{0}$

(3.) $\underline{2}$. $\underline{-\ 3}$. $\underline{-\ 1}$. $\underline{2}$. $\underline{2}$. $\underline{-\ 3}$. $\underline{-\ 1}$. $\underline{2}$.

8. a. 5   FORMAT(5F10.0/(10I8))   b. 5   FORMAT(2F10.0,I5)
    c. 5   FORMAT(3F10.0/1000(10I6/),2X,F5.0,I3)

9. a. Valid; 3 records.   b. Valid; 5 records.   c. Valid; 18 records.
    d. Invalid K − 1 (compilation error).   e. Invalid; integer variable read with
    real format code (execution-time error).   f. Valid; 30 records.
    g. Valid; 2 records.   h. Valid; 5 records.

10. a.   WRITE(3,5)(A(I),I = 1,100)   DO 10 I = 1,100,2
       5   FORMAT(T10,F5.0,1X,F5.0)   10   WRITE(3,5)A(I),A(I + 1)

    b.   WRITE(3,5)(A(I),A(I + 50),I = 1,50)   DO 10 I = 1,50
       5   FORMAT(T10,F5.0,1X,F5.0)   10   WRITE(3,5)A(I),A(I + 50)

    c.   WRITE(3,5)(I,A(I),I = 1,100)   DO 10 I = 1,100
       5   FORMAT(T10,I1,1X,F5.0)   10   WRITE(3,5)I,A(I)

    d.   WRITE(3,5)(A(I),I = 2,100,2),(A(I),I = 1,100)
       5   FORMAT(100(T10,F5.0/)//(2X,10F5.0))

11. a. Value of J is undefined; could destroy a memory location and blow
       program.
    b. Value of J is undefined; cannot blow program, results may be meaningless.
    c. Program may blow since values will be read into A(101),A(102), $\cdots$,
       A(110) which have not been reserved for the array A.
    d. The initial values of A(2),A(3),A(4) and A(5) will be destroyed by suc-
       cessive values.

12. The value of the subscript I is negative. This can be "caught" only at execu-
    tion time since the compiler has no knowledge of the value of I.

TWO- AND THREE-DIMENSIONAL ARRAYS

9-1 Problem Example

Widgets, Inc., manufacturer of widgets of all kinds, utilizes three identical shops in its production facilities. Each shop is comprised of five machines required in the manufacture of widgets. The company has compiled the repair records on all the machines and has tabulated the number of hours lost on each machine in each shop as shown below:

			Machine		
Shop	1	2	3	4	5
1	6	3	1	0	2
2	9	7	2	6	2
3	0	3	7	10	5

For example, in shop 3 no hours have been lost on machine 1, while 3, 7, 10 and 5 hours have been lost respectively on machines 2, 3, 4 and 5. Write a program to calculate and print the average hours lost for each type of machine. Each row of the above table is punched onto one data card. The data is stored into a two-dimensional array A. In each reference to an element of the array A, the first sub-script indicates the shop; the second subscript indicates the machine. In the pro-gram of Figure 9-1, a one-dimensional array S is used to store the sums of lost hours, which is then used later to compute the averages of lost hours for the five machines.

```
      DIMENSION A(3,5),S(5)
      DO 10 I = 1,3
10    READ(1,3)(A(I,J),J = 1,5)
3     FORMAT(5F2.0)
      DO 35 J = 1,5
      S(J) = 0
      DO 30 I = 1,3
30    S(J) = S(J) + A(I,J)
35    S(J) = S(J)/3.0
      DO 40 I = 1,3
40    WRITE(3,4)(A(I,J),J = 1,5)
4     FORMAT(20X,5F6.0)
      WRITE(3,5)(S(J),J = 1,5)
5     FORMAT('0AVERAGES',T21,5F6.0)
      STOP
      END
```

Read $A(1,1),A(1,2),A(1,3),A(1,4),A(1,5),A(2,1) \cdots$.

Zero out array S.
For each machine J, compute the hours lost in each shop, i.e., $S_J = A_{1J} + A_{2J} + A_{3J}$.
Compute the average of hours lost for each machine.

Figure 9-1 Average hours lost by machine.

9-2 FORTRAN Statements

9-2-1 Two-Dimensional Arrays

So far, all the arrays we have considered have been one-dimensional or linear ar-rays; only one subscript is used in addressing elements of the array. Many times when writing programs it is necessary to work with data arranged in table form (rows or columns of information). Two-dimensional arrays can be used in FOR-TRAN to represent such data structures. These arrays can be manipulated very conveniently for processing and for input/output purposes through the use of indices or subscripts.

For example, the table of numbers shown in Figure 9-2 could be stored in a two-dimensional array A containing three rows and five columns. The conven-tional method of addressing elements of a two-dimensional array is to write the row number first followed by the column number. Thus the element in the second row and third column of array A would be addressed A(2,3). In general, A(I,J) is the element found in the Ith row and Jth column. Note that the two sub-scripts are separated by a comma and enclosed in parentheses.

	Column 1	Column 2	Column 3	Column 4	Column 5
Row 1	6.	3.	−1.	0.	2.
	A(1,1)	A(1,2)	A(1,3)	A(1,4)	A(1,5)
Row 2	−123.	32.67	−.527	.05	3345.
	A(2,1)	A(2,2)	A(2,3)	A(2,4)	A(2,5)
Row 3	3.1	−456.	2.12	11111.	0.
	A(3,1)	A(3,2)	A(3,3)	A(3,4)	A(3,5)

Figure 9-2 A two-dimensional array.

9-2-2 The DIMENSION statement for Two-Dimensional Arrays

The general form of the DIMENSION statement is

DIMENSION variable(row-limit,column-limit) [,· · ·]

where variable(s) is the name of the array(s).
Row-limit is a positive integer constant specifying the maximum number of rows.
Column-limit is a positive integer constant specifying the maximum number of columns.

Any number of two-dimensional (or one-dimensional) arrays may be specified in a DIMENSION statement. For example, the statement:

DIMENSION B(6,8),C(10),ISUM(10,25)

reserves 48 array locations for the real array B with six rows and eight columns, 10 array locations for array C and 250 locations for the integer array ISUM (maximum row subscript is ten; maximum column subscript is 25).

Any reference to the variable name B or ISUM in an arithmetic statement must include two subscripts. For example, the statement B(I) = 0 is invalid, because only one subscript is included in reference to B.

The row subscript value used in a reference to a two-dimensional array *must* be in the range 1 to the row-limit specified in the DIMENSION statement. A similar restriction applies to the column subscript. For example, given the size of the array A defined by DIMENSION A(3,5), the references A(1,1),A(2,4) and A(3,5) are valid, whereas A(4,1), A(3,6) and A(0,1) are invalid, since one or more of the subscripts is outside the declared subscript range.

Subscript expressions for two-dimensional arrays behave in the same way as one-dimensional subscript expressions. (See Section 8-2-2.) For example, the following references to a two-dimensional array are valid:

$$TABLE(3*K, I + 2)$$
$$B(10*ISUM - 7, J)$$
$$C(K, 5*L)$$

9-2-3 · Processing Two-Dimensional Arrays

Two-dimensional arrays can be processed in essentially the same way as single-dimensional arrays. Suppose, for example, that we wished to determine the number of elements with values less than 50 in an array A of size 4 × 3. The search for values less than 50 can be accomplished by successively examining the first, second, third and fourth row of the array A, as shown in Figure 9-3.

```
      DIMENSION A(4,3)
            ·
            ·
            ·                  K is a counter used to count array elements with
  10  K = 0                    value less than 50.
  20  DO 40 I = 1,4
  25  DO 40 J = 1,3            For a fixed value of I, J spans the columns of A,
  30  IF(A(I,J).GE.50)GOTO40   hence the search in the inner loop scans the rows
  35  K = K + 1                of A; that is, $A_{11}, A_{12}, A_{13}, A_{21}, A_{22}, \cdots$.
  40  CONTINUE
```

Figure 9-3   Processing all elements of a two-dimensional array.

In general, if *all* elements of an array are to be processed, two loops with two indices controlling the row and column of the array are required. The order of these loops in the program is immaterial. The program shown in Figure 9-3 with statements 20 and 25 interchanged would perform the same task. In this case, columns 1, 2 and 3 in that order are searched for elements less than 50.

Another illustration will help clarify the index mechanism of a two-dimensional array. Suppose it is desired to (1) compute the sum of the entries of the Nth row of an array A of size 10 × 17 where N is accepted from input and (2) interchange column 3 with column 17. The row sum to be calculated is SUM = A(N,1) + A(N,2) + A(N,3) + · · · A(N,16) + A(N,17). The row index is fixed to N, while the column index varies from 1 to 17.

The interchange procedure can be accomplished by moving, successively, each element of column 3 into a temporary location TEMP, then moving the corresponding element of column 17 in the vacated column 3 position and finally moving the saved value in TEMP into the corresponding location of column 17, as depicted in Figure 9-4. If no temporary location TEMP were used, the elements of column 3 would be destroyed by the statement $A(I,3) = A(I,17)$, as I ranges from 1 to 10. The code to perform the sum and the interchange procedure is shown in Figure 9-4.

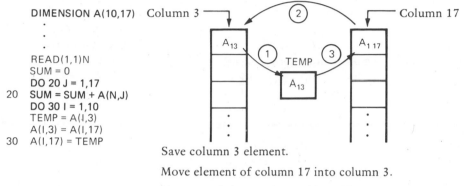

```
DIMENSION A(10,17)
    .
    .
    .
    READ(1,1)N
    SUM = 0
    DO 20 J = 1,17
20  SUM = SUM + A(N,J)
    DO 30 I = 1,10
    TEMP = A(I,3)
    A(I,3) = A(I,17)
30  A(I,17) = TEMP
```

Save column 3 element.

Move element of column 17 into column 3.

Move saved element into column 17.

Figure 9-4 Sum of a row and column interchange procedure.

9-2-4 Input/Output of Two-Dimensional Arrays

The basic task to be accomplished when an input or output operation is to be performed on a two-dimensional array is to specify correctly the proper sequence of the array elements in the READ/WRITE list. There are always alternative ways to accomplish a given task—some ways more compact and efficient than others—but all may be acceptable solutions. For example, consider the data to be processed by the program of Figure 9-1. Information about machines in each shop (row) is recorded on a data card. We may visualize the input data as

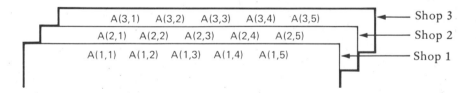

One method to input the above data would be

```
READ(1,3)A(1,1),A(1,2),A(1,3),A(1,4),A(1,5)
READ(1,3)A(2,1),A(2,2),A(2,3),A(2,4),A(2,5)
READ(1,3)A(3,1),A(3,2),A(3,3),A(3,4),A(3,5)
```

Of course, by using a DO loop the above code could be reduced to

```
    DO 2 I = 1,3
2   READ(1,3)A(I,1),A(I,2),A(I,3),A(I,4),A(I,5)
3   FORMAT(5F6.0)
```

Using an implied DO list, the list of variables could be shortened to

$$DO\ 2\ I = 1,3$$
$$2\quad READ(1,3)(A(I,J),J = 1,5)$$
$$3\quad FORMAT(5F6.0)$$

This is the form used in Figure 9-1. FORMAT statement 3 specifies that five variables are to be read from one record; hence there is no real reason for the external DO loop used above. Two implied DO lists could be used, as follows:

$$READ(1,3)((A(I,J),J = 1,5),I = 1,3)$$

Inner loop cycles the fastest
as I = 1, J runs through 1, 2, 3, 4, 5.

Outer loop moves slowest. For each value of I,
the inner index J runs from 1 to 5.

Once again, the implied DO list is nothing more than a compact technique to generate a list of variables. What the DO list actually does is to generate the following code:

$$READ(1,3)A(1,1),A(1,2),A(1,3),A(1,4),A(1,5),A(2,1),A(2,2), \cdots ,A(2,5),A(3,1), \cdots A(3,5)$$

Hence 15 values are to be read in memory. The number of values read per card (record) is specified by the format. FORMAT(5F6.0) specifies that five values are to be read per card. Since 15 variables are to be read, three data cards will be required. Had the FORMAT specified 7F6.0, two cards would have been read, with only one entry on the last card read.

Suppose that in the problem of Section 9-1 the data punched on each card were to represent the hours lost for each machine. The input data might be visualized as

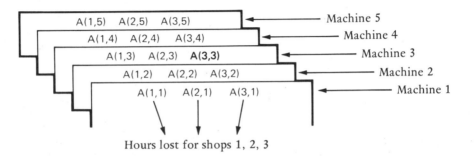

Hours lost for shops 1, 2, 3

To input the above data, the following code might have been used:

READ(1,4) A(1,1),A(2,1),A(3,1)
READ(1,4) A(1,2),A(2,2),A(3,2)
READ(1,4) A(1,3),A(2,3),A(3,3)
READ(1,4) A(1,4),A(2,4),A(3,4)
READ(1,4) A(1,5),A(2,5),A(3,5)

or

DO 2 J = 1,5
2   READ(1,4) A(1,J),A(2,J),A(3,J)
4   FORMAT(3F6.0)

or

DO 2 J = 1,5
2   READ(1,4)(A(I,J),I = 1,3)

or

READ(1,4)((A(I,J),I = 1,3),J = 1,5)

When using implied DO lists for reading or writing data, the beginning programmer should be careful about which index moves fastest in the implied DO list. The following examples show how arrays can be loaded row-wise or column-wise, depending on how the implied DO list is coded:

Fast index   Fast index
              Slow index   Slow index
4   FORMAT(4F4.0)   4   FORMAT(4F4.0)
READ(1,4) (A(I,J),I = 1,4),J = 1,4)   READ(1,4) (A(I,J),J = 1,4),I = 1,4)

When J = 1, I takes on values 1,2,3,4.   When I = 1, J takes on values 1,2,3,4.
When J = 2, I takes on values 1,2,3,4 etc. When I = 2, J takes on values 1,2,3,4 etc.
Hence the array is stored in column   Hence the array is stored in row fashion,
fashion, as in   as in

A_{11} A_{21} A_{31} A_{41} A_{11} A_{12} A_{13} A_{14}

Array is loaded column-wise.   Array is loaded row-wise.

Many implied DO lists can be specified in one READ/WRITE statement. Consider the following, for example:

Example 1

Assume three arrays A,B,C are to be read row-wise, according to the data layout shown below:

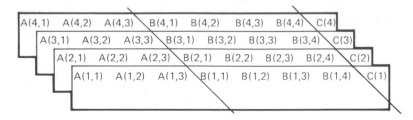

The correct implied DO list might be

```
1    FORMAT(8F5.0)
     READ(1,1)((A(I,J),J = 1,3),(B(I,K),K = 1,4),C(I),I = 1,4)
```

This can be interpreted as

When I = 1, read A(1,J) as J = 1 to 3, then B(1,K) as K = 1,4 and C(1)

or

read A(1,1),A(1,2),A(1,3),B(1,1), · · · ,B(1,4),C(1)

and repeat the above for I = 2,3 and 4.

Altogether, three elements of A, four elements of B and one element of C will be read per card as I ranges from 1 to 4. Hence (3 + 4 + 1)·4 = 32 elements will be read. The list of variables contains 32 elements, and the FORMAT specifies 8 values per card; hence, 4 cards will be read.

Example 2

In this example, the array B is to be read column-wise.

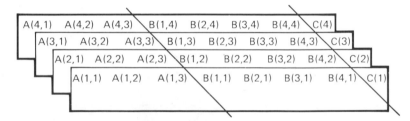

The following code might be used to read the above data:

```
      READ(1,1)((A(I,J),J = 1,3),(B(K,I),K = 1,4),C(I),I = 1,4)
  1   FORMAT(8F5.0)
```

If the beginner finds the above too confusing, he can use a combination of a DO loop and an implied DO list, as follows:

```
          DO 10 I = 1,4
          READ(1,1) (A(I,J),J = 1,3),(B(K,I),K = 1,4),C(I))
  10      CONTINUE
```

Two-dimensional arrays can be used to great advantage when printing tables of numbers that require some form of column/row identification and headings. Consider, for example, the problem in Figure 9-1, where it is desired to print the input data according to the following output:

```
shop 1      XX.X      XX.X      XX.X      XX.X      XX.X
shop 2      XX.X      XX.X      XX.X      XX.X      XX.X
shop 3      XX.X      XX.X      XX.X      XX.X      XX.X
```

The following code could be used to generate the above output:

Shop number   Hours lost

```
      WRITE(3,1) (I,(A(I,J),J = 1,5),I = 1,3)
  1   FORMAT(8X,'SHOP',I2,5X,5F10.1)
```

generates 1, $A_{11},A_{12},A_{13},A_{14},A_{15}$, 2, $A_{21},A_{22}, \cdots 3, \cdots A_{35}$

For the programmer who wishes to generate the more sophisticated output shown below for Figure 9-1, with just one WRITE statement:

MAINTENANCE ANALYSIS

	Machine 1	*Machine 2*	*Machine 3*	*Machine 4*	*Machine 5*
shop 1	XX.X	XX.X	XX.X	XX.X	XX.X
shop 2	XX.X	XX.X	XX.X	XX.X	XX.X
shop 3	XX.X	XX.X	XX.X	XX.X	XX.X
Average	XX.XX	XX.XX	XX.XX	XX.XX	XX.XX

The following code could be used:

Machine numbers   Shop number   Hours lost   Average lost for each machine

```
      WRITE(3,1)(K,K = 1,5),(I,(A(I,J),J = 1,5),I = 1,3),(S(J),J = 1,5)
  1   FORMAT('1',T35,'MAINTENANCE ANALYSIS'//T24,5('MACHINE',I2,2X)//
     * 3(8X,'SHOP',I3,5X,5F10.1/),T25,'AVERAGE',5F11.2)
```

Shop   Number   Data   Average result
         (I)   (A(I,J))   (S(J))   (K)

The beginning programmer may wish to use two or three separate WRITE statements instead of the one shown above!

Another example illustrates the power of the two-dimensional arrays for input/output considerations. Suppose it is desired to print the following multiplication tables:

$1*1 = 1$	$2*1 = 2$	$3*1 = 3$	$\cdots$	$10*1 = 10$
$1*2 = 2$	$2*2 = 4$	$3*2 = 6$		$10*2 = 20$
$1*3 = 3$	$2*3 = 6$	$3*3 = 9$		$10*3 = 30$
.	.	.		.
.	.	.		.
.	.	.		.
$1*10 = 10$	$2*10 = 20$	$3*10 = 30$		$10*10 = 100$

The following code could be used:

```
      DIMENSION MULT(10,10)
      DO 10 J = 1,10
      DO 10 I = 1,10
10    MULT(I,J) = I*J            Compute all entries of multiplication table (row-wise).
      DO 15 J = 1,10
15    WRITE(3,11)(I,J,MULT(I,J),I = 1,10)    When J = 1, the first row of the above
                                             table is printed.
11    FORMAT(10(I2,'*',I2,'=',I3,3X))        When J = 2, the second row of the above
                                             table is printed, etc.
```

9-2-5   Three-Dimensional Arrays

A three-dimensional array is a data structure which can be accessed using three subscripts. A three-dimensional array may be visualized as a cube containing several two-dimensional arrays. Consider an array specified by

$$\text{DIMENSION } Q(3,2,4)$$

We may think of this cube as containing four two-dimensional arrays, three rows and two columns each.

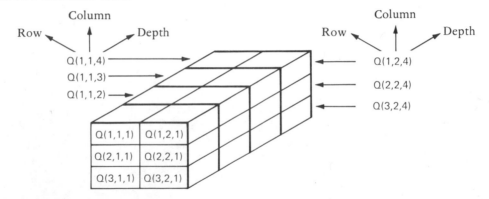

Any element of the cube can be referenced by Q(IR,IC,ID)
where IR indicates the row.

IC indicates the column.

ID indicates the depth, i.e., which of the two-dimensional arrays the element is in.

Input/output and processing techniques for three-dimensional arrays are similar to the techniques for two-dimensional arrays. For example, suppose Widgets, Inc., referred to in Section 9-1, has two factories each containing three shops of five machines each. An array to store the data regarding the repair records of machines could be specified by:

DIMENSION A(3,5,2)

Shop Machines Factory

Suppose the data for each shop has been punched onto data cards, with data for factory 1 preceding data for factory 2. The data may be visualized as

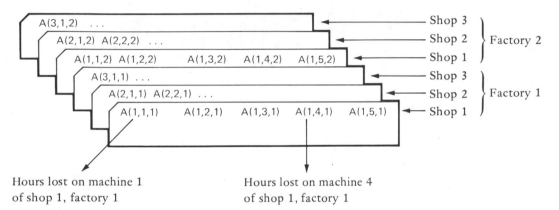

Hours lost on machine 1 of shop 1, factory 1

Hours lost on machine 4 of shop 1, factory 1

The FORTRAN code required to read, compute the average time lost on each machine and write out the results is shown in Figure 9-5.

```
      DIMENSION A(3,5,2),S(5)              Three shops, five machines, two factories.
      READ(1,1)(((A(I,J,K),J = 1,5),I = 1,3),K = 1,2)
   1  FORMAT(5F2.0)
      DO 30 J = 1,5
      S(J) = 0
      DO 20 K = 1,2
      DO 20 I = 1,3
  20  S(J) = S(J)+A(I,J,K)                 S(J) is total of hours lost on machine J.
  30  S(J) = S(J)/6.                       S(J) is the average of hours lost on machine J for the six shops.
      DO 40 K = 1,2
      WRITE(3,2)K
   2  FORMAT('0',26X,'FACTORY NUMBER',I3)
  40  WRITE(3,3)((A(I,J,K),J = 1,5),I = 1,3)
   3  FORMAT(20X,5F6.0)
      WRITE(3,4)(S(J),J = 1,5)
   4  FORMAT('0AVERAGES',T21,5F6.1)
      STOP
      END
```

Figure 9-5 Sample program to process a three-dimensional array.

9-2-6   Internal Representation of Multidimensional Arrays

Internally, two-dimensional arrays are stored as a linear sequence of elements in column order. For example, an array A with three rows and three columns is stored as follows:

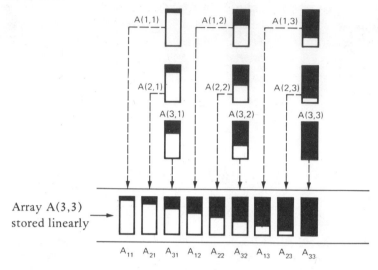

Array A(3,3) stored linearly →

Although the array A is stored column-wise in memory, this does not mean that A has to be read into memory by columns. It can be read row-wise as in READ(1,3)(A(I,J),J = 1,3),I = 1,3).

Three-dimensional arrays are stored linearly in memory. The internal order of storage for the array A(3,5,3) is column-wise across each depth plane.

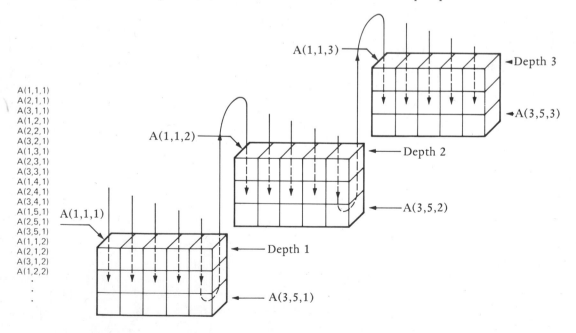

An array name may be used in a READ or WRITE list without subscripts. In that case, the elements are processed in column order.

Example

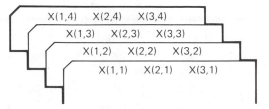

DIMENSION X(3,4)   Note
READ(1,3)X
3   FORMAT(3,F4.0)

This code will result in all 12 elements of X being read, with three data items per card. The data may be visualized as

```
      X(1,4)   X(2,4)   X(3,4)
         X(1,3)    X(2,3)    X(3,3)
            X(1,2)    X(2,2)    X(3,2)
               X(1,1)    X(2,1)    X(3,1)
```

The above array considerations apply for output as well. For example, suppose the array IX contains the following data:

IX =

17	9	8	73
4	6	18	14
5	10	21	5

The following are equivalent WRITE statements:

DIMENSION IX(3,4)   DIMENSION IX(3,4)
.   .
.   .
.   .
WRITE(3,10)IX   WRITE(3,10)((IX(I,J),I = 1,3),J = 1,4)
10   FORMAT(2X,3I3)   10   FORMAT(2X,3I3)

This would produce the following printout:

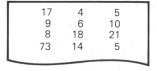

```
      17      4      5
       9      6     10
       8     18     21
      73     14      5
```

A three-dimensional array can also be processed without any subscripts in a READ/WRITE statement. The order in which elements are processed is discussed in Section 9-2-6.

9-3 You Might Want to Know

1. Does FORTRAN allow arrays of more than three dimensions?

   Answer: Some versions of FORTRAN allow 31 dimensions for an array (Burroughs 6700/7700), while others restrict the programmer to three.

2. What will happen to my program if I use a subscript reference which is illegal? For example, suppose my array is declared by DIMENSION X(3,5) and I reference X(5,7).

   Answer: The handling of this problem may differ among FORTRAN systems. Many FORTRAN compilers translate an array reference into an address without checking whether the subscripts are in the range allowed by the DIMENSION statement. If the address is invalid, an execution-time diagnostic will be produced. If the address is valid, the data contained in that location will be fetched and/or changed, depending on whether X(5,7) is to the left or to the right of the equal sign in a replacement statement. The effects of such a mistake might be apparent when the desired output is not produced by the program. The cause of the error may be difficult to determine, since the erroneous output will usually have no clue in it that can be traced to an invalid array reference.

3. Can I initialize two- or three-dimensional arrays in a DATA statement?

   Answer: Most systems will allow it. For example:

   ```
   DIMENSION X(3,2)
   DATA((X(I,J),I = 1,3),J = 1,2)/3*1.,3*2./ or DATA  X/3*1.,3*2./
   ```

   The array X will be initialized to 1's for column 1 and to 2's for column 2.

4. Can I change the implicit mode of a multidimensional array?

   Answer: Yes, in the same way as one-dimensional arrays. For example:

REAL M(4,7),X(3,5)	The elements of M are real.
INTEGER X(3,47)	The entries of X are integer.
DOUBLE PRECISION MAT(3,5)	MAT consists of double precision elements.
LOGICAL X(5,2)	
COMPLEX T(51,4),IT(3,1)	

5. Is there any limit to the size of a multidimensional array?

   Answer: Theoretically, no. Practically, yes. Restrictions on array sizes are dictated by the size of the memory of the particular system. For example, on a system with memory size of 32,000 bytes the statement DIMENSION A(100, 10,10) exceeds the memory size. On larger systems, the operating system may take up a large chunk of memory; the programmer requiring large arrays should check on memory availability at his particular installation.

9-4 Program Examples

9-4-1 A Frequency Distribution

Data regarding the smoking habits of students at a university have been gathered. The student's class (1 = freshman, 2 = sophomore, 3 = junior, 4 = senior, 5 = graduate) and a code representing the student's smoking habits (1 = don't smoke, 2 = one pack or less a day, 3 = more than one pack a day) have been recorded on data cards. Each card contains the student's class and smoking habit. It is desired to write a program to generate a frequency table displaying the frequency of the student's smoking habits by class and response; for example, how many seniors smoke one pack or less a day. To better understand the problem, assume we have the data cards shown below. We could manually record or check off each response in a table of five rows (for the five classes) and three columns (for the smoking habits) as follows:

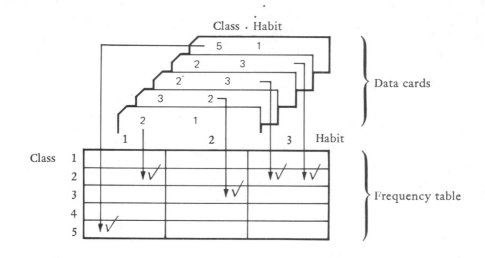

A class code of zero will terminate the input and cause the frequency table to be printed. The output should be arranged as follows:

FREQUENCY DISTRIBUTION

CLASS	DON'T SMOKE	1 PACK OR LESS	MORE THAN 1
1	XX	XX	XX
2	XX	XX	XX
3	XX	XX	XX
4	XX	XX	XX
5	XX	XX	XX

A program to solve this problem is shown in Figure 9-6. The array K is used as a group of counters. The first subscript indicates the class; the second represents the response code. For instance, the count in K(3,2) indicates the number of juniors (3) smoking one pack a day or less (2). Note that both class and smoking codes are used as subscripts of the array K to directly update the frequency count (see statement 30).

```
        INTEGER HABIT
        DIMENSION K(5,3)
        WRITE(3,5)
    5   FORMAT('1',T30,'FREQUENCY DISTRIBUTION'/T10,'CLASS',T20,
      * 'DONT SMOKE',T40,'1 PACK OR LESS',T60,'MORE THAN 1')
        DO 10 I=1,5
        DO 10 J=1,3
   10   K(I,J)=0
    2   READ(1,1)KLASS,HABIT
    1   FORMAT(2I1)
        IF(KLASS)30,20,30
   30   K(KLASS,HABIT)=K(KLASS,HABIT)+1
        GO TO 2
   20   WRITE(3,3)(I,(K(I,J),J=1,3),I=1,5)
    3   FORMAT(T10,I3,T20,I5,T40,I8,T60,I5)
        STOP
        END
```

Figure 9-6   Two-dimensional frequency distribution.

9-4-2   Alphabetic Data

Each card of a deck of no more than 100 cards contains a person's name (20 characters) followed by the person's address (26 characters), state (2 characters) and zip code number. Let us write a program to store all names and addresses in memory and print four sets of mailing labels for each individual. The program to perform this task is shown in Figure 9-7. Since each name may contain up to 20 characters, it is not possible to store each name in a one-dimensional array; five variables are needed, hence a two-dimensional array with NAME(K,1), NAME(K,2), NAME(K,3), NAME(K,4), NAME(K,5) to represent the name of the Kth person. The same is true for the address. Note, however, that the state may be stored in a single-dimension array, since it occupies fewer than four characters.

9-4-3   A Three-Dimensional Array Example

A data processing class consists of ten students. Each student receives a grade on three separate program tests (P1, P2, P3) and on three separate math tests (M1, M2, M3). Compute each student's overall average (combining programming and math test scores) and determine the highest score obtained on the third math test (P3).

To solve this problem, we shall use a three-dimensional array A with three rows (for 3 tests), ten columns (for 10 students) and a depth of two (for program-

```
        INTEGER ADDR(100,4),CITY(100,2),STATE(100),ZIP(100)
        DIMENSION NAME(100,5)
        K=1
   10   READ (5,1,END=20) (NAME(K,J),J=1,5),(ADDR(K,J),J=1,4),
      * (CITY(K,J),J=1,2),STATE(K),ZIP(K)
        K=K+1
        GO TO 10
   20   K=K-1
    C   K IS THE NUMBER OF NAMES/ADDRESSES TO BE PROCESSED
        DO 40 L=1,4
        DO 40 M=1,K
   40   WRITE (6,3) (NAME(M,J),J=1,5),(ADDR(M,J),J=1,4)
      * ,(CITY(M,J),J=1,2),STATE(M),ZIP(M)
        STOP
    1   FORMAT(5A4,4A4,2A4,A2,I5)
    3   FORMAT(1X,5A4/1X,4A4/1X,2A4,2X,A2,3X,I5//)
        END
        .
        .
        .
    BRYAN STANDLEY
    21 E. 4TH
    PENSACOL FL 32503  ◄─── Four of each are printed.
        .
        .
    WILSON HART
    1814 N 12TH
    MILTON FL 36609
        .
        .
        .
```

Figure 9-7 Mailing label program.

ming and math scores). For example, $A(3,9,2)$ refers to the third math test of the ninth student, and $A(3,9,1)$ refers to the third programming score of the ninth student. Data is recorded on data cards in the following sequence:

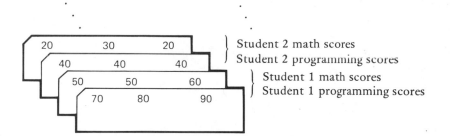

The program to solve this problem is shown in Figure 9-8.

9-5 Probing Deeper

9-5-1 Graphing

It is often very desirable to produce graphic output from a computer program. A scientific problem may require the graph of a function; a business problem might

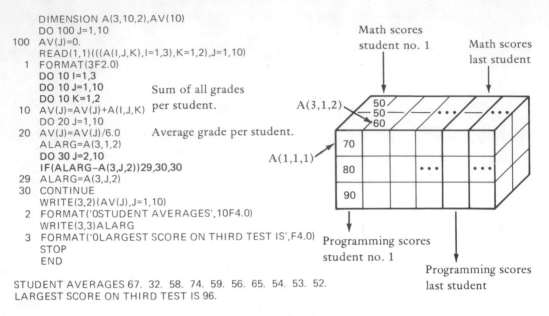

```
      DIMENSION A(3,10,2),AV(10)
      DO 100 J=1,10
100   AV(J)=0.
      READ(1,1)(((A(I,J,K),I=1,3),K=1,2),J=1,10)
  1   FORMAT(3F2.0)
      DO 10 I=1,3
      DO 10 J=1,10
      DO 10 K=1,2
 10   AV(J)=AV(J)+A(I,J,K)
      DO 20 J=1,10
 20   AV(J)=AV(J)/6.0
      ALARG=A(3,1,2)
      DO 30 J=2,10
      IF(ALARG−A(3,J,2))29,30,30
 29   ALARG=A(3,J,2)
 30   CONTINUE
      WRITE(3,2)(AV(J),J=1,10)
  2   FORMAT('0STUDENT AVERAGES',10F4.0)
      WRITE(3,3)ALARG
  3   FORMAT('0LARGEST SCORE ON THIRD TEST IS',F4.0)
      STOP
      END
```

Sum of all grades per student.

Average grade per student.

Math scores student no. 1

Math scores last student

A(3,1,2)

A(1,1,1)

Programming scores student no. 1

Programming scores last student

STUDENT AVERAGES 67. 32. 58. 74. 59. 56. 65. 54. 53. 52.
LARGEST SCORE ON THIRD TEST IS 96.

Figure 9-8   Three-dimensional array program.

require a bar graph. Both types of graph can be produced by FORTRAN programs.

A basic technique that can be used in graphing is to use an array to represent a line of output. Each element of the array stores one character to be printed on the line. The program can then store any desired character into positions on the line prior to printing the line. In this section, we shall examine techniques for producing bar graphs.

Example

Data regarding sales for a week have been tabulated as shown below:

Day	Sales
1	3
2	7
3	10
4	6
5	8
6	2
7	0

Let us write a program to produce a bar graph representing the above transactions. The output of the program should be similar to the following bar graph.

```
DAY    SALES
 1     * * *
 2     * * * * * * *
 3     * * * * * * * * * *
 4     * * * * * *
 5     * * * * * * * *
 6     * *
 7
```

The program shown in Figure 9-9 could be used to generate the bar graph.

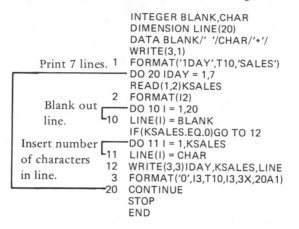

```
                              INTEGER BLANK,CHAR
                              DIMENSION LINE(20)
                              DATA BLANK/' '/CHAR/'*'/
                              WRITE(3,1)
        Print 7 lines.  1     FORMAT('1DAY',T10,'SALES')
                              DO 20 IDAY = 1,7
                              READ(1,2)KSALES
                       2      FORMAT(I2)
        Blank out             DO 10 I = 1,20
        line.         10     LINE(I) = BLANK
                              IF(KSALES.EQ.0)GO TO 12
        Insert number         DO 11 I = 1,KSALES
        of characters  11     LINE(I) = CHAR
        in line.       12     WRITE(3,3)IDAY,KSALES,LINE
                       3      FORMAT('0',I3,T10,I3,3X,20A1)
                       20     CONTINUE
                              STOP
                              END
```

Figure 9-9 Horizontal bar graph example.

The program in Figure 9-9 produces a horizontal bar graph. A vertical bar graph is a little more complex. An approach to the problem is to use a two-dimensional array to represent the entire graph. See Figure 9-10.

The basic technique is to use an array GRAPH of size 10 by 7 (10 for the highest daily sales volume and 7 for the number of days) initially set to blanks. In the first column of the array, we then store three graphic symbols (asterisks for instance), to represent the volume for the first day. In the second column, we store seven graphic symbols to represent the volume of the second day etc. In the last column (column 7), we store no graphic symbols (sales = 0). We then obtain an array G, which looks like:

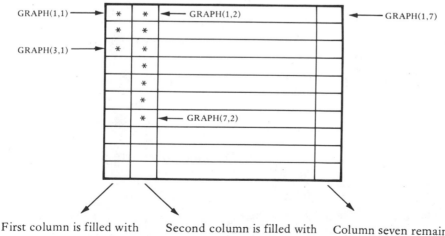

First column is filled with three asterisks to represent volume for day 1

Second column is filled with seven asterisks to represent volume for day 2.

Column seven remains filled with blanks.

The array must then be turned upside down so that the bar graph "peaks" up rather than down. This is achieved by printing the "bottom" of the above array first, i.e., printing row 10 on the first line, row 9 on the second line etc., as shown in statement 30 of Figure 9-10.

```
      INTEGER BLANK,CHAR,GRAPH(10,7)
      DATA GRAPH/70*' '/,CHAR/'*'/          Output
      DO 20 IDAY=1,7
      READ(1,2)KSALES                         *
   2  FORMAT(I2)                              *
      IF(KSALES)100,20,100                    *        *
 100  DO 11 I=1,KSALES                        *        *
  11  GRAPH(I,IDAY)=CHAR                 *    *        *
  20  CONTINUE                           *    *   *    *
      JROW=10                            *    *   *    *
  30  WRITE(3,3)(GRAPH(JROW,J),J=1,7)    *    *   *    *
   3  FORMAT(1X,7(1X,A1))           *    *    *   *    *
      JROW=JROW-1                   *    *    *   *    *   *
      IF(JROW - 1) 110,30,30        *    *    *   *    *   *
 110  WRITE(3,4)(I,I=1,7)
   4  FORMAT('0',7I2)               1    2    3   4    5   6   7
      WRITE(3,5)
   5  FORMAT('0',T4,'DAYS')         DAYS
      STOP
      END
```

Figure 9-10   A vertical bar graph.

9-6 Exercises

9-6-1 Self Test

1. Which of the following are valid array declarations? Specify errors, if any.
   a. INTEGER A(100,3),IB(3,5)
   b. DIMENSION A3(3),A4(4,4)
   c. REAL ST(50,40),J(3,1,7)
   d. DIMENSION Z100
   e. DIMENSION UT(3.,2)
   f. REAL N,X(3,1,N)
   g. DIMENSION Z(1,2,3,4,5,6)
   h. DIMENSION (MIKE)10
   i. DIMENSION BIG(3*10,2)
   j. DOUBLE PRECISION I(1,1)

2. List the internal order of storage for arrays A and B specified by:

$$\text{DIMENSION} \qquad A(2,4),B(3,1,4)$$

3. Using implied DO lists, write the I/O statements corresponding to the following lists of variables:
   a. WRITE(3,10)A(4),A(5),A(6),A(7), · · · ,A(90)
   b. WRITE(3,4)B(1),B(3),B(5),B(7),B(9), · · · ,B(99)
   c. READ(1,2)C(2,1),C(2,2),C(2,3),C(2,4),C(2,5)
   d. READ(1,1)A(1,1),B(1),A(2,1),B(2),A(3,1),B(3)
   e. WRITE(3,5)K,A(1,1),B(1),B(2),B(3),K,A(2,1),B(1),B(2),B(3)

f. READ(1,3)A(1,1),A(1,2),A(1,3),B(2,1),B(2,2),B(2,3),C(1),C(2),C(3)

g. WRITE(3,1)A(1,1),B(1,1),C(1,1),I,A(1,2),B(1,2),C(1,2),I,A(1,3),B(1,3),C(1,3),I

4. Generate the corresponding READ/WRITE list of variables for the following implied DO lists and specify the number of records (cards/lines) that would be processed by the accompanying FORMATs.

  a. (A(I,J),I = 1,3),J = 1,2)   FORMAT(8F3.1)
  b. (A(I,J),I,I = 1,3),J = 1,2)   FORMAT(2(F3.1,I2)/F3.1,I2)
  c. (A(I,J),I = 1,3),J,J = 1,3)   FORMAT(3F3.1,I1/(3F3.1,I1))
  d. (A(I,J),B(I,J),J = 1,2),I = 1,3)   FORMAT(F3.1)
  e. (C(I),(A(I,J),J = 1,3),(P(K,I),K = 1,2), I = 1,2)   FORMAT(6F4.1)
  f. (((A(I,J,K),I = 1,2),K = 1,3),J = 1,2)   FORMAT(11F3.0)

5. Assume arrays A, JSUM and VAR contain the following data:

A(3,4)					JSUM(3,4)					VAR
1.	2.	3.	4.		10	20	30	40		500.
5.	6.	7.	8.		50	60	70	80		
9.	10.	11.	12.		90	100	110	120		

Write the necessary implied DO lists to generate the following output using only the above three arrays (no computations are to be performed). Show formats.

a.   1. 2. 3. 4. · · · 12.   10 20 30 40 · · · 120   500.

b.   1. 2. 3. 4.   10 20 30 40   500.
     5. 6. 7. 8.   50 60 70 80   500.
     9. 10. 11. 12.   90 100 110 120   500.

c.   1. 5. 9.   500.   10 50 90
     2. 6. 10.   500.   20 60 100
     3. 7. 11.   500.   30 70 110

d.   1. 10   2.   20   3.   30   4.   40
     5. 50   6.   60   7.   70   8.   80
     9. 90 10. 100 11. 110 12. 120

e.   1. 10 5. 50 9. 90 2. 20 6. 60 10. 100
     3. 30 7. 70 11. 110 4. 40 8. 80 12. 120

   For part e, you may want to use a combination of a DO loop and an implied DO list.

6. Generate the correct input statements to read the following with one READ statement using DO list.

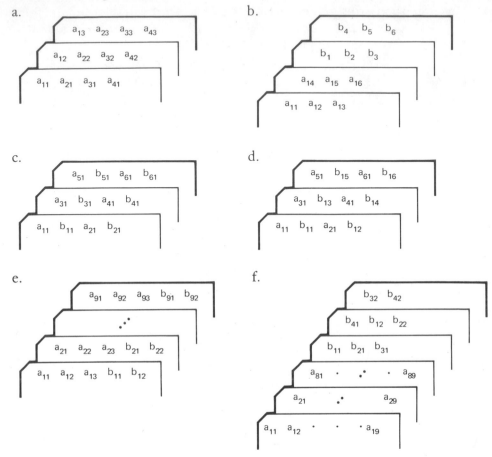

a.

a_{13} a_{23} a_{33} a_{43}

a_{12} a_{22} a_{32} a_{42}

a_{11} a_{21} a_{31} a_{41}

b.

b_4 b_5 b_6

b_1 b_2 b_3

a_{14} a_{15} a_{16}

a_{11} a_{12} a_{13}

c.

a_{51} b_{51} a_{61} b_{61}

a_{31} b_{31} a_{41} b_{41}

a_{11} b_{11} a_{21} b_{21}

d.

a_{51} b_{15} a_{61} b_{16}

a_{31} b_{13} a_{41} b_{14}

a_{11} b_{11} a_{21} b_{12}

e.

a_{91} a_{92} a_{93} b_{91} b_{92}

$\cdot \cdot \cdot$

a_{21} a_{22} a_{23} b_{21} b_{22}

a_{11} a_{12} a_{13} b_{11} b_{12}

f.

b_{32} b_{42}

b_{41} b_{12} b_{22}

b_{11} b_{21} b_{31}

a_{81} $\cdot$ $\cdot$ $\cdot$ a_{89}

a_{21} $\cdot$ a_{29}

a_{11} a_{12} $\cdot$ $\cdot$ a_{19}

7. Write the code to initialize an array A of size 4 × 7 to zeroes.

8. If A is an array of size 16 × 6, initialize the first column of A with 1's, the second column with 2's, the third column with 3's up to column 6 with 6's.

9. A two-dimensional array A of size 5 × 5 is punched one row per data card.
    a. Read in the array and write it out in row form (one row per line). Write out each column on one line, that is, write out the columns in row fashion.
    b. Calculate the sum of the elements in the third row.
    c. Find the largest value in the first column.
    d. Create a linear array B consisting of five elements initialized to zero. Calculate the sum of each column of A storing the result in the corresponding column position of B.

    e. Add corresponding elements of rows 2 and 3 of the array A, storing results in row 3, that is, A(3,1) = A(3,1) + A(2,1) etc.

    f. Interchange column 3 and row 4.

    g. Compute the sum of the entries of the first diagonal. (A(I,I) for I = 1 to 5).

    h. Compute the sum of the entries of the second diagonal and determine the largest entry of that diagonal.

    i. Read values for I and J such that $1 \leqslant I, J \leqslant 5$ and interchange row I with column J.

10. Read in two arrays C and D of size 3 × 3 given the following input description

    $\underbrace{1\ 2\ 3}_{\text{Row 1 of C}}$ $\underbrace{9\ 2\ 4}_{\text{Row 1 of D}}$ $\underbrace{4\ 5\ 6}_{\text{Row 2 of C}}$ $\underbrace{7\ 8\ 9}_{\text{Row 2 of D}}$ ...

11. Write the code to determine the smallest element of an array A of size 10 × 10 and its position in the array (column and row).

12. Assume an array F of size 40 × 17 that already contains data. Write the code to store the rows of the array F sequentially into a one-dimensional array G of size 680 (40 × 17), as follows:

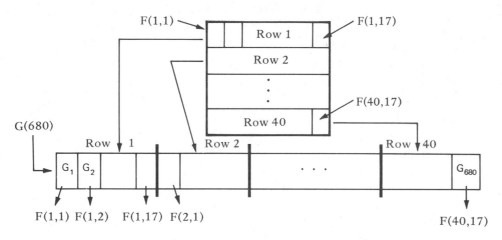

13. Assume the array A(10,3) has been read in; write a program segment to compute the sum of the elements of the array A, and print the following with *one* WRITE statement.

FINAL				
Column 1	Column 2	Column 3	...	Column 10
A_{11}	A_{12}	A_{13}		$A_{1\ 10}$
A_{12}	A_{22}	A_{23}		$A_{2\ 10}$
A_{13}	A_{32}	A_{33}		$A_{3\ 10}$
SUM IS XXX.X				

9-6-2 Programming Problems

9-6-2a   Two-Dimensional Arrays

1. An array A has size 4 × 9. Write a program to interchange the first column with the ninth, the second column with the eighth etc.

2. Write a program to compute and print the total number of hours lost per shop in the example of Section 9-1.

3. Each card in a file consists of six data items organized as follows: a student number, five test scores. There are at most 100 cards. For example:

```
┌ 111    10 20 30 40 50 ┐
│
└ 222    10 10 70 60 40 ┘
```

Student number   5 Test scores

Read the data into a two-dimensional array. (For example, A(3,I), with I ranging from 1 to 6, represents the *third* student's data items.) Compute the average score for each student and the average score on each test. The format for your output is as follows:

Student number	Test 1	Test 2	Test 3	Test 4	Test 5	Student average
111	10	20	30	40	50	30
222	10	10	70	60	40	38
Average/test	10	15	50	50	45	

Test your program with at least five of your own data cards.

4. a. The following diagram represents an island surrounded by water (shaded area). Two bridges lead out of the island. A mole is placed at the black square. Write a program to make the mole take a walk through the island. The mole is allowed to travel only one square at a time either horizontally or vertically. A random number between 1 and 4 should be used to decide which direction the mole is to take. The mole drowns when hitting the water and escapes if she crosses a bridge. What are the mole's chances of getting out of the island safely? (Restart the mole 100 times at the starting block, and count the number of times she escapes, even if she drowned on some of her prior promenades.)

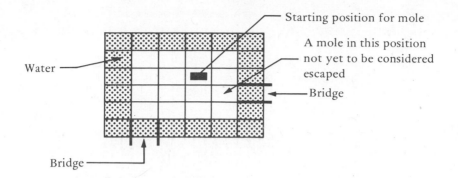

b. This time a mouse is positioned on the black square. The mouse travels in the same fashion as the mole except that when she touches water she bounces right back from where she came taking two steps in the process. The mouse escapes when she sets foot on either of the two bridges. What are the mouse's chances to escape in fewer than 20 moves? Simulate 100 separate mouse trips each restarting in row 3, column 4. Kill the mouse if it stays in the maze over 500 steps.

c. Assume the mouse is clever! Keep track of the different escape routes. After ten escapes select the exit route with the fewest number of steps. Then, when you reposition the mouse in row 3 and column 4, she should, without hesitation, immediately head for the exit. Print all freedom paths.

5. Write a program using two-dimensional arrays to draw the checkerboard illustrated in Exercise 16 of Section 5-6-2.

6. Write a program to draw the various squares shown in Exercise 32 of Section 8-6-2.

7. You own four warehouses across the country, each of which can stock five particular items (see arrangement below). The data is recorded on one record; for example: 14, 15, 25, 5, 15, 20, 25, 3, $\cdots$, 16, 5, 20, 10. Write a program to read the data into a two-dimensional array to produce the following output. Identify any item that has zero stock in three or more warehouses.

		Items				Total/warehouse
	1	2	3	4	5	
Warehouse 1	14	15	5	0	16	50
Warehouse 2	15	20	25	0	5	65
Warehouse 3	25	25	40	30	20	140
Warehouse 4	5	3	10	0	10	28
Totals	59	63	80	30	51	

ZERO STOCK ITEMS IN THREE OR MORE WAREHOUSES: 3

8. Complete Exercise 7 by printing those warehouses and item numbers where the stock is below 10. Given the data of Exercise 7, the output should be similar to:

Warehouse	Item number
1	3,4
2	4,5
4	1,2,4

9. You are calculating returns from a primary election where five candidates were running. Each vote is recorded on one punched card with two entries per card. The first entry is a number identifying the party of the voter (1 = Democrat, 2 = Republican, 3 = Fascist). The second entry identifies the candidate (1, 2, 3, 4 or 5). Write a program to determine:

   a. How many votes did each candidate get from the Democrats, Republicans and Fascists (and print the results).

   b. In the event a candidate obtains more than ten votes from any party, print out the candidate number and the number of votes given to him by that party, as well as his total vote. For example:

CANDIDATE	PARTY	NUMBER OF VOTES	TOTAL VOTES
1	2	15	
1	3	20	43
2	1	11	29
3	1	15	
3	2	15	
3	3	10	40
.	.	.	.
.	.	.	.
.	.	.	.

10. A small airplane has a seating capacity of five rows with three seats per row. Seat reservations are handled by a computer. Seat preferences for each passenger are recorded on cards with the name of the passenger, the row and seat number punched on one card. If a requested seat is vacant, reserve the seat for the passenger and print his name and seat number. If the requested seat is already taken, assign seats in row-wise fashion, starting with seat 1 row 1 and move to the end of the row before starting with the second row etc. Print the passenger's name and his assigned seat and row. Print a message if the plane is fully loaded. For example, given the data cards shown at the top of page 343, the output should be as follows:

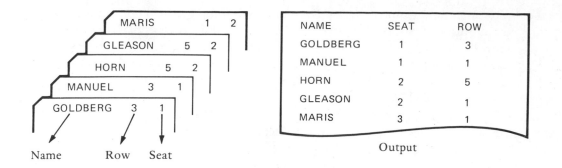

NAME	SEAT	ROW
GOLDBERG	1	3
MANUEL	1	1
HORN	2	5
GLEASON	2	1
MARIS	3	1

Output

11. The Formfit Company manufactures brassieres and girdles. The company employs ten salesmen. Sales, date and amount of sales are recorded by the company on a day-to-day basis whenever sales are made. This data is transcribed into data cards as follows (note that the transactions are *not* sorted by salesman number and can occur in random fashion):

Salesman number	Date of sales	Sales amount
111	012378	100.00
222	012478	250.00
111	012578	300.00
222	012778	200.00
334	012878	57.50

Write a program to produce a monthly sales report summarizing total sales and total sales for each salesman. Transactions must be grouped by salesman number and listed in ascending salesman number order. For example, given the above input the output should have the following format (input records are assumed in date order):

Salesman number	Date of sales	Sales amount	Total amount
111	012378	100.00	
111	012578	300.00	
			400.00
222	012478	250.00	
222	012778	200.00	
			450.00
334	012878	57.50	
			57.50
	Total sales		907.50

12. You are the organizer for the National Swimming Finals, and you would like a computer program to seed swimmers in the correct preliminary heats (races). Each swimmer's name and submitted time is recorded on punched cards. There are 16 swimmers altogether. The swimming pool has four lanes only and hence only four swimmers can race at one time. The procedure for seeding is as follows.

Sort the swimmers by their submitted times and designate their heats as follows: The swimmers in the first heat are those with the 1st, 5th, 9th and 13th fastest time. The swimmers in the second heat are those with the 2nd, 6th, 10th and 14th fastest time. The remaining heats are determined in a similar manner. Each card contains a name (16 characters maximum) and a time. Write a program to read the 16 names into an array N(16,4) with each row containing a name (four words) and the 16 times into the array T(16). Then:

a. Sort both arrays in ascending order by time.

b. Print each heat with list of names for each heat (four names per line).

c. Print names of swimmers with faster than average swim time (one per line).

For example:

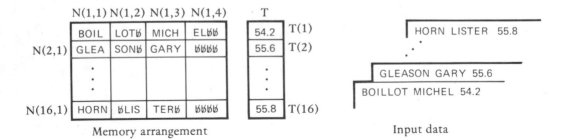

The output should be similar to the following:

```
HEAT    NAMES
  1     Name 1, Name 5, Name 9, Name 13
  2     Name 2, Name 6, Name 10, Name 14
  .
  .
  .
  4     Name 4, Name 8, Name 12, Name 16

SWIMMERS WITH FASTER THAN AVERAGE SWIMTIME
           Name              time
           Name              time
            .                 .
            .                 .
            .                 .
```

13. Rewrite the code for the program of Figure 8-14 to generate a class schedule, using two-dimensional arrays.

14. John Livelong is thinking of buying a six-payment life policy of $20,000 on his twentieth birthday. (Six-payment policy means that annual payments are limited to six years.) John has been told that the earlier you buy life insurance the less expensive it is; nevertheless, he would still like to see for himself the differences in annual payments for ages 20 to 26 (in yearly increments), and the total payments over six years in each case. Write a program to produce the following report, using the table look-up process.

Life insurance premium payments

JOHN LIVELONG

Age	Annual premium	Total premium/6 years
20	—	—
21	—	—
.	.	.
.	.	.
.	.	.
26	—	—

The formula to compute the yearly premium for a $1 policy is:

$$P = \frac{M_x}{N_x - N_{x+n}}$$

where x is the age at issuance of policy
n is the number of payment years
M_x and N_x are given in the table below

Example

The net annual premium for a six-year payment life policy for $1.00 issued at age 22 is:

$$P = \frac{M_{22}}{N_{22} - N_{28}} = \frac{1,784,367}{156,184,676 - 124,748,158} = .0567$$

Hence for a $3,000 life policy the payment would be $3,000 × .0567 = $170.10. Load the M_x and N_x entries into arrays from the following table:

Commutation columns—interest at 2½ percent
(based on 1958 CSO mortality table)

Age, x	D_x	N_x	C_x	M_x
0	10,000,000.0000	324,850,104.9680	69,073.1710	2,076,826.7172
1	9,687,024.4290	314,850,104.9680	16,632.9566	2,007,753.5462
.	.	.	.	.
.	.	.	.	.
.	.	.	.	.
20	5,898,264.9735	167,827,045.8785	10,300.1828	1,804,922.4208
21	5,744,104.7377	161,928,780.9050	10,255.1657	1,794,622.2380
22	5,593,749.4258	156,184,676.1673	10,150.6810	1,784,367.0723
23	5,447,165.8414	150,590,926.7415	10,044.0865	1,774,216.3913
24	5,304,263.9929	145,143,760.9001	9,883.7932	1,764,172.3048
25	5,165,007.9517	139,839,496.9072	9,725.3439	1,754,288.5116
26	5,029,306.7854	134,674,488.9555	9,617.0037	1,744,563.1677
27	4,897,023.7928	129,645,182.1701	9,507.1611	1,734,946.1640
28	4,768,076.9758	124,748,158.3773	9,442.8900	1,725,439.0029
29	4,642,339.5370	119,980,081.4015	9,420.4356	1,715,996.1129
30	4,519,691.3751	115,337,741.8645	9,392.0634	1,706,575.6773
31	4,400,062.8465	110,818,050.4894	9,401.2183	1,697,183.6139
32	4,283,343.0569	106,417,987.6429	9,402.5686	1,687,782.3956
33	4,169,468.7479	102,134,644.5860	9,437.1317	1,678,379.8270
34	4,058,337.1968	97,965,175.8381	9,502.3390	1,668,942.6953

15. Write a program to allow a user to enter his age (x), the number of payments (n), and a dollar amount for a life insurance policy. Compute the annual and total premium for the n years of the policy. The formula to determine the annual premium is shown in Exercise 14. The data should be recorded on a data card as

$$10000 \quad 23 \quad 8$$

Amount of policy   Age   Number of payments

The input data x and n should be restricted to the intervals $20 \leqslant x \leqslant 25$ and $1 \leqslant n \leqslant 9$.

16. To solve the following problem use the table look-up process discussed in Section 9-4-1. An endowment policy provides for the payment of the face value of the policy at the end of the stated period. The annual premium (A) for an n year $1 policy issued at age x is:

$$A = \frac{M_x - M_{x+n} + D_{x+n}}{N_x - N_{x+n}}$$

where M_x, D_x are defined as in the table of Problem 14 above. Write a program to input x and n and the amount of policy, and compute and print out the annual premium and the total of annual premiums over the n years.

17. The region shown below is a two-dimensional model of a section of a nuclear reactor. The point marked S is the source of particles which are free to travel one mesh step in any direction with equal probability. Points marked A are centers of absorption, and any particle reaching such a point is considered to have been absorbed. Points marked R are reflectors and return a particle to the point from which it came taking a total of two steps in the process. Points marked E indicate that a particle has escaped through the absorbing medium. Blank points are scattering centers from which the particle moves one mesh step in any direction with equal probability. Motion may be in the horizontal or vertical direction only. The source is to be considered as a normal mesh point.

```
        E E E E E E
      E .  .  .  .  .  . . A A A
        A .  . A .  .  . . A
      R .  .  .  .  .  .  . . . A
      R .  . A .  . A .  . A E E A A
      R .  .  .  .  .  .  .  .  . . A
      R .  .  .  .  .  .  .  .  . . . A A A
      R .  .  .  .  .  .  .  .  .  .  .  . . E
      R .  .  .  .  .  ·  .  .  .  .  .  . . E
      R .  .  .  .  .  .  .  .  .  .  .  . . E
      R . S .  . A .  . A .  .  .  .  .  . . E
      R .  .  .  .  .  .  .  .  .  .  .  . . E
      R .  .  .  .  .  .  .  .  .  .  .  . . E
      R .  .  .  .  .  .  .  .  .  .  .  . . E
      R .  .  .  .  .  .  .  .  .  .  .  . . E
      R .  .  .  .  .  .  .  .  .  .  . . A A A
      R .  .  .  . . A A A .  .  .  . . E
      R .  . . A .  .  .  . . E A E E A
        E E A A   E A E E E
```

Write a program which starts individual particles one at a time from point S and follows them one at a time to their escape or absorption.

a. Run 500 particles; keep track of each particle in an array which records the number of steps taken and whether the particle was absorbed or escaped.

b. Print out the percentage of particles that escaped.

c. Print out the number of particles that escaped versus the number of steps taken (so many escaped on the fifth step, so many escaped on the sixth step etc.).

d. Print how many particles escaped through the rightmost points.

   e. Print the number of particles absorbed versus the number of steps as in question c.

18. A large computer company decided some years ago to make a study on whether there was any relationship between the major of a college student and his success in the computer field. Four hundred graduates were selected as follows: 70 in mathematics, 156 in engineering and 174 in liberal arts. At the end of the company training period, overall scores revealed the following:

| | *Performance* | | |
	Excellent	*Fair*	*Unsatisfactory*
Mathematics	37	23	10
Liberal arts	56	76	42
Engineering	25	64	67

The formula used to determine whether "major" is a significant factor in success is:

$$x = \frac{1}{4} \sum_{j=1}^{3} \sum_{i=1}^{3} (f_{ij} - e_{ij})^2 = \frac{1}{4} \Big[(f_{11} - e_{11})^2 + (f_{12} - e_{12})^2 + (f_{13} - e_{13})^2$$
$$+ \ (f_{21} - e_{21})^2 + \cdots + (f_{33} - e_{33})^2 \Big]$$

where

$$f_{ij} \text{ is } \frac{(\text{sum of row } i) \cdot (\text{sum of column } j)}{\text{sum of all entries of performance array}}.$$

For example, $f_{23} = \dfrac{(56 + 76 + 42) \cdot (10 + 42 + 67)}{400}.$

e_{ij} is number of students in cell at row i and column j. For example, $e_{23} = 42$.

Write a program to read the given numbers in an array and determine whether or not there is a relationship between "major" and future success. If $x > 9.488$, the relationship exists; otherwise, it does not.

19. Following is a questionnaire used in a survey to determine people's attitude toward abortion:

Abortion attitude survey

Male □   Female □   Married □   Single □
Children □   No children □   Widowed □   Divorced □
Age group: Below 20 □   20–30 □   31–40 □   41–above □

If you are opposed to abortion, answer part A below.
If you are not opposed to abortion, answer part B below.
If in part A or part B there are questions about which you feel undecided, leave both boxes blank.

Part A   If you are opposed to abortion is it:
Yes No

☐ ☐   On religious grounds?

☐ ☐   Because you believe the fetus has an absolute right to life?

☐ ☐   Because you believe physical pain is inflicted on the fetus in the abortion process?

☐ ☐   Do you feel abortion would be justified in specific instances (such as rape, malformed fetus, danger to mother's life etc.)?

Part B   If you are not opposed to abortion, is it because you feel:
Yes No

☐ ☐   A woman has a right to her own body?

☐ ☐   Abortion is a private decision for the parents alone to make?

☐ ☐   Abortion can be a valid means to control population growth?

☐ ☐   No physical pain is inflicted on the fetus in the abortion process?

☐ ☐   Unwanted children should not be born?

☐ ☐   A fetus is an incomplete human being, and as such no moral or legal laws are applicable to it?

☐ ☐   Laws against abortion would increase criminal abortions?

The number of respondents should at least be ten. Either simulate responses or hand out questionnaires to friends to be completed. Before you start writing the program, think of the most efficient way to handle input and special code considerations. Try to use just one two-dimensional array to store the responses of all ten candidates.

a. Determine how many yes, no and undecided responses there were for the four questions to be completed by those opposed to abortion. The print-out should be as follows:

Opposed to abortion

	Yes	*No*	*Undecided*
Question 1	x	x	x
Question 2	x	x	x
Question 3	x	x	x
Question 4	x	x	x

b. Same as a for those favoring abortion (seven questions altogether).

c. Determine the number of undecided responses for each of the respondents and record these as follows:

Respondent 1 ___   Respondent 2 ___   Respondent 3 ___

Respondent 4 ___   Respondent 5 ___   Respondent 6 ___

. . . Respondent 10 ___

d. Determine the percentage of respondents opposed to abortion.

e. Determine the number of females, between 20 and 30 with children, who are opposed to abortion.

f. Were there more males in favor of abortion than there were females?

g. Were there more single females against abortion than married females for abortion?

20. You work for IBM. Top management personnel have some questions related to competitor computer companies that they want answered. You have data, in the format given below, that you can analyze to provide them with answers to their questions. By doing this, you can get promoted to a top management position and get a big raise. If you can't, you get fired.

> *Data:*   (columns)
>   1–8   name of company (aaaaaaaa) [left-justified]
>   10–13 year founded (xxxx)
>   16–20 number of employees (xxxxx)
>   25–30 profit last year in millions of dollars (xxx.xx)
>   31–34 profit-sharing percentage expressed as a decimal (.xxx)

Since you do not know how much data you have, the last data record is followed by a record containing "$" in column 1 to indicate the end of the data. You have at most 15 data records before the "$."

> *Questions:*   How many other companies are older than us? (IBM was founded in 1950)
>   How many companies had profit-sharing percentages less than 2 percent; between 2 percent and 5 percent, inclusive; and over 5 percent?
>   How much profit-sharing money did Univac give its stockholders last year? (To convert from millions of dollars to dollars, use 10.**6.)
>   How much profit did all the companies make last year? (No conversion is needed.)

Write a program to provide an alphabetic listing of all the competitor computer companies analyzed for these answers.

> *Answers:*   (*use this format*):
>   xxx COMPANIES ARE OLDER THAN IBM. (This should start a new page.)

xx COMPANIES HAD PROFIT SHARING PERCENTAGES
LESS THAN 2 PERCENT.
xx BETWEEN 2 PERCENT AND 5 PERCENT INCLUSIVE.
xx GREATER THAN 5 PERCENT.
UNIVAC PROFIT SHARED $xxxxxxxxx.xx LAST YEAR.
xxxxx.xx MILLION DOLLARS WERE MADE IN PROFIT
LAST YEAR BY OTHER COMPANIES. HERE ARE THE
COMPANIES IN THIS SURVEY:
aaaaaaaa
aaaaaaaa

21. A matrix is a rectangular array of numbers. Addition and multiplication of matrices is illustrated in the following examples:

Addition

$$\begin{pmatrix} a_{11} & a_{12} & a_{13} \\ a_{21} & a_{22} & a_{23} \end{pmatrix} + \begin{pmatrix} b_{11} & b_{12} & b_{13} \\ b_{21} & b_{22} & b_{23} \end{pmatrix} = \begin{pmatrix} a_{11} + b_{11} & a_{12} + b_{12} & a_{13} + b_{13} \\ a_{21} + b_{21} & a_{22} + b_{22} & a_{23} + b_{23} \end{pmatrix}$$

Multiplication

$$\begin{pmatrix} a_{11} & a_{12} & a_{13} \\ a_{21} & a_{22} & a_{23} \end{pmatrix} \cdot \begin{pmatrix} b_{11} & b_{12} \\ b_{21} & b_{22} \\ b_{31} & b_{32} \end{pmatrix} =$$

$$\begin{pmatrix} a_{11} \cdot b_{11} + a_{12} \cdot b_{21} + a_{13} \cdot b_{31} & a_{11} \cdot b_{12} + a_{12} \cdot b_{22} + a_{13} \cdot b_{32} \\ a_{21} \cdot b_{11} + a_{22} \cdot b_{21} + a_{23} \cdot b_{31} & a_{21} \cdot b_{12} + a_{22} \cdot b_{22} + a_{23} \cdot b_{32} \end{pmatrix}$$

In general, if A is $m \times n$ (m rows and n columns) and B is $n \times q$ then the product matrix $C = A \cdot B$ is of size $m \times q$. The entry C_{ij} of the product matrix can be computed by multiplying the ith row of A by the jth column of B as follows:

$$j\text{th column}$$

$$i\text{th row} \to \begin{pmatrix} a_{i1} & a_{i2} & \cdots & a_{in} \end{pmatrix} \begin{pmatrix} b_{1j} \\ b_{2j} \\ \cdot \\ \cdot \\ \cdot \\ b_{nj} \end{pmatrix} = a_{i1} \cdot b_{1j} + a_{i2} \cdot b_{2j} + \cdots + a_{in} \cdot b_{nj} = c_{ij}$$

Note: To multiply two matrices A and B, the number of columns in A must equal the number of rows in B. Such matrices are *conformable*.

a. Write a program to read two 4×3 matrices and compute their sum and difference (in the case of subtraction, corresponding entries are subtracted).

b. Write a program to read a 3×3 matrix A and a 3×3 matrix B. Compute $A \cdot B$ and $(A + B) \cdot (A - B)$.

c. Write a program to input N and compute A^N where A is a matrix that has been read in.

$$A^N = \underbrace{A \cdot A \cdot \cdots A}$$

N matrices

d. Read in a square matrix A and print out its transpose A^T (the rows of A^T are equal to the columns of A; row i of A^T = column i of A).

22. The XYZ Company manufactures four products: P_1, P_2, P_3, P_4. Each of these products must undergo some type of operation on five different machines: A, B, C, D, E. The time (in units of hours) required for each of those products on each of the five machines is shown below:

	A	B	C	D	E
P_1	.2	.2	.1	.58	.15
P_2	.26	.1	.13	.61	.3
P_3	.5	.21	.56	.45	.27
P_4	.6	.17	1.3	.25	.31

For example, product P_1 requires .2 hours on machine A, .2 hours on machine B, and .1 hour on machine C, and so on.

a. The XYZ Company has been requested to fill an order for 356 products P_1, 257 products P_2, 1,058 products P_3 and 756 products P_4. Write a program to determine the total number of hours that *each* machine will be used. (Hint: Express the above table as a 4 × 5 matrix; express the order as a 1 × 4 matrix and multiply both matrices.)

b. The XYZ Company is renting the five machines A, B, C, D, E from a tooling company. The hourly rental cost for each machine is as follows:

Machines	A	B	C	D	E
Rental cost/hour	$10.00	$5.75	$3.50	$10.00	$5.76

Write a program to compute total rental expense for all machines. (Hint: Express rental costs as a 1 × 5 matrix and multiply by matrix result of part a.)

23. Write a program to verify that for any conformable matrices X, Y, Z of your choice the following is true:
a. $(X + Y) \cdot Z = X \cdot Z + Y \cdot Z$
b. $(X \cdot Y) \cdot Z = X \cdot (Y \cdot Z)$

24. An $n \times n$ matrix A is said to be *symmetric* if and only if $A = A^T$. (See Problem 21d above.) Write a program to demonstrate that
a. $A \cdot A^T$ is symmetric.
b. $A + A^T$ is symmetric.

25. A triangular matrix can be defined as a square matrix with all entries below the main diagonal equal to zero. Write a program to demonstrate that if A is a 4 × 4 triangular matrix, then $A^4 = A \cdot A \cdot A \cdot A$ is the zero matrix (in general A^n = zero matrix if A is an $n \times n$ triangular matrix).

26. The trace of a matrix is defined as the sum of its diagonal elements. Let A be a 5 × 5 matrix and B be a 5 × 5 matrix. Write a program to demonstrate that $tr(A \cdot B) = tr(B \cdot A)$, where *tr* stands for the trace.

27. A method for computing the inverse of any matrix on a computer is as follows: Let A be an $n \times n$ matrix, $(n \geqslant 1)$. Then

$$A^{-1} = -\frac{1}{c_n} \left(A^{n-1} + c_1 A^{n-2} + c_2 A^{n-3} + \cdots + c_{n-1} I \right)$$

where the c's are all constants defined as
$\quad c_1 = -tr(A)$ (See Exercise 26 for the definition of the trace)
$\quad c_2 = -1/2 \, (c_1 \, tr(A) + tr(A^2))$
$\quad c_3 = -1/3 \, (c_2 \, tr(A) + c_1 \, tr(A^2) + tr(A^3))$
$\quad \cdot$
$\quad \cdot$
$\quad \cdot$
$\quad c_n = -1/n \, \left(c_{n-1} \, tr(A) + c_{n-2} \, tr(A^2) + \cdots + c_1 \, tr(A^{n-1}) + tr(A^n) \right)$

Write a program to compute the inverse of a 5 × 5 matrix A and check that it is indeed the inverse by verifying that $A \cdot A^{-1} = I$ (identity matrix).

For example, the inverse of a 2 × 2 matrix X is $X^{-1} = -\frac{1}{c_2} (X + c_1 I)$ where $c_2 = -1/2(c_1 \, tr(X) + tr(X^2))$ and $c_1 = -tr(X)$.

28. A *graph* is a structure made up of a set of vertices and edges connecting the vertices. A common means of representing a graph is with points and line segments as shown in the example of Figure 9-13. In the example, the vertices are labeled 1, 2, 3, $\cdots$, 8; the line segments connecting the numbered points represent edges. For example, there is an edge connecting vertices 1 and 3. A way of representing a graph in a computer is by means of an *adjacency matrix*. An adjacency matrix has a row and a column for each vertex in the graph. The graph of Figure 9-13 could be represented by the matrix A shown in Figure 9-14. In an adjacency matrix A, the value of a_{ij} is 1 if there is an edge connecting vertices i and j; the value of a_{ij} is 0 otherwise. For example, $a_{13} = 1$ represents an edge connecting vertices 1 and 3.

A *walk* in a graph is defined as a series of vertices connected by edges. In the example of Figure 9-13, 134 would represent a walk since edges exist connecting vertices 1 and 3, and 3 and 4. The sequence 12 would not represent a walk since no edge connects these two vertices. The *length* of a walk is defined as the number of edges traversed in the walk. For example, the walk 134 is of length 2, since the edges 13 and 34 are traversed. The walk 14 is of length 1; the walk 13741 is of length 4. The matrix of Figure 9-14 may be thought of as representing the number of walks of length 1 connecting any two vertices of the graph.

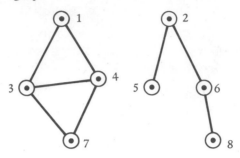

Figure 9-13   Geometric representation of a graph.

	1	2	3	4	5	6	7	8
1	0	0	1	1	0	0	0	0
2	0	0	0	0	1	1	0	0
3	1	0	0	1	0	0	1	0
4	1	0	1	0	0	0	1	0
5	0	1	0	0	0	0	0	0
6	0	1	0	0	0	0	0	1
7	0	0	1	1	0	0	0	0
8	0	0	0	0	0	1	0	0

Figure 9-14   An adjacency matrix for the graph of Figure 9-13.

We wish to solve the problem of counting the number of walks of a specific length connecting any two vertices on a graph. For example, consider vertices 3 and 4. The walks 314 and 374 both connect the vertices and are of length 2. An interesting connection exists between this problem and matrix multiplication. Suppose we multiply row 3 and column 4 of A. The value is calculated as

$$a_{31}a_{14} + a_{32}a_{24} + a_{33}a_{34} + a_{34}a_{44} + a_{35}a_{54} + a_{36}a_{64} + a_{37}a_{74} + a_{38}a_{84} =$$
$$1\cdot1 \;+\; 0\cdot0 \;+\; 0\cdot1 \;+\; 1\cdot0 \;+\; 0\cdot0 \;+\; 0\cdot0 \;+\; 1\cdot1 \;+\; 0\cdot0 \;=\; 2$$

the walk 314   the walk 374

The result of the multiplication represents the number of walks of length 2 connecting vertices 3 and 4. In general, if we multiply A·A = A^2, the element a_{ij} of the matrix A^2 represents the number of walks of length 2 connecting vertex i and vertex j. By extension, entries in A·A·A = A^3 represent the number of walks of length 3 connecting specified vertices; A^n represents the number of walks of length n.

a. Write a FORTRAN program to accept adjacency matrices of any desired size and output the number of walks of length 2, 3, $\cdots$, connecting vertices on the graph. Test your program using the graphs shown in Figure 9-16.

b. Note that a valid adjacency matrix must be symmetric. Add to the program of part a above a procedure to verify the validity of an adjacency matrix.

It is not always possible to proceed from one vertex to another of a graph by walks of any length because connecting edges do not exist. A set of vertices which are connected to one another by at least one walk of some length is called a *connected segment*. In the example of Figure 9-13, vertices 1, 3, 4, 7 and vertices 2, 5, 6, 8 represent connected segments. It is usually easy to recognize connected segments from the geometric representation of a graph, but it is not easy when the adjacency matrix is used. Consider the matrix $B = A^2 + A^3$. The element b_{ij} represents the number of walks of length 2 or 3 connecting vertices i and j. If we compute the matrix $C = A + A^2 + A^3 + \cdots + A^{n-1}$, the element c_{ij} would represent the number of walks of length 1, 2, 3, $\cdots$, $n - 1$ connecting vertices i and j. If n represents the number of vertices in the graph, we can calculate the matrix C and examine the elements c_{ij} to find connected segments. If the element $c_{ij} = 0$, there is no path connecting vertices i and j; if $c_{ij} \neq 0$, there exists at least one walk connecting vertices i and j. (It can be shown that if two vertices are connected by a walk of length greater than or equal to n, then they are connected by a walk of length less than n. Hence it is necessary only to compute powers of A up to A^{n-1}.) For the example of Figure 9-14, the matrix C would be as shown in Figure 9-15. Examination of row 1, for example, shows nonzero entries in columns 1, 3, 4 and 7 indicating a connected segment composed of those vertices.

	1	2	3	4	5	6	7	8
1	220	0	291	291	0	0	220	0
2	0	20	0	0	21	33	0	12
3	291	0	365	366	0	0	291	0
4	291	0	366	365	0	0	291	0
5	0	21	0	0	8	12	0	12
6	0	33	0	0	12	20	0	21
7	220	0	291	291	0	0	220	0
8	0	12	0	0	12	21	0	8

Figure 9-15   The matrix $C = A + A^2 + A^3 + A^4 + A^5 + A^6 + A^7$.

c. Write a program to analyze an adjacency matrix of size n and output all connected segments. (Handle as a special case segments of size one, that is, vertices not connected to any other vertex.) Test your program using the graphs shown in Figure 9-16.

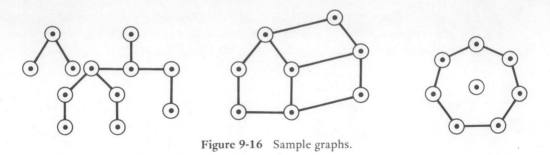

Figure 9-16 Sample graphs.

9-6-2b   Three-Dimensional Arrays

1. Temperatures are read into a 3 × 3 × 4 cube in the sequence shown in Section 9-2-6. Write a program to determine the highest and lowest temperatures.

2. Write a program to print the four diagonals of a 4 × 4 × 4 cube, using an index mechanism using three subscripts.

$$(a_{111}, a_{222}, a_{333}, a_{444} \mid a_{141}, a_{232}, a_{323}, a_{414} \mid \text{etc.})$$

3. Assume each vertical slice of a 3 × 3 cube contains a 3 × 3 matrix (the first vertical slice is matrix A, the second vertical slice is matrix B and the third vertical slice is matrix C).
    a. Compute $D = A + B + C$.
    b. Compute A^3.
    c. Compute $A \cdot B \cdot C$.

4. Write the program of Problem 4, Section 9-6-2a for a cube.

5. Write the program of Problem 17, Section 9-6-2a for a cube.

6. The following is the schedule of a small Pennsylvania airline. Write a program for maintaining passenger reservations for three days (see Figure 9-17).

Flight number	Origin	Stops	Plane capacity	Departure time
700	State College	Harrisburg Baltimore Washington	5	7:05 A.M.
701	Washington	Harrisburg State College	5	9:00 A.M.
430	State College	Harrisburg Baltimore Washington	5	4:15 P.M.
431	Washington	Baltimore Harrisburg State College	5	6:15 P.M.

If a plane is full, assume the passenger will accept the next available flight.

After all transactions have been processed, print a listing by flight and stops of the passengers scheduled. The planes are very small—assume a maximum of five passengers per flight. Use a three-dimensional array to store reservations.

Sample output from your program

Date	Flight		Passenger
2/25	700	State College to Harrisburg	B. Baldrige H. Davis .
		Harrisburg to Baltimore	B. Baldrige H. Davis .
		Baltimore to Washington	H. Davis (Baldrige gets off at Baltimore) .
	701	Washington to Harrisburg	A. Charles . . .
		Harrisburg to State College	(Charles gets off in Harrisburg) . .
	430	State College to Harrisburg	. .
		.	.
		.	.
		.	.
	431	.	.
		.	.
		.	.
		.	.
		.	.
2/26	700	.	.
.	.	.	.
.	.	.	.
.	.	.	.

7. Assume your FORTRAN did not support two-dimensional arrays. Two-dimensional arrays can be simulated by determining the formula to compute the linear position L corresponding to an array element $A(I,J)$. For an array A with IR rows and IC columns, display two formulas for L, depending on

whether the elements of the array are stored row-wise or column-wise in memory.

8. Assume elements of a cube of dimension IR rows, ID depth and IC columns are read into a one-dimensional array in the sequence shown in Section 9-2-6 (vertical slices). Determine the formula to compute the linear position of any element A(I,D,J).

Transactions (requests for seats)

Name	Date Desired	From	To	Flight Number
B. Baldrige	2/25	State College	Baltimore	700
W. Bartlett	2/26	Harrisburg	State College	431
W. Broderick	2/25	Harrisburg	Washington	430
R. Cheek	2/26	Baltimore	State College	431
E. Cooley	2/27	State College	Washington	700
H. Davis	2/25	State College	Washington	700
S. Dalles	2/26	Harrisburg	State College	431
L. Donald	2/25	Baltimore	Washington	700
F. John	2/26	Baltimore	Harrisburg	431
L. Line	2/26	Washington	State College	431
M. Dohert	2/25	State College	Baltimore	700
W. Howard	2/26	Washington	Harrisburg	431
J. Jacks	2/25	Washington	State College	431
J. Jacks	2/26	State College	Washington	430
G. Holland	2/26	Harrisburg	Washington	700
G. Holland	2/27	Washington	Harrisburg	431
C. Italia	2/26	State College	Washington	700
C. Italia	2/26	Washington	Harrisburg	431
H. Kent	2/25	Baltimore	Harrisburg	431
H. Kent	2/27	Harrisburg	Baltimore	430
C. Murray	2/25	State College	Washington	700
C. Murray	2/26	Washington	State College	431
R. Steel	2/25	State College	Washington	700
R. Steel	2/25	Washington	State College	431
A. Charles	2/25	Washington	Harrisburg	701
A. Charles	2/26	Harrisburg	Washington	430
A. Jabbari	2/25	State College	Washington	700
B. Jolly	2/27	Baltimore	Harrisburg	431
J. Hay	2/26	State College	Harrisburg	430
D. Day	2/27	Washington	State College	431
C. Mead	2/25	State College	Baltimore	700
Z . Mattern	2/26	Washington	Harrisburg	431
D. Davidson	2/25	Harrisburg	State College	431
M. West	2/26	State College	Washington	700
L. Mudd	2/27	Baltimore	Harrisburg	431
R. Frat	2/25	Washington	Harrisburg	701

Figure 9-17 Seat requests for airline scheduling problem.

9-6-3 Answers to Self Test

1. a. Legal.   b. Legal.   c. Legal.   d. Missing parentheses.
   e. Real number is invalid for size specification.
   f. Variable may not be used to specify array size.
   g. More dimensions than allowed on most compilers.
   h. Misplaced parenthesis.   i. 3*10 not allowed.   j. Legal.

2. A(1,1),A(2,1),A(1,2),A(2,2),A(1,3),A(2,3),A(1,4),A(2,4)
   B(1,1,1),B(2,1,1),B(3,1,1),B(1,1,2),B(2,1,2),B(3,1,2),B(1,1,3),B(2,1,3),B(3,1,3),B(1,1,4),
   B(2,1,4),B(3,1,4)

3. a. WRITE( )(A(I),I = 4,90)
   b. WRITE( )(B(J),J = 1,99,2)
   c. READ( )(C(2,K),K = 1,5)
   d. READ( )(A(J,1),B(J),J = 1,3)
   e. WRITE( )(K,(A(I,1),(B(J),J = 1,3),I = 1,2)
   f. READ( )(A(1,J),J = 1,3),(B(2,J),J = 1,3),
      *(C(J),J = 1,3)
   g. WRITE( )(A(1,5),B(1,J),C(1,J),I,J = 1,3)

4. a. A(1,1),A(2,1),A(3,1),A(1,2),A(2,2),A(3,2). 1 record.
   b. A(1,1),I,A(2,1),I,A(3,1),I,A(1,2),I,A(2,2),I,A(3,2),I. 4 records.
   c. A(1,1),A(2,1),A(3,1),J,A(1,2),A(2,2),A(3,2),J,A(1,3),A(2,3),A(3,3),J.
      3 records.
   d. A(1,1),B(1,1),A(1,2),B(1,2),A(2,1),B(2,1),A(2,2),B(2,2),A(3,1),B(3,1),
      A(3,2),B(3,2). 12 records.
   e. C(1),A(1,1),A(1,2),A(1,3),P(1,1),P(2,1),C(2),A(2,1),A(2,2),A(2,3),
      P(1,2),P(2,2). 2 records.
   f. A(1,1,1),A(2,1,1),A(1,1,2),A(2,1,2),A(1,1,3),A(2,1,3),
      A(1,2,1),A(2,2,1),A(1,2,2),A(2,2,2),A(1,2,3),A(2,2,3). 2 records.

5. a. WRITE( )((A(I,J),J = 1,4),I = 1,3),(JSUM(I,J),J = 1,4),I = 1,3),VAR
      FORMAT(2X,12F4.0,12I4,F5.0)

   b. WRITE( )((A(I,J),J = 1,4),(JSUM(I,J),J = 1,4),VAR,I = 1,3)
      FORMAT(2X,4F4.0,4I4,F5.0)

   c. WRITE( )((A(I,J),I = 1,3),VAR,(JSUM(I,J),J = 1,3),I = 1,3)
      FORMAT(2X,3F4.0,F5.0,3I4)

   d. WRITE( )((A(I,J),JSUM(I,J),J = 1,4),I = 1,3)   FORMAT(4(F5.0,I5))

   e. WRITE( )((A(I,J),JSUM(I,J),I = 1,3),J = 1,4)   FORMAT(6(F5.0,I5))

6. a. READ( )((A(I,J),J = 1,4),J = 1,3)   FORMAT(4F5.0)
   b. READ( )(A(1,J),J = 1,6),(B(I),I = 1,6)   FORMAT(2(3F5.0/),(3F3.0))
   c. READ( )(A(I,1),B(I,1),I = 1,6)   FORMAT(2(F4.0,1X,F5.0))
   d. READ( )(A(I,1),B(1,I),I = 1,6)   FORMAT(2(F5.0,F6.0))

e. READ( )((A(I,J),J = 1,3),B(I,J),J =
 *1,2),I = 1,9)   FORMAT(3F5.0,2F3.0)

f. READ( )((A(I,J),J = 1,9),I = 1,8),
 *((B(I,J),I = 1,4),J = 1,2)   FORMAT(8(19F3.0/),(3F4.0))

7. DO 1 I = 1,4
   DO 1 J = 1,7 or DATA A/28*0./
  1 A(I,J) = 0.0

8. DO 2 I = 1,16
   DO 2 J = 1,6
  2 A(I,J) = J

9. a. DIMENSION A(5,5),B(5)
    READ(1,1)((A(I,J),J = 1,5),I = 1,5)
   1 FORMAT(5F10.0)
    WRITE(3,2)((A(I,J),J = 1,5),I = 1,5)
   2 FORMAT(2X,5F10.0)

  b. SUM = 0
    DO 3 I = 1,5
   3 SUM = SUM + A(3,I)

  c. ALARG = A(1,1)
    DO 4 I = 2,5
    IF(ALARG.LT.A(I,1))ALARG = A(I,1)
   4 CONTINUE

  d. DO 5 I = 1,5
   5 B(I) = 0
    DO 6 I = 1,5
    DO 6 J = 1,5
   6 B(J) = B(J) + A(I,J)

  e. DO 7 I = 1,5
   7 A(3,I) = A(3,I) + A(2,I)

  f. DO 8 I = 1,5
    HOLD = A(I,3)
    A(I,3) = A(4,I)
   8 A(4,I) = HOLD

  g. SUM2 = 0
    DO 9 I = 1,5
   9 SUM2 = SUM2 + A(I,I)

h.   SSUM = 0
                SLARG = A(1,5)
                DO 16 I = 1,5
                J = 6 – I
                SSUM = SSUM + A(I,J)
                IF(SLARG.LT.A(I,J))SLARG = A(I,J)
    16   CONTINUE

i.   READ(1,3)I,J
    3   FORMAT(2I1)
                DO 17 L = 1,5
                HOLD = A(I,L)
                A(I,L) = A(L,J)
    17   A(L,J) = HOLD

10.   READ(1,3)(C(I,J),J = 1,3),(D(I,J),J = 1,3),I = 1,3)

11.   KROW = 1
                KOLUMN = 1
                ALARG = A(1,1)
                DO 5 I = 1,10
                DO 5 J = 1,10
                IF(ALARG.GT.A(I,J))GOTO5
                ALARG = A(I,J)
                KROW = I
                KOLUMN = J
    5   CONTINUE

12.   DIMENSION F(40,17),G(680)
                   .
                   .
                   .
                K = 1
                DO 10 I = 1,40
                DO 10 J = 1,17
                G(K) = F(I,J)
    10   K = K + 1

13.   DIMENSION A(10,3)
                SUM = 0
                DO 10 I = 1,10
                DO 10 J = 1,3
    10   SUM = SUM + A(I,J)
                WRITE(3,5)(I,J = 1,10),(A(I,J),I = 1,10),J = 1,3),SUM
    5   FORMAT(T30,'FINAL'/T5,10('COL',I3,2X)/3(T5,10F6.1/)/T5,
    *'SUM IS',F5.1)

FUNCTIONS

10-1 Introduction

The reader is probably familiar with many mathematical functions such as the square root, the exponential and the trigonometric functions. These functions, as well as others, are available to the FORTRAN programmer through the use of libraries that are provided by the computer system. FORTRAN also allows the programmer to define and write his own functions, which he may want to incorporate in the library (user or system library). In any event, functions allow the programmer to transfer to a prewritten block of code (routine) to perform a specific task. This can be very convenient when the same task is to be repeated numerous times or at different places in a program. Functions relieve the programmer of writing the code for routine tasks while certain user-written functions can be shared by different users resulting in a significant economy of effort.

In this chapter, we shall examine functions which are included with FORTRAN and also describe procedures for the programmer to define functions of his own. Consider, for example, the following problem. An observer on shore sights a ship one mile away, moving along a line perpendicular to his line of sight. One hour later, he sights the ship and finds an angle of 25° between the two sightings (see Figure 10-1). How far has the ship traveled?

Using trigonometric methods, it can be shown that the distance traveled in one hour is x = tan 25°. A FORTRAN program to perform this calculation is shown in Figure 10-1. The program makes use of the function TAN; the programmer does not have to write a routine to evaluate the tangent function. Note that the argument of the function TAN must be expressed in radians. One radian is equivalent to 57.296° (180° = π radians), hence 25° = 25/57.296 radians.

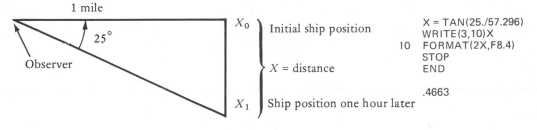

Figure 10-1   Distance calculation.

10-2   FORTRAN Supplied Functions

10-2-1   Definition

A function is a correspondence between one set of numbers, called *arguments*, and another set of numbers, called *values* of the function. For example, the square root function may be used in a FORTRAN statement as follows:

Figure 10-2 illustrates the use of the square root function to produce the square root of the integers 1 through 7.

The mode of the argument depends on the function used; for example, the SQRT function requires its argument to be real (see Figures 10-3 and 10-4). Functions may be part of any arithmetic expressions. The general form of a function reference is

$$\text{function-name (argument-expression } [, \cdots])$$

where   function-name is the name of the function.

The argument-expression (there must be at least one) may take the form of a constant, a variable, another function reference or an expression containing constants, variables, arithmetic operations and function references. The argument

```
        WRITE(3,10)
10      FORMAT('1ARGUMENT',4X,'VALUE')
        DO 20 I = 1,7
        X = I
13      Y = SQRT(X)
20      WRITE(3,11)X,Y
11      FORMAT(2X,F3.0,7X,F6.3)
        STOP
        END
```

```
ARGUMENT        VALUE
    1.          1.000
    2.          1.414
    3.          1.732
    4.          2.000
    5.          2.236
    6.          2.449
    7.          2.646
```

Figure 10-2   Program using function SQRT.

expression is evaluated to a single value, which is then passed to the function as an argument.

Logically, we may think of the function as being evaluated at the point of invocation (where it appears in the statement). Internally, a transfer is made to a set of instructions which calculates the value of the function based on the value of the arguments. Control is then returned at the point at which the function is called. The mode (whether real, integer etc.) of the value returned by the function is determined by the mode of the function name (integer if it starts with I,J,K,L,M or N and real otherwise). Some functions may have more than one argument as in the case of the function MIN0 which selects the smallest value of the integer arguments:

$$AK = MIN0(I,J,K,L,3,5,NT)$$

Function value is stored in AK as a real number.

More than one argument.

The function returns an integer value (Name MIN0 starts with M).

The argument of the function must always be enclosed within parentheses. The argument itself may contain parentheses, as in

Outer parentheses identify the argument.

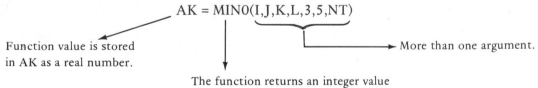

$$Y = SQRT((3.*(X1 + X2 + X3) - (X1 + X2 + X3)**2)/(3.*(3. - 1.)))$$

Expression is to be evaluated as the argument.

FORTRAN-supplied functions are furnished by the computer manufacturer with the FORTRAN compiler. These functions are stored in system libraries on magnetic disks or other types of storage devices. The FORTRAN library of functions consists of mathematical functions and other special functions described in the next two sections.

10-2-2 Mathematical Functions

Common mathematical functions supplied with FORTRAN are shown in Figure 10-3. Note that there are restrictions on the range of values acceptable as arguments, for example, in the square root and logarithmic functions. If an invalid argument is detected by a function, an error message will be printed.

Function	Definition (a represents the argument)	Number of arguments	Name	Mode of	
				Argument	Value of function
Absolute value	$\|a\| = a$ if $a \geqslant 0$ $-a$ if $a < 0$	1	IABS ABS DABS CABS	Integer Real Double precision Complex	Integer Real Double precision Real
Square root	$\sqrt{a}$, $a \geqslant 0$	1	SQRT DSQRT CSQRT	Real Double precision Complex	Real Double precision Complex
Exponential	e^a note $e = 2.718 \cdots$	1	EXP DEXP CEXP	Real Double precision Complex	Real Double precision Complex
Natural logarithms	$\ln(a)$, $a > 0$	1	ALOG DLOG CLOG	Real Double precision Complex	Real Double precision Complex
Common Logarithms	$\log_{10}(a)$, $a > 0$	1	ALOG10 DLOG10	Real Double precision	Real Double precision
Sine	$\sin(a)$ a is expressed in radians	1	SIN DSIN CSIN	Real Double precision Complex	Real Double precision Complex
Cosine	$\cos(a)$ a is expressed in radians	1	COS DCOS CCOS	Real Double precision Complex	Real Double precision Complex
Tangent	$\tan(a)$ a is expressed in radians	1	TAN DTAN	Real Double precision	Real Double precision

Figure 10-3 Some FORTRAN supplied mathematical functions.

Examples

Y = SQRT(A**2 + B**2)	Evaluate the expression $\sqrt{a^2 + b^2}$.
IF(ABS(Y).LT.0.01)GOTO5	If the value of Y is in the range $-0.01 <$ $Y < 0.01$, go to statement 5.
I = COS(X)**2 + C*EXP(−SIN(X))	Evaluates to $\cos^2 x + c\, e^{-\sin x}$. The result is truncated since it is stored in I.
Q = ALOG(R)	The natural logarithm (base e) is computed. If R is negative, an error message will be printed, since logarithms of negative numbers are not defined.

The following are invalid references to mathematical functions:

J = IABS(R)	The function IABS must have an integer argument.
K = SQRT(3)	The function SQRT must have a real argument.

10-2-3 Special Functions

Certain other functions shown in Figure 10-4 are also included in the FORTRAN libraries. The mode conversion functions are used to change the mode of an argument. This mode conversion can, of course, be accomplished by use of a replacement statement in which the mode of the expression on the right is different than that on the variable on the left. The mode conversion functions allow this operation to be performed within an arithmetic expression.

Example

If J = IFIX(A/B) + IFIX(A/4.) and A = 3. and B = 2. then J = 1
                1   +   0   =   1

The transfer of sign and positive difference functions requires two arguments. Consider the following:

Function reference	Value	Function reference	Value
ISIGN(3,−2)	−3	IDIM(3,−2)	5
ISIGN(3,2)	3	DIM(3.,2.5)	.5
SIGN(−3.,−2.)	−3.	IDIM(−3,−2)	0
ISIGN(−3,2)	3	IDIM(−3,2)	0

The functions which return the largest and smallest of a sequence of arguments require at least two arguments and may have any number of arguments.

Example

Suppose J = 3 and K = −2

Function reference	Value
MIN0(3,9,7,−1,4)	−1
MAX1(3.,9.,7.,−1.,4.)	9
AMIN0(J,K,J*K,J + K)	−6.
MAX0(J,K,J*K,J + K,14)	14

Function	Definition $(a_1, a_2$ represent arguments)	Number of arguments	Name	Mode of Argument	Mode of Value of function
Mode conversion	Conversion to integer	1	INT or IFIX IDINT	Real Double precision	Integer Integer
	Conversion to real	1	FLOAT SNGL REAL	Integer Double precision Complex	Real Real Real
	Conversion to double precision	1	DFLOAT DBLE	Integer Real	Double precision Double precision
Transfer of sign	$\|a_1\|$ if $a_2 > 0$ $-\|a_1\|$ if $a_2 < 0$	2	ISIGN (a_1, a_1) SIGN DSIGN	Integer Real Double precision	Integer Real Double precision
Positive difference	$a_1 - a_2$ if $a_1 > a_2$ 0 if $a_1 \leqslant a_2$	2	IDIM (a_1, a_1) DIM DDIM	Integer Real Double precision	Integer Real Double precision
Choose the largest value	The largest of $(a_1, a_2, \cdots)$	$\geqslant 2$	MAX0 AMAX1 DMAX1 AMAX0 MAX1	Integer Real Double precision Integer Real	Integer Real Double precision Real Integer
Choose the smallest value	The smallest of $(a_1, a_2, \cdots)$	$\geqslant 2$	MIN0 AMIN1 DMIN1 AMIN0 MIN1	Integer Real Double precision Integer Real	Integer Real Double precision Real Integer
Remainder function	Remainder of the division of a_1 by a_2: $r = a_1 - INT(a_1/a_2)$ $*a_2$	2	MOD (a_1, a_2) AMOD DMOD	Integer Real Double precision	Integer Real Double precision

Figure 10-4   Other FORTRAN supplied functions.

10-3 You Might Want to Know

1. Can an argument expression contain a reference to another function?

    Answer: Yes. For example:

    $$SQRT(ABS(X)) \text{ and } SQRT(SQRT(Y))$$

2. Is it better to use SQRT or **.5 to calculate the square root?

    Answer: In general, SQRT is more efficient if not more accurate than exponentiation. In either case, results will be a close approximation to the actual square root. Logarithms are used to perform exponentiation in most systems; iterative methods may be used in evaluation of SQRT.

3. What other functions are available?

Answer: The listing of functions in Figures 10-3 and 10-4 are by no means exhaustive. The reader is referred to the manufacturer's reference manual for the FORTRAN system available to him for a complete listing. Also, most installations have available packages of statistical and other mathematical functions with a wide variety of capabilities. When available, such functions may considerably reduce the amount of effort involved in program development.

4. Can an array element be used as a function argument?

Answer: Yes. For example, if A and XYZ are arrays, the following are valid function references:

$$SQRT(A(4)), \quad ABS(XYZ(L,J)), \quad SQRT(ALOG(X + T))$$

5. Can the MAX/MIN functions return the value of the largest/smallest value contained in an array?

Answer: Yes, but each element of the array must be listed as a separate argument. For example:

$$SMALL = AMIN1(X(1),X(2),X(3),X(4),X(5),X(6),X(7))$$

It would, of course, be better for the programmer to write a function which would accept the array as an argument to return the smallest element (see Section 9-5).

6. Are all FORTRAN-supplied functions stored in the system library?

Answer: No. Some functions, such as ABS, INT, are said to be *in-line* functions, while others are said to be *out-of-line* functions. In-line functions are inserted by the FORTRAN compiler in the FORTRAN program itself whenever a reference to that function is made, i.e., the compiler itself generates the code for the function during the compilation process. An out-of-line function on the other hand is stored in the system library, and the FORTRAN compiler generates external references to it; that is, the compiler generates the necessary instructions to link the FORTRAN program to the library function program so that transfer can be established between the two programs.

7. What if I dimension an array SIN(10), and in my program I refer to Y = SIN(X); will the sine function of X be computed?

Answer: No. The compiler will treat any reference to SIN as an array reference. There are no "reserved words" in the FORTRAN language.

10-4 Programming Examples

10-4-1 Prime Numbers

The program in Figure 10-5 provides a list of all the prime numbers between 5 and 10,000. A prime number is a number which is only divisible by 1 and by it-self. To determine whether a number N is prime, it suffices to check whether N is divisible by any integer up to and possibly equal to $\sqrt{N}$. For example, to deter-mine whether 43 is prime one only needs to check if 43 is divisible by 3,4,5 and 6.

   Note in Figure 10-5 the use of the FLOAT function in statement 11 to make the argument of the square root function a real argument. Note also the use of the MOD function to determine whether I (possible prime candidate) is divisible by J. If I is divisible by J, I is not a prime.

```
      DO 5 I = 5,10000,2     Skip all even numbers.

      K = SQRT(FLOAT(I))    Determine √I. Argument of SQRT must be real.
      DO 4 J = 3,K,2         Check if I is divisible by any integer
  12  IF(MOD(I,J))4,5,4      up to and possibly including √I.
   4  CONTINUE
      WRITE(3,31)I           Number is prime; print it.
  31  FORMAT(I25)
   5  CONTINUE
      STOP
      END
```

Figure 10-5 List of prime numbers.

10-4-2 Break-Even Analysis

Systems analysts at the XYZ Company computed the revenue function associated with the manufacture and marketing of a new company product. A cost function was also projected for that product. Both functions are given as below:

$$\text{Revenue function:} \quad y = 15xe^{-x/3} + 0.5$$

$$\text{Cost function:} \quad y = \frac{x^3}{16} - \frac{x^2}{2} + \frac{7x}{4} + 4$$

Determine graphically the break-even point(s). A solution to the problem is shown in Figure 10-6. Note that

$$y = \frac{x^3}{16} - \frac{x^2}{2} + \frac{7x}{4} + 4 = \frac{x^3 - 8x^2 + 28x + 64}{16}$$

The numerator is then factored to yield $((x - 8)x + 28)x + 64$ as in statement 2 in Figure 10-6. The latter expression of the cost function is more efficient in terms of computations, since it contains only two multiplications and one division as opposed to four and three respectively in the original cost function. Both the cost and revenue functions are graphed for values of x ranging from 0 to 11.

In Figure 10-6, the array KLINE is used to print each line of the graph. This array is initially filled with 70 blanks. The integer value J of the revenue function and the integer value L of the cost function are then computed for X = 0,1,2, $\cdots$, 11. Each time, the graphic symbols R and C are inserted in position J and L of the array KLINE (statements 7 and 8). The array is then printed:

```
      DIMENSION KLINE(70)          Read the three characters "R", "C" and " " (blank)
      READ(1,100)IR,IC,KBLANK      from 1 data card.
100   FORMAT(3A1)
      WRITE(3,10)
10    FORMAT('1 X',2X,'REVENUE',2X,'COST')
      X = 0
2     C = ((((X – 8.)*X + 28.)*X + 64)/16.)
      R = 15.*X*EXP(–X/3.) + 0.5
      DO 1 I = 1,70
1     KLINE(I) = KBLANK    Blank out the line before inserting character.
      J = R + 0.5               Round off.
7     KLINE(J) = IR    Insert the graphic character "R" on the line.
      L = C + 0.5
8     KLINE(L) = IC    Insert the graphic character "C" on the line.
      WRITE(3,11)X,R,C,KLINE
11    FORMAT(1X,F3.0,3X,F4.0,3X,F4.0,3X,70A1)
      X = X + 1
      IF(X – 12)2,3,3
3     STOP
      END
```

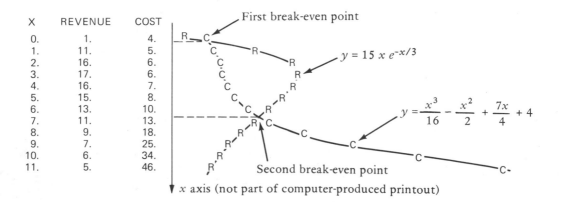

X	REVENUE	COST
0.	1.	4.
1.	11.	5.
2.	16.	6.
3.	17.	6.
4.	16.	7.
5.	15.	8.
6.	13.	10.
7.	11.	13.
8.	9.	18.
9.	7.	25.
10.	6.	34.
11.	5.	46.

First break-even point

$y = 15\ x\ e^{-x/3}$

$y = \dfrac{x^3}{16} - \dfrac{x^2}{2} + \dfrac{7x}{4} + 4$

Second break-even point

x axis (not part of computer-produced printout)

Figure 10-6 Break-even analysis.

10-4-3   A Graph of the TAN Function

Figure 10-7 shows a program which produces a rough graph of the function $y = \tan(x)$ in the interval $0, 2\pi$ for values of x in steps of .2 radian. Special precautions must be taken, however, since in that interval $\tan x$ is $\pm \infty$ at $\pi/2$ and $3\pi/2$, as shown below:

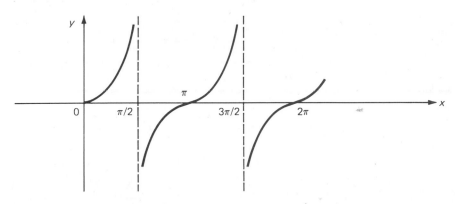

The programmer must decide what portion of the graph he wants to retain, since he cannot graph all those points close to the asymptotes. He may decide as in the program of Figure 10-7 to graph only those points that fall in the area where y lies between -9 and 9. When writing the program, this means that the programmer must test the values for y and graph only those points falling in the restricted area.

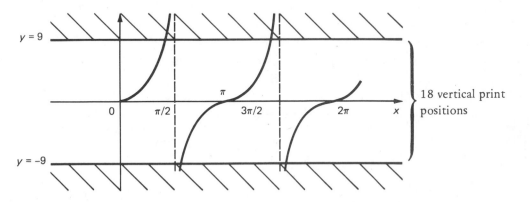

Since graphs are printed on the printer output form with the y axis horizontal and the x axis vertical, only 18 print positions (-9 to 9) would be used to print $y = \tan(x)$. To magnify the graph for a better graphic display, a scale factor of 4 is applied to make use of 72 print positions (4×18) instead of just 18. The graph is then drawn one horizontal line at a time using the array LINE to print a line of blanks except for the graphic character * inserted at position (TANx + 9)*4 on that line:

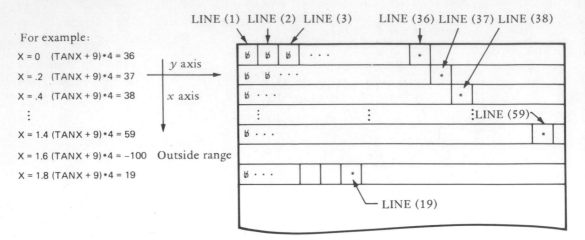

For example:

X = 0 (TANX + 9)*4 = 36

X = .2 (TANX + 9)*4 = 37

X = .4 (TANX + 9)*4 = 38

⋮

X = 1.4 (TANX + 9)*4 = 59

X = 1.6 (TANX + 9)*4 = –100 Outside range

X = 1.8 (TANX + 9)*4 = 19

In Figure 10-7, the variable J (statement 16) is used to place the asterisk at the Jth position in the array LINE (the asterisk will be in LINE(J)). If J is negative or J ≥ 72, the asterisk cannot be graphed, since it is outside the designated interval 1–72 for the array LINE.

10=5 Programmer-Defined Functions

10-5-1 Programming Example

As a promotional gimmick, every patron of the Circle K gas station gets a lucky card with three numbers on it ranging between 10 and 10,000. The station manager then draws at random a number between 1 and 10,000. If any of the customer numbers matches the one drawn by the manager, the customer gets a dollar amount equal to 1/10 of his lucky number. Write a program to read ten customer lucky cards and determine the dollar amount of any lucky winner. For example, if the lucky card contains the numbers 50, 100 and 200 and the manager draws the number 50, the customer wins 5 dollars.

To solve this problem, we will write:

1. A function called IRAND[1] which will generate random numbers between two specified integers named IBEG and ITER. This function can be copied by the user to generate his own random numbers if his installation does not have a random number generator.

2. A function called WIN to determine whether the customer has a lucky number and in the affirmative compute the dollar win.

---

[1] The function IRAND can be used on any computer system to generate random numbers.

```
      DIMENSION LINE(72)
      READ(1,1)KBLANK,KAST          Read the graphic characters.
 1    FORMAT(2A1)
      X = 0
 3    Y = TAN(X)
      DO 4 I = 1,72
 4    LINE(I) = KBLANK
16    J = (Y + 9)*4 + 0.5           .5 is added to take care of round-off.
      IF(J)11,5,5                   Check for outside the range.
 5    IF(J – 72)6,6,11
 6    LINE(J) = KAST
      WRITE(3,15)X,Y,LINE
15    FORMAT(1X,F4.1,2X,F5.1,T13,72A1)
12    X = X + .2
      IF(X – 7.0)3,3,8
 8    STOP
11    WRITE(3,15)X,Y                Print X,Y if outside the range.
      GOTO12
      END
```

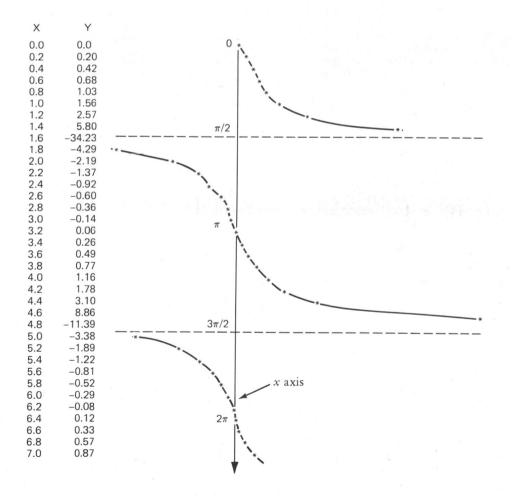

X	Y
0.0	0.0
0.2	0.20
0.4	0.42
0.6	0.68
0.8	1.03
1.0	1.56
1.2	2.57
1.4	5.80
1.6	−34.23
1.8	−4.29
2.0	−2.19
2.2	−1.37
2.4	−0.92
2.6	−0.60
2.8	−0.36
3.0	−0.14
3.2	0.06
3.4	0.26
3.6	0.49
3.8	0.77
4.0	1.16
4.2	1.78
4.4	3.10
4.6	8.86
4.8	−11.39
5.0	−3.38
5.2	−1.89
5.4	−1.22
5.6	−0.81
5.8	−0.52
6.0	−0.29
6.2	−0.08
6.4	0.12
6.6	0.33
6.8	0.57
7.0	0.87

Figure 10-7 Graph of the TAN function.

A program to accomplish the above is shown in Figure 10-8. Note the following:

1. The way in which IRAND and WIN are invoked (called) and how the arguments (parameters) are passed to the functions with the same name.

2. The way in which the FUNCTION statement is used to declare that the program is a function subprogram.

3. The way in which the function value in the function subprogram is returned to the calling program through the name of the function itself.

The complete program shown in Figure 10-8 consists of three independent blocks of code (or subprograms), which perform very specific tasks. The main program, which acts as a coordinator between the other two subprograms; the IRAND program, which generates random numbers, and the WIN program, which computes an amount won or lost.

Read the ten cards one at a time.
Call the function IRAND to choose a random number between 1 and 10,000. The arguments of the random routine are 1 and 10,000. The function WIN computes the amount won. If the customer loses AMT = 0. The array CARD is transmitted to the function WIN as well as the lucky number K, which is the random number returned by the function IRAND.

```
      DIMENSION CARD(3)
      DO 15 I = 1,10
      READ(1,1)(CARD(J),J = 1,3)
      K = IRAND(1,10000)
      AMT = WIN(CARD,K)
      WRITE(3,11)AMT
11    FORMAT('OYOU HAVE WON',F10.0,'CENTS')
15    CONTINUE
1     FORMAT(3F5.0)
      STOP
      END
```

The array SLIP in the function WIN really refers to the array CARD in the calling program. Similarly, N is just a dummy name for the variable K defined in the calling program.
If no match exists between the numbers on the card and the number drawn by the manager, the value of the function is WIN = 0. If there is a match, WIN is one-tenth of the lucky number.
Note how the name of the function WIN returns the value of the function to the calling program.

```
      FUNCTION WIN(SLIP,N)
      DIMENSION SLIP(3)
      DO 15 I = 1,3
      IF(SLIP(I) – N)15,3,15
15    CONTINUE
      WIN = 0
      RETURN
3     WIN = SLIP(I)/10
      RETURN
      END
```

Function IRAND returns any integer value between IBEG and ITER (IBEG < ITER). In the case of this program, IBEG and ITER take on those values passed by the calling program, i.e., IBEG = 1 and ITER = 10,000. The value X, as a result of the computations is always a real number between 0 and 1. The value IRAND becomes any number between 1 and 10,000. Note how IRAND transmits the function value to the calling program.

```
      FUNCTION IRAND(IBEG,ITER)
      DATAIM,IB,IA/2511,32768,19727/
      IA = MOD(IM*IA,IB)
      X = FLOAT(IA)/FLOAT(IB)
      IRAND = X*(ITER – IBEG + 1) + IBEG
      RETURN
      END
```

Figure 10-8   Random number lucky win.

All three programs are compiled independently of one another. Through the function invocation statement, data (such as the specific range of the desired random numbers) is passed from one program to another by means of arguments or parameters specified in the function invocation statement and also in the FUNCTION definition statement. Other information, such as the three customer numbers, is stored in an array CARD in the main program, which can be accessed from the function WIN through a "dummy" argument array name SLIP. The flowpath between the three blocks of code or programs can be visualized as shown in Figure 10-9.

Note, through the use of functions, how it might be possible to avoid duplication of code. Whenever a procedure (task) is to be performed, a transfer is made to that procedure (program), which, when completed, returns control to the program which called the procedure. In the case of the program in Figure 10-8, it is conceivable that the main program might need to call on the random number generator routine, later on, for other purposes. In that case, instead of writing the code to generate random numbers many times, only one block of code is written to perform this task, which can be called any number of times by the main or other subprograms.

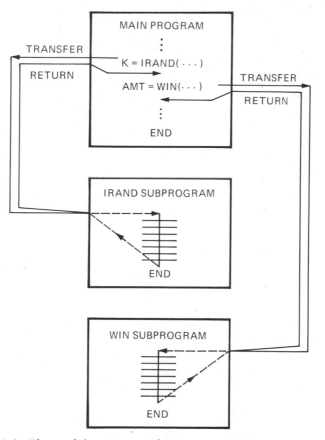

Figure 10-9 Flowpath between a main program and function subprograms.

10-5-2   Function Subprograms

One form of a programmer-defined function is the function subprogram; another form is the arithmetic statement function, which will be discussed in Section 10-5-8. The function subprogram is a separately compiled program which may be executed by another program. The prefix *sub-* in subprogram implies that the function subprogram is not really a complete program; if it were executed all by itself, it would not produce meaningful results. Function subprograms are usually written to carry out generalized procedures that are data independent; for example, determining the largest element of any array, computing the average or the standard deviation of any set of grades etc. Parameters or arguments (sometimes called *dummy* arguments because they are used as place holders) are used to illustrate the way in which the procedure (function) is to be carried out. These arguments in turn must be specified by the program wishing to make use of the generalized procedure; for example, what is the name of the array whose largest element must be found? what is the exact number of grades for which an average is to be calculated? etc. A function subprogram should be viewed as one logical component (module) of a total program that might consist of numerous other logical components (subprograms).

   Function subprograms can be catalogued in the system or user libraries if these functions are to be shared by other users or used repeatedly by the programmer (in the same way as the mathematical functions are stored in the libraries). They may also be part of the jobstream, i.e., part of the deck that is submitted each time the program is to be run. Functions may be accessed or executed from another program (main program or other subprograms) by invoking the name of the function and by specifying a list of arguments.

10-5-3   The Invocation Statement

The general form of a function invocation statement is

$$\text{function-name } [(a_1, a_2, a_3, \cdots, a_n)]$$

where   function-name is the name of the function (any valid variable name).

   $a_1, a_2, a_3, \cdots, a_n$ are arguments to be passed to the function subprogram.

   These arguments can be variables, subscripted variable names, array names, constants, expressions or function names.
   The value of the function is returned in the name of the function (acting as a variable).
   The mode of the value of the function is implicitly defined by the function name. If the name begins with I,J,K,L,M or N, the function value is integer; otherwise, it is real.

Consider, for example, the following:

X = 3.*SUB(Y)/SAM + 3	One argument is passed to the function.
AX = A(T,J,3) + B(X**2,1.5)	The function A has three arguments, while the function B has two arguments.
IF(TRAP(X,K) − 8)1,1,3	The function TRAP is part of an IF statement. It is first evaluated and its value is compared to 8.
Z = S1(A,B(1),3*I + K,J)	S1 has four arguments.
T = SUB2(SIN(X),Y) − SUB2(3.1,0.)	Arguments can be functions, too.

The reader may wonder how the compiler differentiates between a function and a reference to an array. For example, B(3*I − 1,2) could be a reference to a function or to an element of the array B. If the variable B is dimensioned, then B is an array; if B is not dimensioned, the compiler will treat any reference to B as a reference to a function subprogram.

10-5-4   The FUNCTION Definition Statement and the RETURN Statement

The first statement in every function subprogram is the FUNCTION statement. The general form of this statement is

$$[type] \text{ FUNCTION function-name } [(p_1,p_2,p_3, \cdots ,p_n)]$$

where   function-name is the name of the function.

$p_1,p_2,p_3, \cdots ,p_n$ are dummy arguments used to pass the data to and from the calling program. These arguments can either be variable names, array names or function names. Subscripted variables such as X(I) and constants are not permitted as arguments in the function definition. Type is an optional parameter which specifies the mode of the value returned by the function. If type is omitted, the mode of the value of the function is implicitly defined in the function name. If the name starts with I,J,K,L, M or N, the value is integer; otherwise, it is real.

The dummy arguments used in the subprogram are the names for the actual arguments defined in the calling program and listed in the invocation statement. When the function is executed, the dummy arguments take on the values of the "real" arguments specified in the calling program. More precisely, the function processes directly the real arguments through the dummy arguments.

The arguments in the invocation statement *must* correspond in number, mode and order with the arguments in the FUNCTION statement. The argument names may be the same or different. If an argument in a function subprogram is an array name, the array should be declared in a DIMENSION statement in the function subprogram.

Return to the calling program is effected by the RETURN statement, which returns control to the statement in the calling program where the invocation was made. Many RETURN statements may be included in a function subprogram (see, for example, the program in Figure 10-8). A distinguishing feature of the function subprogram is that at its conclusion the statement to which the return is made is variable (unlike the GO TO statement). The return point depends on the statement at which the function was called (invoked).

The last statement in every function subprogram must be the END statement. Following are some examples of function subprograms:

Example 1

Calling program	Function subprogram
.	FUNCTION ALARG(A,B)
.	IF(A.GT.B)GOTO5
.	ALARG = B
Z = ALARG(X,Y)	RETURN
WRITE(3,3)Z	5 ALARG = A
.	RETURN
.	END
.	
IF(ALARG(Z,T) − 3.1)1,1,2	This function returns the largest value of any two arguments. Note how the function value is returned by the function name ALARG.
.	
.	

Example 2

INTEGER QUIZZ	INTEGER FUNCTION QUIZZ(J,K,L)
.	QUIZZ = (J + K + L)/3.
.	RETURN
.	END
IF(QUIZZ(30,40,50).GT.T)GOTO2	
.	
.	Note the INTEGER specification in both programs.
.	
Y = QUIZZ(J,30,L)	QUIZZ returns an integer value.

Example 3

I = 2	FUNCTION BAKER(X,Y,J)
A = 7.0	.
Y = BAKER(3.2,9.8*A,I)	. The arguments of BAKER must be two real values followed by an integer value. When BAKER is executed X = 3.2, Y = 9.8*7 = 68.6 and J = 2.
.	
.	
.	

Example 4

In this example, the function name participates as a variable in the subprogram.

```
DIMENSION A(10),B(10)                    FUNCTION SUM(Z)
        .                                DIMENSION Z(10)
        .                                SUM = 0.
        .                                DO 10 I = 1,10
X = SUM(A)                          10   SUM = SUM + Z(I)
        .                                RETURN
        .                                END
Y = SUM(B)
        .
        .
```

Note the DIMENSION statement required in the subprogram. SUM (name of the function) is used as an accumulator.

Example 5

```
DIMENSION A(10),B(10)                    FUNCTION ALARG(X)
        .                                DIMENSION X(10)
                                         ALARG = X(1)
X = ALARG(A) + ALARG(B)                  DO 10 I = 2,10
                                         IF(ALARG.LT.X(I))ALARG = X(I)
                                    10   CONTINUE
                                         RETURN
                                         END
```

When the RETURN statement is executed, control is passed to the point at which the function was invoked. First ALARG(A) is executed, then ALARG(B), then the sum of the two largest numbers is stored in X.

Example 6

This example illustrates the use of several RETURN statements.

```
        .                                FUNCTION RATE(Q)
        .                                RATE = 1.0
Y = RATE(3.2)                            IF(Q.GT.3.0)GOTO3
        .                                RETURN
        .                           3    IF(Q.GT.5.0)GOTO7
        .                                RATE = 2.0
        .                                RETURN
Z = RATE(9.8)                            RETURN
                                    7    RATE = 3.0
                                         RETURN
                                         END
```

The function RATE results in $\text{RATE}(Q) = \begin{cases} 1 \text{ if} & Q \leqslant 3 \\ 2 \text{ if } 3 < Q \leqslant 5 \\ 3 \text{ if} & Q > 5 \end{cases}$

Note the use of the multiple RETURN statements, but only one END statement as the very last statement.

It is often necessary to write function subprograms which will process arrays of varying sizes. In this case, it is possible to use an integer variable to specify the size of the array in the DIMENSION statement. A more detailed and complete discussion of variable dimension for multidimensional arrays is presented in Section 11-5-2. In the following example, the subprogram will process arrays of varying sizes. The rows and columns are passed as the second and third arguments.

Calling program	*Function subprogram*
DIMENSION CLASS1(10,10)	FUNCTION AVER(ARAY,NR,NC)
DIMENSION CLASS2(5,5)	DIMENSION ARAY(NR,NC)
DIMENSION CLASS3(7,17)	AVER = 0
A = AVER(CLASS1,10,10)	DO 5 I = 1,NR Variable dimension
B = AVER(CLASS2,5,5)	DO 5 J = 1,NC
C = AVER(CLASS3,7,17)	5 AVER = AVER + ARAY(I,J)
TOT = (A + B + C)/3	AVER = AVER/(NR*NC)
	RETURN
	END

The function AVER computes the average of the grades stored in ARAY. Being able to use the variable dimension in the function subprogram allows the user to write one subprogram to find the average of any array of any size. The reader is cautioned to check his technical FORTRAN reference manual to ascertain whether the variable dimension feature is available at his installation.

The following are invalid function references or function definition statements:

Calling program	*Function subprogram*	
X = AMAX(2.1,3,4.)	FUNCTION AMAX(X,Y,Z)	"3" is integer and "Y" is real.
INTEGER SMALL . . X = SMALL(3.1,X)	FUNCTION SMALL(T,X)	SMALL should be declared as INTEGER in the subprogram.
S = COT(A,B,T(3))	FUNCTION COT(X,Y,Z) X = COT(T,Z,P)	Function cannot invoke itself.
DIMENSION Q(100) C = DAM(Q(1),Q(2),−4)	FUNCTION DAM(T(1),T(2),J) DIMENSION T(100)	Subprogram arguments may not be subscripted variable names.
MIM = SUB(X,2*J,9.8)	FUNCTION SUB(X,J)	Arguments disagree in number.
DIMENSION CART(10) . . X = TIP(3.9,X,CART)	FUNCTION TIP(X,Y,Z) TIP = (X + Y)/2 .	Z must be dimensioned in the function subprogram.

Since subprograms are separate programs that are treated independently by the compiler, variable names appearing in both the calling and called program may be identical with no risk of confusion possible; likewise, duplicate labels are permissible, since the programs are compiled separately. For the same reason, if, in a function subprogram, the programmer wishes to refer to a variable that is defined in the calling program, he cannot use the same name and hope that it will refer to the variable with identical name in the calling program. The only way to "communicate" variables between programs is either through the COMMON statement (see Section 11-2-4) or by passing the variable name as an argument in the function calling sequence. Consider the following examples:

Example 1

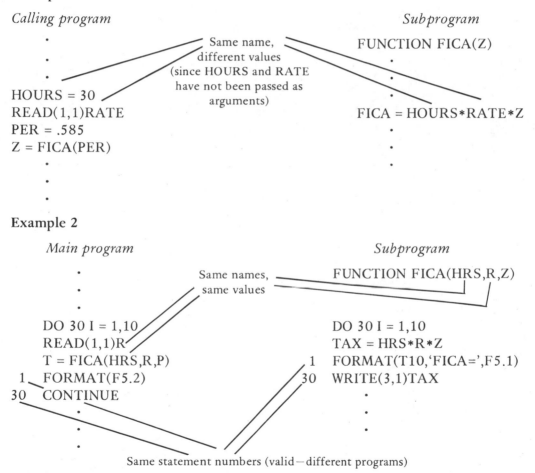

Calling program   *Subprogram*

Same name,   FUNCTION FICA(Z)
different values
(since HOURS and RATE
have not been passed as
arguments)

HOURS = 30
READ(1,1)RATE   FICA = HOURS*RATE*Z
PER = .585
Z = FICA(PER)

Example 2

    Main program   *Subprogram*

Same names,   FUNCTION FICA(HRS,R,Z)
same values

    DO 30 I = 1,10   DO 30 I = 1,10
    READ(1,1)R   TAX = HRS*R*Z
    T = FICA(HRS,R,P)   1   FORMAT(T10,'FICA=',F5.1)
1   FORMAT(F5.2)   30   WRITE(3,1)TAX
30   CONTINUE

Same statement numbers (valid—different programs)

10-5-5   Position of the Function Subprogram in the Job Deck

All user-defined function subprograms are separate physical and logical entities and as such are compiled independently of one another. The compiler treats each function subprogram as a new program in the job deck. Special system control cards (job control, work flow etc.) may physically separate each program from one another as depicted in Figure 10-10. The student should determine the proper control cards required by his computer system.

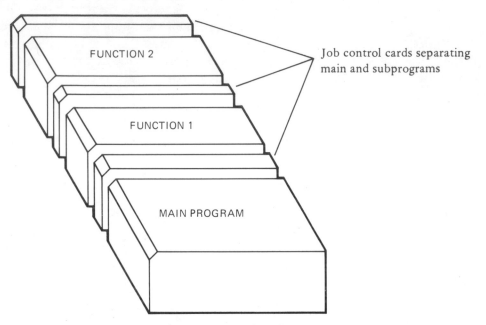

Figure 10-10 Job makeup.

10-5-6 Program Example

Write a program to compute the binomial expression $C(n,m) = \dfrac{n!}{m!(n-m)!}$

$C(n,m)$ represents the number of ways to choose m objects from n different objects. For example, if six persons are on a ship and the lifeboat can hold only two persons, then:

$$C(6,2) = \frac{6!}{2!4!} = \frac{6 \cdot 5 \cdot 4 \cdot 3 \cdot 2 \cdot 1}{(2 \cdot 1) \cdot (4 \cdot 3 \cdot 2 \cdot 1)} = 15$$

This represents the number of different combinations of people who could be saved. One approach to the problem is shown in the program of Figure 10-11.

The factorial calculation must be repeated three times to compute the result. The program is greatly simplified by use of a function subprogram to perform the calculation of factorials as shown in Figure 10-12. Note in the program of Figure 10-12 that the function FACT is declared explicitly to be of integer mode in the subprogram. In the main program, FACT must also be included in an INTEGER statement to specify that it represents integer data.

```
        INTEGER COMB
        READ(1,1)N,M
    1   FORMAT(2I2)
        NFACT = 1
        DO 10 I = 1,N
   10   NFACT = NFACT*I
        MFACT = 1
        DO 20 I = 1,M
   20   MFACT = MFACT*I
        NM = N – M
        NMFACT = 1
        DO 30 I = 1,NM
   30   NMFACT = NMFACT*I
        COMB = NFACT/(MFACT*NMFACT)
        WRITE (3,2)N,M,COMB
    2   FORMAT('1 COMBINATIONS OF ',I3,' OBJECTS TAKEN',I3,' AT A TIME IS ',
       *I4)
        STOP
        END
```

} Factorial computation.

} Factorial computation.

} Factorial computation.

COMBINATIONS OF 6 OBJECTS TAKEN 2 AT A TIME IS 15

Figure 10-11   Combination without function subprogram.

```
        INTEGER COMB,FACT
        READ(1,1)N,M
    1   FORMAT(2I2)
        COMB = FACT(N)/(FACT(M)*FACT(N – M))
        WRITE(3,2)N,M,COMB
    2   FORMAT('1 COMBINATIONS OF ',I3,' OBJECTS TAKEN',I3,' AT A TIME IS ',
       *I4)
        STOP
        END

        INTEGER FUNCTION FACT(N)
        FACT = 1
        DO 10 I = 1,N
   10   FACT = FACT*I
        RETURN
        END
```

COMBINATIONS OF 6 OBJECTS TAKEN 2 AT A TIME IS 15

Figure 10-12   Combination with function FACT.

10-5-7   Why Use Function Subprograms?

A subprogram can be an aid in writing shorter and more compact programs. The programmer can break his program in smaller logical components that are easier to work with, resulting in a more readable program. A subprogram can result in an economy of code for procedures or tasks that are to be performed repeatedly at different places in a program(s). The code for the procedure is written just once and is not recoded wherever it is needed in the program.

Function subprograms that are to be used frequently should be compiled, debugged and thereafter included in the program in object deck form (or stored in a library). This saves computer time, since the subprogram need not be recompiled each time it is to be used. Subprograms may be written and shared by users through "share" libraries. A brief subprogram description and its use (calling sequence) should be included in the listing of the subprogram through comment cards.

In long, complex problems, it may be possible to segment the tasks that make up a complete program; the programmer can write these tasks as subprograms and verify that each subprogram executes properly. The complete program can then be constructed using the already written and debugged subprograms.

10-5-8 Statement Functions

As we have seen, FORTRAN allows the programmer to define his own functions through the use of function subprograms. The function subprogram, in general, may require several lines of code and can produce several answers (more than one RETURN statement), even though only one value can be returned to the calling program. In some cases where the function is so simple that it can be expressed in one line of code and can only produce one possible answer, the statement function can be used to great advantage. Statement functions are generally used when a particular arithmetic expression needs to be evaluated for different values of the variable at different places in the program. Unlike function subprograms, which are compiled independently, statement functions are defined within (part of) the program that uses the statement function. For example, if it is needed to evaluate a second-degree polynomial several times in a program for different values of the variable, the statement function POLY could be used as follows:

Program without statement function	*Program with statement function*
X = ___	POLY(X) = 2.1*X**2 − 3*X + 1
Y = 2.1*X**2 − 3*X + 1	Y = POLY(X)
X = 2.12347	.
	.
IF(2.1*X**2 − 3*X + 1 − TOT)1,1,3	IF(POLY(2.12347) − TOT)1,1,3
.	.
.	.
.	.
T = 10.6	T = 10.6
SUM = SUM + SQRT(2.1*T**2 − 3*T + 1)	SUM = SUM + SQRT(POLY(T))

The general form of the statement function definition is

$$\text{function-name } (a_1, a_2, a_3, \cdots, a_n) = \text{expression}$$

where   function-name is the name of the function (any variable name).

$a_1, a_2, a_3, \cdots, a_n$ are dummy arguments which must be nonsubscripted variable names.

expression is any arithmetic expression that does not contain any subscripted variables. This expression will contain $a_1, a_2, a_3, \cdots, a_n$ as well as possibly other variables or constants, or references to function subprograms or previously defined statement functions.

The statement function definition should precede the first executable statement of the program but follow such specification statements as DIMENSION, INTEGER etc. The statement function definition can be visualized as follows:

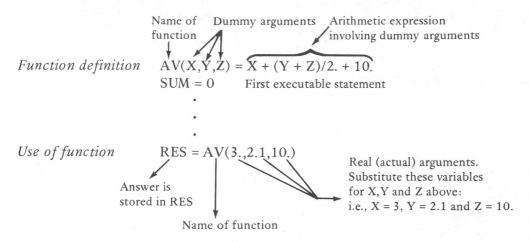

Function definition $AV(X,Y,Z) = X + (Y + Z)/2. + 10.$

Use of function $RES = AV(3., 2.1, 10.)$

When a statement function is executed, the value of the real (actual) arguments replaces the dummy arguments in the expression of the function definition. If variables other than the dummy arguments are used in the expression, then their current values will be used when the function is evaluated. The use of a variable as a dummy argument does not preclude its use as a variable later in the program. The only purpose of the dummy argument is to illustrate the way in which the real arguments are manipulated to produce the function value.

In the expression of the function definition, the dummy arguments must be nonsubscripted variable names. In the calling statement of the function, the real arguments *can* be subscripted variables or arithmetic expressions. As with function subprograms, the real arguments must agree in number, order and in mode with the dummy arguments in the function definition. The mode of the value returned is determined implicitly by the name of the function but may be changed by appropriate specification statements.

Examples

a. $F(X) = (X + 2)/(X - 2) + X**2$ $F(X) = \dfrac{X + 2}{X - 2} + X^2$

    Y = F(4.0)   The value of Y will be 19.
    Y = F(T)   The value of Y is computed, substituting T for X in the function definition.

b. $BETA(Y) = A*Y**2 + B*Y + C$ The expression involves variables
                                                     other than the formal argument Y.

```
      READ(1,1)A,B,C
      DO 10 IX = 1,10
      Q = BETA(FLOAT(IX))
   10 WRITE(3,2)IX,Q
```

The values of A,B, and C are established. The function will be evaluated
for values of IX varying from 1 to 10.
Note that the mode of the actual
argument and the formal argument
must be the same. The FLOAT function converts the integer IX to real
mode.

---

c. $RAD(DEGREE) = DEGREE/57.296$ RAD converts degrees into radians.

$Y = SIN(RAD(30.))$ Statement functions may be used as
                                                     arguments of any other functions.

---

d. $B1(Y) = ABS(Y - 1.)$ Statement functions may reference
    $B2(Y) = LOG(B1(X))/10.$ other previously defined statement
                                                     functions. B1 and B2 are functions.

$Z = B2(-5)$ $Z = LOG(|-5 - 1|)/10 = LOG(6)/10$

---

e. $COMB(N,M) = FACT(N)/(FACT(M)*FACT(N - M))$ The COMB function could be used in
                                                     the program of Figure 9-12. Note the
                                                     use of the user-defined function
                                                     subprogram FACT.

$K = COMB(8,2)$

---

f. $PAY(HRS,RATE) = HRS*RATE + BONUS$

```
BONUS = 50.
X = PAY(40.,5.)                                      X = 5*40 + 50 = 250
BONUS = BONUS + 10
Y = PAY(50.,4.)                                      Y = 4*50 + 60 = 260
```

---

g. $FAHR(C) = 9./5.*C + 32.$ The variable C is used as an ordinary
                                                     variable in the program, even though
                                                     it is also used as a dummy argument.

```
C = 0.
TEMP = FAHR(100)
C = C + 1.                                           The value of C is 1.
```

h. REAL INT

   INT(R,N) = PRIN*(1. + R)**N

         .

   DUE = INT(A(3),K*360 + J)

The FORTRAN supplied function INT is redefined as a user function. Note the use of the subscripted variable A(3). In this case, R = A(3) and N = K*360 + J.

---

i. T(X) = SQRT(X**2 + 9.) + A

   A = 11

   S = T(4) + SQRT(T(5))

$S = \sqrt{25} + 11 + \sqrt{34} + 11$

The following are examples of invalid statement function definition or invalid references to statement functions:

a. PAY = HRS*RATE

   RES = PAY(40,5)

No arguments.

b. CONS(X,3) = 3*X + 1

3 is an invalid dummy argument.

c. DUE(X,A(1),Z) = A(1) + X + Z

Subscripted variable as dummy argument.

d. MERDE(X,Y) = (X + Y)**13 − A(4)

Subscripted variable name in expression.

e. DOG(X,Y,Z) = X + Y*DOG(C,D,F)

Recursive definition of DOG—a function cannot reference itself.

f. A(X) = T(X) + 1

   T(Y) = Y*3 + K

T(X) is not previously defined. Interchange the two statements.

g. TRUE(NCY) = NCY*3/256

   DIMENSION A(100)

Statement functions should follow specification statements.

h. SIGN(X) = −X

   Y = SIGN(3)

Arguments differ in mode.

i. BRA(VO,S) = (VO + S)**3

   Z = BRA(3.12*X)

Arguments differ in number. Only one argument in BRA.

10-5-9 Program Example

The program in Figure 10-13 illustrates the use of a statement function to solve a set of linear equations of the form

$$a_1 x + b_1 y = c_1$$
$$a_2 x + b_2 y = c_2$$

The program uses the Gauss–Seidel iteration procedure, which involves starting with an approximation x_0, y_0 of the solution and computing successive approximations for x and y using the formulas

$$x_{n+1} = \frac{1}{a_1}\left(c_1 - b_1 y_n\right)$$

$$y_{n+1} = \frac{1}{b_2}\left(c_2 - a_2 x_{n+1}\right)$$

It can be shown that this sequence of approximations x_i, y_i converges towards the solution of the system of linear equations if

$$|a_1| \cdot |b_2| > |b_1| \cdot |a_2|$$

The program in Figure 10-13 accepts as input the values $a_1, b_1, c_1, a_2, b_2, c_2$ and tests to see if the Gauss–Seidel iteration procedure will converge. If it will not converge, an appropriate message is produced; if it will converge, the first eight terms of the sequence are computed.

Program	Output
	8.X + 2.Y = 18.
	1.X + 1.Y = 3.

```
        XNEW(Q) = (1./A1)*(C1 – B1*Q)
        YNEW(Q) = (1./B2)*(C2 – A2*Q)
  10    READ(1,1)A1,B1,C1,A2,B2,C2,LC
        IF(LC – 9)11,200,11
  11    WRITE(3,2)A1,B1,C1,A2,B2,C2
        IF(ABS(A1)*ABS(B2) – ABS(B1)*ABS(A2))190,190,12
  12    WRITE(3,3)
        Y = 0
        DO 100 N = 1,8
        X = XNEW(Y)
        Y = YNEW(X)
        WRITE(3,4)N,X,Y

 100    CONTINUE
        GOTO10
 190    WRITE(3,5)
        GOTO10
   1    FORMAT(6F2.0,T80,I1)
   2    FORMAT(2X,F3.0,'X +',F3.0,'Y =',F4.0)
   3    FORMAT('0',2X,'N',3X,'XN',4X,'YN')
   4    FORMAT(2X,I2,2X,F5.2,2X,F5.2)
   5    FORMAT('0',2X,'SYSTEM WILL NOT CONVERGE')
 200    STOP
        END
```

N	XN	YN
1	2.25	0.75
2	2.06	0.94
3	2.02	0.98
4	2.00	1.00
5	2.00	1.00
6	2.00	1.00
7	2.00	1.00
8	2.00	1.00

3.X +–4.Y = –1.
2.X + 6.Y =   8.

N	XN	YN
1	–0.33	1.44
2	1.59	0.80
3	0.74	1.09
4	1.12	0.96
5	0.95	1.02
6	1.02	0.99
7	0.99	1.00
8	1.00	1.00

2.X + 6.Y =   8.
3.X +–4.Y = –1.

SYSTEM WILL NOT CONVERGE

Figure 10-13   Gauss–Seidel method.

10-6 Exercises

10-6-1 Self Test

1. Write FORTRAN statements to translate each of the following:

   a. $a = \sin^2 x - \cos^2 x$
   b. $z = e^x - e^{-x}$
   c. $x = \sqrt{|p - q|}$
   d. Find the largest of A, B, C, D and E.
   e. Find the smallest of I, J, K and 3.

2. How could IFIX be used to round to the nearest hundred? to the nearest thousandth? to the next largest integer?

3. What will be the value of each of the following if A = 100. and B = −2.4 and C = 81, D = 0?

   a. SQRT(C)
   b. SQRT(SQRT(C))
   c. IFIX(B)
   d. SIGN(A,B)
   e. SIGN(B,A)
   f. DIM(A,B)
   g. DIM(B,A)
   h. AMIN1(A,B,C,D)
   i. AMAX1(A,B,4.*B,C,D)
   j. ABS(B) + ABS(C)
   k. ALOG10(A)
   l. SIN(D) + COS(D)

4. In the graph of Figure 10-7, what would be the difference if instead of using $J = (\tan x + 9)*4$ to determine the position of the graphic character on the line we used $J = \tan x + 35$. Why do you think it is necessary to have a magnifying factor such as 4 in this case?

5. What statement in the program of Figure 10-7 would you change in order to display the graph of the tangent function in 126 print positions instead of 72?

6. Determine which of the following function subprograms are invalid. Give reasons.

   a. X = MAX(2.1,3.1,4)   FUNCTION MAX(X,Y,Z)
   b. IF(LOW(I,J,K))1,2,3   FUNCTION LOW(K,I,J)
   c. REAL MALL   FUNCTION MALL(X,T)
      X = MALL(X,T)
   d. DIMENSION A(5)   FUNCTION A(I,J,T)
      INTEGER X,S
      Z = A(X,K,3*S)
   e. T = BAD(1,2 + S,3*I)   FUNCTION BAD(I,J,K)

f. M = TUT(SQRT(R),S)	FUNCTION TUT(RT,T)
g. S = MAD(3.,2*S,−1)	FUNCTION MAD(X,Y,K)
h. P = MAT(ABS(K),2,SIN(T))	FUNCTION (X,I,T)
i. S = COT(A,B,COT(3))	FUNCTION COT(X,Y,Z)
j. DIMENSION Q(100)	FUNCTION DAM(T(1),T,J)
T = DAM(Q(1),Q,−4)	DIMENSION T(100)
k. WRITE(3,11)FUNC(1.,2.)	FUNCTION FUNC(X,Y)
l. MIM = SUB(X,2*J,9.8)	FUNCTION(X + K,S)
m. SON = OF(A,GUN)	FUNCTION OF(A,NON)
n. DIMENSION B(5)	FUNCTION TIP(A,B,C)
X = TIP(B(1),X,B(5))	DIMENSION A(5)
o. DIMENSION A(5)	FUNCTION CAN(T,J,3)
Z = CAN(T,3,6/L)	
p. A = PAT(L,M,N)	FUNCTION PAT(N,M,L)
	N = 1
	M = 1
	L = 3
	RETURN
q. S = LARG(2,LARG(3,4))	FUNCTION LARG(I,J)
r. X = COT(X)	FUNCTION COT(X)

7. Which of the following function subprogram declarative statements are incorrect? State the reason in each case.

a. FUNCTION AD(A,B,C + D)   e. FUNCTION A(A,B,C)

b. FUNCTION SORT(X,Y,Z)   f. FUNCTION B(A,C(1))

c. FUNCTION FUNCTION(X)   g. FUNCTION (A,AA,B)

d. FUNCTION SQRT(I)   h. FUNCTION C(A,B,B)

8. Which of the following statement function definition statements are invalid? State reasons.

a. SOME(A(I),B) = A(I)*2

b. SQRT(A,B) = SQRT(A) + SQRT(B)

c. T(Y) = Y**2 + 2
    A(X) = T(X) + 1

d. SQRT(X) = X**0.5

e. ROOT = −B + SQRT(B*B − 4*A*C)
    C(B) = B**2 + FUN

f. LONE(I,J,K) = I*J*K
    L = LONE(1,2,3) + I*J*K

g. HI(1,2,3) = A + 1 + 2 + 3

h. A(L) = L + AL + SIM
    Y = A(K) − AL − SIM

i. ADD(X,Y,Z) = X + Y + Z
    T = ADD(X*Y,T)

j. C(X + 1,A) = (X + 1)*3 + A

k. MIX(K) = LOG(K + 1)
    S = MIX(3.1) + 3

9. Determine whether the following statements are true or false.

a. The mode of a FORTRAN-supplied mathematical function is determined by its arguments.

b. The argument of the ABS function must be real.

c. In-line functions are part of the function libraries.

d. Y = SQRT(3) could mean store the third element of array SQRT into Y if SQRT is dimensioned.

e. The trigonometric-supplied functions are actually function subprograms.

f. The END statement in some cases is not needed in function subprograms.

g. Function subprograms can return only one value to the calling program.

h. The function reference I = STAN(X,Y) is invalid, since I and STAN are not of the same mode.

i. In some cases, function subprograms can be compiled concurrently with the calling program.

j. Since only one value can be returned by a function subprogram, only one RETURN statement is allowed in the subprogram.

k. In the definition of a function subprogram, a dummy argument may not be a subscripted variable name.

l. Array names are permitted as arguments in a function subprogram.

m. Statement functions are compiled independently of the program in which they are used.

n. A statement function can be coded in only one statement.

o. Real arguments used in a reference to a statement function can be subscripted variables.

10. Define one statement function that could be used for all statements 5,6,7,8.

```
5   Y = 3*X**2 + 2*X − 1.
    WRITE(3,1)Y
6   T = I*X**2 + 7*X − TOT
7   S = 3*X**2 − K(2)*X + SIN(T)
    SUM = S + T
8   IF(17*X**2 + MIN1(A,B)*X − SQRT(A))1,2,3
```

11. Same exercise as 10, except that statement 5 is coded as Y = 3*T**2 + 2*T − 1.

12. Write a function to perform the following:

   a. $C^2 = A^2 + B^2 - 2AB \cos(C)$ Length of one side of a triangle.

   b. $A = P(1 + I/J)^{J \cdot T}$ Compound interest: P is fixed.

   c. $A = P(1 + R)^N$ Simple interest: P is fixed.

   d. $1/R = 1/R1 + 1/R2 + 1/R3$ Total resistance.

   e. $Q = .92A(T_i - T_0)/H$ Heat flow: H is fixed.

   f. $e^x = 1 + X + X^2/2! + X^3/3!$

   g. $Y = Be^{-ax} \cos(\sqrt{b^2 - a^2} x - t)$

13. Specify the output obtained by the following two programs:

a.
```
        IMPLICIT INTEGER(A-Z)
        READ(5,7)A,B,C
   7    FORMAT(2I2,I3)
        DO 10 I = 1
        Y = (10 - I)*POL(A,B,C,-I)
   10   WRITE(6,14)Y
   14   FORMAT(1X,I7)
        STOP
        END
        INTEGER FUNCTION POL(A,B,C,X)
        INTEGER A,B,C,X
        POL = A*X**2 + B*X + C
        RETURN
        END
```

Data:
   +2+3−1

b.
```
        IMPLICIT INTEGER(A-Z)
        INTEGER ITEM(3)
        REAL PRICE(3)
        DO 10 I = 1,3
   10   READ(5,11)ITEM(I),PRICE(I)
   11   FORMAT(I4,E4.2)
        READ(5,12)J
   12   FORMAT(I4)
        L = FIND(ITEM,J)
        IF(L.LT.0)GOTO8
        WRITE(6,15)ITEM(L),PRICE(L)
   15   FORMAT(1X,I4,2X,F5.2)
        STOP
   8    WRITE(6,13)J
   13   FORMAT(1X,I4,1X,'COULD
   *       NOT BE FOUND')
        STOP
        END
        INTEGER FUNCTION FIND(A,B)
        INTEGER A(3),B
        FIND = -1
        DO 10 I = 1,3
        IF(A(I).EQ.B) FIND = I
   10   CONTINUE
        RETURN
        END
```

Data:
   11461733
   1172 845
   1166142
   1172

10-6-2 Programming Problems

1. Find the square roots of a group of ten positive real numbers one to a card

(card columns 1–5, with a decimal point punched in the field). Remember there are two roots: a positive and a negative root.

2. Modify the program in Figure 10-1 to produce a table showing the distance traveled by the ship for angles varying from 1° to 45°. How is the program changed if the ship is two miles off shore?

3. You are dealt 13 cards. They are punched on one data card in the following manner: the numbers 01–13 represent the spades from the 2 to the ace; 14–26 represents the hearts from the 2 to the ace; 27–39 diamonds from the 2 to the ace; 40–52 clubs from the 2 to the ace. The 13 numbers are not in order. How many kings are there? Use the MOD library function.

4. The number of different poker hands of five cards which could be dealt from a deck of 52 cards is $\dfrac{52!}{5!(52-5)!}$ (where $52! = 52 \cdot 51 \cdot 50 \cdots 1$). Write a function subprogram to compute the factorial of any positive number and use that function to calculate the above formula.

5. A deck of cards contains an employee name, a number of hours worked and a rate of pay. Write a main program to read the cards and call a function subprogram to compute each employee's pay. Hours in excess of 40 are paid time and a half. The printout should list the employee name, number of hours, rate of pay and pay.

6. A salesman is assigned a commission on the following basis:

Sale	Commission
$ 0.00–$ 500.00	1%
$500.01–$5000.00	5%
over $5000.00	8%

Write a main program to read a sale (one per card) and use a subprogram to compute the commission.

7. Same exercise as 6 with the difference that eight sales are recorded on one card.

8. Write a function subprogram to calculate the difference between the largest and smallest elements of an array of variable length.

9. Write a function subprogram to evaluate a 2 × 2 and a 3 × 3 determinant.

10. Write a function subprogram to evaluate C(N,M) (see Section 10-5-6).

11. The first card in a data deck contains the current date. Each succeeding card contains (among other items) the date of the last time an item was sold, the number of items on hand, the cost per item and the regular selling price. A store plans a sale to try to sell slow-moving items. The purpose of the program is to produce a report showing recommended sale price as follows:

If item has not been sold in last 30 days, discount is 10 percent.
If item has not been sold in last 60 days, discount is 20 percent.
If item has not been sold in last 90 days, discount is 40 percent.

However, any item which has sold in the last 30 days is not to be put on sale. If there is only one (1) of an item left in stock, it is not to be placed on sale no matter when the last date of sale was. The amount of discount allowed is also subject to the following rule: Sale prices may not be lower than cost. Write a subprogram to return the cost of a particular item using a main program to read the data and to produce a finalized report for all items read.

12. You have 50 students. For each student, you have his name and ten test scores. The student is allowed to drop his lowest score to figure his average. Use a subprogram to find the sum of his scores and another subprogram to find his minimum score. Print the student's name and his average. (The sum subprogram should be *general* to allow an array of any dimension.)

13. Write a program to read two sets of data on two cards. The first entry on the first card (card columns 1–2) is N and represents the number of numbers to be read from the first card for the first set of data. These N numbers are punched on one card (3 columns each with 1 implied decimal place) starting in card column 3. N may not exceed 25. The second card is arranged in similar fashion. Write a main program to compute the average of each of the sets of data and then of the combined set of data using a subprogram to compute the average of each set of numbers. The input and output could be visualized as follows:

| 02 | 80 | 60 |
| 04 | 195 | 40 | 60 | 805 |

Four numbers

N = 4
N ⩽ 25

Input

Data set 1
19.5
40.0
60.0
80.5
Average data set 1 is 50.0
Data set 2
80.0
60.0
Average data set 2 is 70.0
Combined average is 56.6

Output

14. Given $ax^2 + bx + c = 0$, the roots (values for x which make the statement true) are found by $\dfrac{-b \pm \sqrt{b^2 - 4ac}}{2a}$. The main program will read values for a, b, c. If a is 0, then there is only one real value for x ($x = -c/b$). If $b^2 - 4ac$ is negative, then there are two complex roots for x. If $b^2 - 4ac$ is positive or

zero, then there are "two" real roots for x as found by the above formula. Write a subprogram that returns a 1 if $a = 0$; returns a 2 if $b^2 - 4ac$ is negative and returns a 3 if $b^2 - 4ac$ is positive or zero. Then, depending on what is returned, write an appropriate message or answer.

15. Write a function to calculate the standard deviation of a set of data items contained in an array of variable length (see Section 6-4-3).

16. Write statement functions for each of the following:

   a. $V = \pi r^3$
   b. $y = ax^3 + bx^2 + cx + d$
   c. $q = x \sin(x) + x^2 \cos(x)$ where x is to be expressed in degrees.
   d. The difference between the largest and smallest values in a list of six real values.

17. Use a statement function to compute the square root of 43, using the formula $x = \dfrac{1}{2}(x + \dfrac{43}{x})$ starting with $x = 1$ until $|x^2 - 43.| < .01$.

18. Input values for a and t. Write a program using statement functions wherever possible to compute x as follows:

   $$\text{if } a > 1, \text{ compute } x = at + t^2 + at + \frac{a}{2} + (a - 1)t^{-1} + \left(a - \frac{1}{2}\right)t^{-2}$$

   $$\text{if } 0 < a \leqslant 1, \text{ compute } x = t^2 + at + \frac{a}{2} + (a - 1)t^{-1} + \left(a - \frac{1}{2}\right)t^{-2}$$

   $$\text{if } a < 0, \text{ compute } x = \log(|a| \cdot t) + t^2 + at + \frac{a}{2} + (a - 1)t^{-1}$$

   $$+ \left(a - \frac{1}{2}\right)t^{-2} + \sin(at)$$

   (These formulas are used to determine the stress coefficient of certain plastics undergoing dilation by heat.)

19. Iterative methods for solving systems of linear equations (illustrated in Figure 10-13) can be terminated in either of the following methods:

   a. When $|x_{n+1} - x_n| < \epsilon$ and $|y_{n+1} - y_n| < \epsilon$ where ϵ is a prescribed degree of accuracy.
   b. When x_n and y_n are substituted back into the equations and the numerical results are within ϵ of the constants on the right-hand side of the original system of equations.

   Write a program using the Gauss–Seidel method to solve a system of equations and use programmer defined functions to terminate the iterative process using both of the above termination criterion. Set $\epsilon = .01$.

20. It can be shown that

$$\sin(x) = x - \frac{x^3}{3!} + \frac{x^5}{5!} - \frac{x^7}{7!} + \cdots$$

where x is expressed in radians. Write a program to calculate values of $\sin(x)$ using the first five terms of the equation for values of x ranging from $0°$ to $90°$ in increments of $10°$. Compare the value you get with the value returned by the FORTRAN function SIN.

21. The number e can be defined as the limit of $\left(\frac{n+1}{n}\right)^n$ as n tends to infinity:

$$e = \lim_{n \to \infty} \left(\frac{n+1}{n}\right)^n$$

Using this definition of e write a program to determine n such that

$$\left|e - \left(\frac{n+1}{n}\right)^n\right| < .001 \qquad \text{Use the function EXP for } e.$$

22. Write a program to show that as n gets larger and larger, the following expressions converge to one limit. Can you guess at the limits from your printouts?

   a. $\dfrac{n^2 + 1}{n + 1}$

   b. $\dfrac{\log(n)}{n}$

   c. $n \cdot \log\left(1 + \dfrac{1}{n}\right)$

23. Write a program to determine the limits of the following expressions as x approaches 0. (Let x range from $1°$ to $.1°$ in steps of $.1°$.)

   a. $\dfrac{\sin(x)}{x}$ d. $\dfrac{x \cdot \sin(x)}{1 - \cos(x)}$

   b. $\dfrac{\tan(x)}{x}$ e. $\dfrac{15t}{\tan(6t)}$

   c. $\dfrac{\tan(2x)}{\sin(7x)}$

   Recall that x must be expressed in radians.

24. Using the exponential function EXP(X) compute EXP(1). The value of e to eight places is 2.71828182. Can you obtain a better approximation than EXP(1) by using the series definition:

$$e^x = 1 + \frac{x}{1!} + \frac{x^2}{2!} + \frac{x^3}{3!} + \cdots + \frac{x^n}{n!} + \cdots$$

How many terms of the series do you need to improve on EXP(1)?

25. The president of the XSTAR Company realizes that the company's present accounting procedures are too slow, too inefficient and not sufficiently accurate to deal with the increasing annual volume of processing of the company. Plans have been made to replace manual accounting operations with a wholly computerized system. The current total manual operating costs in dollars in terms of annual processing volume is given by $y = x + .5$ (where y is the dollar cost and x the annual processing volume). Projected total computerized cost is given by the formula $y = .75x + 2$. The anticipated annual processing volume will be close to four units. Write a program to:

   a. Determine graphically whether the president's decision to switch to a computerized system is economically sound (graph both lines).

   b. Determine graphically the break-even point (the annual volume of processing which would justify the president's plan for changing methods of operation).

   Realizing that an annual volume of processing of four units is not sufficient to warrant such a change in operations, a compromise is effected. The new operational procedures will involve both manual and computer operations. The cost attached to such a new system is given by $y = .445x + 1.5$. Write a program to:

   c. Determine graphically whether such a system would be economically beneficial to the company.

   d. Determine graphically the break-even point for the total computerized system versus the computer manual plan.

26. The Toystar Corporation is marketing a new toy. Expected revenues are approximated by the function $y = 3\sqrt{x}$. Costs associated with the production and the sales of the toy are defined by the function $y = 2 + x^2/4$. Write a program to determine graphically the break-even point for the production of the new toy.

27. Write a program to graph the total profit function of the example in Exercise 26. The total profit function is defined as the difference between the cost and revenue function, that is, $T(x) = |R(x) - C(x)|$, where R, C and T are respectively the revenue, the cost, and the total profit functions. In the case of Exercise 26, identify on the total profit graph the point at which profit is maximum.

28. Sometimes it is helpful to expand or contract a graph. Scale factors are used for this purpose. Rewrite the break-even analysis program of Section 10-4-2 to change both graphs by using the functions

$$y = n \left(15xe^{-x/3} \right) \quad \text{and} \quad y = n \left(\frac{x^3}{16} - \frac{x^2}{2} + \frac{7x}{4} + 4 \right)$$

where n is a scale factor accepted from input. If $n = 1$, the graph should be identical to the one depicted in Figure 10-6. If $n = 10$, the graph should be steeper, and if $n = .5$ the graph should be wider (more elongated). Try various scale factors.

29. Determine graphically the roots of $y = x \sin(x)$ as x varies from 0 to 3π. You may have to use a scale factor. Remember this will not affect the roots.

30. What scale factors could you use on $y = 1/x$ to get a feel for the shape of the graph of that function? Experiment by graphing that function.

31. Write a program to plot a circle. Hint: The equation of a circle of radius r centered on the y axis passing through the origin is given by:

$$(y - r)^2 + x^2 = r^2 \quad \text{or} \quad y = \pm\sqrt{r^2 - x^2} + r$$

Plot both branches by adding .5 to the y positive branch and $-.5$ to the y negative branch. Use $r = 4.5$ initially.

32. Generalize Exercise 31 by accepting the radii from input.

10-6-3 Answers to Self Test

1. a. $A = \text{SIN}(X)**2 - \text{COS}(X)**2$ b. $Z = \text{EXP}(X) - \text{EXP}(-X)$
   c. $X = \text{SQRT}(\text{ABS}(P - Q))$ d. $\text{ALARG} = \text{AMAX1}(A,B,C,D,E)$
   e. $\text{KSMAL} = \text{MIN0}(I,J,K,3)$

2. To round the value in A to the nearest hundred:
   $A = 100*\text{IFIX}((A + 50.)/100.)$.

   To round the value in A to the nearest thousandth:
   $A = \text{IFIX}((A + .005)*1000.)/1000$.

   To round the value in A to the nearest whole number:
   $A = \text{IFIX}(A + .5)$.

3. a. 9.   b. 3.   c. −2   d. −100.   e. 2.4.   f. 102.4.   g. 0.
   h. −2.4.   i. 100.   j. 83.4.   k. 2.   l. 1.

4. The values for tan$x$ for values of x close to 0, π, 2π etc. would appear to fall on a straight line, because the differences among successive values of the function are small in these intervals. The factor 4 is needed to "magnify" the differences so that they are visible on the graph.

5.   DIMENSION LINE(120)
      .
      J=(Y+9)*7+0.5
      .
   5 IF (J−120)6,6,11

6. a. Invalid: 4 and z different mode.   b. Valid.   c. Mode of function must be the same in the calling program and in the function definition.   d. Valid: no reference to a function is made since A is an array in the main program. e. 2 + S and J are mixed modes.   f. Valid.   g. Valid.   h. Function has no name.   i. COT(3) should have three arguments.   j. Invalid: subscripted variable T(1).   k. Function reference cannot occur in I/O statement list.   l. Number of arguments do not agree.   m. GUN, NON different mode.   n. C should be declared as an array in function.   o. Dummy argument must not be a constant.   p. Function is not assigned a value. q. Valid.   r. Valid.

7. a. Dummy argument cannot be an expression.   b. Valid.   c. Function name too long.   d. Valid (user defines own SQRT).   e. Function name and argument cannot be the same.   f. Argument cannot be subscripted variable.   g. Function name is missing.   h. Valid.

8. a. Dimensioned variable cannot be in dummy argument list.   b. Function cannot refer to itself and number of arguments must be the same as in function definition.   c. Valid.   d. Valid.   e. Function definition must precede executable statements.   f. Valid: dummy variables may be used as actual variables in a program.   g. Dummy arguments may not be constants.   h. Valid.   i. Number of arguments in function reference and in function definition does not match.   j. Expression (X + 1) cannot be used as a dummy argument.   k. Mode of actual arguments must match mode of dummy arguments.

9. a. F.   b. T.   c. F.   d. T.   e. T.   f. F.   g. T.   h. F.   i. F. j. F.   k. T.   l. T.   m. F.   n. T.   o. T.

10. FN(L,J,A) = L*X*X + J*X – A

11. FN(L,J,A,Y) = L*Y*Y + J*Y – A

12. a. SIDE(A,B,C) = A*A + B*B + 2.*A*B*COS(C)
     b. A(T,AI,J) = P*(1 + AI/J)**(J*T)
     c. SINT(R,N) = P*(1 + R)**N
     d. R(R1,R2,R3) = 1./R1 + 1./R2 + 1./R3
     e. HF(A,TI,T0) = .92*A*(TI – T0)/H
     f. E(X) = 1. + X + X*X/2. + X**3/6.
     g. F(A,B,ASM,X,T) = A*EXP(–ASM*X)*COS(SQRT(B*B – ASM**2*X) – T)

13. a. 90,112.   b. 1172,8.45.

11

SUBROUTINES

11-1 Problem Example

A deck of cards consists of two subdata decks, each containing grades obtained by two different classes. Each subdeck is identified by a header card specifying the class and the number of students for the particular class. One student grade is punched per card. No class is expected to contain more than 100 students. Write a complete program to determine each class's grade average and the number of grades below the average and provide a listing of grades with appropriate headings. The reading of the data cards must be performed in the main program. One subroutine will take care of all output functions, while another subroutine will calculate the class average and the number of grades less than the average. Both the input and desired output can be visualized as shown on page 401. A program to solve the above problem is shown in Figure 11-1.

In the program of Figure 11-1, note the use of

1. The CALL statement, which is used to call for the execution of a subroutine and to pass parameters (arguments) to the subprogram.

2. The SUBROUTINE statement, which is used to declare that a program is a subroutine.

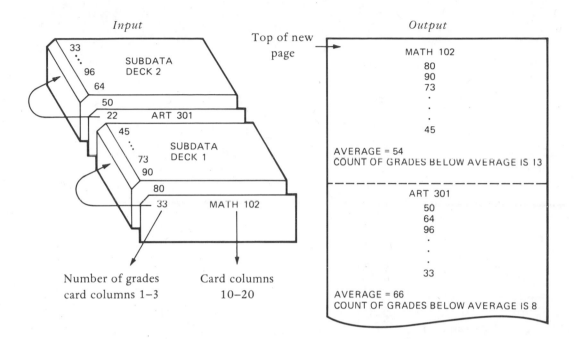

The complete program shown in Figure 11-1 consists of three independent program segments, which perform specific tasks. These program segments are

1. The main program, which coordinates the use of the two subroutines.

2. The AVRGE program, which computes the average of a set of scores and determines the highest score.

3. The PRINT program, which performs all output functions.

All three program segments are compiled independently of one another. Through the CALL statements, information (such as the grade array) is passed from the *calling* program to the *called* program by means of arguments or parameters specified in the CALL statement and also in the SUBROUTINE definition statement. Arguments can be used as two-way or one-way communication links between the calling and the called program. In the PRINT program, all arguments are one way (main program to subroutine); the main program specifies the values of all arguments, and these are not changed in the subroutine. In the case of the AVRGE routine, two arguments, GRADE and N, are used to transmit data to the subroutine, while two other arguments, AV and LOW, are used to transmit results from the subroutine back to the main program. Results between programs are then passed by means of arguments. The flowpath of data between the three blocks of code may be visualized in Figure 11-2.

Note how it is possible, through the use of subroutines, to avoid duplication of code as shown on the right side of Figure 11-2. Whenever a procedure (task) is to be performed, a transfer is made (through the CALL statement) to that pro-

The array HEADER is used to store the different class sections.

No more than 100 students (grades) per class.

Read and process both subdecks.

Read the number of grades, section number and grades one subdeck at a time.

Transfer control to subroutine AVRGE.

GRADE,N,AV,LOW are called *arguments*; they are used in the subroutine to determine the grade average and highest score. In the subroutine, the dummy argument SCORE is used to refer to GRADE (defined in the main program). Both of these variables identify the same memory locations. Similarly L, SUM and LOW1 refer to N,AV and LOW respectively. The average and number of grades below the average are computed in the subroutine in SUM and LOW1, which in effect stores the results in AV and LOW.

Transfer to subroutine PRINT and print N grades with a header (class/ number), the average AV and the count of grades < average. At the conclusion of the PRINT routine, return is made to the main program at the instruction following CALL PRINT.

Subroutine AVRGE will compute the average of L grades stored in an array SCORE and store the result in SUM. The count of grades below the average is stored in LOW1. Initially, LOW1 is set to 0.

The array SCORE is really the array GRADE, which has been read in the main program, and L (or N) is the number of grades to be processed. Note that the subroutine does not change the array SCORE and the variable L, and hence these are not changed in the main program. The

```
      DOUBLE PRECISION HEADER(2)

      INTEGER GRADE(100)

      DO 5 I = 1,2
      READ(1,6)N,HEADER,(GRADE(I),I = 1,N)
6     FORMAT(I2,2X,A6,A5/(I3))

      CALL AVRGE (GRADE,N,AV,LOW)




      CALL PRINT(N,GRADE,HEADER,AV,LOW)


5     CONTINUE


      STOP
      END
```

```
      SUBROUTINE AVRGE(SCORE,L,SUM,LOW1)
      INTEGER SCORE(100)
      SUM = 0.

      LOW1 = 0
      DO 1 I = 1,L
1     SUM = SUM + SCORE(I)
      SUM = SUM/L
      DO 2 I = 1,L
      IF(SCORE(I).LT.SUM)LOW1 = LOW1 + 1
2     CONTINUE
      RETURN
      END
```

Figure 11-1 Main program calling two subroutines.

average and highest score are returned
to the main program in AV and LOW
via SUM and LOW1.

Subroutine PRINT will print a heading
found in H(1) and H(2) on a new page,
with N grades listed vertically. The
average of grades AV and LOW (count
below average) will also be printed.
Note that none of the arguments are
changed in the subroutine (set to any
value).
The array H is another name for the
array HEADER defined in the main
program.

```
        SUBROUTINE PRINT(N,GRADE,H,AV,LOW)
        DOUBLE PRECISION H(2)
        INTEGER GRADE(100)
        WRITE(3,5) H(1),H(2),(GRADE(I),I = 1,N)
    5   FORMAT('1',T48,A6,A5/(T53,I4))
        WRITE(3,6) AV,LOW
    6   FORMAT(T50,'AVERAGE IS',F8.1/
       *T50,'COUNT OF GRADES BELOW AVERAGE IS',I3)
        RETURN
        END
```

Figure 11-1 (cont.)   Main program calling two subroutines.

cedure which, when completed, returns to the program (that called the procedure). In the case of the program in Figure 11-1, instead of writing the code to
determine the average and the count of scores below the average three times, one
block of code is written which is called three times by the main program.

11-2   FORTRAN Statements

11-2-1   Subroutines

A subroutine is an independently compiled block of code sometimes called a *subprogram.* The prefix *sub-* implies that a subroutine is not really a complete program, in the sense that if it were executed all by itself it would not produce
meaningful results. Subroutines are usually written to carry out generalized procedures that are data-independent; for example, sorting or merging of any arrays,
computation of averages for any set of grades etc. Parameters or arguments (sometimes called *dummy arguments*) are used to illustrate the way in which the procedure is to be carried out in the subroutine. These arguments must be specifically
identified by the program wishing to make use of the generalized procedure. The
name of the particular array to be sorted and the exact number of grades for
which an average is to be computed are examples of arguments which might be
passed to a subroutine.

A subroutine should be viewed as one logical component of a total program
that might consist of numerous other logical components (subprograms). A subroutine can be accessed (executed) from another program (main program or other
subprogram) through the use of the CALL statement.

The main differences between the subroutine and function subprograms are

1. The manner in which they are called. A function is called implicitly by using the name of the function; a subroutine is called explicitly by the CALL statement.

2. The method used to return values to the calling program. A function generally returns a single value to the calling program; a subroutine may return any number of values by changing the contents of one or more of the variables that are used as arguments. For example, the subroutine AVRGE in Figure 11-1 returns two values (LOW and AV) to the calling program.

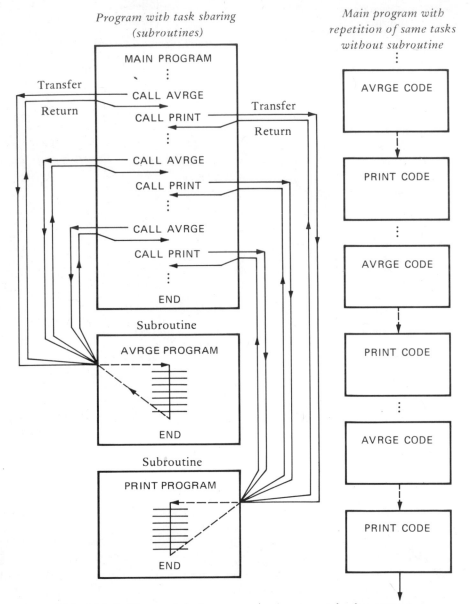

Figure 11-2 Flowpath between a main program and subprograms.

The general form of the CALL statement is

$$\text{CALL}\qquad \text{subroutine-name}\,[(a_1,a_2,a_3,\cdots,a_n)]$$

where CALL is a required key word.

subroutine-name is the name of the subroutine (any valid variable name).

a_1, a_2, $\cdots$, a_n are arguments to be passed to the subroutine. These arguments may be variables, subscripted variables, array names, constants, expressions or function names. Arguments are used to either transmit data from the calling program or to receive data (values, results) from the called program. Arguments are optional.

Examples

CALL SUB(X)	One argument is passed to the subroutine called SUB.
CALL XRAY	No arguments are passed to XRAY.
CALL S1(A,B(1),3*I+K,J)	Four arguments are passed to the subroutine. $3*I + K$ is evaluated and passed to the third argument of S1.
CALL SUB2(SIN(X),Y)	The sine of X will be evaluated and the value passed to SUB3 as the first parameter.

11-2-3   The SUBROUTINE Statement

The SUBROUTINE statement must be the first statement in every subroutine subprogram. The general form of the SUBROUTINE statement is

$$\text{SUBROUTINE}\qquad \text{subroutine-name}\,[(p_1,p_2,p_3,\cdots,p_n)]$$

where SUBROUTINE is a required key word.

subroutine-name is the name of the subroutine (any valid variable name).

$p_1,p_2,p_3,\cdots,p_n$ are dummy arguments used to communicate data to and from the calling program. These arguments can either be variables, array names or function names (no subscripted variable names or constants).

If an argument is an array name, the array name should be declared in a DIMENSION statement within the subroutine. The size of that array should be the same as the size of the corresponding argument (array) in the calling program (see Section 11-5-2 for exceptions). The dummy arguments used in the subroutine refer to the actual names or arguments listed in the invocation statement of the calling program. When the subroutine is executed, the dummy arguments take on the values of the "real" arguments specified in the subroutine CALL in the calling program. More precisely, the subroutine processes directly the real arguments through the dummy arguments.

The arguments in the CALL statement should correspond in number, order and mode with the dummy arguments of the SUBROUTINE statement. The names used may be the same or different. The order of the arguments in the CALL statement and in the SUBROUTINE statement must be the same; that is, there must be a one-to-one correspondence between both sets of arguments.

integer integer

real ↑ real ↑ real

CALL SUB(X , 2 , T , L , 3.5)

One-to-one correspondence between arguments.
Five arguments in calling and called program.
Mode between corresponding arguments preserved.

SUBROUTINE SUB(XX , J , S , K , Z)

real ↓ real ↓ real

integer integer

XX is same as X.
J is same as 2 (J = 2).
S is same as T.
K is same as L.
Z is same as 3.5 (Z = 3.5).

Example 1

Main program	Subprogram	Comments
DATA X,Y/3,4/	SUBROUTINE ADD(A,B,C)	
CALL ADD(X,Y,R)	C = A + B	
WRITE(3,1)R	RETURN	The value of R is 7.
CALL ADD(X,R,Z)	END	
WRITE(3,1)Z		The value of Z is 10.

In the first call to ADD, A, B and C correspond to X, Y, and R respectively.
In the second call to ADD, A, B and C correspond to X, R, and Z respectively.

It should be emphasized again that the subroutine can change values in the main program. Consider the following example:

Example 2

Main Program	Subprogram
	SUBROUTINE TRI(X,C)
.	.
.	.
.	.
A = 4.	X = 7.
CALL TRI(A,B)	C = 3.1
WRITE(3,1)A	RETURN
.	END
.	

A is 4 when the CALL is made to the subroutine; on return to the main program, the value for A will be 7.

The value of any expression in the CALL statement is calculated before passing values of parameters to the subroutine.

Example 3

Main program	*Subprogram*
.	SUBROUTINE(A,B,C)
.	
X = 3.	
Y = 2.	
CALL SUB4(X,X + Y,3.*Y)	

The value of A will be 3.; the value of B will be 5.; the value of C will be 6.

If an array is to be passed to a subroutine, the name of the array is specified in the CALL statement. The array name used in the subroutine must be specified in a DIMENSION statement and its size must equal the size of the corresponding array in the calling program.

Example 4

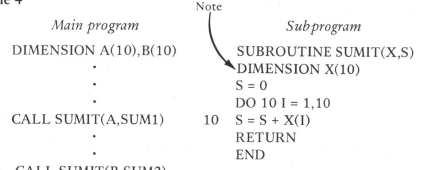

Main program	Note	*Subprogram*
DIMENSION A(10),B(10)		SUBROUTINE SUMIT(X,S)
.		DIMENSION X(10)
.		S = 0
.		DO 10 I = 1,10
CALL SUMIT(A,SUM1)	10	S = S + X(I)
.		RETURN
.		END
CALL SUMIT(B,SUM2)		

Two calls to subroutine SUMIT are made. As a result, SUM1 and SUM2 will contain the sum of the elements of array A and B respectively.

The following are incorrect SUBROUTINE statements:

Main program	*Subprogram*	*Comments*
CALL SUM(A,B,C)	SUBROUTINE SUM(A,B)	Invalid. Two subroutine arguments.
CALL PROD(A,3,N)	SUBROUTINE PROD(X,Y,I)	Y is real; should be integer.
CALL TOT(X,3.1,2)	SUBROUTINE TOT(X,B(1),J)	B(1) not allowed as argument.
CALL SIS(T(3),M)	SUBROUTINE SIS(S,4)	4 is not a variable name.
CALL TW(A + B,C)	SUBROUTINE TW(X + Y,D)	X + Y is an invalid argument.

The RETURN statement returns control to the statement immediately following the CALL statement in the calling program. Many RETURN statements may be included in a subroutine. A distinguishing feature of the subroutine is that at its conclusion the statement to which transfer (return) is made in the calling program is variable (unlike the GO TO statement). The return point depends on the statement at which the subroutine was called. The last statement of a subroutine must always be the END statement.

Since subprograms are really separate programs that are treated independently by the compiler, variable names appearing in both the calling and called program may be identical with no risk of confusion possible; for instance, in the following example the variables HOURS and RATE are used in both the calling and called program but there is no relationship between them. The content of the variable Z is directly related because it is used as a dummy argument and as a real argument.

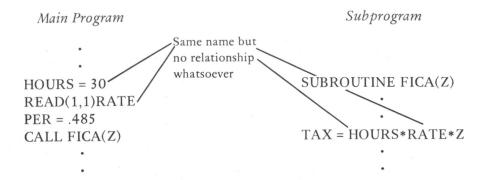

In the same way, duplicate labels are permissible since the programs are compiled independently. For example

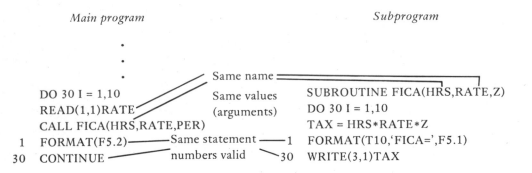

11-2-4   The COMMON Statement

One method that can be used to pass data from one subprogram to another is by specifying each data item (variable) in the argument list of the CALL and SUB-ROUTINE statements. It should be noted that the "dummy variables" (arguments) of the subroutine do not really have a fixed memory address. When a "dummy variable" is encountered in the subroutine, the system must look up the address of the corresponding argument in the calling program and process the contents (value) of that memory location or use it for storage. The "address" of the dummy variable changes depending on the argument in the main program that it represents. For example:

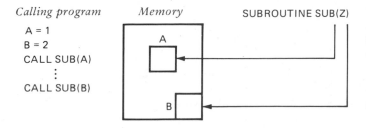

Calling program   *Memory*   SUBROUTINE SUB(Z)

A = 1

B = 2

CALL SUB(A)

⋮

CALL SUB(B)

As a result of the first call to SUB, Z points to the address of A in memory.

As a result of the second call to SUB, Z points to the address of B in memory.

Another method to pass data from one subprogram to another is by means of the COMMON statement. Variables to be shared among subprograms are declared in a COMMON statement. COMMON may be thought of as a block of memory locations which can be accessed (shared) by any programs containing a COMMON statement. The names of variables used to refer to the data in the COMMON block may be different in the various subprograms. It is the ordering of the variables in COMMON which will determine which names in one program will be associated with which names in another program. The use of COMMON in a subprogram offers immediate access to data in memory; there is no "look-up address" procedure as in the case of dummy variables (subroutine arguments), as each variable in COMMON has a predetermined (fixed) memory address:

Example 1

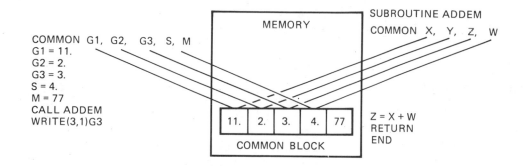

COMMON G1, G2, G3, S, M

G1 = 11.

G2 = 2.

G3 = 3.

S = 4.

M = 77

CALL ADDEM

WRITE(3,1)G3

MEMORY

| 11. | 2. | 3. | 4. | 77 |

COMMON BLOCK

SUBROUTINE ADDEM

COMMON X, Y, Z, W

Z = X + W

RETURN

END

G1 and X identify the first element of the COMMON block, G2 and Y refer to the second element of the COMMON block, G3 and S refer to the third and fourth elements of the COMMON block, just as Z and W do. M refers to the fifth element of the block. The subroutine is adding the first and fourth element of the COMMON block and storing the result in the third location. Hence Z = 11. + 4. = 15. . In the main program the name of the third element of the COMMON block is G3. Hence G3 = 15. Note that M is not shared by the subroutine ADDEM.

Example 2

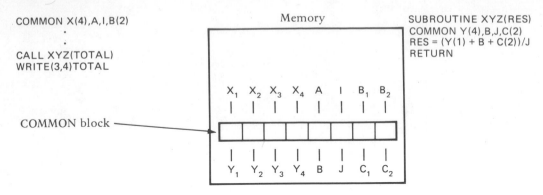

```
COMMON X(4),A,I,B(2)
        .
        .
CALL XYZ(TOTAL)
WRITE(3,4)TOTAL
```

Memory

```
SUBROUTINE XYZ(RES)
COMMON Y(4),B,J,C(2)
RES = (Y(1) + B + C(2))/J
RETURN
```

COMMON block

X_1 X_2 X_3 X_4 A I B_1 B_2

Y_1 Y_2 Y_3 Y_4 B J C_1 C_2

As a result of the WRITE statement in the main program, TOTAL = (X(1) + A + B(2))/I.

Example 3

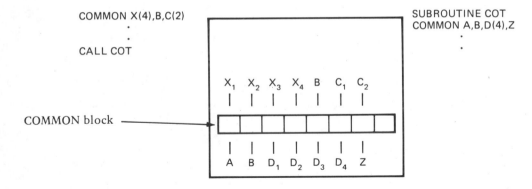

```
COMMON X(4),B,C(2)
        .
        .
CALL COT
```

```
SUBROUTINE COT
COMMON A,B,D(4),Z
        .
        .
```

COMMON block

X_1 X_2 X_3 X_4 B C_1 C_2

A B D_1 D_2 D_3 D_4 Z

Note the correspondence between the variables in COMMON.
The general form of the COMMON statement is

COMMON   list-of-variables

where the list-of-variables can either be variables, array names or subscripted variables.

Arguments transmitted between programs defined in a calling sequence or in a subroutine argument list must not be declared in the COMMON statement.
All the variables in the COMMON list are allocated to the COMMON data storage area.
The COMMON statement may be used in lieu of a DIMENSION statement if desired. The following three coding sequences are identical:

DIMENSION X(100)   REAL X(100)   COMMON X(100)

COMMON X   or   COMMON X   or

However, the following is illegal:

DIMENSION X(100)
COMMON X(100)

COMMON may be used to great advantage when there is a data base which is needed by several subprograms. It is often more convenient to transmit a lengthy sequence of variables to be shared between programs by a COMMON statement rather than as arguments in a calling sequence. A deck of COMMON cards can be duplicated and included in the various subprograms requiring it.

If in a subroutine the programmer wishes to refer to a variable (or change a variable) that is defined in the calling program, he cannot use the same name in the subroutine and hope that it will refer to the variable with identical name in the calling program. The only way to "communicate" variables between programs is either through the COMMON statement or by passing the variable name as an argument in the calling sequence.

11-2-5 Position of Subprograms in the Job Deck

All user-defined function or subroutine subprograms are separate logical entities and as such are compiled independently of one another. The compiler treats each subprogram as a new program in the job deck. Special system control cards (job control, workflow etc.) will physically separate each program from one another as depicted in Figure 11-3. The student should determine the proper control cards required by his computer system.

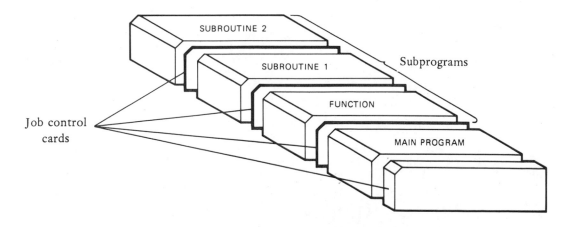

Figure 11-3 Subprogram job make-up.

11-3 You Might Want to Know

1. Why use subroutines?

    Answer: A subroutine can be an aid in writing shorter and more compact programs. The programmer can break his program in smaller logical components that are easier to work with, resulting in a more readable program. A subroutine can result in an economy of code for procedures or tasks that are to be performed repeatedly at different places in a program(s). The code for the procedure is written just once and is not recoded wherever it is needed in the program.

    Subroutines that are to be used frequently should be compiled and tested until thoroughly debugged and thereafter included in the program in object deck form (or stored in a library). This saves computer time, since the subroutine need not be recompiled each time it is to be used. In that perspective, subroutines may be written and shared by users through "share" subprogram libraries. A brief subroutine description and its use (calling sequence) should be included in the listing of the subprogram by means of comment cards.

2. There are no repetitive tasks in most of the programs I write. Are subroutines of any value to me?

    Answer: Perhaps, particularly in long or complex problems. It may be possible to segment the tasks that make up the complete program, write subprograms to perform these tasks and verify that each subprogram executes properly. The complete program can then be constructed using the already written and debugged subprograms.

3. What statements may be used in a subroutine?

    Answer: Any FORTRAN statements except other SUBROUTINE or FUNCTION declarative statements.

4. Is a STOP statement necessary after the RETURN statement?

    Answer: No. Logically the STOP instruction cannot get executed, since RETURN will pass control back to the calling program.

5. If an argument in a CALL statement is just used by the subroutine to pass a particular result to the calling program, need that argument be initialized to a specific value in the calling program?

Answer: No. For example:

> CALL ADD(X,Y,RES)   SUBROUTINE ADD(A,B,RES)
>   RES = A + B

There is no need to initialize RES to any value in the calling program.

6. If I use a DATA statement to initialize a variable in a subroutine, will that variable be reinitialized every time the subroutine is called?

Answer: No. For example:

> CALL TX(Y,3)   SUBROUTINE TX(X,K)
>   •   DATA SUM/0./
>   •   SUM = SUM + K
> CALL TX(Y,4)   RETURN

As a result of the first call to TX, the value of SUM is 3. The second time through TX, SUM will equal 7, not 4. If you need to reset SUM to 0, use the statement SUM = 0.

7. Can a subroutine use a STOP statement?

Answer: Yes. Consider the following example:

> SUBROUTINE QUAD(A,B,C,X,ROOT1,ROOT2)
>   •
>   •
>   •
>
>   DISC = B**2 − 4*A*C
>   IF (DISC) 1,2,1
> 2 WRITE(3,11)
> 11 FORMAT(T20,'ROOTS ARE IMAGINARY')
>   STOP ←
> 1 ROOT1 =   Note the STOP statement.
>   •
>   •
>   •

The practice of using the STOP statement in a subroutine is *not* recommended, as many programmers feel it should be the privilege of the main program to stop execution of the complete program. A flag can be used in the subroutine and tested in the main program if there is cause for immediate termination of the job.

8. Can a subroutine call another subroutine or a function subprogram?

Answer: Yes, as long as the subroutine does not call itself. Nor can a subroutine call a subroutine which calls the original subroutine. You must avoid calling sequences which result in a closed loop, such as

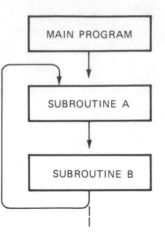

9. How many COMMON statements may be contained in a program?

   Answer: As many as desired. Locations in COMMON are allocated sequentially in the order encountered in the lists of the COMMON statements.

   Example

   COMMON X(4)
   COMMON A,B
   COMMON Z(2)
   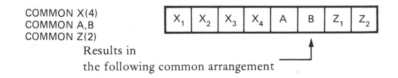
   Results in
   the following common arrangement

10. Is a subroutine permitted to change the value of any parameter?

    Answer: Yes. However, care must be exercised to avoid problems such as shown in the following example:

Main program	*Subprogram*
•	SUBROUTINE SUB(X,N,Y)
•	•
•	•
CALL SUB(A,3,B + C)	N = 6
•	Y = 6
•	•
	•

    Invalid

    The value of the second parameter is changed to 6 by the subroutine; however, the actual parameter is a constant 3. This can have an unpredictable effect in the program. Similarly, the value of the third parameter is changed by the subroutine, but the actual parameter is an expression and not a storage location.

11. Can the COMMON statement be used with function subprograms?

Answer: Yes. It is used in exactly the same way as in subroutine subprograms. Remember that a dummy variable should not be listed in the COMMON statement.

12. FUNCTIONs and SUBROUTINEs seem to have a lot in common. Could I change the value of a parameter in a function subprogram as I can in a subroutine subprogram?

    Answer: Yes, you could write a function to perform the exact same tasks as a subroutine; however, this is contrary to the purposes of a function subprogram. A function is generally used to return a single value to the calling program via the function name. A subroutine should be written when the value of more than one variable is to be changed.

13. Why would I ever want to write a subroutine without arguments such as CALL SUB?

    Answer: Perhaps you might want to write a subroutine just to set up headings for each page of a lengthy computer-generated report or to control the printer for special editing effects, or you might want to use SUB in conjunction with a data set defined in a COMMON statement, to operate directly on that common data.

14. Can a subroutine use arrays that are not declared as arguments or in a common statement?

    Answer: Yes. For example:

    ```
    SUBROUTINE SUB(A,B,K)
    DIMENSION A(100),C(50,10)
    DATA C/500*0/
    ```

    The array C is to be used in the subroutine even though it is not part of the argument list of the subroutine.

11-4 Programming Examples

11-4-1 An Investment Decision

Mr. X. must decide whether to buy a house now at a relatively high interest rate or wait one year and buy at what is anticipated to be a lower interest rate. He is looking at a $30,000 house which he can purchase with 10 percent down and a 30-year mortgage at 8.5 percent. The current rate of inflation for housing is 10 percent per year; thus in one year the house is expected to be worth $33,000. However, the interest rate may decline to 7.5 percent in the next year. Should Mr. X. buy the house now or wait? The program in Figure 11-4 could be used to help make the decision. Note the use of a subroutine to calculate the total cost for each option. The formula to compute the monthly payment is

$$\text{monthly payment} = \frac{\text{principal} \cdot \dfrac{\text{interest}}{12}}{1 - \left(1 + \dfrac{\text{interest}}{12}\right)^{-12 \cdot \text{years}}}$$

```
      REAL I1,I2
      DATA I1,P1,I2,P2/.085,30000.,.075,33000./
      WRITE(6,5)
5     FORMAT(T4,'INTEREST',2X,PRINCIPAL,2X,'MONTHLY PAYMENT',2X,'TOTAL')
      CALL CALC(I1,P1,PAYMT,TOT1)
      WRITE (6,1)I1,P1,PAYMT,TOT1
1     FORMAT(T5,F5.3,T15,F6.0,T29,F6.2,T40,F10.2)
      CALL CALC(I2,P2,PAYMT,TOT2)
      DIF = TOT1 - TOT2
      WRITE (6,1)I2,P2,PAYMT,TOT2
      WRITE (6,2)DIF
2     FORMAT('0THE DIFFERENCE IN TOTAL COST IS',F9.2)
      STOP
      END

      SUBROUTINE CALC(I,P,PAYMT,TOT)
      REAL I,LOAN
      LOAN=.9*P
      PAYMT=LOAN*(I/12./(1.-(1.+I/12.)**(-360.)))
      TOT=PAYMT*360+.1*P
      RETURN
      END
```

INTEREST	PRINCIPAL	MONTHLY PAYMENT	TOTAL
0.085	30000.	207.61	77738.39
0.075	33000.	207.67	78060.02

THE DIFFERENCE IN TOTAL COST IS –321.62

Figure 11-4 Investment decision program.

11-4-2 Solution to a Quadratic Equation

The two solutions to quadratic equations of the form $ax^2 + bx + c = 0$ are given by the formulas

$$x_1 = \frac{-b + \sqrt{b^2 - 4ac}}{2a} \qquad\qquad x_2 = \frac{-b - \sqrt{b^2 - 4ac}}{2a}$$

If $b^2 - 4ac < 0$, then the solutions are complex. The program shown in Figure 11-5 uses a subroutine to solve quadratic equations. If the solution cannot be found, because the roots are complex or because the equation is not a quadratic ($a = 0$), the subroutine sets a flag which can be tested by the main program. Otherwise, the two solutions are calculated.

```
        INTEGER FLAG
100     READ(1,10)A,B,C,LC
        IF(LC−9)1,99,1
        FORMAT(3F10.0,T80,I1)
 10     CALL QUAD(A,B,C,X1,X2,FLAG)
        WRITE(3,11)A,B,C
 11     FORMAT('0A =',F11.0,2X,'B =',F11.0,2X,'C =',F11.0)
        IF(FLAG−1)20,30,20
 20     WRITE(3,13)X1,X2
 13     FORMAT('+',T50,'X1 =',F11.3,2X,'X2 =',F11.3)
        GO TO 100
 30     WRITE(3,12)
 12     FORMAT('+',T50,'NO SOLUTION')
        GO TO 100
 99     STOP
        END

        SUBROUTINE QUAD(A,B,C,X1,X2,FLAG)
        INTEGER FLAG
        FLAG=0
        IF(A)1,20,1
  1     DISC=B**2−4.*A*C
        IF(DISC)30,2,2
  2     X1=(−B+SQRT(DISC))/(2.*A)
        X2=(−B−SQRT(DISC))/(2.*A)
        RETURN
 20     X1=−C/B
        X2=X1
        RETURN
 30     FLAG=1
        RETURN
        END
```

Figure 11-5   Solution of quadratic equations.

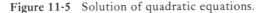

11-4-3   Sort Example

Mr. X. has calculated the final grades for two data-processing classes. He wishes to sort the grades for each class into ascending sequence and also to produce one list with the grades for the two classes merged and sorted into ascending sequence. Since the code for sorting is fairly long and the program needs the sorting procedure performed several times, utilization of a subroutine for sorting is an efficient way to construct the program. Also, since the output of an array is performed several times, the code to produce the output can also be placed in a subroutine. A program using a subroutine to perform the sorting and a subroutine to perform output is shown in Figure 11-6. A header card in the data deck indicates the number of grades of each class. Grades are recorded one per card. Assume there will be no more than 50 students in each class.

```
        DIMENSION GRADE1(50),GRADE2(50),GRADE(100)
        READ(1,1)N1,N2,(GRADE1(I),I=1,N1),(GRADE2(I),I=1,N2)
    1   FORMAT(2I2/(F3.0))
        CALL SORT(GRADE1,N1)
        CALL OUTPUT(GRADE1,N1)
        CALL SORT(GRADE2,N2)
        CALL OUTPUT(GRADE2,N2)
        DO 30 I=1,N1
    30  GRADE(I)=GRADE1(I)
        DO 40 I=1,N2
        J=N1+I
    40  GRADE(J)=GRADE2(I)
        CALL SORT(GRADE,N1+N2)
        CALL OUTPUT(GRADE,N1+N2)
        STOP
        END

        SUBROUTINE SORT(G,N)
        DIMENSION G(100)
        M=N-1
        DO 10 I=1,M
        LIM=N-I
        DO 10 J=1,LIM
        IF(G(J)-G(J+1))10,10,1
    1   Q=G(J)
        G(J)=G(J+1)
        G(J+1)=Q
    10  CONTINUE
        RETURN
        END

        SUBROUTINE OUTPUT(G,N)
        DIMENSION G(100)
        WRITE(3,1)
    1   FORMAT('0DATA SET')
        WRITE(3,2)(G(I),I=1,N)
    2   FORMAT (2X,10F6.0)
        RETURN
        END
```

} Merge grades in one array.

Figure 11-6 Sort program with subroutines.

11-5 Probing Deeper

11-5-1 Flowchart Symbols for Subroutines

The predefined process block ⌷▭⌷ is used to show a branch to a subroutine in a program flowchart. For example, ⌷CALL SUB(X,Y)⌷ could be translated into a FORTRAN program as CALL SUB(X,Y).

The terminal block ⬭ is used in a program flowchart to show the entry point and exit point(s) in a subroutine. The entry point corresponds to the first instruction in the subroutine and could be indicated by placing the name of the subroutine in a begin/end block and a list of the dummy arguments such as

(SUB(X,Y))

An exit point corresponds to the use of the RETURN instruction and would be shown on the program flowchart as ⟨ RETURN ⟩. A complete program flowchart for the program of Figure 11-6 is shown in Figure 11-7.

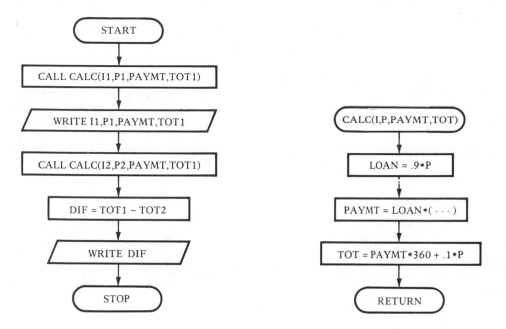

Figure 11-7   Flowchart for investment decision program.

11-5-2   Variable Dimension

Arrays that are passed as arguments from one program to another through the CALLing sequence (or COMMON statements) must be declared as arrays in the subroutine through the DIMENSION statement. If the size of the array to be processed in the subroutine is to be always of the same size as the corresponding array in the main program (or calling program), the size of the subroutine array can be set to the size of the array defined in the calling program. Suppose, for example, we wished to add two arrays A and B of the same size (adding corresponding elements) and store the resulting entries in a third array C. The following code could be used:

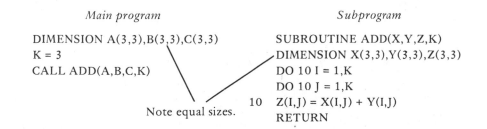

Main program

```
DIMENSION A(3,3),B(3,3),C(3,3)
K = 3
CALL ADD(A,B,C,K)
```

Note equal sizes.

Subprogram

```
SUBROUTINE ADD(X,Y,Z,K)
DIMENSION X(3,3),Y(3,3),Z(3,3)
DO 10 I = 1,K
DO 10 J = 1,K
10   Z(I,J) = X(I,J) + Y(I,J)
RETURN
```

The only drawback to subroutine ADD is that it is coded to add only arrays of size 3 × 3. This restricts somewhat the generality of the subroutine, since it does not permit one to add arrays that are of size 2 × 2, 5 × 5 etc. Consider the following example:

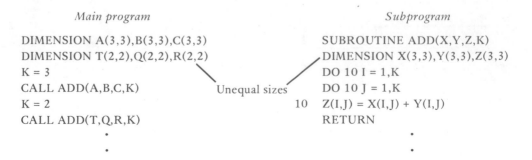

Main program

```
DIMENSION A(3,3),B(3,3),C(3,3)
DIMENSION T(2,2),Q(2,2),R(2,2)
K = 3
CALL ADD(A,B,C,K)
K = 2
CALL ADD(T,Q,R,K)
        .
        .
```

Unequal sizes

Subprogram

```
   SUBROUTINE ADD(X,Y,Z,K)
   DIMENSION X(3,3),Y(3,3),Z(3,3)
   DO 10 I = 1,K
   DO 10 J = 1,K
10 Z(I,J) = X(I,J) + Y(I,J)
   RETURN
        .
        .
```

In the case of arrays A, B, subroutine ADD will add correctly the two arrays and store the resulting array in C. In the case of arrays T and Q, however, the subroutine will add these two arrays *incorrectly*. The reason for this is due to the way the compiler translates a two-dimensional address (row, column) into a one-dimensional (or linear) address. The subroutine array $X(3,3)$ is represented by the compiler as a linear structure of nine elements arranged in column order, as follows:

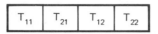

Hence the linear address of X_{22} is 5, since X_{22} is the fifth element of the linear array. Similarly, the address of X_{23} is 8, since X_{23} is the eighth element of the linear array. The array T in the main program, on the other hand, is stored columnwise in linear fashion as

| T_{11} | T_{21} | T_{12} | T_{22} |

T_{12} is the third element of the linear array.
T_{22} is the fourth element of the linear array.

However, because of DIMENSION $X(3,3)$ in the subroutine, the linear addressing scheme used to address array elements X is based on a one-dimensional array of size 3 × 3 = 9. This then means that the subroutine ADD expects the elements T_{11}, T_{21}, T_{12}, T_{22} to be stored linearly in the main program as

 Contents actually not defined in the main program, since T is 2 × 2.

So, as far as the subroutine is concerned, T_{12} is four positions away from the beginning of the array. T_{22} is five positions away from the start of the array.

In the main program, however, the story is different. The fourth element from the beginning of the array is not T_{12}, as the subroutine thinks, but T_{22}. Similarly, the fifth element from the beginning of the array T is not T_{22}, but *garbage*, since the array T in the main program only consists of four elements. Hence the correspondence between elements is ill defined.

One way to correct the problem is to make use of the variable DIMENSION feature (variable DIMENSIONs are not available on all compilers), which allows the user to adjust the size of the array defined in the subroutine to the size of the corresponding array in the main program (calling program). Integer variables in the subroutine DIMENSION statement are used to reflect the varying sizes of the arrays.

For example, the problem of adding corresponding elements of two arrays could have been coded as follows:

Main program	*Subprogram*
DIMENSION A(3,3),B(3,3),C(3,3)	SUBROUTINE ADD(X,Y,Z,M,N)
DIMENSION T(2,2),Q(2,2),R(2,2)	DIMENSION X(M,N),Y(M,N),Z(M,N)
M = 3	DO 10 I = 1,M
N = 3	DO 10 J = 1,N
CALL ADD(A,B,C,M,N)	10 Z(I,J) = X(I,J) + Y(I,J)
.	RETURN
.	END
.	
CALL ADD(T,Q,R,2,2)	

Note that in the program above it is now possible to add arrays that are not necessarily square.

It should be noted that in the case of one-dimensional arrays it is not necessary to use variable DIMENSION, since one-dimensional arrays are addressed linearly. Consider the following valid code:

Main program	*Subprogram*
DIMENSION A(10),B(50),C(200)	SUBROUTINE SUB(X,K)
.	DIMENSION X(1)
.	.
.	.
CALL SUB(A,10)	.
.	
.	
N = 36	
CALL SUB(B,N)	
.	
.	
CALL SUB(C,175)	

Note that the DIMENSION statement in the subroutine could just as well have been DIMENSION X(100), DIMENSION X(10000). The compiler does not reserve memory storage for arrays defined as arguments in subroutines, since storage is already reserved for those arrays in some other subprograms. The DIMENSION statement, however, must be present in the subroutine if any arguments are arrays. This is required for addressing purposes for the compiler. Variable dimension should be used when writing subroutines that process variable size two or more dimensional arrays. Unfortunately, some versions of FORTRAN do not allow for the variable DIMENSION feature. When writing programs for such systems, it is necessary to simulate the procedure used by the compiler in calculating the address of a two- or more-dimensional array element reference.

The formula to compute the linear address of an array element X(I,J) of an array X of size NR rows and NC columns can be computed as follows: Consider the array X:

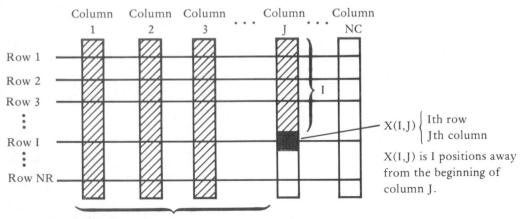

DIMENSION X(NR,NC)

number of rows
number of columns
(NR,NC are supposed to represent integer constants)

Column 1   Column 2   Column 3   · · ·   Column J   · · ·   Column NC

Row 1
Row 2
Row 3
⋮
Row I
⋮
Row NR

I

X(I,J) { Ith row
          Jth column

X(I,J) is I positions away from the beginning of column J.

(J − 1) full columns before we get to column J

Since two-dimensional arrays are stored column-wise in a single-dimensional array, the linear position or address L of the element X(I,J) is (J − 1) full columns from the origin plus I positions down in the Jth column. Since each column consists of NR elements, the linear address L of X(I,J) is

$$L = (J - 1)*NR + I \qquad \text{hence A(L) is equivalent to A(I,J)}$$

Consider the following array A stored in memory as a one-dimensional array.

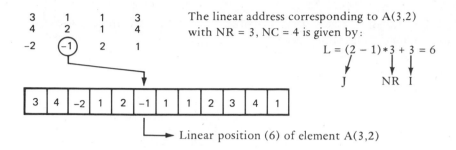

The linear address corresponding to A(3,2) with NR = 3, NC = 4 is given by:

$$L = (2 - 1) * 3 + 3 = 6$$

Linear position (6) of element A(3,2)

Let us now write a subroutine TOT to compute the sum of the elements of any two-dimensional array and return the total in an argument SUM.

Main program	Subprogram
DIMENSION A(3,3),B(17,13)	SUBROUTINE TOT(X,SUM,NR,NC)
•	DIMENSION X(1)
• Note	SUM = 0
• dimension.	DO 10 I = 1,NR
CALL TOT(A,RES1,3,3)	DO 10 J = 1,NC
•	L = (J − 1)*NR + I
• 10	SUM = SUM + X(L)
CALL TOT(B,RES2,17,13)	RETURN
•	
•	

For three-dimensional arrays, the formula used by the compiler to calculate the linear address of an element A(I,J,K) of an array A of NR rows, NC columns and ND depth is given by

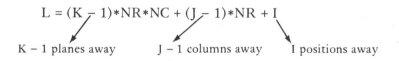

$$L = (K - 1)*NR*NC + (J - 1)*NR + I$$

K − 1 planes away   J − 1 columns away   I positions away

For example, given DIMENSION A(2,3,4), the linear position L of A(1,3,2) is

$$L = (2 - 1)*2*3 + (3 - 1)*2 + 1 = 11$$

Similar formulas can be written for arrays of higher dimensions.

11-5-3 Named COMMON Blocks

Recall that variables located in COMMON are available to any program containing the COMMON statement. In many instances, the number of variables contained in COMMON may be quite large and all subroutines may not require access to all variables. In such cases, it is possible to construct named blocks of COMMON. These named COMMON blocks allow subroutines to access only those COMMON blocks that are needed.

Example

Main program	Subprograms
COMMON/BLK1/X,Y/BLK2/Q,R	SUBROUTINE SUB1
·	COMMON/BLK1/X,Y
·	·
·	·
CALL SUB1	END
·	SUBROUTINE SUB2
·	COMMON/BLK2/Q,R
·	·
CALL SUB2	·

In this example, two blocks of COMMON are defined in the main program. Note that the subroutines do not share any common area with one another; however, each shares a separate common area with the main program.

The general form of the COMMON statement is:

COMMON [/block-name/] list-of-variables [/block-name/] list-of-variables · · ·

where COMMON is a required key word.
        'block-name' is the name of the block COMMON.
        slashes (/) are a required part of the statement.
If the block name is omitted, the variables are placed in unnamed (sometimes called *blank*) COMMON.

Examples

COMMON/XYZ/X(10),Y(100)/ABC/RR(100)
COMMON A,B,C(10)/BLOCK3/Q,R,S

Three blocks of COMMON are named XYZ,ABC and BLOCK3, while blank COMMON contains the variables A,B and ten elements of C.

11-5-4 The EQUIVALENCE Statement

The EQUIVALENCE statement can be used to give more than one name to a memory location. For example, EQUIVALENCE(A,B) causes the variables A and B to have the same address, i.e., any reference to A is equivalent to a reference to B and vice versa. A and B may be thought of as different names for the same memory location. Consider the following example:

```
EQUIVALENCE(A,B)
A = 1.
B = 3.
WRITE(3,11)A    The value written for A will be 3.
```

The general form of the EQUIVALENCE statement is

$$\text{EQUIVALENCE (list-of-variables)} \cdots$$

Here, each variable in the list-of-variables is declared to be equivalent to the others. The variables can be subscripted variable names. The EQUIVALENCE statement must appear after the DIMENSION and COMMON statements but before any executable statements. Any equivalenced variables should be of the same mode.

Example

$$\text{EQUIVALENCE (X,Y),(ZZZ,R,STU)}$$

The variables X and Y share the same memory location. ZZZ, R and STU all refer to the same storage location; they are synonymous names for the same variable.

Arrays, or parts of arrays can be equivalenced by specifying the starting location at which sequential matching between array elements is desired. For example, assume arrays A and B are to be equivalenced:

DIMENSION A(5),B(5)

EQUIVALENCE (A(1),B(1))   yields the pairing $\begin{matrix} A_1 & A_2 & A_3 & A_4 & A_5 \\ B_1 & B_2 & B_3 & B_4 & B_5 \end{matrix}$

EQUIVALENCE (A(3),B(3))   yields the pairing $\begin{matrix} A_3 & A_4 & A_5 \\ B_3 & B_4 & B_5 \end{matrix}$

In this case, separate memory locations are reserved for A_1, A_2 and B_1 and B_2.

EQUIVALENCE (A(2),B(3))   yields the pairing $\begin{matrix} A_2 & A_3 & A_4 \\ B_3 & B_4 & B_5 \end{matrix}$

In this case, A_1, A_5, B_1, B_2 are all assigned separate memory locations. The pairing of elements terminates as soon as an array has reached its DIMENSION size (5 in this case for array B). In the case of two-dimensional arrays, the matching sequence is performed according to the linear memory sequence in which multi-dimensional arrays are represented. For example:

DIMENSION A(2,2),B(3,2) $\quad A_{12} \quad A_{21} \quad A_{12} \quad A_{22}$

EQUIVALENCE (A(2,1),B(3,1)) $B_{11} \quad B_{21} \quad B_{31} \quad B_{12} \quad B_{22} \quad B_{32}$

Hence A_{12}, B_{11}, B_{21}, B_{32} are assigned separate memory locations.

The EQUIVALENCE statement is sometimes used when two or more programmers working independently on program segments have used different names for the same variable. Rather than rewrite the entire program with the same variable names, the EQUIVALENCE statement can be used. Similarly, the EQUIVALENCE statement allows the programmer to reuse arrays that might otherwise be used only once in a program. To reuse the same array for a different purpose and to avoid name confusion, the same array can be given a different name. Consider the following example:

```
DIMENSION A(10,10),AINVER(10,10),TEMP(10,10)
EQUIVALENCE (AINVER(1,1),TEMP(1,1))
    .
    .
    .
WRITE(3,1)AINVER
    .
    .
    .
READ(3,11)TEMP
```

The inverse matrix has now been computed. Write it out. At this point in the program, AINVER is no longer needed.
Let us use it to read in some temperatures. Calling the array AINVER could be misleading, so we call it TEMP.

11-6 Exercises

11-6-1 Self Test

1. What would happen if you tried to execute a subroutine all by itself?

2. List two distinct differences between function and subroutine subprograms.

3. What advantages are there in using subroutines?

4. What are two ways to pass data to a subroutine?

5. Why can't you write the code equivalent to a subroutine in the main program and branch to it whenever you want to execute that code?

6. Would the statement DIMENSION X(N) be valid in a main program? a subroutine? a function subprogram? What restrictions would be placed on X and N?

7. Find the error in each of the following:

Main program	*Subprogram*
a. INTEGER A(10),B(10)	SUBROUTINE SUB(I,J)
.	DIMENSION I(10),J(10)
.	DO 10 K = 1,10
.	10 I(K) = J(K)
CALL SUB(A,3.)	RETURN
.	END
.	

	Main program	Subprogram

b. DIMENSION X(100)

      •
      •
      •

   CALL SUB(X,14.)

```
        SUBROUTINE SUB(A,X)
        DIMENSION A(100)
        X = 0
        DO 3 I = 1,100
3       X = X + A(I)
        RETURN
        END
```

---

c. DIMENSION X(10,10),Y(3,4)

      •

   CALL SUBC(X)

      •

      •

   CALL SUBC(Y)

```
        SUBROUTINE SUBC(A)
        DIMENSION A(10,10)
             •
             •

        RETURN
        END
```

---

d. DIMENSION A(15)

      •
      •
      •

   CALL SUBD(A,B)

      •
      •
      •

```
        SUBROUTINE SUBD(P,Q)
        DIMENSION Q(15)
        DO 10 I = 1,15
10      Q(I) = P
        RETURN
        END
```

---

e. DIMENSION X(3,4)

      •
      •
      •

   CALL SUBE(X)

      •
      •

```
        SUBROUTINE SUBE(X,N,M)
        DIMENSION X(N,M)
             •
             •
             •
```

---

f. DIMENSION X(3,4)

      •
      •

   CALL SUBF(X,3,4)

      •

```
        SUBROUTINE SUBF(X,A,B)
        DIMENSION X(A,B)
             •
             •
             •
```

Main program	*Subprogram*
g. REAL JSUM(10) • • CALL SUB(JSUM,N,3.1) • •	SUBROUTINE (JSUM,K,R) DIMENSION JSUM(1) REAL JSUM • • •

h. DIMENSION A(5),B(5),C(5),E(5,5) COMMON D(3) • • CALL SUB(B,E,3,D) • • •	SUBROUTINE SUB(B,E,K,DD) COMMON DD(3) DIMENSION E(1) • • •

8. Which of the following statements are invalid or false? If incorrect, state the reason.
   a. SUBROUTINE(A,X,Z,3.126)
   b. CALL A(X,Y,Z(JNE))
   c. COMMON A/I,J,K,L
   d. EQUIVALENCE TABLE(100)
   e. SUBROUTINE ANT(X,Y,2.)
   f. COMMON /W/X
   g. ⎰ DIMENSION A(10,10)
 ⎱ EQUIVALENCE/A(5),B(5)/
   h. SUBROUTINE BC(K,L(10),M)
   i. COMMON W/T/
   j. ⎰ DIMENSION A(10),B(10)
 ⎱ EQUIVALENCE (A(5),B(8)),(MSUM,TSUM)
   k. The statement DIMENSION A(10),B(5,5),C(P) is valid in some cases.
   l. Only one RETURN is allowed in a subroutine.
   m. Two-dimensional arrays are stored in memory in column sequence.
   n. The COMMON statement may be placed anywhere in the program before the first executable statement.
   o. It is possible for subroutines to have no arguments.
   p. Arguments in a subroutine argument list may be declared in a COMMON statement.
   q. EQUIVALENCE and COMMON statements really mean the same thing.
   r. Arguments in a calling sequence and in a subroutine must always agree in number and mode.

s. Subroutine names cannot have more than six characters.

t. The EQUIVALENCE statement can be put anywhere before the first executable statement.

u. More than one COMMON statement is allowed per subroutine.

v. If a statement number is the same in a main program and in a subprogram, there will be a syntax error.

w. In a subroutine, the statement END is not necessary, because of the RETURN statement.

x. Subscripted variable names cannot be used in a subroutine declaration statement.

y. At least one RETURN statement should immediately precede the END statement in a subroutine.

z. The French revolution took place in 1791.

9. Determine what the following program does.

```
          INTEGER A(4),B(4),BLOOD(4),TYPE
          COMMON A,B,BLOOD
          DO 10 I=1,4
   10     READ(5,11)A(I),B(I),BLOOD(I)
   11     FORMAT(2A4,2X,A3)
          READ(5,12) TYPE
   12     FORMAT(A3)
          WRITE(6,13) TYPE
   13     FORMAT(1X, 'THESE PEOPLE HAVE BLOOD',2X,A3)
          CALL SEARCH(TYPE)
          STOP
          END
          SUBROUTINE SEARCH(L)
          INTEGER N1(4),N2(4),BLOOD(4),L
          COMMON N1,N2,BLOOD
          DO 10 I=1,4
          IF(BLOOD(I).EQ.L)WRITE(6,19)N1(I),N2(I)
   10     CONTINUE
   19     FORMAT(T3,2A4)
          RETURN
          END
```

Data:

```
MICHELLEₒₒ+Aₒ
MICHAELₒₒₒ+Oₒ
MARCₒₒₒₒₒₒ+AB
ROBERTₒₒₒₒ+Aₒ
+Aₒ
```

11-6-2   Programming Problems

1. A toy store sells 20 different toys. Write a main program to read the costs of toys into a one-dimensional array and

   a. Write a subroutine to print all items over $5.00.

   b. The store decides to run a sale on all its merchandise; everything is reduced to 60 percent. Write a subroutine to output the new prices.

2. Write a subroutine which accepts a one-dimensional array and returns the largest and the smallest element of that array.

3. Write a subroutine which accepts a one-dimensional array and returns the position of the largest and the position of the smallest element.

4. Same as Exercise 2, with a two-dimensional array.

5. Same as Exercise 3, with a two-dimensional array.

6. Rewrite the program of Figure 11-6 without subroutines. Compare the length and the complexity of the two programs. Is there any advantage in using subroutines in this instance?

7. Rewrite the program of Figure 11-1 without arguments for either subroutines.

8. Modify the program of Figure 11-4 to find the break-even point for the future interest rate. How low does the interest rate have to go before it does not matter whether Mr. X. buys now or waits? Also generalize the program to enter a variable interest rate, a house purchase cost and a percentage of house purchase price for down payment.

9. Write and test subroutines to perform the following tasks on two-dimensional arrays.

   a. Set all elements of an array to a constant.

   b. Add corresponding elements of two arrays storing results in a third array.

   c. Multiply each element of an array by a constant.

10. Write a subroutine which accepts a one-dimensional array and reverses the elements of the array.

11. Write a subroutine which accepts any integer and sets a flag to 1 if the integer is a prime number and sets a flag to zero otherwise.

12. Each card of a deck of cards (no more than 50) contains a name (maximum of eight characters). Read the names and corresponding grades in a 50 × 2 double-precision array with names in column 1 and grades in column 2. For example:

K(1,1) ——	MARTIN	30.5	—— K(1,2)
K(2,1) ——	JONATH	96.0	—— K(2,2)
	.	.	
	.	.	
	.	.	

Write a subroutine to sort this data on demand either by name or by grade in ascending fashion and let the main program produce a table of names and corresponding grades.

13. Write a main program to call a subroutine A to compute the real roots of $ax^2 + bx + c = 0$. If $b^2 - 4ac < 0$, subroutine A should call subroutine C to compute the complex roots. In any event, the main program prints out all roots.

14. Write a subroutine to accept a number between 1 and 10 and return a character array(s) spelling out the number; for example, 3 yields THREE.

15. Write a subroutine to accept a number between 20 and 99 and return character arrays which will print the number in letter form. Use two alphabetic arrays to store the words one, two, three, $\cdots$, nine, and the words twenty, thirty, $\cdots$, ninety.

16. Write a subroutine to compute a standard deviation and apply it to solve Exercise 30, Section 6-6-2.

17. Write a subroutine to multiply two arrays (matrices) as illustrated in Exercise 22, Section 9-6-2.

18. Write a subroutine to accept the coordinates of up to 100 ships and determine which two ships are the closest. If (X_1, Y_1) are the coordinates of ship 1 and (X_2, Y_2) are the coordinates of ship 2, then the distance d separating the two ships is given by

$$d = \sqrt{(X_1 - X_2)^2 + (Y_1 - Y_2)^2}$$

19. In a particular class, grades are based on homework, quizzes and tests. For each student, there is a card with his name, eight homework scores, four quiz scores and three test scores. Print out each student's name, homework average, quiz average and test average. To do this, write a *general* subprogram to find the average of an array of real numbers. There are at most 100 students.

20. Given three values, A, B, C on a card. Write a subprogram to determine if they make up the sides of a triangle (the sum of any two is more than the third). If they do, let $K = 1$ and find the area of the triangle where area $= \sqrt{S*(S - A)*(S - B)*(S - C)}$ and $S = .5(A + B + C)$. If the three values do not make up the sides of a triangle, let $K = 0$ and let the area = 0. Then, if they do make up a triangle, write another subprogram to determine if it is a

right triangle—let RIGHT = 1 if it is; let RIGHT = 0 if it is not. The main program should print out appropriate messages and answers.

21. Write a subroutine to update inventory. From the main program, seven cards will have the item number and amount in stock at the beginning of the day. These cards are followed by cards that have the item number, amount shipped out or amount received, and a code with value 1 if the item was received and 2 if the amount was shipped out. These cards are not in any order, and some items may not have been shipped out or received and some items may have had several orders shipped out or received. A blank card indicates the end of these cards. When the inventory has been updated, punch the new inventory on cards, including item number and quantity. (Use the COMMON statement.)

22. On the first card of a deck of cards, we have punched the answers (1, 2, 3, 4) to a multiple choice test of ten questions. On the second card is the number of students (card columns 1–4). On each of the next cards is a student name (eight characters) followed by the student's ten answers to the ten questions. Write a main program to read the data cards, using a subroutine to determine the percentage of correct answers for each student and another subroutine to determine the grade (90–100 = A, 80–89 = B, 60–79 = C and below, a D). The output should be performed by a subroutine to print the student name, the letter grade and percentage. The input and output might be viewed as follows:

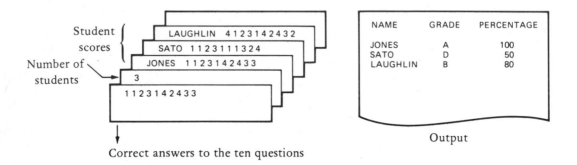

Correct answers to the ten questions

23. LUXURMART is an exclusive clothing store where Luxurmart members are required to maintain $1,000 in their accounts at all times. Members charge all purchases on Luxur credit cards. Write a main program to create a master member file consisting of member names (eight characters maximum) with an initial $1,500 credit for all members. Some members frequently return merchandise which must be credited to their accounts; others may purchase items that cause their credit to fall below $1,000, in which case a message is to be printed requesting the member to write a check for an amount bring-

ing his credit back to $1,000. In some cases, a member name may not be on the master file and an appropriate message should be printed.

Write a subroutine to update each customer's account. Transaction cards contain member names and dollar amounts for credit or debit. The subroutine tells the main program whether a message is to be printed. The main program performs all output functions and should produce an updated member file after all transaction records have been processed. For example, input and output data are shown as follows:

Master file

HOWARD	1500
NIARCO	1500
PELLON	1500
ROCKER	1500

Transaction file

NIARCO	−5
HOWARD	−600
NIARCO	−10
MOCKER	500
PELLON	106

Output

```
**NO MATCHING NAME FOR MOCKER**
−−HOWARD MUST PAY 100 NOW −−

    UPDATED MASTER FILE
    HOWARD    900
    NIARCO    1485
    PELLON    1606
    ROCKER    1500
```

24. Same exercise as above with the following variation: to simplify and minimize transcription errors, tag numbers for items purchased or returned are recorded on transaction cards instead of dollar amounts. A "D" and "C" signify debit and credit respectively. For example:

| HOWARD | 9 D | means debit HOWARD's account by whatever item 9 costs. |
| NIARCO | 10 C | means credit NIARCO's account by the value of item 10. |

Create a table of costs for the different items. For example:

Item tag	Cost
1	44.50
2	100.75
3	
.	
.	
.	
10	46.00

25. The Stayfirm Company accounting system keeps sales records for each salesman on a day-to-day basis. This data is transcribed on data cards as follows:

Salesman	Date of sale	Amount of sale
MONISH	011578	100.00
MONISH	011378	50.00
GLEASON	012778	10.00
MONISH	012778	150.00
GLEASON	012678	190.00
HORN	011378	100.00

Note that the transactions are not arranged alphabetically by salesman name. Also note that the dates are not sorted in ascending order. (Assume dates only cover a 30-day period starting with the first day of the month to the thirtieth day of that month.)

Write a program using a sort subroutine to produce a monthly sales report summarizing total sales and total sales for each salesman. Entries in the report must be listed by salesman name in alphabetical order, and these in turn must be sorted by date of sales. For example, given the above data, the output should be as follows:

Salesman	Date of sales	Sales amount	Total amount
GLEASON	012678	190.00	
	012778	10.00	
			200.00
HORN	011378	100.00	
			100.00
MONISH	011378	50.00	
	011578	100.00	
	012778	150.00	
			300.00
		Total sales	600.00

26. Write a subroutine to multiply any two matrices without making use of the variable dimension feature (use the linear index mechanism).

27. Write a subroutine to compute the trace of a matrix as described in Exercise 27, Section 9-6-2, and use it to compute the inverse in Exercise 28 of Section 9-6-2.

28. Write a subroutine which will accept an integer number and return via an array all permutations of the digits which make up the number. The subroutine should compute the number of digits and return this value also.

Example

Input	321	
Output	NUMBER OF DIGITS	3
	PERMUTATIONS	1 2 3
		1 3 2
		2 1 3
		2 3 1
		3 1 2
		3 2 1

29. Dr. X. has unusual grading practices. He assigns random grades (1–100) to his class of N students (where N is accepted from input). Each student gets three random test scores for three tests. Write a program to compute the average grade of each student and the average of the entire class. The results should be tabulated in page form as follows:

				Page 1
Student	*Score 1*	*Score 2*	*Score 3*	*Average*
#1	20	30	40	30
#2	20	80	20	40
.	.	.	.	.
.	.	.	.	.
.	.	.	.	.
#15	1	0	98	33

1 dotted line   — — — — — — — — — — — — — — — — — — —

2 blank lines ⟶

				Page 2
Student	*Score 1*	*Score 2*	*Score 3*	*Average*

1 blank line ⟶

#16	50	60	70	60
#17	.	.	.	.
.	.	.	.	.
.	.	.	.	.
.				
#30				

2 blank lines ⟶
1 dotted line   — — — — — — — — — — — — — — — — — — —

				Page 3
Student	*Score 1*	*Score 2*	*Score 3*	*Average*
.	.	.	.	.
.	.	.	.	.
.	.	.	.	.

A subroutine should be used to simulate for automatic ejection to the top of a new page, to provide a page number, headings, and a demarcation line. The average class grade should be printed all by itself on a new numbered page. Would you expect the class average grade to be close to 50?

30. Write a program that will read in a bridge hand for each of four players (West, North, East and South in that order). Each hand has 13 cards. Each hand is on its own data card (therefore, there are four data cards). A data card will look like this:

02   14   41   12   42   01   49   48   22   21   13   40   24

Each two-digit number represents one playing card in that player's hand. The numbers 1–13 represent the spades 2–ace (example: 1 represents 2 of spades, 11 represents the queen of spades and 13 represents the ace). The numbers 14–26 represent the hearts 2–ace; the numbers 27–39 the diamonds and 40–52 the clubs (example: 25 represents the king of hearts). These 13 numbers should be stored in an INTEGER array. Call a subroutine SORT to sort the numbers in ascending order (notice that by representing the cards this way, SORT arranges the cards into their separate suits, and puts them in ascending order *within* the suits). Call an INTEGER function ITOTAL to calculate the number of points in this hand. WRITE the name of the hand (West, North, East or South in that order) *in the main program* and then call a subroutine SHOW to write out the contents of the hand and the number of points in the hand as per the instructions and coding form below. Repeat all of above for each hand.

Write a *general* subroutine SORT that will take *any* integer array and return a sorted array in ascending order of the same elements. An example of a call to SORT is

CALL SORT(array, length-of-array)

where both array and length-of-array are INTEGERS.

Write a *general* INTEGER *function* ITOTAL that calculates the number of points in a given hand. This subprogram has two arguments. An example of a call to ITOTAL is

IX = ITOTAL(array, length-of-array)

where both array and length-of-array are INTEGERS.
The points are calculated as follows:

4 pts for each ace
3 pts for each king
2 pts for each queen
1 pt for each jack

(Hint: the MOD function might help in this routine.)

Write a subroutine SHOW with two arguments. The first argument is an INTEGER array of length 13 which contains the sorted cards and the second argument is an INTEGER variable containing the number of points in the hand. An example of a call to SHOW is:

CALL SHOW(array, number-of-points)

Subroutine SHOW prints the contents of the hand passed to it as an argument and prints the number of points in the hand. It prints out the cards by suit and in ascending order within a suit. The order of the suits at printout is spades, hearts, diamonds and then clubs. Print the information according to the sample shown below. Note: The array will have already been sorted into ascending order of spades, hearts etc. by the subroutine SORT; subroutine SHOW is merely a "print" routine.

Print the cards so that an 'A' is printed when an ace is present and a 'K' when there is a king. Likewise a 'Q' for queen and 'J' for jack. Output for sample data card given is shown below:

```
WEST
                SPADES
                2
                3
                K
                A
                HEARTS
                2
                9
                10
                Q
                DIAMONDS
                CLUBS
                2
                3
                4
                10
                J
                NUMBER OF POINTS xx
    NORTH
                    .
                    .
                    .
```

31. a. Store into a three-dimensional array K(9,7,6) the geometric sets representing the digits 1–9 as follows:

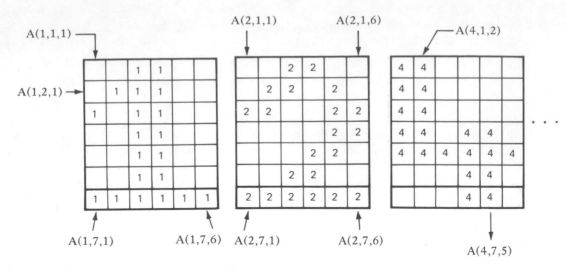

Read a card containing three digits and write a subroutine to display the three digits as a continuous geometric ensemble. For example, if the digits 2, 1, 4 are read, the subroutine should produce the following output:

```
    2 2              1  1         4  4
      2 2    2      1 1 1         4  4
  2 2       2 2   1   1 1         4  4
        2 2                1  1   4  4    4  4
          2 2              1  1   4  4  4 4  4  4
      2 2                  1  1        4  4
  2 2 2 2 2 2    1 1 1 1 1 1           4  4
```

b. (This exercise is for patient artists only.) Represent each letter of the alphabet as a geometric ensemble (as in the above exercise) and write a subroutine to accept a name and print its corresponding geometric symbols as above.

32. If you have access to a conversational computing system, write a program to play tic-tac-toe. The program should allow the user to make the first move, then calculate its next move and so forth. Can you make the program always win? If not, can you design the program so that it can never lose?

33. If you have access to a conversational computing system, write a progam to play blackjack. The program should deal cards from the deck in a randomized fashion. You may choose to start with a new deck for each hand or keep track of all cards dealt until the entire deck has been used. The program should act as the dealer and include routines to evaluate its own hand to

determine whether to deal itself more cards or stand pat. It must also evaluate the player's hand to determine the winner of each hand.

34. a. Write separate subroutines to print each of the following geometric symbols:

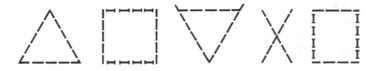

b. Write a main program to generate primitive art artificially (through random generator routine) by vertical spacing of the above geometric symbols in random fashion. For example:

35. Same exercise as 32, except that two symbols must be printed per line.

11-6-3 Answers to Self Test

1. The dummy variables are not initialized properly and might destroy memory; also, the return address is unknown.

2. a. A function generally returns one value; a subroutine returns many values.
   b. A subroutine is invoked by the CALL statement, whereas a function is invoked implicitly in an expression.

3. a. Program segmentation.   b. Utilization of coding segments from program libraries.

4. a. COMMON   b. Argument lists.

5. Return to a variable point (location) using the GO TO statement is not possible.

6. A variable as a size declarator is valid in a subprogram. X and N must be dummy variables.

7. a. Mode of real and dummy arguments must match.
    b. Value of the constant 14. cannot be changed in the subprogram.
    c. Dimension of an array in a subprogram must match dimensions in the calling program (except for one-dimensional arrays).
    d. P should be dimensioned instead of Q.
    e. Number of arguments does not match.
    f. Mode of size declarator in DIMENSION must be integer.
    g. Mode of real and dummy arguments do not match.
    h. A dummy argument may not also be in COMMON (D).

8. a. Subroutine name is missing; also, constant is found in list of dummy arguments.
    b. Valid.   c. Missing "/" at end of variable list.
    d. Improper syntax.   e. Constant in list of dummy arguments.
    f. Improper syntax.   g. Use parentheses instead of slashes.
    h. Dimensioned variable in list of dummy variables.   i. Valid.
    j. Array B should be dimensioned 13.   k. T.
    l. As many RETURN statements as desired can be used, although it is preferable to have one RETURN and many GO TO statements addressing the RETURN statement.
    m. T.   n. T.   o. T.
    p. True, but both methods may not be used in the same subprogram.
    q. F.   r. T.   s. T.   t. T.   u. T.
    v. Statement labels are independent among main programs and subprograms.
    w. The END statement is required at the end of every main program or subprogram.   x. T.   y. F.   z. F (1789).

9. The printout will be as follows:

THESE PEOPLE HAVE BLOOD +A
MICHELLE
ROBERT

FILE PROCESSING

12-1 Introduction

12-1-1   File Concepts

Many applications of computers, particularly in business environments, require the storage and processing of large amounts of data. Typically, there is too much data to store in memory at one time; therefore, external storage for the data is utilized. The very earliest computers used punched cards and magnetic tapes for storage of data. Later computers utilized magnetic disks and drums as external storage devices.

Data is organized into *records* containing related data items. Groups of related records compose a *file.* For example, a personnel file might contain one record for each employee in a company. Each record would be composed of such data items as the employee name, social security number, age, date hired and so on. For convenience in processing, the data items in each record are stored in the same order.

Records within a file are organized in such a way that they can be easily accessed to process the data they contain. One data item is designated as the *record key* and is used as the basis for the file organization. In the example above, the employee social security number might be the record key (see Figure 12-1). The file might then be organized sequentially, randomly or in any one of a num-

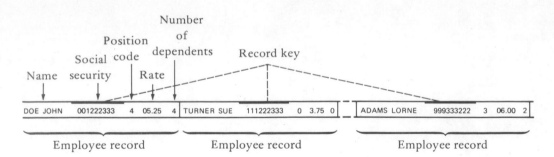

Figure 12-1 Personnel file on magnetic tape.

ber of other schemes. Using sequential organization, records are placed in the file in order by record keys; each record has a record key value larger than that of its predecessor. A file that is organized sequentially is usually processed sequentially; a program processes each record in turn, starting with the first record in the file. Using random organization, records are placed in the external storage device at a location which is calculated from the value of the record key. This organization allows a program to have random access to any specified record within a file without processing other records in the file. This type of file organization is not commonly supported in FORTRAN systems. Direct access file organization offers a compromise between the limitations of sequential and the advantages of random organization. Direct access files are discussed in Section 12-5.

Regardless of the type of file organizations and the device used for storage, certain tasks are commonly performed in a file-processing environment. Initially, the file must be created and stored on the external storage device. Programs may be required to merge the contents of two files, insert records into an existing file, delete records from a file, change data items on individual records in a file and generate reports based on the data contained in the file.

12-1-2 Program Example

Mr. X. wishes to maintain data regarding the number of parts on hand at his company's warehouse. The company has just taken inventory, so the number of parts on hand at the present time is known. This data is entered into the computer system and retained in a file. A short FORTRAN program shown in Figure 12-2 is used to create this file on external storage. The physical device used for storage will vary from one system to another. The device-number used on the WRITE statement will be associated by the operating system with an appropriate file storage device. New features introduced in the program of Figure 11-2 include the END FILE statement, and the unformatted WRITE.

Later, as parts are used from or added to the inventory, it will be necessary to update the data recorded in this file. A second program shown in Figure 12-3

```
      INTEGER PARTN,QTY
C THIS PROGRAM IS USED TO CREATE A PARTS INVENTORY FILE
      WRITE(3,3)
100   READ(1,1,END = 44)PARTN,QTY
      WRITE(7)PARTN,QTY
      WRITE(3,2)PARTN,QTY
      GOTO100
 44   ENDFILE7
      REWIND7
      STOP
  1   FORMAT(I6,I3)
  2   FORMAT(1X,I6,3X,I3)
  3   FORMAT('1PART   #',2X,'QUANTITY')
      END
```

Read a record from the card reader.
Write it on file 7.
Write same record on printer.

```
PART  #    QUANTITY
111111       20
222222        3
333333       25
444444      123
```

Figure 12-2 File creation program.

```
      INTEGER P(100),Q(100),PART,QUANTY
C LOAD CONTENTS OF FILE 7 INTO ARRAYS P AND Q
      DO10N = 1,100
      READ(7,END = 11)P(N),Q(N)
10    CONTINUE
11    N = N – 1
12    READ(1,1,END = 21)PART,QUANTY
14    DO13I = 1,N
      IF(P(I).EQ.PART)GOTO15
13    CONTINUE
      WRITE(3,2)PART
      GOTO12

15    Q(I) = Q(I) + QUANTY
      GOTO12
21    REWIND7
      DO 30 I = 1,N
      WRITE(7)P(I),Q(I)
30    CONTINUE
      ENDFILE7
      REWIND7
      STOP
  1   FORMAT(I6,I3)
  2   FORMAT('0INVALID PART NUMBER',I7)
      END
```

Store into appropriate arrays all part numbers and associated quantities.

N represents the number of records.
Read a change record.

Find a part number in the file which is equal to the part number on the change record. If the part number is not on the file, write the appropriate error message.

Update appropriate quantity.

Reposition file 7.

Rewrite file 7 with updated data.

INVALID PART NUMBER 234567

Figure 12-3 File update program.

could be used for this purpose. New features introduced in this program include the unformatted READ statement and the REWIND statement.

Finally, a program will be required to list the contents of the file for determining how many parts are available, how many should be ordered and so forth. Such a program is shown in Figure 12-4. A system flowchart showing the relationships among these programs is shown in Figure 12-5.

```
      INTEGER PARTN,QTY
      WRITE(3,1)
10    READ(7,END = 99)PARTN,QTY
      WRITE(3,2)PARTN,QTY
      GOTO10
99    REWIND7
      STOP
1     FORMAT('1PART   #',2X,'QUANTITY')
2     FORMAT(1X,I6,3X,I3)
      END
```

PART #	QUANTITY
111111	26
222222	3
333333	25
444444	223

Note change in quantities which resulted from the file update.

Figure 12-4 Listing program.

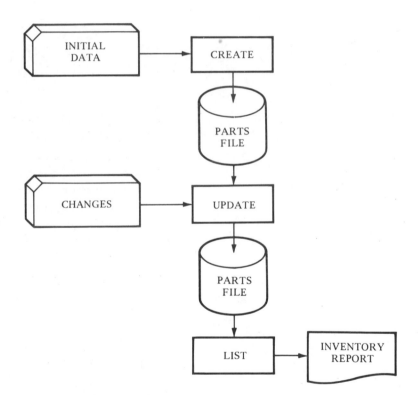

Figure 12-5 System flowchart for inventory system.

12-2 File Processing Statements

12-2-1 Formatted vs Unformatted I/O

If the format statement number is omitted from the READ or WRITE statement, data is read or written without undergoing translation by FORMAT specifications. FORMATs are required to translate data in character form to internal form for input and from internal form to character form for output. Numerical data on data cards is in character form and hence must be translated into internal number representation before it can be processed by the arithmetic unit. The printer requires its data in character form so FORMATs must be used to translate an internal number representation into character form before it can be printed. Data may, however, be stored on devices such as tapes and disks in either internal or character form (see Figure 12-6). The unformatted WRITE statement will write the internal form of the numbers onto the storage medium. Data which has been written out in the internal form on a storage medium does not need to be retranslated when it is read, and hence the unformatted READ statement is used. Using unformatted data whenever possible may save space on the external storage device being used and speed up the processing of data by the program.

Example   READ(7)A,B,K

Three values will be read from a record on device 7. No translation will take place; the data will be assumed to be in internal form.

WRITE(10)X,Y,LL,KK

Four values in internal form will be written on device 10.

12-2-2 The END = Option

The general form of the READ statement with the END = option is

READ (device-number,[format-statement-number,] END = branch-statement-number) variable-list

where branch-statement-number is the number of the statement to be executed when the system end-of-file record is read.

Note that the END = option can be used with either the unformatted or formatted READ statements.

Example
```
         SUM = 0
    1    READ(10,END = 75)A
         SUM = SUM + A
         GOTO1
   75    WRITE(3,11)SUM
```

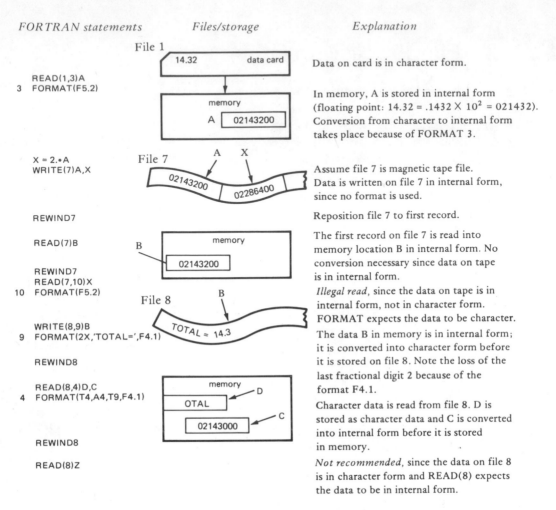

| FORTRAN statements | Files/storage | Explanation |

File 1

14.32   data card — Data on card is in character form.

READ(1,3)A
3 FORMAT(F5.2)

memory
A   02143200

In memory, A is stored in internal form (floating point: $14.32 = .1432 \times 10^2 = 021432$). Conversion from character to internal form takes place because of FORMAT 3.

X = 2.*A
WRITE(7)A,X

File 7   A   X

02143200   02286400

Assume file 7 is magnetic tape file. Data is written on file 7 in internal form, since no format is used.

REWIND7 — Reposition file 7 to first record.

READ(7)B   B

memory

02143200

The first record on file 7 is read into memory location B in internal form. No conversion necessary since data on tape is in internal form.

REWIND7
READ(7,10)X
10 FORMAT(F5.2)

Illegal read, since the data on tape is in internal form, not in character form. FORMAT expects the data to be character.

File 8   B

TOTAL = 14.3

WRITE(8,9)B
9 FORMAT(2X,'TOTAL=',F4.1)

The data B in memory is in internal form; it is converted into character form before it is stored on file 8. Note the loss of the last fractional digit 2 because of the format F4.1.

REWIND8

READ(8,4)D,C
4 FORMAT(T4,A4,T9,F4.1)

memory   D

OTAL

02143000   C

Character data is read from file 8. D is stored as character data and C is converted into internal form before it is stored in memory.

REWIND8

READ(8)Z

Not recommended, since the data on file 8 is in character form and READ(8) expects the data to be in internal form.

Figure 12-6   Formatted vs unformatted READ/WRITE.

The code (p. 445) will cause the entire file to be read on device 10. When the end-of-file record is read, statement 75 will be executed. The END = option is not used when a last record check is incorporated into the logic of the program.

12-2-3   The END FILE Statement

Every file must have a system end-of-file record following the last data record of the file. The END FILE statement is used to write this record when a disk or tape file is being created by a FORTRAN program. The general form of this statement is

END FILE device-number

where device-number is the number associated with the disk or tape file.

Example

```
   1    READ(1,10,END = 100)A,B,C
        SUM = A + B + C
        WRITE(7)A,B,C,SUM
        GOTO1
 100    ENDFILE7
  10    FORMAT(3F5.0)
                .
                .
                .
```

Statement 100 will cause the system end-of-file record to be written on device number 7.

12-2-4   The REWIND Statement

A major advantage of a disk or tape file is that it can be processed repeatedly by a program. The REWIND statement causes the next input operation addressed to a file to return to the program the first record of the file. When the file is on tape, the tape is physically rewound and repositioned so that the first record of the file is available at the next operation. When the file is on disk, the rewinding is logical rather than physical. The result, however, is the same; the first record of the file is the next one available for processing. The general form of the REWIND statement is

REWIND device-number

where   device-number is the number associated with the file to be rewound.

Example

```
                .
                .
                .
 100    ENDFILE7
        REWIND7
   2    READ(7,END = 1000)A,B,C,SUM
        WRITE(3,110)A,B,C,SUM
        GOTO2
1000    STOP
```

After processing of the file on device 7 is terminated, the file is rewound and processed again (statement 2).

12-3 You Might Want to Know

1. Is there any way to get the system to backspace a record in processing a file?

   Answer: Yes. The BACKSPACE statement causes the system to back up one record at a time from the current position of the file. For example, to backspace four records in a file the following code could be used:

   ```
           DO10I = 1,4
   10      BACKSPACE 7
   ```

2. Can a file be used as both an input file and an output file in the same program?

   Answer: Yes. For example, combine the program segments in Sections 12-2-3 and 12-2-4. This program would create a file, rewind it and read it back.

3. Can I skip files if there are more than one on a tape?

   Answer: Yes. For example:

   ```
   10      READ(7,END = 88)DATA
           GOTO10
   88      __
   ```

4. How can I read data from more than one file using one READ statement?

   Answer: Instead of using an integer constant to represent the logical input unit, use an integer variable name, as in

   ```
           GOTO(1,2),K
   1       N = 5
           GOTO7
   2       N = 1
   7       READ(N,8)A,B,C
   ```

5. What is the advantage of using unformatted READ/WRITE statements as opposed to formatted READ/WRITE statements?

   Answer: Time is saved by unformatted READ, since no translation of the data read is necessary. Unformatted WRITE may save space, since less space may be used by the internal form of a data item than the character form.

6. Can I write formatted and unformatted records on the same file? For example:

   ```
           WRITE(7)A
           WRITE(7,4)B
   4       FORMAT(2X,'SUM IS',F4.2)
   ```

   Answer: Yes. See discussion in Section 12-5-2.

12-4 Programming Examples

12-4-1 File Creation

In the following program examples, we shall assume that a file MASTER (device-number 7) has been established, containing payroll data records including identification number, name and hourly wage. The program used to create the file is shown in Figure 12-7; the program used to list the file is shown in Figure 12-8. In both examples, the END = option is used to control the program when end of file is reached; no special last record is needed.

```
C THIS PROGRAM CREATES THE FILE MASTER FROM CARD INPUT
      DIMENSION NAME(5)
  1   READ(1,100,END = 60)ID,NAME,H
      WRITE(7)ID,NAME,H                          Create file 7 in unformatted form.
      GOTO1
  60  ENDFILE7
      REWIND7
      STOP
  100 FORMAT(I9,5A4,F5.2)
      END
```

Figure 12-7 File creation program.

```
C THIS PROGRAM PRODUCES A LISTING OF THE FILE MASTER
      DIMENSION NAME(5)
      WRITE(3,10)
      WRITE(3,11)
  1   READ(7,END = 100)ID,NAME,H          Access to file 7 is made through an
  2   WRITE(3,12)ID,NAME,H                unformatted READ, since this was the way the
      GOTO1                               file was initially created.
  100 WRITE(3,13)
      STOP
  10  FORMAT('1',60('*'))
  11  FORMAT(1X,'ID NUMBER',5X,'NAME',16X,'HOURLY WAGE')
  12  FORMAT(1X,I9,5X,5A4,2X,F7.2)
  13  FORMAT(1X,60('*'))
      END
```

```
***************************************************************
ID NUMBER          NAME              HOURLY WAGE
123456789          DOE JOHN             5.00
222222222          BROWN JIM            2.50
333333333          GREEN MARY           7.25
456789000          SMITH SAM            4.21
***************************************************************
```

Figure 12-8 File-listing program.

12-4-2 Merging

As new employees are hired, it will be necessary to add items to the file MASTER. If no ordering is assumed in the file MASTER, adding records at the end of the file presents no special difficulties. However, in most cases it is advantageous to store a file in ascending order by record key. Note that the sample file listed in Figure 12-8 is sorted into ascending sequence by identification number. We will write a program which will accept new items to be added to the file and then merge the new items with the old items in such a way as to preserve the order of the records in the new file.

Throughout this discussion, it is assumed that there are too many items in the file MASTER to be stored into arrays. If such storage were available, techniques like those used in the program of Section 12-1 would be appropriate. In this program, we will assume that there is sufficient space available in memory for the new items to be added to the file. The program shown in Figure 12-9 will accept new items to be added, store these in arrays and print a listing of each new item. When all new items have been entered, the program will merge the new items with the old and create a file NEW MASTER (device-number 8) containing the new file.

If tapes are being used for file storage, a common procedure would be to store the file MASTER as a backup in case errors are discovered and use the file NEW MASTER in subsequent processing. If disk storage is used, there may not be room to store both the file MASTER and NEW MASTER permanently. In this case, a typical procedure would be to copy the contents of the file MASTER onto tape for backup storage and copy the file NEW MASTER onto MASTER. The file MASTER is used in subsequent processing; the area used by the file NEW MASTER is released for other usage. The program in Figure 12-9 assumes that disk storage is used and that a backup copy of the file MASTER has been produced prior to execution of this program; hence the program copies the contents of NEW MASTER into MASTER.

In the program of Figure 12-9, it is assumed that the new items are in ascending sequence. If this is not the case, a sort algorithm could be used prior to merging the new items. In all file processing, it is important to institute error checks with appropriate messages, to ensure that erroneous data do not enter the system. Note, for example, the checking in the program of Figure 12-9 which ensures that employees with duplicate identification numbers are not allowed to enter the file. If a duplicate identification number appears, a message is written on the report. The new contents of the file MASTER are shown in Figure 12-10.

12-4-3 Report Generation

A second file (HOURS) is to be created containing records in the form:

Identification-number, hours-worked

```
      DIMENSION N ID(100),NEWNAM(100,5),WAGNEW(100)
      DIMENSION NAME(5)
      DO10I = 1,100
      READ(1,100,END = 20)NID(I),(NEWNAM(I,J),J = 1,5),WAGNEW(I)   Store new records into arrays.
10    WRITE(3,102)NID(I),(NEWNAM(I,J),J = 1,5),WAGNEW(I)
20    N = I–1                          N represents the number of items to be added.
      I = 1
21    READ(7,END = 50)ID,NAME,H        Read a record from master file.
23    IF(ID.EQ.NID(I))GOTO33           Check for duplicate identification numbers. If ID on master file
      IF(ID.GT.NID(I))GOTO30           is less than new record ID, then output master file record onto
      WRITE(8)ID,NAME,H                new file.
      GOTO21
30    WRITE(8)NID(I),(NEWNAM(I,J),J = 1,5),WAGNEW(I)        If ID on master file is greater than
22    I = I + 1                        new record ID, then output new record onto new file.
      IF(I.GT.N)GOTO40
      GOTO23                           If all new records have been used, go to 40; otherwise continue
33    WRITE(3,101)ID                   the loop.
      GOTO22                           Write error message.
50    IF(I.GT.N)GOTO60
51    WRITE(8)NID(I),(NEWNAM(I,J),J = 1,5),WAGNEW(I)        Output remainder of new records when
      I = I + 1                        master file has been exhausted.
      GOTO50
40    WRITE(8)ID,NAME,H                Output remainder of master file when all new records have been
      READ(7,END = 60)ID,NAME,H        exhausted.
      GOTO40
60    ENDFILE8
      REWIND8                          New file has been completed.
      REWIND7
61    READ(8,END = 70)ID,NAME,H        Copy new file onto master file.
      WRITE(7)ID,NAME,H
      GOTO61
70    ENDFILE7
      REWIND7
      REWIND8
      STOP
100   FORMAT(I9,5A4,F5.2)
101   FORMAT(2X'DUPLICATE ID',I10)
102   FORMAT(2X,I9,2X,5A4,F7.2)
      END
```

```
100000000      ABLE BAKER          3.00
222222222      BROWN JIM           2.50
555555555      JONES MARK          7.50
DUPLICATE ID   222222222
```

Figure 12-9 File-merging program.

```
*****************************************************************
ID NUMBER       NAME                HOURLY WAGE
100000000       ABLE BAKER              3.00
123456789       DOE JOHN                5.00
222222222       BROWN JIM               2.50
333333333       GREEN MARY              7.25
456789000       SMITH SAM               4.21
555555555       JONES MARK              7.50
*****************************************************************
```

Figure 12-10 New contents of file MASTER.

The program used to create and list the file HOURS is shown in Figure 12-11. Note the use of the REWIND statement to enable processing the file after its creation.

```
C THIS PROGRAM CREATES AND LISTS THE FILE HOURS
    1   READ(1,100,END = 20)ID,HOURS
        WRITE(8)ID,HOURS                        Create the file HOURS on device-number 8.
        GOTO1
   20   ENDFILE8
        REWIND8
        WRITE(3,101)
   21   READ(8,END = 30)ID,HOURS               List the file HOURS.
        WRITE(3,102)ID,HOURS
        GOTO21
   30   WRITE(3,103)
        REWIND8
        STOP
  100   FORMAT(I9,F6.2)
  101   FORMAT('1',40('*')/'0','ID NUMBER',3X,'HOURS WORKED')
  102   FORMAT(1X,I9,5X,F7.2)
  103   FORMAT('0',40('*'))
        END
```

```
****************************************************************
ID NUMBER        HOURS WORKED
123456789            40.00
222222222            53.00
444444444            30.00
456789000            24.00
555555555            50.00
****************************************************************
```

Figure 12-11   Creation of the file hours.

A report is needed which shows the employee's name, identification number, hourly wage, hours-worked and gross pay. The program in Figure 12-12 could be used to generate the required report. It is assumed that there is more data in both files than can be contained in memory; hence items regarding one employee at a time are read from each of the files. When identification-numbers match, a line of the report is written. In this case, there are two end-of-file problems to consider. When end of file is detected in the file HOURS, this signifies the end of the report. When end of file is detected on the file MASTER, however, there may be items left on HOURS which have not been processed. This case is treated as an error condition.

```
C THIS PROGRAM READS THE FILE HOURS AND MASTER AND PRODUCES GROSS PAY REPORT
        DIMENSION NAME(5)
        WRITE(3,100)
    1   READ(7,END = 700)MASTID,NAME,WAGE
    2   READ(8,END = 600)ID,HOURS
    3   IF(MASTID−ID)4,200,4
    4   IF(MASTID−ID)190,190,5
    5   WRITE(3,101)ID
        GOTO2
  190   READ(7,END = 500)MASTID,NAME,WAGE
        GOTO3
  200   PAY = HOURS*WAGE
        WRITE(3,102)ID,NAME,WAGE,HOURS,PAY
        GOTO1
  500   WRITE(3,101)ID
        READ(8,END = 600)ID,HOURS
        GOTO500
  700   READ(8,END = 600)ID,HOURS
        WRITE(3,101)ID
        GOTO700
  600   WRITE(3,103)
        REWIND7
        REWIND8
        STOP
  100   FORMAT('1',70('*')/2X,'ID NUMBER',3X,'NAME',17X,'HOURLY WAGE',
       #5X,'HOURS',5X,'PAY')
  101   FORMAT(2X,'NO MATCHING RECORD ID NUMBER',I10)
  102   FORMAT(2X,I9,3X,5A4,2X,F7.2,6X,F7.2,2X,F8.2)
  103   FORMAT(1X,70('*'))
        END
```

Read a record on MASTER file.

Read a record on HOURS file.

If ID's are equal, go to 200.

If MASTER ID is greater than HOURS ID, write error message.

Read new record on MASTER file if MASTER ID is less than HOURS ID.

Compute pay and write report line when MASTER ID is equal to hours ID.

If end is reached on MASTER, current hours record and remaining HOURS records are in error.

If end is reached on MASTER, remaining HOURS records are in error.

```
*********************************************************************************
ID NUMBER        NAME                 HOURLY WAGE        HOURS       PAY
123456789        DOE JOHN                 5.00           40.00       200.00
222222222        BROWN JIM                2.50           53.00       132.50
NO MATCHING RECORD ID NUMBER 444444444
456789000        SMITH SAM                4.21           24.00       101.04
555555555        JONES MARK               7.50           50.00       375.00
*********************************************************************************
```

Figure 12-12 Gross pay report.

12-5 Direct Access Files

12-5-1 Definition

Records contained on a direct access file may be accessed by specifying a number which is associated with each record. The number corresponds to the position of the record in the file—a program can access the fifth record, the tenth record etc. without processing any other records in the file. Hence, records are accessed directly; any record in the file may be read or written at will.

Associated with each direct access file is an integer variable called the *cursor.* The cursor points to the record in the file which is available for processing without repositioning of the file. Each read or write operation on a direct access file causes the cursor to point to the record immediately following the one just processed. Direct access files may be created in formatted form, unformatted form or a mixture of the two. The number of records and the size of each record must be specified in the program.

There may be additional operating system considerations in setting up a direct access file. The reader must consult locally available references for further details.

12-5-2 The DEFINE FILE Statement

The DEFINE FILE statement is a specification statement which is used to specify certain parameters for a direct access file. The general form of the statement is

DEFINE FILE device-number (length, size, mode, cursor) [, · · ·]

where   device-number is the number associated with the file and used as a device-number in all READ/WRITE statements for the file.
length is the maximum number of records to be stored on the file.
size is the size of each record.
mode is either E, U or L specifying whether records are stored in formatted form (E), unformatted form (U) or a mixture of the two forms (L).
cursor is an integer variable which will be associated with the file to point to the next available record. After any READ/WRITE operation, the value of the cursor variable is automatically set by the system to the record number of the next record in the file.

The specifications for length and size must be unsigned integer constants. When the mode is E (formatted) or L (mixed), size specifies the number of characters in a record; when the mode is U (unformatted), size specifies the number of words in a record.

Examples

DEFINE FILE 8(1000,4,U,KPOINT)

The file on device-number 8 will contain 1,000 records. Records will be written and read without format control. Each record will be four words long. (A record of length four words would ordinarily accommodate four variables unless double precision variables are used.) The variable KPOINT is associated with the file:

DEFINE FILE 9(5000,60,E,N9),10(1050,70,L,N10)

The files on device-numbers 9 and 10 are declared to be direct access files. File 9 records will be in formatted form; file 10 records may be in either formatted or unformatted form. File 9 records are 60 characters in length; file 10 records are 70 characters in length.

12-5-3 Direct Access READ and WRITE

Direct access files must be processed with special direct access READ and WRITE statements. The general form of the direct access READ and WRITE statements is

    READ(device-number'record-number[,format-statement-number])list-of-variables
    WRITE(device-number'record-number[,format-statement-number])list-of-variables

where device-number is the number of the device associated with the file.
    record-number is an integer expression specifying the position of the record on the file.
    list-of-variables is a list of the variables to be read/written.

Examples

$$READ(8'14)A,B,C$$

This statement will read the variables A,B,C from the fourteenth record of a direct access file on device-number 8.

$$K = 132$$
$$READ(9'K,16)P,Q,R$$

Record 132 will be read from a direct access file on device-number 9.

$$L = 14$$
$$K = 2$$
$$READ(10'L*K + 2)X,Y$$

The value of the expression $L*K + 2 = 14*2 + 2 = 30$ specifies which record of the file is to be read.

$$WRITE(8'95)A,B,C$$

The values of A,B and C will be written in unformatted form onto record 95 of the file on device-number 8.

$$K = 97$$
$$WRITE(9'K,160)P,Q,R$$

The values of P,Q,R as interpreted by format statement 160 will be the 97th record on the file on device-number 9.

12-5-4 Program Example

Direct access files are very convenient to use when a direct correspondence can be set up between the record key and the position of the record in the file. For example, suppose we must create a file to store payroll data for a small company with employee identification numbers ranging from 001 to 999. The employee identification number can be used to point to the position of the record in the file (see the program in Figure 12-13). The program could be used to create the file or add records to the file. Compare this program to the merging program for sequential files in Figure 12-9. Note in the program of Figure 12-13 that the cursor associated with file 8 is K8, but the program uses the variable ID to determine the record to be written. Although the system automatically sets the value of K8 after each READ or WRITE, the program may use any integer variable to specify the record to be accessed in the file.

At first glance, it would seem to be superfluous to write the value of the ID into the record, since the position of the record corresponds to the value of ID. However, suppose we now wish to list the contents of the file. The file contains 1,000 records, although some (or many) may not be used. (The contents of unused records is dependent on the operating system.) One way to test for unused records is to compare the position of the record with the contents of ID when the record is read. If they are equal, the record is in use; if they are not equal, the record is not used. This approach is used in the program of Figure 12-14. Note that no sorting of records is required to produce a sequentially stored file.

```
C THIS PROGRAM CREATES A DIRECT ACCESS FILE
      DIMENSION NAME(5)
      DEFINE FILE8(1000,6,U,K8)
  1   READ(1,100,END = 20)ID,NAME,RATE
      WRITE(8'ID)ID,NAME,RATE              The value in ID.
      GOTO1
 20   STOP
100   FORMAT(I3,5A4,F5.2)
      END
```

Figure 12-13   Direct access file creation.

```
C THIS PROGRAM LISTS A DIRECT ACCESS FILE
      DIMENSION NAME(5)
      DEFINE FILE8(1000,6,U,K8)
      DO10I = 1,1000
      READ(8'I)ID,NAME,RATE
      IF(I−ID)10,11,10
 11   WRITE(3,100)ID,NAME,RATE
 10   CONTINUE
      STOP
100   FORMAT(2X,I3,2X,5A4,2X,F7.2)
      END
```

```
100   ABLE BAKER              3.00
123   DOE JOHN               5.00
222   BROWN JIM              2.50
333   GREEN MARY             7.25
456   SMITH SAM              4.21
555   JONES MARK             7.50
```

Figure 12-14   Direct access file listing.

The cursor could be used to read the entire file, since it always points to the next sequentially numbered record in the file. The program in Figure 12-14 could be rewritten as shown in Figure 12-15. Note that after the READ operation the value of the cursor is one larger than the position of the record just read, since it is incremented automatically as a part of the READ statement execution.

Suppose that we now wish to produce a gross pay report based on an input file containing records with employee identification and hours worked. As each hourly record is read, the associated record from the direct access file is read and the data from the two records is used to produce a line on the report. Compare the logic used in the program of Figure 12-16 with that required to process sequential files (see Figure 12-12). Again note the fact that the ID must equal the record position; otherwise, the record is an unused record.

```
C THIS PROGRAM USES THE CURSOR TO LIST A DIRECT ACCESS FILE
      DIMENSION NAME(5)
      DEFINE FILE8(1000,6,U,K8)
      K8 = 1
   1  READ(8'K8)ID,NAME,RATE
      IF(ID.NE.K8 –1)GOTO11
      WRITE(3,100)ID,NAME,RATE
  11  IF(K8.LE.1000)GOTO1
      STOP
 100  FORMAT(2X,I3,2X,5A4,2X,F7.2)
      END
```

Since K8 is incremented automatically after each READ, the value of the ID just read should be K8 − 1 if the record contains valid data.

Figure 12-15   Use of cursor in direct access file listing.

```
C THIS PROGRAM PRODUCES A GROSS PAY REPORT
C FROM A DIRECT ACCESS FILE
      DIMENSION NAME(5)
      DEFINE FILE8(1000,6,U,K8)
   1  READ(1,100,END = 20)NUM,HOURS
      READ(8'NUM)ID,NAME,RATE
      IF(ID.NE.NUM)GOTO10
      PAY = HOURS*RATE
      WRITE(3,101)ID,NAME,RATE,HOURS,PAY
      GOTO1
  10  WRITE(3,102)NUM
      GOTO1
  20  STOP
 100  FORMAT(I3,F6.2)
 101  FORMAT(2X,I3,2X,5A4,2X,F7.2,2X,F8.2)
 102  FORMAT(2X,'NO MATCHING RECORD FOR EMPLOYEE',I4)
      END
```

Read data from record number NUM. If valid data is not contained on this record, write error message.

Figure 12-16   Gross pay report.

12-5-5 System Flowcharts

The flowchart technique has also been applied to describe the relationship among programs and file in a data-processing system. In a computing system various devices may be used to store a file. In a system flowchart, different symbols (blocks) are used to represent files stored on these devices (see Figure 12-17).

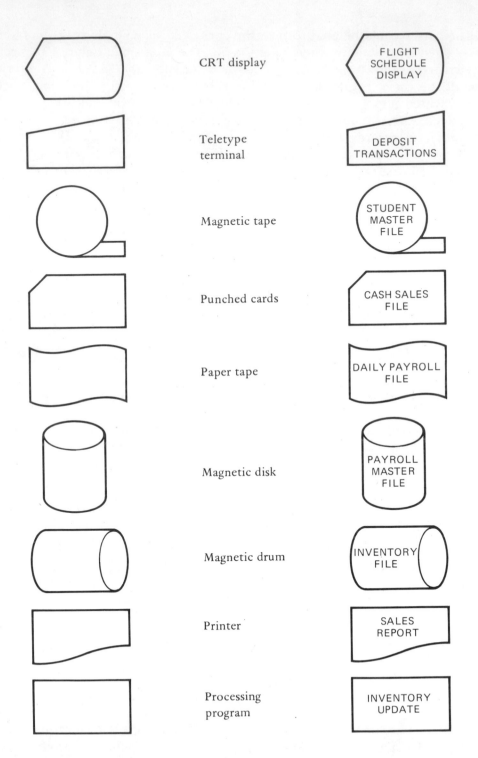

Figure 12-17 System flowchart symbols and examples.

Inside the block, the type of data contained in the file is identified. A processing step is symbolized by use of a rectangle. Within the rectangle, the name of a processing program is printed.

The flow of data from files to processing programs and from programs to files is symbolized by flowlines such as

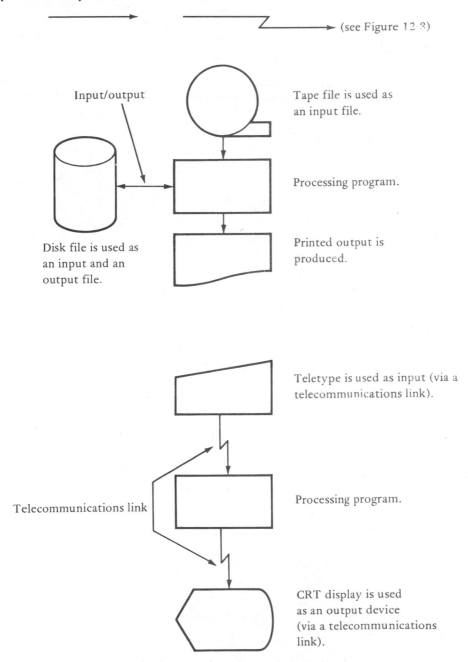

(see Figure 12-8)

Input/output

Tape file is used as an input file.

Processing program.

Disk file is used as an input and an output file.

Printed output is produced.

Teletype is used as input (via a telecommunications link).

Telecommunications link

Processing program.

CRT display is used as an output device (via a telecommunications link).

Figure 12-18   System flowchart flowlines.

If the head of the flowline points away from the file and toward a processing block, the file is an input file for the program. If the head of the flowline points away from the processing block and toward a file, the file is being produced as output from the program. A file may be used for both input and output by a program; in this case, a double-headed flowline such as ⟷ is used.

If no telecommunications link is used between the CPU and the input/output device used for the file, a straight flowline is used. If telecommunications is used, a flowline such as

may be used to signify that telephone lines (or other link) are being used to transmit data. For example, the system flowchart is Figure 12-19 illustrates a data-processing system in which two programs are used to produce paychecks. The DAILY PAYROLL UPDATE PROGRAM is used daily to record the time worked by each employee from the DAILY TIMECARDS input file. This data is recorded on records in the PAYROLL MASTER FILE. Periodically, this file is used as input for the PAYCHECK PROGRAM which actually produces CHECKS.

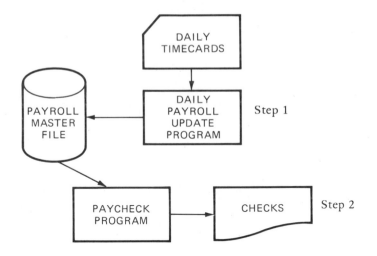

Figure 12-19 A simple payroll system.

The system flowchart in Figure 12-20 illustrates a typical system in which the FORTRAN programming system accepts FORTRAN statements from a Teletype terminal and transmits results to the same terminal. In many systems, the programming system is capable of storing the user's statements on a disk file for later recall and execution. In this case, the disk file is used for both input and output. Such systems may also be capable of processing several users on a time-sharing basis. See Figure 12-21 for a system flowchart of such a system.

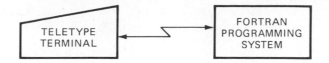

Figure 12-20   A simple telecommunications system.

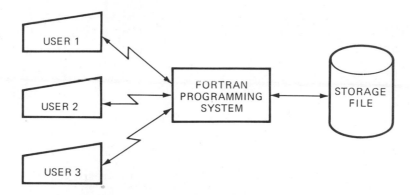

Figure 12-21   A more complex system.

12-6   Exercises

12-6-1   Self Test

1. What purpose is served by each of the following features of FORTRAN?
    a. The END = option
    b. The END FILE statement
    c. The REWIND statement
    d. The BACKSPACE statement

2. What is the difference between formatted and unformatted processing of data?

3. What is a record key? Why is it important?

4. Differentiate among the following: data item, data record, data file.

5. What are the disadvantages of sequential access to data? Are there advantages?

12-6-2   Programming Problems

1. Write a program to perform addition of records, deletion of records and changing of existing records for the inventory file discussed in Section 12- Use a code on the input record to indicate the action to be performed. F example, you might use 1 for addition, 2 for deletion and 3 for change.

2. In the example of Figure 12-9, suppose the new items are not in sorted sequence. Add logic to perform the sort.

3. Write a program to delete items from the file MASTER discussed in Section 12-4.

4. Write a program to process changes in name and hourly wage for the file MASTER discussed in Section 12-4.

5. Rewrite the program of Section 8-4-3 using a file to store the students' names and grades.

6. Write programs for the Widget Manufacturing Company's sales information system. A sales file is to be created with records in the following format:

   salesman-number, amount-of-sale

   A master file must also be created with records in the format:

   salesman-number, name, amount-of-sales-to-date

   Programs are needed to
   a. Create the files.
   b. Update the master file from data in the sales file.
   c. Produce a report showing each salesman's totals to date.

7. Dr. X. teaches an introduction to computers course to 15 students. Three equally weighted tests are given in the course. A file is created for the class; each record consists of a student name followed by the student's grade. Records are sorted by name in alphabetical order. Each time a test is given, the file is updated to reflect the total score (sum of grades) obtained by each student so far. At the end of the semester, Dr. X. computes the average of the three scores and assigns letter grades as follows:

90 and above	A
80–89	B
70–79	C
60–69	D
Below 60	F

   a. Write a program to create a class file for Dr. X. Initially, the students' scores are all zero.
   b. Simulate three sets of test scores for the 15 students; update the class file three times.
   c. Produce a listing of names with their corresponding averages and letter grades.

    d. Write a program to input a student's name and print out that student's total test score so far.

8. In Exercise 7 above, make necessary changes to the student's record and to the program to allow for the following message to be printed out when assigning the letter grade for each student: "Cannot determine student's final grade. Student did not take all three tests."

9. A bank maintains its accounts master file with items in the following format:

account-number, name, present-balance

Checks must be processed against the master file. Write a program which accepts information about checks to be processed as input and updates the master file. Note that checks will be presented in any order so that some sorting will be required before updating the file. Also note that more than one check may be processed against an account. What type of error conditions may be encountered? If your system supports random access binary files, this problem may be greatly simplified.

10. Rewrite the airline reservation problem of Exercise 6, Section 9-6-2b to allow maintenance of passenger reservation information in files.

11. The Grand Order of Beavers bills its members for dues on a monthly basis. The Vice-Exalted Flat Tail has been performing this task by hand, but since a computer system has become available he feels that the billing could be made more efficient using a computerized system. Design and implement a system to maintain membership rolls and produce bills and associated reports. Payments should be processed in small batches as they are received. Include a feature for dropping a member if his dues are in arrears by three months or more.

12. Consider the program examples of Section 12-5-4. Suppose the identification number is nine digits rather than three digits in length. Will the same approach still be practical? Can you think of a solution to the problem?

13. Modify the program of Exercise 6 above to use direct access files. Make an appropriate assumption about the salesman number field.

14. Modify the programs for Exercise 7 above to use direct access files. Add an appropriate student number field.

15. Modify the program for Exercise 9 above to use direct access files. Make an appropriate assumption about the account number field.

12-6-3 Answers to Self Test

1. a. The END = option allows automatic branching when the end-of-file record is read.

    b. The END FILE statement causes an end-of-file record to be written.

    c. The REWIND statement causes a file to be repositioned so that the first record in the file is available for processing.

    d. The BACKSPACE statement causes the repositioning of a file one record backwards.

2. Unformatted processing of data works with data in its internal form; formatted processing of data causes translation of data between internal and external forms.

3. A record key is a field in a record. It is important because it is used to retrieve data from a file.

4. A data file is a collection of data records. A data record is composed of data items.

5. Sequential access to data requires that each record in a file be processed (read) to obtain any record from the file. It is the only file access method available on certain devices (e.g., tape). There is less overhead involved in accessing a sequential file than in using other methods.

STRUCTURED PROGRAMMING

13-1 Introduction

Structured programming has become a very important concept in the art of program design. Structured programming originated in the observation that the unrestricted use of the GO TO statement results in programs which are difficult to follow, difficult to debug and even more difficult to modify. It has been shown that programs which are developed using structured programming concepts prohibiting or restricting the use of the GO TO are less likely to contain logical errors, are developed more rapidly and are easier to maintain than programs using traditional developmental methods.

Some programming languages have a sufficiently rich repertoire of constructs to permit the writing of programs without the GO TO statement. FORTRAN is not one of these languages. It is possible, however, to make use of the ideas of structured programming and to implement them in FORTRAN using the GO TO only where necessary.

Structured programming makes use of *top-down* program design. At each stage in the development process, a program is described as a sequence of one or more tasks. Each task may then be respecified as a sequence of tasks describing what is to be done at a slightly higher level of detail. Finally, when all tasks have been specified in sufficient detail, the program can be coded in a programming language.

The language used to develop programs written in this manner is sometimes called *pseudo code*. A program written in pseudo code is a description of the procedures (tasks) which must be carried out. Tasks are executed sequentially unless the program makes use of certain structured constructs as IF THEN ELSE, DO WHILE, DO UNTIL or SELECT.[1] (Note that GO TO is not included in the above list.) These constructs are not yet a part of the FORTRAN language, but they may be implemented in FORTRAN in a very straightforward manner. A program written in structured pseudo code may be read from beginning to end like a book or essay. There are no jumps or GO TOs to interrupt the logical flow of the statement of the algorithm.

13-2   Structured Programming

13-2-1   Pseudo Code

When writing a program in pseudo code, a *task* is defined as any procedure which can be logically considered as a whole. It does not matter that the FORTRAN implementation of the task may require one statement or one hundred statements. We shall follow the convention of expressing tasks in lowercase characters while reserving uppercase characters for structured constructs. The following are examples of tasks:

> compute pay
> process transaction record
> update master file record
> initialize counters
> increment appropriate counter
> interchange x and y
> x = 0
> $y = x^2 + 3$

Note that these tasks may actually be quite simple or very complex when the final coding is written.

A *process* is defined to be a logically related set of tasks. A program is a process, but any logically related set of tasks within a program may also be referred to as a *process*. Top-down program design may be viewed as the repeated redefinition of processes, with each redefinition yielding tasks that are more detailed than those given at the preceding level.

---

[1] Top-down program development and program design without GO TO statements are logically two separate ideas; however, both are utilized by most practitioners of structured programming. These two concepts form the major theme of this chapter.

Example

Initial specification of a process	*First redefinition as a sequence of tasks*
write paycheck for employee	read employee data record
	compute pay
	write check

The top-down method of program development is illustrated in the above example. The initial specification of the process "write paycheck for employee" is rewritten as a set of more detailed tasks. Any process which is not a sequentially executable set of tasks must make use of one or more of the following constructs: IF THEN ELSE, DO WHILE, DO UNTIL and SELECT.

13-2-2   IF THEN ELSE

The construct IF THEN ELSE is used to test for a condition and take appropriate action. It has the general form

IF condition THEN process 1 ELSE process 2

If the condition is true, process 1 is performed; if the condition is false, process 2 is performed. After either of the two processes is performed, the task following the IF THEN ELSE statement is performed (see Figure 13-1).

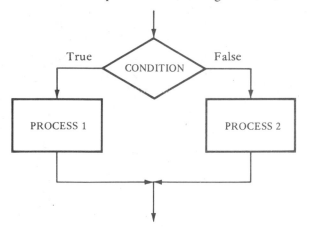

Figure 13-1   IF THEN ELSE flowchart form.

Examples

IF sex is male THEN add 1 to counter for males
                    ELSE add 1 to counter for females
IF number is greater than 60 THEN add number to accumulator
                                 write number
                    ELSE write error message

Note that the process performed in the THEN or ELSE parts may consist of one task or several tasks.

Example

First redefinition

read employee data record
— compute pay
write check

The task "compute pay" is respecified using the IF THEN ELSE construct.

Second redefinition

read employee data record
→ IF hours worked ≤ 40 THEN compute regular pay
                           ELSE compute pay for 40 hours
                                  compute overtime pay
                                  add overtime pay to regular pay

write check

The flowchart equivalent of IF condition THEN process 1 ELSE process 2 is shown in Figure 13-1.

In FORTRAN, the GO TO statement is required for implementation of the IF THEN ELSE construct as follows:

```
     IF (condition) GO TO s1
     process 2
     GO TO s2
s1   process 1
       .
       .
       .
s2   _____
```

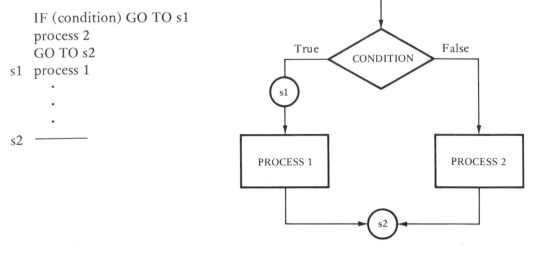

Pseudo code may be included as comments within the FORTRAN program.

Example 1

Pseudo code — Condition

                                               process 1
IF sex is male THEN add 1 to counter for males ←   process 2
             ELSE add 1 to counter for females

FORTRAN Code

```
C   IF SEX IS MALE THEN ADD 1 TO COUNTER FOR MALES
C                    ELSE ADD 1 TO COUNTER FOR FEMALES
C
            IF(SEX.EQ.1)GOTO30
            NF = NF + 1
            GOTO40
        30  NM = NM + 1
        40     .
                .
                .
```

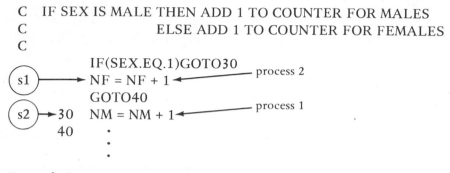

Example 2

Pseudo code

read employee data record
IF hours worked ≤ 40 THEN compute regular pay
                    ELSE compute pay for 40 hours
                        compute overtime pay
                        add overtime pay to regular pay
write check

FORTRAN code

```
C   READ EMPLOYEE DATA RECORD
C
            READ(1,10)NUM,HRS,RATE
C
C   IF HOURS WORKED < = 10 THEN COMPUTE REGULAR PAY
C                            ELSE COMPUTE PAY FOR 40 HOURS
C                                COMPUTE OVERTIME PAY
C                                ADD OVERTIME PAY TO REGULAR
C                                PAY
C
        IF(HRS.LE.40)GOTO300
        REGPAY = 40.*RATE
        OTPAY = (HRS − 40.)*RATE*1.5
        REGPAY = REGPAY + OTPAY
        GOTO500
    300 REGPAY = HRS*RATE
C
C   WRITE CHECK
C
    500 WRITE(3,11)· · ·
                .
                .
                .
```

13-2-3 DO WHILE

The DO WHILE construct enables a program to perform a process while a condition is true. The condition is tested *before* execution of the process. The general form of the construct is

DO WHILE condition
process

The execution of the construct may be shown in flowchart form as in Figure 13-2.

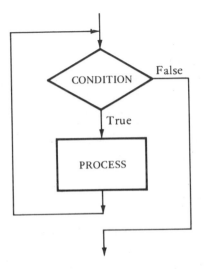

Figure 13-2   DO WHILE flowchart form.

Example

count = 0
DO WHILE count < 100
process a data record
increment count

The above pseudo code describes a procedure for processing 100 data records. The process performed in a DO WHILE construct must modify the condition which will be used to terminate execution of the process; otherwise, an endless loop will be created.

Example

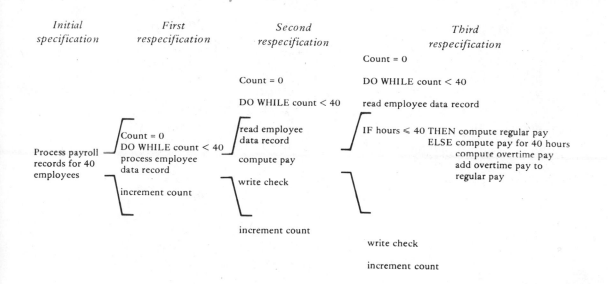

| Initial specification | First respecification | Second respecification | Third respecification |

Third respecification:

Count = 0

DO WHILE count < 40

read employee data record

IF hours ≤ 40 THEN compute regular pay
ELSE compute pay for 40 hours
compute overtime pay
add overtime pay to
regular pay

write check

increment count

Second respecification:

Count = 0

DO WHILE count < 40

read employee data record

compute pay

write check

increment count

First respecification:

Count = 0
DO WHILE count < 40
process employee data record

increment count

Initial specification:

Process payroll records for 40 employees

The above example illustrates top-down refinement of a payroll problem. The DO WHILE construct may be implemented in FORTRAN by

```
s1   IF(.NOT.condition)GOTO s2
     process
     GOTOs1
s2      .
        .
        .
```

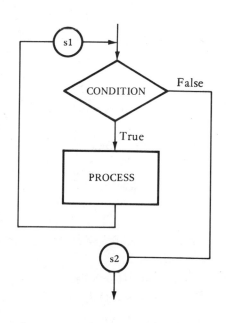

Example 1

Initial specification

Calculate and print the sum of ten
elements of an array

FORTRAN code

```
      DIMENSION ARRAY(10)
           .
           .
           .
```

Respecification

```
sum = 0                              SUM = 0
count = 1                            KOUNT = 1
DO WHILE count ≤ 10            C
        sum = sum + array(count)  C   DO WHILE KOUNT < = 10
        count = count + 1         C
                                  2    IF(.NOT.KOUNT.LE.10)GOTO3
print sum                              SUM = SUM + ARRAY(KOUNT)
                                       KOUNT = KOUNT + 1
                                       GOTO2
                                  3    WRITE(3,5)SUM
```

Example 2

Initial specification

```
read n                               READ(1,1)N
calculate n!                         KFACT = 1
print result                         K = 2
```

FORTRAN code

Respecification

```
                                  C
                                  C   DO WHILE K < = N
read n                            C
fact = 1                          50   IF(.NOT.K.LE.N)GOTO60
count = 2                              KFACT = KFACT*K
DO WHILE count ≤ n                     K = K + 1
        fact = fact*count              GOTO50
        count = count + 1
print fact                        60   WRITE(3,5)KFACT
```

Note that in the above example the fact that the test is made before execution
of the procedure ensures that the value of 1! and 0! is one.

13-2-4 DO UNTIL

The DO UNTIL construct enables a program to perform a process until a certain
condition is true. The condition is tested *after* execution of the process. The
general form of the DO UNTIL construct is

$$\text{DO UNTIL condition}$$
$$\text{process}$$

The execution of the construct may be illustrated in Figure 13-3. When the condition is met, the repetition of the process is terminated.

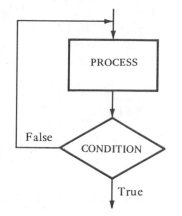

Figure 13-3   DO UNTIL flowchart form.

Example 2

Initial process specification

process payroll file to produce checks

First respecification

DO UNTIL end of file
        read payroll file

Example 1

Initial process specification

find record for employee number 123

Respecification

DO UNTIL employee number = 123
        read employee file

Second specification

        DO UNTIL end of file
            read payroll file

        IF end of file THEN exit
            ELSE process data record

In the example above, the test for end of file is required so that the end-of-file record is not processed as a data record. The task "exit" is used when there are no other tasks to be performed in a process. It can be implemented in FORTRAN by the CONTINUE statement. (There may be several ways to formulate a program using the structured programming constructs.) The above program could be restated as

> read payroll file
> DO WHILE not end of file
> > process data record
> > read payroll file

In FORTRAN, the construct

> DO UNTIL condition
> > process

may be coded as

> s1   process
> IF(.NOT.condition)GO TO s1

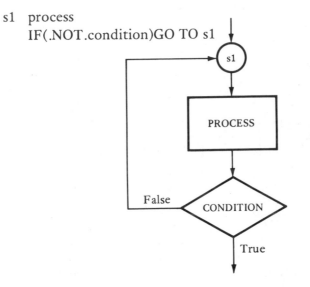

Example 3

Pseudo code

```
count = 1
DO UNTIL count > 10
         read data record
         count = count + 1
```

FORTRAN code

```
      KOUNT = 1
C
C   DO UNTIL KOUNT > 10
C
   16    READ(1,1)X,Y,Z
         KOUNT = KOUNT + 1
         IF(.NOT.KOUNT.GT.10)GOTO16
```

When counting is used for loop control, the FORTRAN DO statement offers an acceptable implementation of the DO UNTIL construct. The above example could be coded as

$$DO\ 16\ K = 1,10$$
$$16\quad READ(1,1)X,Y,Z$$

When other techniques are used for loop control, the FORTRAN DO statement is not satisfactory and the programmer must resort to the general FORTRAN implementation.

Example 4

Initial process specification

find the first integer value of $x < 11$ such that $x^2 - 2x - 3 < 0$

Respecification

```
x = 11
DO UNTIL y < 0
          x = x - 1
          y = x² - 2x - 3
```

FORTRAN code

```
      X = 11.
C
C   DO UNTIL Y < 0
C
   20   X = X - 1.
        Y = X**2 - 2.*X - 3.
        IF(.NOT.Y.LE.0)GOTO20
```

Example 5

Initial specification

find largest value in an array

Respecification

```
large = array(1)
count = 2
DO UNTIL count > 10
          IF array (count) > large THEN large = array(count)
                              ELSE exit
          count = count + 1
```

FORTRAN code

```
      ALARG = ARRAY(1)
      KOUNT = 2
C
C   DO UNTIL KOUNT > 10
C
  10  IF(ARRAY(KOUNT).GT.ALARG)ALARG = ARRAY(KOUNT)
      KOUNT = KOUNT + 1
      IF(.NOT.KOUNT.GT.10)GOTO10
```

Since counting is used for loop control, the example above could be recorded using the DO statement.

13-2-5 SELECT

The SELECT construct is used to select an appropriate action based on a set of mutually exclusive conditions. A flowchart form of the SELECT construct is shown in Figure 13-4.

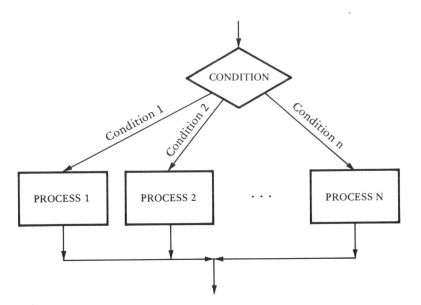

Figure 13-4 Select flowchart form.

For example, suppose we wish to tabulate the number of persons who are single (S), married (M), widowed (W), or divorced (D). Using the IF THEN ELSE construct, the process could be written as

IF single THEN s = s + 1
      ELSE IF married THEN m = m + 1
            ELSE IF widowed THEN w = w + 1
                  ELSE IF divorced THEN d = d + 1
                        ELSE write error

Although this approach is certainly correct, mutually exclusive conditions are found frequently enough to warrant the inclusion of the SELECT construct to describe this logic. The general form of the construct is

SELECT CASE condition 1
        process 1
    CASE condition 2
        process 2
        .
        .
        .
    CASE condition n
        process n

The process corresponding to whichever condition is true will be executed. The above example could be described using the SELECT construct by

SELECT CASE single
        s = s + 1
    CASE married
        m = m + 1
    CASE widow
        w = w + 1
    CASE divorced
        d = d + 1
    CASE other
        write error message

One of the CASEs will be true, and the appropriate action will be taken.
    In FORTRAN, the SELECT construct may be implemented as follows:

```
                        IF(condition 1) GO TO s1
                        IF(condition 2) GO TO s2
                                 ·
                                 ·
                                 ·
                        IF(condition n) GO TO sn
              s1    process 1
                    GO TO s
              s2    process 2
                    GO TO s
                                 ·
                                 ·
                                 ·
              sn    process n
              s          ·
                         ·
                         ·
```

Example

Pseudo code

```
SELECT CASE deposit
            balance = balance + amount
        CASE withdrawal
            balance = balance − amount
            IF overdrawn THEN write appropriate message
                        ELSE exit
```

FORTRAN code

```
C   SELECT CASE
C
        IF(KODE.EQ.1)GOTO10
        IF(KODE.EQ.2)GOTO20
C
C   DEPOSIT
C
   10   BAL = BAL + AMT
        GOTO30
C
C   WITHDRAWAL
C
   20   BAL = BAL − AMT
        IF(BAL.LT.0)WRITE(3,100)BAL,AMT
   30      ·
           ·
           ·
```

In some instances, when the variable being used to differentiate among cases assumes values 1,2,3 · · · , the computed GOTO can be utilized to implement the CASE statement. For example, the above code could be replaced by

```
        GOTO(10,20),KODE
10      BAL = BAL + AMT
        GOTO30
20      BAL = BAL - AMT
        IF(BAL.LT.0)WRITE(3,100)BAL,AMT
30          .
            .
            .
```

13-3   You Might Want to Know

1. What languages are better than FORTRAN for implementing structured programs?

    Answer: Any block structured language such as
    COBOL (*CO*mmon *B*usiness *O*riented *L*anguage)
    ALGOL (*ALGO*rithmic *L*anguage)
    PL/I (*P*rogramming *L*anguage *I*)
    APL (*A P*rogramming *L*anguage)

    These languages have features which closely resemble the IF THEN ELSE and DO WHILE or DO UNTIL constructs.

2. I believe I can write simpler programs traditionally than those generated by translating pseudo code into FORTRAN. What good is this approach to me?

    Answer: In some instances, it may be possible to write more compact code using the traditional approach. The value of structured programming is seen most clearly in the development of large programs. The top-down approach enables the identification of relatively independent program modules (processes). Such modules may be coded and tested separately. The use of structured constructs imposes a discipline on programmers enabling the separately constructed modules to fit together without mutual interference. A team working on a programming project can be assigned separate modules. Errors can also be traced more easily than in a traditional setting where the flowpath may be very circuitous and difficult to follow. Note, for example, that in the implementations of each of the constructs, all GO TOs are quite local in scope—the target is contained within the process being implemented. There is no chance that a GO TO statement in one module will cause an erroneous branch into another module.

3. But I don't work on large programming projects! What good is structured programming to me?

Answer: Pseudo code serves as documentation for the program. Since pseudo code is written in a compact and straightforward manner, it is easy to understand and easy to change in the event changes are necessary. Pseudo code may be written at a relatively high level with many details of implementation omitted. Such a program statement is a very effective way to communicate the essential elements of an algorithm to others. It also sharpens the ability of the programmer to think logically, by breaking down a problem into distinct processes.

4. I am still not convinced. Is there any evidence that structured programming does what you say?

Answer: Yes. Top-down program design together with the use of structured constructs in program implementation have resulted in significant decreases in program development time and cost and in an increase in program dependability in a number of software design projects in business and industry. Pseudo code has become the standard way for expressing algorithms in computer science publications. Although structured programming is only a few years old, it has gained wide acceptance among computer users.

5. The FORTRAN implementation of structured constructs requires the use of the GO TO following one or more process implementations. These processes may be quite lengthy. Doesn't this wide separation of the GO TO statement and its target make the "structured" program as difficult to follow and debug as the nonstructured?

Answer: Yes. The solution is to implement lengthy processes with subprograms. In this way, the main program can be kept compact enough to retain visibility of its structure.

6. Is there any chance that FORTRAN will be enhanced to enable easier implementation of structured programs?

Answer: Such enhancements are being tried experimentally at many universities and research institutions. They have not as yet been incorporated into standard FORTRAN. Whether they will be in the future is unknown as of now.

13-4 Programming Examples

13-4-1 File Merging

Write a program in pseudo code to merge the contents of two sequential files (FILE 1 and FILE 2) containing records in ascending sequence. The program shown in Figure 13-5 could be used. Note the two independent processes present in this program. These processes could be coded separately if desired.

```
read file 1 record
read file 2 record
DO UNTIL end of file 1 or end of file 2
            IF record key 1 < record key 2 THEN write file 1 record on output file
                                                 read file 1 record
                                            ELSE write file 2 record on output file
                                                 read file 2 record
SELECT CASE end of file 1
            DO UNTIL end of file 2
                  write file 2 record on output file
                  read file 2 record
        CASE end of file 2
            DO UNTIL end of file 1
                  write file 1 record on output file
                  read file 1 record
```

Figure 13-5   File-merging program.

13-4-2 Sorting

Write a program in pseudo code to sort n elements of an array into ascending sequence using the sort algorithm described in Section 8-4-4. The program in Figure 13-2 could be used. Note how compact and straightforward the program is when expressed in pseudo code.

```
k = n
DO WHILE k > 1
        j = 1
        DO WHILE j < k
                IF array(j) > array(j + 1) THEN interchange array(j) and array(j + 1)
                                           ELSE exit
                j = j + 1
        k = k - 1
```

Figure 13-6   Sort program.

13-5 Exercises

13-5-1 Self Test

1. Write FORTRAN code for each of the following:
    a. IF a < b THEN x = x + 1
              ELSE y = y + 1

b. IF $s < t$ THEN write s,t
          ELSE IF $s > t$ THEN write t,s
               ELSE write s

c. a = 1
   x = 0
   DO WHILE $a \leqslant 10$
          x = x + a
          a = a + 1

d. DO UNTIL end of file
        read a,b,c
        IF not end of file THEN write a,b,c
                  ELSE exit

e. a = 1
   x = 0
   DO UNTIL $a > 10$
          x = x + a
          a = a + 1

f. c1 = 0
   c2 = 0
   c3 = 0
   SELECT CASE $x < 10$
          c1 = c1 + 1
       CASE x = 10
          c2 = c2 + 1
       CASE $x > 10$
          c3 = c3 + 1

g. n = 0
   z = 0
   p = 0
   DO UNTIL end of file
        read num
        IF end of file THEN exit
                ELSE SELECT CASE $num < 0$
                         n = n + 1
                    CASE num = 0
                         z = z + 1
                    CASE $num > 0$
                         p = p + 1

2. Is it necessary to have mutually exclusive conditions when using the CASE construct? Why?

3. In what cases will it be possible to delete the CONTINUE statement which is generated by the task "exit"? In what instances is it not possible?

4. What advantages may be expected from the use of structured concepts in program development? Are there disadvantages?

5. Write FORTRAN implementations of the programs in Figures 13-1 and 13-2.

13-5-2 Programming Problems

Any programming problem from any chapter may be approached from the structured point of view.

13-5-3 Answers to Self Test

1. a.
```
        IF(A.LT.B)GOTO10
        Y = Y + 1
        GOTO20
    10  X = X + 1
    20  ___
```
b.
```
        IF(S.LT.T)GOTO30
        IF(S.GT.T)GOTO40
        WRITE(3,1)S
        GOTO50
    40  WRITE(3,2)T,S
        GOTO50
    30  WRITE(3,2)S,T
    50  ___
```

c.
```
        A = 1
        X = 0
   100  IF(.NOT.A.LE.10)GOTO200
        X = X + A
        A = A + 1
        GOTO100
   200  ___
```
d.
```
    3   READ(3,1,END = 4)A,B,C
        WRITE(3,2)A,B,C
        GOTO3
    4   ___
```

e.
```
        A = 1
        X = 0
    5   X = X + A
        A = A + 1
        IF(.NOT.A.GT.10)GOTO5
```
f.
```
    C1 = 0
    C2 = 0
    C3 = 0
    IF(X.LT.10)C1 = C1 + 1
    IF(X.EQ.10)C2 = C2 + 1
    IF(X.GT.10)C3 = C3 + 1
```

```
g.          N = 0
            Z = 0
            P = 0
   10   READ(1,2,END = 100)NUM
        IF(NUM.LT.0)N = N + 1
        IF(NUM.EQ.0)Z = Z + 1
        IF(NUM.GT.0)P = P + 1
        GOTO10
   100  CONTINUE
```

2. In using the CASE structure, the first condition which tests TRUE will be the applicable condition. If cases are not mutually exclusive, the order in which the tests are made will affect the outcome.

3. It is possible to delete the CONTINUE statement unless the statement is being used at the foot of a DO loop and the deletion would force an invalid statement (IF,GOTO etc.) to become the foot of the loop.

4. See "You Might Want to Know" section.

5. Figure 13-1: program essentially as shown in Figure 12-9.
   Figure 13-2: program essentially as shown in Figure 8-11.

INDEX

A

A format code   220, 226
Absolute error   250
Absolute value   365
Abundant number   219
Accumulation   196
  using arrays   268
Accumulator   37
Accuracy vs. precision   234
Addition   53
  of matrices   351
Address of memory location
  4
Adjacency matrix   353
Adjustable dimension arrays
  380, 421, 220, 226
ALGOL   7
Algorithm   26
ALPHA key   17
Alphabetic characters   50
Alphabetic data   332
Alphanumeric data   223, 228
  in DATA statement   226
Alphanumeric variables   226
American National Standards
  Institute (ANSI)   7
Amortization schedule   213
AND   236

Annotation block   123
APL   7
Apostrophe in literal   76
Applications programs   16
Approximation
  area under a curve   218
  e 217, 396
  fractional numbers   119
  $\pi/4$ 216
  $\sin x$ 217
  square root   136
Area
  circle   86
  triangle   431
Argument   363
  function   377, 385
  subroutine   403, 405
Arithmetic expression
  definition   52
  evaluation of   54, 56
Arithmetic IF   112
  restriction in DO loops
  190
Arithmetic/logical unit   3
Arithmetic operations   53
  precedence   54, 238
Array   260
  adjustable dimensions
  380, 421

Array (cont.)
  elements   260
  initialization   266, 336
  internal representation   328
  subscript   260, 265
  three-dimensional   326
  two-dimensional   318
Ascending sequence   211
Associative property   258
Automatic end of file   148,
  156, 271
Average   36, 197

B

BACKSPACE   448
Balance sheet   88, 133
Bar graph   281, 334
BASIC   7
Batch processing   19
Benefit cost ratio   213, 301
Binary   220
Binomial expression   382
Bit   220
Blanks
  in FORTRAN statements
  119
  input of   117
Branching   8

Break-even analysis 180, 369
Bridge 436
Bubble sort 285
Bug 75
BYE 20

C

Calculation 8
CALL statement 400, 405
Calling/called program 401
Card reader 14
Carriage control characters 79
Centigrade 86
Central Processing Unit (CPU) 3
Channel 12
CHARACTER statement 245
Character string 224
Characters per word 224
Circle
    area of 86
    graph of 398
COBOL 7
Coding form 57
Collating sequence 245
Combinations 382
COMMENT statement 90, 122
COMMON statement 410
    named 423
    use of 408, 414
Compilation 95
Compile-time error 72
Compiler 4, 15
Complex
    data 240
    functions 241
    input/output 241
    square root 246
COMPLEX statement 240
Compound interest 33, 87, 120
Computed GO TO statement 123

Computer errors 6
Computer program 26
Conditional branching 8
Conformable matrices 351
Connected segment of a graph 355
Connector block 31
Constant
    complex 240
    double-precision 232
    integer 50
    logical 234
    real 50
Continuation 125
CONTINUE statement 192
    placement of 198
Control cards 94
    subprograms 382, 411
Control unit 2
Convergence 136, 388, 396
Conversational processing 19
Cosine function 366
Counting 145
    for file control 154
    initialization 161
CPU 12, 13
CRT 14
Cursor 454

D

D format code 234
Data 2
    alphabetic 332
    alphanumeric 223
    complex 240
    deck 94
    format codes 64
    logical 234
    representation 220
DATA statement 141, 143
    H code in 226
    placement of 144, 275
    use of 160, 161
Debug 75
DEC System 10 CPU 13
Decision block 28, 30

DEFINE FILE statement 454
Deficient number 219
Depth of three-dimensional array 327
Device number 62
DIMENSION statement 261, 263, 319
    use of variable in 419
Direct access files 453
    READ statement for 455
    WRITE statement for 455
Disk system flowchart symbol 458
Distance formula 89, 431
Division 53
    by zero 73
DO statement 187
    flowchart symbol for 201
    implied 269, 272, 322
    range 189
DO UNTIL 472
DO WHILE 470
Double-precision data 232, 244
Drum system flowchart symbol 458
Dummy arguments 377, 385, 403, 405
Duplication factor 124

E

E format code 230
Easter Sunday date 87
EBCDIC 224, 245
Edge of graph 353
Edit format code 64
END FILE statement 446
End of file 148
    automatic 148, 156, 271
    last card code 151, 152, 155, 271
    trip record 150, 156
END = option 150, 445
END statement 29, 47, 71, 74
    functions 378

End-statement (cont.)
  placement of 107
  subroutines 408
Entry point 31
Equations, systems of 136,
  388, 395
EQUIVALENCE statement
  425
Errors 72
  abolsute 250
  arrays 290
  execution-time 72
  relative 250
  round-off 250, 257
Executable statement 160
Execution-time error 72
Executive 16
Exit from DO loop 189,
  191
Explicit mode specification
  143
Exponential form 229
  computation of function
  396
Exponentiation 53
  negative numbers 75
Expression 52
  logical 235, 236
  mixed mode 56

F

F format code 66, 98
Factorial 37, 199, 395,
  472
Fahrenheit 86
FALSE 235
Field 148
  width error 66, 68
File 148, 441
  creation 443, 449, 456
  direct access 453
  listing 456
  merge 450, 480
  update 443
Fixed point 220
Floating point 220, 249
Flowchart 26

Flowchart block 29
  annotation 123
  connector 28, 31
  decision 28, 30
  DO statement 201
  END 29
  entry point 31
  flowlines 31
  input/output 28, 29
  literal data 33
  loop 33
  nonstandard symbols 33
  predefined process 418
  processing 28, 30
  READ 29
  replacement statement 30
  START 29
  STOP 29
  system 33, 457
  tabulation 34, 35
  terminal 28, 29
  transfer point 31
  WRITE 30
Flowlines 28, 31
FORMAT code
  A 226
  D 234
  data 64
  duplication factor 124
  E 230
  edit 64
  F 66, 98
  I 65, 97
  L 239
  literal data 69
  relationship with variable
    list 202
  slash (/) 156
  T 69, 100
  X 64, 101
FORMAT statement 47, 63,
  97
  error 66, 68
  placement of 63, 96
  reuse 291
FORTRAN 4
  character set 50

FORTRAN (cont.)
  coding form 57
  constant 50
  continuation 125
  job 60
  program 21, 94
  variable 51
  versions 7

FORTRAN statements
  arithmetic IF 112
  BACKSPACE 448
  CALL 405
  CHARACTER 245
  COMMENT 122
  COMMON 410, 424
  COMPLEX 240
  computed GO TO 123
  CONTINUE 192
  DATA 143
  DEFINE FILE 454
  DIMENSION 263, 319
  direct access READ 455
  direct access WRITE 455
  DO 187
  DOUBLE PRECISION 233
  END 71
  END FILE 446
  EQUIVALENCE 425
  FORMAT 63, 97
  FUNCTION 377
  GO TO 101
  IMPLICIT 164
  INTEGER 143
  LOGICAL 235
  logical IF 102, 108, 238
  READ 95, 150, 445
  REAL 143
  replacement 55
  RETURN 377
  REWIND 447
  statement function defi-
    nition 384
  STOP 71
  SUBROUTINE 405
  WRITE 61

Fractional numbers 119

Frequency distribution 280, 331
Function 363
    complex 241
    computation of e 396
    computation of $\sqrt{\ }$ 136, 395
    in-line 368
    invocation 376
    mathematical 365
    out-of-line 368
    position 382
    RAND 205
    RANDOM 205, 214
    reference 363
    special 366
    typed 377, 383, 387
FUNCTION statement 377, 384
Function subprogram 376
    position of 381
    use of 383

G

Gauss-Seidel method 388
Geometric progression 77
GO TO statement 92, 101
    in structured programming 465
GOODBYE 20
GPSS 7
Graph 353, 371
    bar 281, 334
    circle 398
    line 289
    scaling 397
Group relationships 179

H

H code in DATA statement 226
Hardware 12
Headings 71
High-level languages 4
Hollerith, Herman 17
Hollerith code 18
Hypotenuse 86

I

I format code 65, 97
IBM 029 keypunch 18
Identification field 58, 78
IF statement
    arithmetic 112
    logical 92, 102, 108, 238
    restrictions 190
IF THEN ELSE 467
Implied DO 269, 272, 322
    in DATA statements 276, 330
Implicit mode
    function names 376, 385
    variables 51, 164
IMPLICIT statement 164
Index 262
    in DO loop 187
Input
    operation 8
    unit 2
Input/output
    alphabetic data 220, 226
    logical 234
    one-dimensional array 269
    READ 29, 92, 95, 150
    two-dimensional arrays 321
    WRITE 30, 47, 61
Integer
    arithmetic 52, 75
    constant 50
INTEGER statement 141, 143, 277
Integrated circuits 12
Interchange maximum/ minimum sort 287
Interest
    compound 33, 87
    simple 86, 164
Inventory 183, 311
Inverse of matrix 353
IRAND 372
Iteration methods
    Gauss-Seidel 388
    linear equations 136, 137
    roots of a polynomial 137
    square root 136

J

Job 21
    control 21, 61, 94
    make up
        function 382
        main 61, 94
        subroutine 411
Julian date 86, 302

K

keypunch 18

L

L format code 239
Language translator 4
Last-card code 151, 152, 155, 271
Life insurance 345
Limits 396
Line graph 289
Line printer 14
Line spacing 79
Linear equations 136
Literal data 33, 224
    apostrophe in 76
    format code 69
Loading 95
Logical
    constants 234
    data 234, 236
    error 72
    expression 235, 236
    operators 236
Logical IF statement 102, 108, 238
LOGICAL statement 220, 235
Logarithm function 365
Loop 33, 145
    control 145
    nested 195

M

Machine
    instruction 60

Machine (cont.)
language 4
Magnetic
disk 458
drum 458
tape 458
Main program 377, 401, 403
Mass storage device 12
Mathematical function 365
Matrix 351
Maturity value of a note 88, 180
Median 179
Memory unit 2
Merge 450, 480
using arrays 269
Metric system 132
Mixed mode
expression 56, 233
input 100
replacement statement 56
Mode 50, 178
explicit specification 143
implicit 51, 164
Model programs 152
Modem 19
Monitor 16
Monthly payment formula 134, 177, 416
Multiplication 53
of matrices 351
Multiprogramming 15

N

Named COMMON 424
Nanosecond 5
Nested loops 195
Nonexecutable statement 160
NOT 236
Nuclear reactor 347
Number generation 148
Numeric
characters 50
punch 17
NUMERIC key 17

O

Object code 60
Octal counting 180
On line 15
Operating system 15
functions of 16
instructions 21
Operation code 4
Operators
arithmetic 53
logical 236
relational 103
OR 236
Output
operation 8
unit 3
Overflow 74
Overtime pay 93

P

Paper tape 458
Parameter 403
Parentheses 53, 73
nested 75
Percentage 162
Perfect number 219
PL/I 7
Plotter 14
Polynomial 137
Precedence 54, 234
Precision 234
Predefined process block 418
Premium of life insurance policy 345
Prime number 211, 369
Printer 458
Process 466
Processing block 28, 30
Program 2, 4
main 377, 403
model 152
source 60
sub 376, 400
system flowchart symbol 458
Programmer 4

Programming, structured 465
Pseudo code 466
Punched card 17
columns 17
rows 17
system flowchart symbol 458

Q

Quadratic equation 120, 249, 394, 416

R

Random numbers 205, 214, 372
Range of DO statement 189
READ statement 29, 92, 95, 150
unformatted 445
Real
arithmetic 52, 75
constant 50, 229
data representation 244
input/output 65, 97, 66, 98
REAL statement 143, 277
Record 148, 441
key 441
Reed, Adam V. 7
Relational
expression 103
operators 103
Relative error 250
Replacement statement 47, 55
logical 236
mixed mode 56
Report generation 450
RETURN statement 377
multiple 379
REWIND statement 447
Right justification 66, 67, 97, 98
Roots of a polynomial 137
Round-off error 250, 257
Rounding off 243, 398
RPG 7

S

Scaling, graph 397
Search 269, 279
SELECT statement 476
Sign-off procedure 20
Sign-on procedure 20
Significant digits 242, 250
Simple
  discount 180
  interest 164
Sine function 365
Slash (/) format code 156,
  291
SNOBOL 7
Software 15
Sort 285, 417, 481
Source
  code 60
  deck 94
Special
  characters 50
  functions 366
Specification statement
  142, 164, 277
Square root 365
  iterative procedure 136,
  395
  of complex number 246
Standard deviation 200, 304
START 29
Statement (*see* FORTRAN)
  executable vs. nonexecutable
  160
  function 384
  number 58
STOP statement 29, 47, 71,
  74, 107, 118
  in subprograms 412, 413
String of numbers 215
Structured programming
  465
  constructs 467
  DO UNTIL 472
  DO WHILE 470
  IF THEN ELSE 467
  SELECT 476

Subprogram 376, 403
  position of 382, 411
  use of 412
Subroutine 403
  flowchart symbol for 418
  position 411
SUBROUTINE statement
  400, 405
Subscript 260, 262, 265
Subtraction 53
Supervisor 16
Switching circuit 246
Symmetric matrices 352
Syntax error 72
System flowchart 33, 457
  equations 136, 388, 395

T

T format code 69
t test 218
Table look-up 280
Tabulation 34, 35, 146
TAN function 363, 371
Tape 458
Task 466
Telecommunication 12
  system flowchart symbol
  for 459
Teletype 14
  system flowchart symbol
  for 458
Terminal block 28, 29
Termination operation 10
Three-dimensional array 326
Timesharing 15
Top-down program design
  465
Trace of a matrix 353
Transfer point 31
Translator program 15, 60
Transpose of a matrix 352
Triangular matrix 353
Trip record 150, 156
Truncation 57
Two-dimensional array 318
  input/output 321
  processing 320

Type statements
  COMPLEX 240
  DOUBLE PRECISION 233
  INTEGER 143
  LOGICAL 235
  REAL 143
Typed functions 377

U

Unconditional branch
  8, 101
Underflow 74
Unformatted input/output
  445

V

Value of a function 363
Variable 29
  complex 240
  DIMENSION 419
  explicit mode 143
  implicit 51, 164
  integer 51
  logical 235
  name 51
  real 52
  subscripted 260, 262,
  265
Vertex of a graph 353
Volume
  cone 86
  cube 86

W

Walk in a graph 353
WATFIV 7
WATFOR 7
Workflow 61, 94
WRITE statement 30, 47,
  61
  unformatted 445

X

X format code 64, 101

Z

Zero, division by 73
Zone punch 17